WICK

WICKED!

The
Prince Naseem
Phenomenon

Gavin Evans

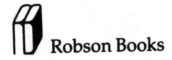 Robson Books

First published in Great Britain in 1999 by Robson Books, 10 Blenheim Court, Brewery Road, London N7 9NT

An earlier edition of this book was published by Robson Books in 1996.

British Library Cataloguing in Publication Data
A catalogue record for this title is available from the British Library

ISBN 1 86105 161 1

Printed and Bound in Great Britain by Creative Print and Design (Wales)

THE PRINCELY PARADOX

Naseem Hamed is a conundrum, or at least I hope he is. Most of us have our contradictions, but with this little prince these are magnified beyond the normal call of duty. Here's a young man who can appropriately be described as boyishly charming and teeth-grittingly obnoxious, generous and stingy, public-spirited and self-obsessed, a man who loves the adulation but sometimes hates the crowd, who has concern for the underdog and no compunction about kicking sand in his face, who gives time and money to cancer victims and plants his cars in disabled parking spaces; who displays an astonishing level of self-belief and yet frequently behaves with defensive insecurity, who talks with passion about his god and his community, yet whose driving force is his own self-advancement; who attracts adoration and contempt in equal portions. Even in his line of work, it is hard to know which manifestation will turn up: Steve Robinson's defensive genius who is near impossible to hit and never puts a foot or glove wrong, or Kevin Kelley's wrong-footed klutz who is an open target and wins on power alone.

None of this detracts from the media phenomenon that is 'Prince Naseem' today. If anything, the signs of vulnerability and inconsistency within the ropes, and of unpredictability beyond them, have added to his allure, helping to break open the American market while keeping the home crowd titillated. His arrival as new kind of British sporting supernova seems to go against the grain, while being at the same time in tune with several important strands of the public mood. Past British boxing heroes came to be defined, perhaps unfairly, within the worthy trier/brave loser couplet. Certainly Henry Cooper and Frank Bruno, the last two heavyweights to capture the public imagination in a way which transcended their sport and all sport, fitted this description for much of their careers. What they also had in their favour was their overt Englishness, their status as big men and their ability to talk. Naseem Hamed is a tiny fellow, making his mark within a weight range that the American public has come to ignore and within a sport supposedly in decline on both sides of the Atlantic. Yet he has not only made himself the highest-earning sportsman in Britain but one of the richest in the world, soaking up massive advertising endorsements, his billboard sneer a feature in New York and London, his face adorning stamps in Sana'a.

Even in the early stages of his career he seemed to have transcended boxing in a way which other non-heavies could only dream of – attracting advertising contracts, constantly featured on television chat shows and in glossy magazines, drawing younger, trendier punters to the sport and building a reputation for himself as a kind of fashion icon, a music fundi, a snooker whiz, a nightclub regular. Part of his allure at that stage was the non-stop tattoo of over-the-top verbiage, the cocky posturing, the attitude, the marvellously naff displays of style he would come up with, and the superb promotional job his people were doing for him.

The immediate comparison, made ill-advisedly by Hamed and some of his less perceptive acolytes, is with Muhammad Ali. If you strip away the thick layers of sentimentality covering our collective memory of Ali the fighter, it might be conceded that in terms of pure boxing prowess today's most famous featherweight compares favourably with history's best known sportsman. You might also draw superficially valid comparisons in terms of public persona: the childlike self-absorption, the desire to humiliate opponents, the flamboyance, the lip, the willingness to predict the round. But if history repeats itself, it is, as Marx noted in his musings on the two Napoleons, first time as tragedy, second time as farce. Ali, a child and icon of the altruistic sixties, transcended the ring, only to be brought down by it. He drew his strength from his love of unfiltered human contact, only to be let down and ripped off by many of those he gave most to. In his prime he defied his parents' religion, his country's laws and his nation's sense of self to confront the values of the white establishment, all the way to refusing to fight in its army, until, released from this curse, he fought on, and on, and on, until it did him no good. In contrast to Ali's transcendent altruism, one way of looking at the contemporary Hamed is as a product and in a sense a symbol of the Thatcherite 1980s – a carefully packaged human product, wary of outsiders and protected from the crowd, and a man who has, as yet, taken a stand for no-one bigger than his 5ft 3in self.

One dimension of this is captured in the response of his crowd when he is about to fight. He attracts a more upwardly mobile fan who is nevertheless far from exempt from excesses of the traditional variety. Any foreigner making a debut attendance at a major 'international' fight in Britain, particularly one involving Hamed, is likely to be shocked by the crowd reaction to the visiting boxer. American, European, Australian, Mexican or South African crowds do not routinely boo the opposition (not unless there is a particularly cogent reason for it, like their home-town worthies being insulted by, say, Prince Naseem). Among larger British fight crowds, however, this is standard fare and at Hamed fights it is particularly virulent. Unless you are part of this spirit, or amused by it, there is something distasteful in the barking dog, beer-fuelled, pack machismo that settles on the local hero, and with the swaggering little Prince, in his role as the local David against the visiting Goliaths, this harsh, youthful edge is seldom absent.

Yet there is more to the Hamed phenomenon than a gratuitous exchange of greed, avarice and selfishness. There is also an aspect of his identity which is in harmony with the more inclusive, multi-cultural Britain of the late 1990s. For a start, he is hardly a snug fit for Norman Tebbit's obnoxious 'cricket test' of pristine national identity. He is a first-generation immigrant child, as loyal, in public, to the Arab world as he is to the English. He is a Muslim at a time in Europe when Muslims are subject to the crudest forms of prejudice. And he comes from a close-knit community whose values and political identity are the antithesis of Thatcherism. These elements have been pulled together to establish a multi-faceted identity that includes being British, Yemeni, Arab, Muslim, black and a son of Sheffield. Over the past decade, boxing has been largely free of the harshest edges of jingoistic racism which are still seen in football and even cricket, but there is nevertheless something reassuring in seeing an Arab boxer, fighting under two flags, attracting this kind of national loyalty in Britain.

This yin and yang dichotomy seems to be represented in the different aspects of his personality which create such confusion among those who write about his exploits – in short, whether, as he claims, he is a 'totally different person outside the ring' or whether his extra-mural personality is a dull reflection of that between the ropes. To complete the paradox, I would have to say that after five years of following his exploits, I have come to the conclusion he is both, and neither.

In the course of my first long interview with him, early in 1995, I was charmed by his mixture of gauche bravado, honesty and religious faith. Before we got down to business, he told me he was feeling peckish and would I mind if he picked up a few sandwiches? I watched as he shook his head on observing that only ham sandwiches were left and then carefully removed the offending pig meat from between the bread, while apologizing for holding me up. He explained how his fighting prowess was a gift from Allah, before filling me in about his love of shopping and snooker and explaining how the none-too-pious way he related to women was because, as he put it, 'at the end of the day I'm only human, just like the rest.' We were interrupted by the chance crossing of the still-active, forty-something former WBC light-heavyweight champion Dennis Andries, who came over to say hello. When Dennis went on his way, I asked Naseem whether he intended to emulate men like Andries by boxing on until middle age. 'You *never* know how long I might be around,' he replied. 'I'm very ambitious and there's no knowing what I might do. I would never set a time limit on it. When it is assigned to me to retire – and retire undefeated that is, because I can't see myself ever getting beat – then I will retire. Until that point I'm just going to keep on bringing the world titles back to Sheffield and will become the first great fighter Britain has ever had.' He paused to give me an intense look and reminded me that while no one could predict their future, he was certain of one thing: 'I will definitely become a legend.' And what about after that, I wondered. Where do legends go when they retire? Is there life after boxing for the Prince? 'Oh, most definitely,' he replied indignantly. 'After my boxing career I will probably devote my life, myself, to the religions. Obviously!' We both thought about this for a few seconds and I tried to imagine the Prince as a preacher. At that moment he deflated a bit and qualified his assertion. 'I'm not sure, you know. I may go into different things, into acting, there's talk of music. Loads of things come up on the pipeline.' Then, after another pause, he returned to his look of absolute conviction and, like so many fighters, reduced the question to an intangible they call destiny. 'Whatever happens to me after I retire is written, and written from God.' And just to make sure I didn't miss the thread, he added: 'I do believe God will give me a great life.'

There was something appealing in this mixture of childlike, egotistical faith in his status as a chosen one and the realization of his flawed humanity, but when I interviewed him again at the end of the year, the idea of mortality seemed to be in doubt. He had just had the first of his grand predictions confirmed by out-classing Steve Robinson to lift his maiden 'world' title, and would go on to tell me that he had the stuff to beat America's Oscar de la Hoya right then and there. Initially he was haughty and stand-offish but gradually relaxed when talking about his love for his family, and he seemed eager to impress on me that he was, indeed, a completely different character outside of his place of business. 'I'm not arrogant, not selfish, not bombastic. I have nothing to prove outside the ring. I'm just an ordinary, totally down to earth, rich guy.' A few minutes later I observed a tiny test of this assertion. An old Arab man recognized him and came over. Naseem politely chatted away for ten minutes, eager to show respect to an elder he'd never met before. Three days on we met up again at an apartment he was renting in London. Once more he was late, but this time he made a point of apologizing and stayed for an hour longer than promised. As he was leaving to go and watch *Grease*, the doorman stopped him for a chat and, again, I watched Naseem showing deference and politeness when there was nothing to gain from them. Little signs of grace like these seemed to indicate he was what he said – a nicer human being than his public and fighting demeanour suggested.

At this point I also got to know and like Naseem's mentor, manager and trainer, Brendan Ingle, who offered a different perspective on what made his young charge the fighter he was. Brendan is an Irishman in England who appreciates the signifi-cance of heritage, symbols and identities. He understands these things not only for what they are worth to an individual but also as marketing tools. In a game where fighters are products or they are nothing, Brendan has an instinctive feel for the market that few can touch, an ad man's gift for images to tease the punter. Sometimes he will milk the irony in national identity – big, black English boxers with leprechaun names was a favourite. Fidel Castro Smith was too bland a name for his future British super-middleweight champion, he decided, so he rechristened him Slugger O'Toole; Paddy Reilly from Balyjamesduff had more of ring about it for a seventeen-stone English heavyweight than boring old Clifton Mitchell. He may also play on the reversal of accepted images (giving the slippery Herol Graham the *nom de guerre* 'Bomber') or he'll use a minor, fortuitous advantage as a major marketing tool (dressing the heavyweight Pele Reid in the Brazilian colours to highlight his name).

When the moment demands, Ingle can also play the game with his tongue a little further from his cheek, as with Naseem Hamed's early identity as the 'Arabian Knight', milking the notion of Middle Eastern mystique (and perhaps believing it). Brendan liked to make the point that Naseem's gifts, his fighting style, and certainly his mental approach, were drawn from his Yemeni heritage, from his Arab genes even. Ingle would warm to his theme, extending it beyond its natural limits, and inevitably move onto his favourite little roots vignette: 'You know, in that part of Yemen where his people come from, they can be totally vicious if they have to. You have to shoot 'em to lick 'em, and I tell you, this fella is like that too. If you break his hands, he'll kick you. If you break his legs, he'll bite you. If you pulls his teeth, he'll nut you. He has that will to win and the ruthlessness to go with it, and he's so accurate and strong that people can't understand it. He carries his own referee in both hands, so no matter what angle they move, he can counter them.'

Quite why this martial spirit and talent settled on little 'Naz' – by several inches the smallest of the nine Hamed children – rather than on his three other brothers who tried their hand at the sport, Brendan doesn't venture to explain, because metaphors like his are only supposed to be taken so far. The broader point, though, is a valid one. Naseem Hamed is very much a product of this rich heritage and it is something he himself frequently acknowledges. His own perspective, though, is that his roots are rather more diverse than Brendan's tales of Arabian Knights suggested. His identity is multi-layered, with each aspect having been absorbed with obvious pride and usually without prejudice against the others. The Arab world, Yemen, Britain, Sheffield and Britain's black communities – each have their place in his self-image. As Naseem explained it to me: 'I see myself as a British Arab, born and bred in Britain and I am proud to be British, I'm proud to be Arab, I'm proud to be black and I'm proud to be from Sheffield.'

The security and direction he gains from his belief in God and an after-life is another key aspect of his identity. Coming from a relatively liberal Islamic community and family, he is never bombastic about his religious belief and regularly breaches its commandments, seldom allowing it to act as a barrier to his access to the secular world. In fact, he prefers to keep quiet on the details rather than to proselytize, but he always makes it clear that Islam is a major source of his strength and direction. 'It's very important for me to be religious and to believe in God,' he says. 'It's one of the biggest parts of my life because at the end of the day, what are you living for? Why are you on earth, on this planet? I think it's all a test, which is why it is very important that I keep my life so clean. A lot of people ask me what's the secret of my success and I can honestly say I think I've been given this gift from God and I use it to the best of my ability. It's not something you can prove one way or another – you either believe it or you don't, and that's what I believe. I thank God for the position I'm in today. I've got so much belief in God and I think God's got so much belief in me.'

Another major element of who he is and how he sees himself is generational – the boyish young man whose formative teen years covered the late 1980s and early 1990s. In a typically eclectic way, he has absorbed some of the tastes and attitudes of his youth generation in Britain. This dimension of his identity is apparent in his sense of himself as one who can't be pushed around, who has *attitude* in abundance. Even now that he is in his mid-twenties, he cuts the posture of the swaggering youth, the lad who can't be *dissed*, the one who *knows*. It is also apparent in his fashion statements, the mix of street style and designer labels he enjoys; in the pseudo-American patois he sometimes fall into; and even more so in his musical interests: 'That's a great inspiration in my life – music. I like all kinds of music and I always have my sounds with me, in the car, the gym, everywhere. I've always got a wicked rhythm or beat about me – I hear the music and I'm there. I like a lot of soul bands. I've always been into swing and soul and reggae, and now jungle and hip-hop. It depends on the mood I'm in – like, if you catch me right before a fight, I wouldn't be listening to soul. It would probably be jungle or ragga, but not aggressive kind of music. I like a lot of garage, pumping music with a great beat to get the adrenaline going, and I can dance to anything from jungle to cha cha.'

The more intimate units of identity – as a member of Sheffield's Yemeni community, his local mosque, Brendan Ingle's gym and in particular his family – were vitally significant in his up-bringing. Certainly, when he speaks of his own family it is always with a warmth and respect which few other subjects inspire. 'We're a large and very stable family and I am very close to them,' he says. 'I love my family and my family loves me. My family is great.' During his childhood he also displayed love and respect for his 'second' family, the Ingles, although this diminished significantly when Brendan's mentor role was no longer required – after which his first family regained its hegemony. From the age of seven he was a feature of their household, eating and some-times sleeping at their house, travelling the country with Brendan and his son John and receiving daily lectures on morality and life skills. 'It was like father and son basically, in a different sort of way,' he said. 'I learnt more from Brendan than I did in my whole school career, and without him I don't know where I would have been. He was like a second father really, and his sons John and Dominic are great too. They were there for me and I was there for them, so it clicked in as a very good relationship.'

Until he was well into his professional career there were few signs of contradiction or discord in the way all these different elements were absorbed. The overwhelming impression was that each added to his sense of self. It may be true that his constant quest for adulation, his strutting *bragadaccio*, his relentless desire to prove himself and his insatiable egotism speak of something other than contented inner security. There were obviously areas of discomfort. Perhaps his transition from being the baby in the family for four years to being an older brother of three siblings contributed to his attention-seeking behaviour. Maybe he over-compensated for a genetic card which left him a good deal shorter than his older, and then younger, brothers and sisters, as well as his father. Possibly even, he would have preferred a flatter pair of ears. But none of that is exceptional and Naseem's inner demons seem to be adequately caged little fellows. He is certainly no Mike

Tyson man-child, reeking of inner turmoil and pain. Beyond the ring lights and television cameras the arrogance is definitely never far from the surface, and even in the private domain there are hints of the swagger and petulance that are so much part of his public persona and which his current success, fame and wealth and the mass adulation, as well as the absence of failure, have encouraged. But when you see him without an audience, there is sometimes also a calmness about him. This can be endearing while at other times coming across as merely smug, but it suggests he is capable of self-contentment, even if he has shown little sign of the realistic self-reflection which life's setbacks tend to foster. He certainly over-emphasizes the distinction between the private and the public Naseems with his wishful mantra 'I'm a totally different person outside the ring', but at the same time he is capable of giving the impression of being a young man unusually at ease with himself, and his surroundings, wherever he might be.

In most respects his upbringing was, by the standards of his profession, safe, settled, secure, comfortable and free from conflict. Despite his playground scraps and occasional street fights, he did not grow up in an environment where fighting was a matter of life and death or where other human beings were regarded as physical obstacles to survival. In the strictest sense, coming from a family who had risen to the ranks of the old petty bourgeoisie (shopkeepers), Naseem was not even working class. What is clear is that his will to succeed has not been a response to any extremes of deprivation – either material or emotional – as it is with so many great fighters. Rather, his extraordinary, religiously-inspired sense of destiny transcended traditional motivational categories.

My initial take on him, therefore, was that he was very much a one-off phenomenon. Not always a very nice one, but still, an uncomplicated example of pure brilliance within the confines of his line of work. It was this that stood out in my exchanges with him before he became world champion.

Soon after, however, I began to see signs of the more unattractive side to the princely conundrum. It seemed that, contrary to his assertion that his feet would always remain on the ground, they were being planted firmly in his mouth or on other people's heads, including former friends and close associates. For a start there was the steady stream of 'off the ball' incidents discussed in the later chapters of this book. While in most cases excuses or denials were offered, the negative impression from these was exacerbated by what many of those around him were saying, usually off the record as the fear factor set in. Several of his gym-mates, associates and sparring partners had become openly critical of his behaviour, while even his former friends seemed more qualified and cautious in their praise. From what I observed of Naseem's treatment of those he encountered, from friends to autograph seekers, there was a volatility in his behaviour: here warm, understated and friendly; there aggressive, sarcastic and conceited. He was capable of treating his stablemates and his trainers with contempt. His displays of rude and aggressive behaviour in public, and occasionally in private, were leaving a bad taste in the mouths of many, contributing to a marked diminution of his reputation within his home town, not to mention his home gymnasium.

As a result, his relationship with the British public deteriorated, even if he was continuing to attract the crowds and television ratings. The excesses of a precocious boy were less endearing in a grown man, and there was little evidence that the passing years were adding to his sense of perspective or even his emotional maturity. He was still capable of putting in passable media turns, but the vibrant originality of his early days had been replaced by a suspicious, sneering and supercilious image, invariably propped up by boringly boastful clichés along the lines of 'End of the day, I knocked him spark out. It was a wicked performance. What more can I say? I'm gonna be a legend.' Within a year of winning his first world title he had become openly antagonistic to all but the most obsequious sections of the press, and seemed incapable of accepting criticism or even taking a joke at his own expense. The result was that his family minders were screening out messengers who were filing in the bad news. A fortress-Prince mentality was developing, where most of those around him were afraid to point to the folly of his course. Fame and fortune, it seemed, were treating him in the worst way possible.

Yet in terms of his own definitions of success, none of this really counted. It was on his standing as a fighting man that his future rested, and therefore it is primarily on this score that he has been, and will be, judged. So it is worth taking a step back and examining what was, what might have been, and what might still be for Naseem the boxer.

The first full thrust of Naseem's magnificent potential was revealed to me when, soon after his twentieth birthday, I watched him dishing up a playfully painful beating to the world-rated bantamweight Vincenzo Belcastro for twelve rounds without taking more than a headbutt in reply. Over the next eighteen months he put in a series of brilliantly devastating performances against a string of fringe contenders. I vividly recall watching from the Shepton Mallet ringside with gaping awe as he twisted his body into impossible angles to avoid the oncoming traffic from Mexico's Enrique Angeles before taking him out with a series of punches from equally impossible angles which landed with a force I had never before seen in one so small. Eight weeks later I was at the ringside of a packed Royal Albert Hall to see him evaporate when former world champion Juan Polo-Perez tried anything serious, only to re-emerge to take out this genuine player with contemptuous ease.

When I was growing up, like many children in the early 1970s I adopted Muhammad Ali as my personal sporting hero. But whenever my adulation got out of hand, my father would make a point of reminding me that the greatest fighter ever to set foot on this earth was Sugar Ray Robinson. Sugar Ray the original, forties and fifties master, could do it all – dance and slug, knock you out going backwards, take trip-hammer blows without breaking – and was smart and pretty to boot. Watching those old black and white re-runs of his battles as a child, I was inspired to box, and kept at it, on an off, for over a decade, finally 'retiring' at the age of twenty-two, after which I preferred to write about other men taking their shots rather than absorb any more myself. Of course, it did not take me long to realize that the only time I could ever be a Sugar Ray Robinson was in my shadow-boxing dreams, but then I thought there never could be another Sugar Ray; not even the superb Ray Leonard could quite match the brilliance of the original master. On that score I knew, for once, my father was right – until I saw Naseem Hamed in action in 1994 and 1995.

Obviously, I am overstating things. In retrospect it seems more than a little ludicrous to suggest a valid comparison between a novice barely out of his teens and the finest fighter the world had ever seen. But for me at least, those first few glimpses of Naseem in action were something of revelation; confirmation of the view that boxing, like every other sport, had moved on, that the day would come – if it hadn't already arrived – when there would be better fighters than the Sugar Rays and Muhammad Alis, just as the best efforts of the Jack Johnsons, Jack Dempseys and Joe Louises had long been surpassed. I realized it was possible that in Naseem's lithe little body lay potential of a kind that Britain had never seen. Soon I was gushing away to anyone who would listen that I had never seen anyone with this level of innate potential. I had been in the United States in 1978 to watch the young Sugar Ray Leonard and in 1986 to see the budding Mike Tyson, but neither of them compared, at least not in terms of capacity for brilliance.

Brendan would tell me how Naseem imagined he was Muhammad Ali, Sugar Ray Leonard and, yes, Sugar Ray Robinson, when he was shadow-boxing. But the Alis and Sugar Rays were not confined to his dreams – he was living those dreams and going several steps further. Ingle, in fact, honestly believed Naseem was already there with the gods, and this was a man in his late middle age who worshipped Robinson and Ali. After watching Hamed knocking the spots off men nearly twice his size in sparring and discovering that the legends about him beating up heavyweights were (mostly) true, and seeing more of his astonishing acrobatic grace, middleweight power, almost psychic reflexes, hand-eye co-ordination, time-distance perception and instinct for the kill, I wondered whether this young man's predictions that he would win world titles at three, four or five weights were not unduly modest. It was hard to escape the impression that the boxer still known as Prince could do the business better than any I had ever seen.

After returning from Cardiff where I had watched him degrade and then crush Steve Robinson, I interviewed Naseem again for various magazines. My last residue of doubt had disappeared and I wrote an early biography. By then I had heard the best and the worst about him, but from everything I had seen in the ring and in the gym, and from all he and those around him had told me, it seemed almost inconceivable that he would not deliver in something close to the terms he had set out, barring a chance collision with an eighteen-wheeler (and even then I was not sure I'd bet on the truck). In my early interviews with Hamed, he told me, in essence, his aims were to be the greatest boxer who ever lived, to win a clutch of world titles, to earn £40 million (or maybe £400 million) and to retire, undefeated, with his bucks and his marbles still intact.

The money has come even faster than expected, but the dreams of unbeaten glory have always seemed an extremely tall order in this sport where young men grow old very quickly, often without realizing it. Sugar Ray Robinson said more or less the same thing, but after a spell of tap dancing with Bojangles, he returned and eventually retired at forty-four, and died close to penniless of boxing-related Alzheimer's disease. Ali also dreamed of retiring undefeated, but could not stay away from the adulation of the crowds and the challenge of the ring and eventually bowed out at thirty-nine. Though far from poverty-stricken, he lost most of his money along the way and today has boxing-exacerbated Parkinson's Syndrome. Naseem believed he was different, that he had learnt from the mistakes of boxing's past, and perhaps that he didn't really need to learn. He had an absolute faith in his destiny which helped make him seemingly fearless when climbing through the ropes, something I had never seen before. In his boxing style, as well as in his personal style, he was, genuinely, very different from any other boxer I had ever interviewed, spoken to or watched, and this helped to make him such an interesting subject, though only for as long as he was delivering in the boxing ring. With all this, and no evidence of failure, it was easy to understate his considerable propensity for self-destruction, which was also starting to seep through.

Then, on the day the book hit the shelves, I grimaced from ringside as this capacity came precariously close to being realized when the quick-fisted Daniel Alicea dumped him on his back. There were excuses a-plenty, and of course he rose to wipe out the fragile-chinned Puerto Rican, but the boxer who spoke of never losing his commitment had cheated on the gym. The Prince who had spoken so often about always having his feet on the ground arrived on a sedan chair throne. A couple of months later in Dublin the excuse (a severe chest infection) was more legitimate, but the fact that he fought in that condition in the first place showed a dangerously cavalier arrogance. This time the former and future IBF featherweight champion Manuel Medina got off the canvas to dish out a boxing lesson, rocking Naseem's head back continually and wobbling him. In the end Hamed's extraordinary power and courage saved him, but it was a further indication that all was not well in his world. He made believers out of the American cynics by unifying the WBO and IBF titles with a clean eighth-round knockout over Tom Johnson, but those of us who had seen him on the way up were underwhelmed. Again he was dropped, though without taking a count, and his own attack seemed to have sacrificed finesse for the sake of power. He was working hard for the fights but no longer between them, with the result that he had lost some of the elusive ease which was once his trademark. It was an impression confirmed by his American debut when he knocked out Kevin Kelley in four rounds at Madison Square Garden. The outcome was emphatic enough, but by the time it was over he had taken three more counts.

After the Kelley fight I wrote a couple of magazine stories on Naseem's worrying signs of drift both inside and outside the ring. As a result I was confronted in person by two of his brothers, Riath (his business manager) and Nabeel (his fan club director). First one then the other harangued me about my temerity in having criticized their young sibling in this way. 'You've spent time interviewing him. You wrote a book on him. You know what he's like,' said Riath, to which Nabeel added: 'Did you get out of bed on the wrong side the morning you wrote that?' Both seemed genuinely astonished that anyone who had broken bread with their brother could fail to give him anything other than a fulsome endorsement. While irritated by this presumption, I was nevertheless intrigued by the absolutist assumption of innocence. It got me thinking that if his two older brothers were so sure on this score, then perhaps, after all, he had not lost all of the charm that coexisted with his less endearing qualities. I had seen and heard enough of the bad side to know it was not an aberration from the real, but maybe something of the good remained. It was time for a second look.

In the ring, in his next encounter against triple 'world' champion Wilfredo Vasquez, he delivered a solid performance. It was not quite up to the 1994–95 standard, but in seven rounds he took only one big punch, for the most part resisted the temptation to go for broke, and ended it in style. But in his following bout, a points win against Wayne McCullough six months later, he flopped by his standards, missing wildly, lacking the precision timing of earlier years, and getting hit too often. It reinforced the over-arching impression of inconsistency since becoming world champion rather than linear decline. At times it all flows beautifully and at times it falls apart.

His personal life has had a similar pattern. When he was under pressure or feeling insecure, such as during his 1997 break-ups with his girlfriend and future wife Eleasha Elphinstone, a coldly, aggressively defensive side emerged, and the car crashes, extramural fights and public rows came to the fore. But when he was feeling loved and at ease with the world, such as when things with his Eleasha were going smoothly, he could be charming, generous and likeable. He was willing to give time and money to charity and was even capable of mildly self-deprecating ribaldry. One suspects he will always have that younger son's impetuosity and impatience, along with the defensive aggression which was no doubt exacerbated by his being the smallest and yet the strongest in his large family. There are still times when he gives every impression of being a prat, and for those who haven't seen him beyond the gaze of the fisheye lens, and for some who have, it is forgivable to think that is all there is to him. But from. following his path for five years, I have realized that Naseem can be kind as well as cruel, wise and silly, bullying and gentle, a big man and a little one. There are indications that marriage and fatherhood, combined with a realization of the possibility of failure, have boosted the adult form of this calmer, less aggressive and, frankly, nicer exterior. Then again, as his embittered, swaggering, press-baiting form before and shortly after the McCullough fight indicated, the adult Naseem is just as capable of narcissistic nastiness as the boy of old.

The spills, near-disasters, Ferrari crashes, the break-ups with Brendan Ingle, and the and extra-mural battles have all created a valid impression that he may be one punch, or one crash away from oblivion, but so far he has risen to ride again and gradually some of the lessons are being learned. Or at least I hope so. He may still retain the egotistical faith in being chosen for a mission by the Almighty, but he has apparently discovered this is imperilled without his own application. He may still not train as often or as consistently as he used to, but he now seems to understand that there is a cost to cutting too many corners. In this sense, his recent quest for maturity may even help him reach his 'gonna be a legend' goal.

Boxing, as Ingle puts it, can be a 'filthy, rotten business'. It is an extremely brutal game, which rewards and honours one thing above all others: the ability to fight. The best fighters are not often the best people, though they are not necessarily the worst either. At the human level, his sport has produced its share of villains and a few heroes too, and Naseem Hamed is capable of both extremes. What counts more than his life outside the ring is that he is capable of being one helluva boxer. So far the ride has been well worth observing and with the stakes getting higher and higher, and the opposition more dangerous, the last few laps should be even more compelling.

1

LITTLE BOY FOUND

Like most of us, Naseem Hamed views himself from overlapping angles. He's a Yemeni, Muslim, English Arab man, boy, son, lad, father, husband, provider, rebel, joker, player, dancer, racer, fighter from Sheffield. He's brave, cruel, kind, cool, generous, wicked, cynical, trusting, funny, loving, hating, arrogant, rebellious, obedient, good and bad. None of this would mean anything to rest of us, were it not for one crucial piece of what makes Naseem: He is a boxer. Obviously. It is this fact which allows him to construct a range of further identities which few of us would dare to, or want to, share: a legend in the making, a man chosen by God, the finest fighter on earth – stuff like that. Without it, he might have been a telephone technician, or a small-scale businessman, or perhaps something less desirable, and few outside his family would be interested. As with most things in life, there was nothing inevitable about his fighting destiny. The fact that he ever laced on a boxing glove is something most people would put down to luck, fortune and circumstance, and he puts down to the will and design of Allah. Whatever version you prefer, this is how it started.

In the late 1950s, Aden was a British colony. It later became communist South Yemen and after 1989 part of the unified Republic of Yemen, but at the time this colonial status facilitated its use as a source of cheap labour for Britain, particularly in Sheffield's steel industry which was expanding rapidly at a time of industrial boom. Yemen has long been a country of extreme wealth and extreme poverty, as well as one of chronic political instability with frequent outbreaks of war and social unrest. For many young men at the time, the prospect of emigration to Britain represented the hope of regular employment and a better life, even if the jobs they were going to in the Sheffield steel mills were hard, dangerous and extremely unhealthy – so much so that local men were reluctant to accept them under the conditions offered. The Yemenis were a godsend for the fretful steel bosses and the trickle of immigration, which started in the late forties, slowly turned into a flow.

Salem Ali Ahmed Kashmeem Hamed, or Sal, as Naseem's dad likes to be called, was one of these young émigrés. Born in 1933, he was raised in a family of farmers in the village of Malah, 120 miles from North Yemen's capital, Sana'a. From an early age he showed an assertively entrepreneurial spirit, even running his own small shop from the age of twelve. Soon he was making regular trips to Sana'a, usually travelling on a donkey which would take almost a week, in order to purchase supplies. While still in his teens he travelled over the mountains and across the country to Aden. He later heard about the opportunities available in Britain and travelled to Djibouti in an overcrowded boat which capsized several times on the way, before boarding a ship to Madagascar. He then worked his way around the East African ports before taking a long voyage around the Cape and up the west coast of Africa to the Mediterranean and Marseilles before working his way through several of England's industrial towns. In 1958, at the age of twenty-five, he arrived in Sheffield and found work in the steel mills. Like most Yemenis, he sent all he could back home to his wife, Caria, until, four years later, she joined him, and by 1967 they had formally emigrated.

Sheffield grew from the outside in, with communities emerging on the surrounding hills before the still-small central business district took shape. The result is that even today one gets a sense of permanence, coherence and even insularity in its suburbs, which is unusual for a large British city. The Hameds were among the first Yemenis to move into the working-class area of Wincobank, within walking distance of the steel foundries in the valley below. Wincobank was a more recent creation than the more established sections of the city, built to serve the labour needs of the steel industry, but it too has an insular, self-contained dimension. Despite its pockets of poverty, and the rise in unemployment through the closure of the mills in the 1980s, there is less social dislocation here than in districts with a similar socio-economic profile elsewhere in the country – fewer single parent households, less violent crime or overt expressions of racism and an easier social mix. Most of the houses in the Hameds' section of Wincobank are small and double-storeyed, with little gardens in the front or back. The street is fairly wide and not too busy, allowing children to play football and generally to hang out without too much danger of being run over.

Sal and Caria are people with immense drive and ambition. They worked extremely hard, scrimped and scraped and saved whatever they could to create the best possible life for their rapidly expanding family. Their first daughter, Mona, was born in 1965, followed two years later by a second daughter, Noele, and then in quick succession by their first son Riath and second son Nabeel, after which Sal and Caria used their savings to buy a small general dealer's store in Newman Road – the same long street where the Ingle home and the St Thomas's Boys Club gym are found. Being the only store in the area for several years, it was always busy and the Hameds earned a reasonable living and were soon occupying a position of some importance in the surrounding neighbourhoods, despite being one of the first 'ethnic' families in this community. There was a gap of three years before the third daughter, Fozia, was born, followed on 12 February 1974 by the boy who was to be the smallest of their children, Naseem Salem Ali.

Family legend has it that on the night of the new baby's birth, Sal fell asleep and had a vivid dream about a sports car with shining headlights. When he woke, he claims to have said to himself, 'I got me a son.' He named the boy after a close family friend. Ironically, in Arabic Naseem means 'gentle breeze', yet almost from the start he proved to be anything but. He was extremely confident, out-going, physically adventurous, petulant and a born show-off. These apparently innate characteristics were enhanced or exacerbated by the way he was indulged as the baby of the family for the next three and a half years. The Hameds lived in cramped conditions above the shop, where Sal and Caria worked extremely long hours, but as Naseem grew older, their circumstances gradually improved. By the time he was four years old they had saved enough to buy the adjacent house and join the two premises, to make more room for themselves. Shortly before this, Naseem's third brother, Ali, was born during a two-year visit to the Yemen, robbing Naseem of his status as the pampered baby of the family. Murad and finally a fourth sister, Sabba, followed.

The environment the Hamed children were raised in was loving and, as a result of his parents' long working hours, not over-controlled. The older siblings tended to look after the younger ones, with Riath, as the oldest boy, taking particular responsibility for his younger brothers. Naseem says his self-assurance comes from both parents, and is fulsome in his public devotion to them. 'I praise my mum and dad so much for the way they raised me,' he says. 'I really had the very best upbringing possible. I was given a glorious childhood – as near to perfection as it's possible to be, so I have a great deal to thank my parents for.' He stresses that they were the prime source of his ethical and religious values, doing their best to keep him somewhere near the straight and narrow. When he was ten, for instance, his father went into a rage when he discovered him playing with slot machines. When he calmed down, he explained to the lad that gambling was contrary to their religion, and Naseem never played again. 'My parents were strict, yes. I'd get a clip around the ear if I deserved it. They taught me morals and ethics and the way to conduct myself. I believe good manners make a man. They taught me right from wrong, to apply myself to the full with everything I attempted. I don't lie or cheat, rob, drink or take drugs.'

He professes great admiration for the sacrifices his parents made and for their struggle to create a better life for their family and would never publicly contradict or criticize them, although on several occasions he has asserted his independence by defying their preferences. Without embarrassment he describes his father as his hero and will talk at length about Sal's determination and drive. He particularly loves the story of his dad's travels from Yemen to Sheffield. 'I admire all the work he had to do to bring us all up as a nice, stable family. He's a wonderful man. Sometimes I look at him and say to myself, "I wish I was you". It's a real achievement travelling 7,000 miles from Arabia to get over here, to work as hard as he did, to get established, to earn so much money, to get off his feet and eventually have a good standard of living. I think this achievement of the goals my parents had – the way they worked so hard all their lives and with such determination – has been an influence on me in the way I devote myself to my sport. They urge me to put as much into my profession as I ever did. I think it is the mental strength they gave me that helps carry me through.'

When he discusses his mother, he emphasizes her positive spirit and devotion to the family and enjoys talking about how she spoils him with her attention and wonderful cooking, and how he now has the means to spoil her by buying her anything she wants (from a new kitchen to a new house and a gift of half a million pounds in cash, carried home in a binliner). Until he met his future wife, he'd tell you, tongue in cheek, his mother was the only woman in his life and more seriously that she was one of his prime sources of direction. 'My mum is a very confident woman, and that's where I get it from. We Hameds are all confident,' he says. 'She's really cool. She prays for me before every fight, for the round I'll win in, and often it comes true.'

Sal is a deeply religious man who has long played a central role in the affairs of their small local mosque, a converted house in Rothay Street about half a mile from their home. His children were raised from birth with a strong emphasis on the tenets of Islam – a belief in a single omnipotent God, in Mohamed being his last and greatest prophet, chosen to deliver God's final message to mankind through the Koran, all the words of which are believed to be divinely inspired. They believe God created the heavens and the earth, rewards good and punishes evil, and that on the day of judgement there will be a resurrection of the dead and God will decide the fate of each soul – whether they are to have eternal life in heaven or to burn in the fires of eternal damnation – according to their deeds on earth, and according to whether they have asked for forgiveness while alive. Naseem has no doubt where he is ultimately headed and has said he views life as 'just a test' and 'looks forward to the afterlife – which is to go to heaven.' Heaven, incidentally, will be 'absolutely brilliant', and although he is unsure of the precise form of its brilliance, perhaps transport will take the form of flying horses, which would make a 'wicked entrance'.

English is the first language of the Hamed children and they speak it with a strong south Yorkshire accent, but from an early age they were required to recite passages of the Koran and learn Arabic – the language of the Koran, as well as being the Yemeni *lingua franca*, in a modern form – through classes at the Yemeni Community Centre, for two hours an evening, five days a week. Although Naseem regularly skipped these sessions to attend to his boxing education, he eventually mastered the language and usually uses it to speak to his parents and other Yemeni elders.

The children were taught to marry fellow Muslims, say their daily prayers on their prayer mats five times a day, and fast at Ramadan – although Naseem no longer follows these rituals and famously defied his family's advice by marrying a woman who, until a final hour conversion and marriage, was not a Muslim. In some respects his upbringing was not rigidly Islamic in an orthodox sense, nor did it conform to many Yemeni traditions. His sisters are not veiled, and although his attitudes to women could euphemistically be described as traditional in the Yorkshire working class male sense, he laughs at the idea of arranged marriages, believing that 'love is blind'. And on many social issues, ranging from sex outside marriage to the death penalty, his views are relatively liberal. As he put it: 'We're not in Yemen, we're not living in the Promised Land, we're in the Western world; but we've got our morals, we've got our ethics, we're clean-living people.'

Naseem does not attend mosque on a weekly basis, swears prodigiously and has done his share of womanizing. He also claims his fight schedule limits the time he devotes to his faith, particularly when it comes to prayer and fasting: 'There are allowances, where you don't have to pray at the exact time as long as you follow up and do a prayer at a different time, but you can't really fast if you're boxing. Obviously, if you're fighting it's going to interrupt the schedule of your eating, so, yes, that is one clash with my religion, but it's the only one.' Dr Abdul Shaif, a community leader who has known him since early childhood, said Naseem 'takes the best out of religion' – particularly the discipline, the work culture and the respect for elders – and sifts out the rest. 'It's not as if Naseem spends the whole day in the mosque, because he doesn't and there's no point beating about the bush and claiming he does. Naseem spends a great deal of time in the gym, and I know he has his own private life as well, which may contradict what is happening in Islam,' he said prior to Hamed's marriage. 'But he has certainly absorbed many things from Islam, and his identity stems from this. Being Yemeni means being Muslim, and I think he has picked the best bits out.'

So it would be a mistake to describe Naseem as devout in the sense that, say, Muhammad Ali is – but there is no doubt that the spiritual and ethical framework of Islam has provided a setting for his single-minded sense of destiny. He says his relationship with his god is 'personal, private but very strong – I believe in the Creator so much that it's untrue. I am deeply religious but I prefer to keep my religion to myself in the sense that you don't like to get people upset.' However, he says he carries a copy of the Koran in his kit bag to fights, and that he reads it occasionally, and has also made the unlikely claim that one of his post-boxing options is some kind of full-time Islamic commitment. He frequently stresses his view that his success is a gift from God, provided because his parents were so worthy: 'I think God picked me out because my parents worked so hard and done so much, and deserved it more than anybody, and being Muslims, I reckon God gave them a son who can basically give them anything they want.' He describes his focus and determination as a product of his Islamic upbringing: 'It's very important for me that religion has kept my life so clean. It's just great for boxing and for all sport. You can't drink alcohol or do any drugs whatsoever, or anything that can twist your mind to a different angle. That's why I'm such a clean-living guy.'

Naseem remembers little of his two years in the Yemen (between the ages of two and four), but Sheffield's 4,000-strong Yemeni community was integral to his life throughout his youth. During the 1950s and 1960s, the Yemenis were treated almost as a pocket of *gastarbeiters* by their host city, and despite increasing social and health problems, particularly in terms of industrial disease, they received minimal support. In the late 1960s, the community began to find its collective voice. Sal Hamed was part of a group of activists and elders who formed the Yemeni Community Association with the aim of catering for the cultural, political and economic needs of the community and providing assistance for its youth and its poor. From the start he was a member of its management committee and subsequently became its chairman, while Riath managed its cultural centre. At the time of its formation its membership was largely working class, Arabic-speaking, Muslim, and broadly socialist in orientation, with most of its members coming from the communist south. The association included a strong core of younger activists who ensured that it was tightly organized and that its mission extended beyond the community's own parameters. It received support from both the Labour Party and Communist Party and made common cause with the trades union movement, while attempting to develop a sense of identification between the Yemenis and the broader black community through the city's Black Community Forum. Today they share offices with the forum and have pictures of Martin Luther King and Malcolm X on their walls.

Dr Shaif, its main spokesman, said the association was central to Naseem's development. 'Its origins go back before Naseem was born, so he came into the association from birth, as a member of the Yemeni community'. 'Sal was always pretty active, so Naseem was exposed to the association from the start.' He stressed that the community helped provide Naseem with the direction and focus that contributed to his success. 'One of our aims is to look for talents and to try and harness them, and to give people support and encouragement and help them to develop a sense of confidence, and I think Naseem owes a lot to the Yemeni community for that. There is a sense of work culture and discipline in the Yemeni community, and politicization, that goes far beyond that in any other community in Sheffield.' Naseem was enormously proud of his father's status within the community. As he put it, in the glowing hyperbole of an uncritical sixteen-year-old: 'My dad is a busy man. He is president of all the Arabs in England. He tells them what to do. He's in charge of an Arab school for kids. We hardly ever see him. ... We only usually see him at night.'

Shaif, who knew Naseem from birth, said the assertiveness, the overt pride and the swagger were part of the package from the moment Naseem could string a sentence together. 'He was always cheeky. He had the arrogance when he was very young, but to me personally he has always been very respectful. He always stopped and shook my hand from when he was very little, and he would run over and say, "Hello, how are you?" whenever I would see him, and then I would give him 50p or something. He was always a nice and gentle young boy; very caring about his family and friends, and about the community, but always with the arrogance and the talents which would develop as he grew up. From an early age, I knew this boy was going to go somewhere. I'd always thought he had talents, but I never knew they were going to be in boxing.'

In June 1978, soon after the family returned from their time in Yemen, Naseem began his formal education at the Wincobank Infants School, four blocks from his home, which he was to attend for the next four years. While he eventually settled in, it was not always easy. Being Muslim, Arab and brown-skinned made him different at an age when difference can become an excuse for exclusion. He was the target of occasional racist name-calling, being dubbed 'chocolate drop' and 'Paki' by some of his peers, although as he became accepted the more affectionate 'Nabby' replaced these pejorative terms. One of the reasons the Hamed brothers began boxing was their father's concern about racist name-calling, although Naseem says stories of his own exposure to racism have been overstated and that it was seldom a major issue for him. However, this does not detract from his awareness of racism in British society, his self-identification as a black man and his willingness to take a public stand on the issue. 'But personally, I've never had *major* problems with racism and racist remarks. Maybe in infant school, yes, but then I got a reputation for myself and I never got no trouble, and no racial problems, and basically I got on with everybody.'

Naseem created strong impressions during his four years at Wincobank Infants School. Brenda Barley, the school secretary, got to know all the Hamed children and their parents, and says her memories of Naseem are particularly vivid. 'He was a lovely kid – very impish and mischievous, but you couldn't help but love him. He had these big brown eyes and one of his teachers, Mrs Fry, was always saying how she wanted to take him home with her, she loved him so much. He was a real little scamp, but not really naughty and never in real trouble. In fact, they were all great kids. They were a very close-knit family and you could see they loved each other very much, though the children used to fight with each other a bit. Basically, it was a very loving home and I think it came out in the children.' Dorothy Clark, who gave Naseem library instruction when he was seven and eight years old, also has a clear picture of him: 'I remember him as being fairly quiet, or at least quite shy with me, so he was difficult to get through to, but he definitely wasn't one of the problem children. He didn't much like doing work with pencils – where you had to keep still and concentrate – and he wasn't very academically inclined, but he used to spark up if it was anything more active, if we were making something, say, and he was always very physical. I don't remember him being one of those who got into many fights, but I used to watch him in the playground and he loved games and was always very quick on his feet, very fast, very agile.'

Great legends tend to follow great fighters, thinkers and doers. Often they are invented as a way of explaining their achievements or providing moral lessons. Alfred the Great had his burnt cakes, Isaac Newton his falling apple, George Washington his moment of honesty after felling the cherry tree. Boxers are never legends, but they frequently trade in them. Theirs is a sport addicted to mythology. So we know that Muhammad Ali made his start as a twelve-year-old who tearfully turned to a police boxing trainer after his new bicycle was stolen. The young 'fairy boy' Mike Tyson had the first taste of his destiny when he could no longer contain his anger after a larger bully pulled off the head of one of his pigeons. As it happens, both of these incidents probably do owe more to fact than fiction – a distinction that once mattered. In the media-wise late twentieth century, where the lines between image and reality, truth and fantasy are more blurred than ever, myths are as much the stuff of star-making as they were in King Alfred's days.

So we come to the story of Naseem Hamed's start on the path to glory. It has been told scores of times, in disparate versions, but this is the way Brendan Ingle gave it to me: 'I'm travelling up Newman Road towards my house, sitting on the top deck of the bus, and it stops at the stop outside the school. I just happen to look outside and I see this young lad who I thought was Pakistani – looked about six years old – fighting off these three bigger white kids, and I had to laugh because he was darting in and out and dashing around and they couldn't touch him and he was hitting them. This tiny fella was too fast for them. I was very impressed, and I thought to meself, "This fella has the makings of a great boxer in him – he can really move." Well, a week later I passed his father's shop and got talking. Both of his older brothers, Riath and Nabeel, were boxers, but they'd been away from the gym for a while and I was asking Sal why, and so on. Then I see this little kid who comes up to say hello, and straight away I recognize him as the lad from the fight outside the school. It is definitely the same kid, and then I realize he's Riath and Nabeel's younger brother, so I ask him to come down to the gym and that's how he gets started.'

One of the common additions to this version of the tale is that the bullies were shouting racist abuse at Naseem, calling him a 'Paki.' As Brendan once put it: 'Naz's father says, "Brendan, can I have a word with you?" and I says, "Sure Sal," and he says, "My boys are at school and they are getting called names and I want to bring them down to the boxing club." So I says, "No problem." So he brought the three of them out – one was Riath, Nabeel and the little fella who was the fella I saw in the school yard.' A thirteen-year-old Naseem gave a similar version to a local newspaper: 'He saw me fighting three boys who had called me names. I was skipping and moving to keep out of their way. Brendan got off the bus and spoke to my dad. Then he went home and told his wife: "I've just seen a champion." Next day I went to his club and I've wanted to be become a boxer ever since.' There are several other variations, but however the story is told, the central tenet is the same: Even the untrained Naseem was a little warrior with the natural speed, agility and elusiveness to beat off several bigger lads.

Today, however, Naseem says it was pure myth: 'Basically, I think it's a load of rubbish. I never had major racist problems and I've never got bullied at all in my life. Never. The story was a good publicity stunt and created a lot of interest at the time – people wanted to hear the story and it worked and gave my career a big amount of interest, and now everybody's familiar with it – but to tell you the truth, I can't remember that incident at all. I think it was made up. I can't remember fighting three guys in the schoolyard – I don't know where that came from, but that's Brendan's story and Brendan will stick to it. What he saw, he saw, but I can't remember doing it. What I do remember is that just down the road from our house was Brendan's gym and there was a lot of success coming from there. My father just brought me down with my brothers – he wanted to start me in self-defence, so I went there, went in the gym and started boxing.' Brendan, on the other hand, insists there was no exaggeration and his son, John, backs him up. 'Naz was the only Arab or Pakistani boy his age in the school at the time, and my father definitely recognized him, because he told us about it when it happened. I think Naz has just forgotten.'

Whatever the truth, all that really matters is that Naseem did indeed have his first boxing lesson early in 1981, at the age of seven, at the St Thomas's Road Boys Club under Brendan Ingle's tutelage. He walked into this large, dark converted church hall with its boxing ring in the far corner, its collection of heavy bags, the pear ball, the speed ball, the pull-up bars, and the odour of decades of sweat absorbed into the splintered floor and chipped walls – all covered with posters and clippings from a game where time passes fast, and fighters age even faster. There he found a kind of ordered informality that is a feature of most boxing gyms, but especially Brendan's, and this immediately appealed. He watched a bunch of boys and men sparring, hitting the bags, punching the pads, shadow-boxing, practising moves, doing ground exercises and the like, and now and then Brendan was shouting instructions to keep the flow going, or approaching one of the fighters to provide some individual tuition or to make a point about some aspect of life and living.

But there was far more to it than that. Go to the same gym today and you'll see things you won't find in any other. For a start, the methods of tuition are very different. The boxers learn unusual combinations and unorthodox punches from an early age. You'll see Brendan calling a group of young boxers together for an exercise where they shadow-box round and round circles painted on the floor, moving their feet back and forth, in and out. It's a strange ritual and one that seems to contradict the traditional iron rule of never going off balance by crossing your feet, but for Ingle there is a paradox here because the exercise is all about remaining in balance whatever position you're in. 'It's about footwork, flexibility, movement and posture,' he explains, not entirely helpfully, though the evidence can be seen in the balance and ability to switch effortlessly from orthodox to southpaw and back, which his better proteges share. There are other unusual exercises too. Some boxers go round after round with their sparring partners firing on both cylinders, and all they're allowed to do is avoid the punches. They tend to dangle their hands comfortably at waist level when outside the fray and they are all encouraged to learn acrobatic manoeuvres – backflips, rope leaps, somersaults and the like – for agility, self-confidence and market-ability.

Like most boxing trainers, Ingle takes the constant threat of brain damage from boxing very seriously. Unlike most, he has a practical solution. As he puts it, 'Punishment in the ring is cumulative. If water drips long enough on a rock, it will crack.' And where most of the drips fall is in the sparring ring, which is why 'open' sparring is a rarity in his domain and why defensive excellence is such a prized commodity there. He explains to each batch of novices why body-sparring is preferable to head-hunting: 'Ya see here, lads, it's better off learning that way than having wars. All the damage is done through open sparring. You can have a bit of controlled open sparring, but you get in there and start bashing each other up, and you're not going to learn anything. And if you damage me, I'm going to try and damage you, and I damage you, you're going to try and damage him, and it just goes on.' He looks at them one by one with his intense, quizzical, wise but childlike eyes. 'You *got* to learn the skill, and what I'm going to try is just to make you see that there's an easier way of doing it than finishing up getting bashed up. If my nose is bashed up, I'm not going to want to spar tomorrow, or if I'm sparring to the body and you hit me accidentally on purpose in the face, what chance is there I'm not going to hit you back? You got me?' That stare again, demanding affirmation, and this time the novices nod as his eyes pass over them, before he seals the point. 'That's the way it goes,' he says emphatically, and then takes a verbal step back to round off the day's lesson. 'Being in here thirty-odd years, I've completely changed the whole lot. You get a workout and you don't what?' – he pauses for the answer that never comes – 'Beat up. Understand? And you learn the skills. Consequently, when you get to box, you enjoy it better and, please God, you don't get hurt. All right. Off you go,' and he waves them off and proceeds to instruct young professionals in the finer points of his craft. Ingle fervently believes his methods are 'taking this sport through to the twenty-first century'.

But his tuition goes far beyond the art of self-defence. On a wall opposite the St Thomas's Boys Club gym you can see the remains of a spraypainted National Front sign that has not been fully erased, giving a hint of a right-wing presence in the area. But this impression is misleading. For the most part Wincobank is free from major racial tensions, partly because of the vigorous efforts of schools, community groups and sports clubs like St Thomas's. Teachers from the three schools Naseem attended say that while theft, drugs, absenteeism and other tensions associated with poverty are rife in some areas of Wincobank, overt racism has never been a particular problem. Within the gym there are frequently tensions over a wide range of other issues, from theft of property (rife in the gym) to 'theft' of girlfriends, but Brendan has made sure that racism and religious bigotry have never been allowed to surface. Black and white, Catholics, Protestants, Hindus and Muslims mix easily. His one trick is to make a bit of a joke about it – always referring to himself as a 'stupid Mick', for example – and in this way get them all immunized to the pet racist terms of insult. But just to make sure, when boxers join the gym they are told emphatically that 'religion and politics is personal and private' and should be left at the door.

Most of these boys were and are from the toughest and poorest sections of Wincobank, with backgrounds more deprived than anything the Hameds experienced. Some are from children's homes, others are young criminals on probation, many come from the 'Flower Estate', where the local council once placed what it considered to be its real welfare hard cases, only to discover too late that this wasn't such a smart idea, with consequences in crime and problems for the local schools which seemed impossible to cope with. The rise in unemployment through the closure of the steel mills meant that in some sections crime became one of the major male pastimes and in this male-oriented community, the sins of the fathers were carried over to the sons. When all else failed, the sons would be deposited at Brendan's door. 'If anyone's got a shot at putting the lad straight, it'll be Brendan,' they'd say. He wouldn't put them straight with a 'tough love' regime, but rather with a mixture of humour, reason, team building and patience. When the boys are caught stealing – and they nick everything from handwraps and jockstraps to shoes, money and equipment there – they are not kicked out. They have to return what they have stolen, stand in the ring, announce their crime and apologize. With each boxing lesson he mixes in a lesson in what he calls 'life skills, social skills, communication skills and how to interact and treat people.' Every would-be world champion gets his chance to climb in the ring, announce his name, tell everyone about his last fight, and do a frontflip or some other antic, before offering a rendition of 'I Can Sing a Rainbow.' They're not allowed to mumble, they have to say please, thank you and sorry, and they're taught to be proud of who they are, tolerant of other races and religions, and to believe that Britain is the best place in the world (and this is coming from an Irishman who tells you he once hated the English).

Ingle sometimes despairs about 'human nature' and the way it manifests itself in his gym, but he still gives the boys their daily lectures on the Seven Deadly Sins and he repeats the lessons over and over again, believing that this is the way to learn – don't steal, lie, or mix boxing with too much sex, or hang out with the 'wrong crowd', or even swear in the gym. Most of these lessons are ignored, but a little gets through. Some of the boys come to learn how to defend themselves against bullies, and, if they stick at it, seldom go away disappointed. Others, probably most, arrive in the gym as lads with an aptitude for fighting and an inclination to use their fists to settle a dispute, and Ingle places great stress on avoiding extra-mural battling and bullying. 'They almost all have had fights outside the gym at one time or another,' he says. 'Naz also had a few scuffles when he was a kid – he always fancied fighting – but the emphasis, the pressure, is on disciplining themselves to learn that sticks and stones will break your bones but words won't hurt you, and to learn to walk away. Of course they get guys having a go at them – Naz will have had that growing up – but the point is that if you can fight, people respect you and they will leave you alone.'

When Naseem arrived there in 1981, these were the lessons he was immediately confronted with, and he took to the whole experience instantly. From then on he could not keep away. As he remembers it, the ethos impressed him enormously but he was there to box, and was particularly transfixed by the sparring – not just the punching but the skill in avoiding punches. 'I remember that first time well,' he recalls. 'I went into the gym and I thought it looked like a great sport, a great art, a great craft – where a fighter could hit another fighter and not get hit back. So I thought, "If you can be like that – get good with your hands and good on your feet – you're not hardly going to be hit, and then obviously you can have a long career and you're going to be successful." So it was a great feeling that first time and I got into it from the start. I thought, "This is the sport for me", and very soon I gathered I was a natural – a natural fighter, natural mover, with natural speed and agility and the attitude for the game, so I knew I was going to go far, and right from the beginning I knew I was going to be a professional boxer and a world champion. That's when the dream started.'

Riath gave up after a few months. Nabeel was more committed and kept at it, on and off, for nearly eight years, ending his amateur career with a record of thirteen wins and four losses. But from the start it was the youngest of the three Brendan focused on, viewing him as a potential world champion from the outset. As Riath recalls it: 'I started boxing, then Nabeel followed, and then Naz got going. But we drifted out, while, as you can see, he hasn't looked back.' Naseem says he was simply more dedicated than his brothers, and had more natural talent. 'Riath didn't have it in his heart and drifted from the game. Nabeel had it in his heart, but drifted too. But I went there to the gym and looked at it at a different level and I kept it up, because that was what I wanted to do.'

He was not immediately popular in the gym, and in fact other than Ingle, Herol Graham and Johnny Nelson, most of the boxers did not take to the little youngster at first. 'From day one, when he first came here, he's always said "I'm going to be world champion," and he was always as brash and cocky as he is now and he hasn't changed at all,' Nelson recalls with an affectionate grin. 'The only thing is, that when he arrived here he had nothing to back it up with, and people scorned him and looked down at him because of what he was saying, because they found it all to be a bit presumptuous.' Graham, the hero of the gym for many years, remembers Naseem as an extremely self-assured child, who had no compunction about assuming his friendship, and making demands on it: 'I lived just down the road from him and he used to come to my house, knock on the door and say, "Come on, we're going training", and I would go. Even then, he was so sure of himself, very forward. He knew what he wanted, he ruled, and that was that.'

With anyone other than Ingle, it is possible that Naseem too might have drifted. But the relationship between this tiny seven-year old Muslim shop owner's son and the wizened forty-one-year-old Catholic socialist was set in stone from day one. Naz just loved 'Old Irish', and Ingle couldn't stop singing the praises of this precocious little lad. There are many boxers in the past who have fallen out with Ingle, who encountered his darker side when he believed they'd crossed him, or who became upset about the financial deals, or failed to understand his convoluted logic and the stories that seemed to have no point unless you listened all the way through to the bite at the end. But Naseem felt sure he would never become one of them. He always knew there were no greener pastures than those he was grazing on, and that for his character and talents he had the best cultivator in the business.

The path that had led Brendan Ingle to Newman Road was

similar to the one followed by Sal Hamed. Raised in Dublin as one of fifteen children of a working-class family, he left school when he was fourteen, and tried his hand at every job he could find – van delivery boy, casual gardener, decorator's assistant, errand runner and general dogsbody for anyone with some heavy work needing attention and a few pence to spare. He also learnt to fight from an early age, having to defend himself against the taunts of his peers because his surname was inherited from an English, Protestant grandfather (who had converted to Catholicism): 'They would say to me, "Your grandfather's English and a turn-coat," and I would have to fight, and then they'd say, "Ah, you think you're tough just because all your brothers box," and I would say, "No, I fight my own fights," and then we'd start fighting again.' He chuckles a little ruefully and adds: 'So I've had it from all sides every time I've opened my mouth, and the same over here because I was Irish.' He left Ireland for England at the age of eighteen in 1958, the year of Sal Hamed's arrival, because his prospects of a regular job in Ireland seemed negligible. His brother, a professional boxer, had settled in Sheffield and one day returned to Dublin waving around £300 and with three new suits in his bag. He told Brendan the city of steel was thriving, so the tough teenager packed his bags, took a job on a building site in Sheffield, and found a room in the Manor – the poorest section of the city, which at the time was covered by layers of soot and smoke which seemed to leave everyone with a permanent cough.

He eventually decided Sheffield was home, and except for a couple of months in Dublin a few years later, he has remained there ever since. 'It was the best thing I ever done. I love Ireland and when I left I used to think the English were the biggest bastards on two legs – tricky, cunning, crafty, devious.' However, a couple of years after arriving he surprised himself by falling for a conservative, English, Anglican, middle-class, well-schooled young woman Alma, whom he later married. Among other things, she persuaded him to further his education by joining the library, which he did with customary relish. 'Now I know they're the cleverest race. What the English done in Ireland was terrible, but now I realize that was the situation at the time, and if it had been the Spaniards or French it would still have been terrible,' he says, shaking his head and then smiling like someone who has found a universal truth. 'Now I'm British by choice, and I am so glad I came here because I have learnt so much about people, but

I'm still Irish.' Ingle's speech and methods are full of such paradoxes. Once a supporter of communism, and still a union-backing socialist, he also strongly admires Margaret Thatcher and some of her policies and opposes nationalization. He's an Irish nationalist who opposes armed struggle and is not convinced by the wisdom of unification; a crypto-pacifist whose hero is Nelson Mandela; a fighting man who passionately abhors violence; a rich 'miser' known for his generosity and community spirit; a 'slow learner' at school who is now a self-made intellectual, always eager to discuss world history, politics, literature or current affairs; and a boxing trainer who alternatively describes his sport as a 'filthy, rotten game' and as being 'so pure there's nothing quite like it'.

In 1961, when Alma was the St Thomas's church secretary, the vicar, the Rev Fred Herrington, asked Brendan to start a youth club in the church hall. Having boxed as an amateur since the age of eight, and having followed the sport fanatically since he was three, he certainly knew the ropes (and didn't know much else), so the youth group became a boxing club. He bought some equipment with his own money, but it didn't take long before most of this was stolen or destroyed. Gradually he developed a core of loyal lads and the club took off. In 1965, two years after the married Alma, the money from Brendan's job as a steelworker was short and the family was growing, so he made the decision to turn professional. He was already twenty-five – a bit old to start a boxing career – but he won his first fight against a gypsy called Dick Griffiths (for a princely purse of £11, after deductions). He stuck at it for eight years, having over thirty outings at welter-weight and middleweight, winning two-thirds of them but retiring at the end of 1973, when he was nearly thirty-four, after a trio of losses in Dublin, London and Copenhagen. At the time he was rated the number eight middleweight contender in Britain. Brendan had a formidable reputation as a fearless streetfighter, and although he never reached great heights as a professional boxer, he was certainly better than most, and what he learnt about the trade he passed on to his youngsters.

After retiring, he built up his own stable of professionals as well as continuing to work with the amateurs, something that was technically forbidden by the stuffy amateur establishment, though they tended to turn a blind eye to the practice. But some of the amateur authorities were unhappy with the mix of professionals and amateurs in Ingle's gym; others did not like the switch-hitting, hands-down style his boxers adopted, or his lack of deference to their authority, or his Irishness, or the fact that he was receiving sponsorship which they felt should have gone into other coffers – and there was particular resentment about a large grant the club received from the Sports Council for its work among underprivileged youth. In June 1978, soon after Herol Graham won the senior ABA middleweight title, it all came to a head and his club was disqualified by the Engish Amateur Boxing Association, on the grounds that amateurs and pro-fessionals were being trained in the same gym. Ingle was beside himself with fury and there were some who feared his dark side would emerge with unfortunate consequences. Even today, he remains bitter about the experience and retains his suspicion of the amateur authorities. 'Up and down the country – all over England – amateurs trained with the pros, without them blinking an eye. I thought if they can do it, then I can do it, but you see, I was a trouble causer, an *Irish* trouble causer, and some of them felt humiliated by the success of my methods. So they told lies about me and used the excuse of the professional thing, and of the Sports Council grant, to disqualify me.' ABA secretary Colin Brown, who was not involved at the time, confirmed that the main issue was professionalism: 'There was a big inquiry and they were suspended. All the tension that led to this conclusion was about amateurs being trained by professionals. People say there is bias, and that's what he may think, but don't ask me why. He's a professional trainer and he shouldn't have been involved with amateurs.' After several days of rage, Alma sat him down, quoted the Bible to him, and Brendan's unusual logic got to work. He decided what he needed was to give up tea-drinking to prove his self-discipline. 'I used to drink gallons of it and then in 1978, when they disaffiliated the club and told all those lies, I didn't want it to get me down – so I thought if I can discipline meself to stop drinking tea, I can discipline meself to do anything.'

Eventually the Ingles found their way back in through the back door. From then on Brendan officially restricted himself to the professionals while his son John took over the amateurs, who boxed under a new flag of convenience – the Unity Amateur Boxing Club – in ABA and schools tournaments. However, they continued to spar with the professionals, who were starting to achieve impressive results, rapidly surpassing anything that had previously been achieved in Sheffield. In the 100 years before Ingle arrived on the scene, the city had produced just three British champions, but over the past seventeen years, Ingle has produced a steady flow of world, British, Commonwealth, European and international champions. Overall, Ingle's has been a record which few, if any, trainers in Britain can compare with, and the reason relates both to his methods and to his personality and character.

The St Thomas's Road gym never developed a formalized hierarchy. Amateurs and pros, boys and men, novices and veterans are all in it together. They mix easily, share jokes and insults and trade punches. But those who make a name for themselves tend to get placed a little higher in the informal pecking order and when Naseem first arrived, the undisputed star was Herol Graham, who may well have been the best British fighter since Jim Driscoll never to win a world title and was probably Britain's finest middleweight and light middleweight of the past two or three decades – better, at 160lbs, than subsequent 'world' champions Nigel Benn, Chris Pyatt and Chris Eubank. There is a strong sense in Sheffield – which Graham shares – that he would have been given far better breaks if the southern English 'establishment' had backed him. He had been a professional for over a decade and had won forty-one out of forty-two fights before he was given his first world title shot, only to lose by a majority decision as a result of a point controversially deducted for turning his opponent, to one of the finest ever middleweights, Mike McCallum. The top London managers did their best to keep their budding stars away from the 'Bomber.' Eubank avoided him after being outclassed in several sparring sessions, and Benn wasn't interested. 'The word got around – keep away from Bomber Graham,' Herol recalls, 'and Naz is the same – not a lot of people want to box him, because he has the ability to move, dance around them and dictate the fight.' The difference, Graham argues, is that Ingle now understands the power politics of the game better than he did in the early 1980s. 'At the time I started, Brendan didn't know a lot about that, really. He's learnt it through having me, and he made sure the same things didn't happen to Naz, but it's a shame he didn't know it then when I was around because I've missed out on a lot ... But there you go, you live your life and make it as merry as you can.'

When the seven-year-old Naseem first made his entrance, Graham at twenty-one was already British light-middleweight champion, with an 18–0 record (which would increase to 38–0 before he lost a decision to future WBA champion Sambu Kalambay six years later after leaving Brendan's stable for the first time). He was a brilliant defensive boxer, the first major exponent of what became known as the 'Ingle style' of switch-hitting and leaning away from punches without ever going off balance, and despite his lack of explosive natural power, most of his wins ended inside the distance as a result of his impeccable timing. At his best, between 1981 and 1990, even the finest light middleweights and middleweights in Britain and the world struggled to land a glove on him, and when he returned to the ring in his late thirties, in 1997 and 1998, he was still good enough to beat a couple of world rated super-middleweights and came close to winning the IBF world title.

In 1992, Brendan and Herol parted ways permanently. The immediate catalyst was the boxer's objection to the sale of his contract to Barney Eastwood for £75,000, but the tensions arose far earlier, from a domestic incident when Graham was living at the Ingle home in the early 1980s which Brendan admits brought him close to the point of carrying out a plan to murder his protégé. Graham says the division is deep and irreparable. 'Look there's tension in everything we do, and yeah, there's still tension with Brendan. It's about life, really. I mean, I want to forget about it. The more I talk about it, the more it stirs a load of things up. I know what's happened and I've paid my consequences, and now I must get on with my life.' Ingle still harbours a deep grudge against Herol but is reluctant to discuss the incident on the record: 'He knows what he did, and he has to live with it.' Ingle often warned the young Naseem not to follow Graham's example outside the ring, but despite this, the younger man still doffs his cap to his first hero. 'Herol was a great boxer. I learnt a lot from him,' he says, which is about as effusive as he gets about another fighter. Hamed's cruiserweight friend Johnny Nelson believes Graham was one of the prime influences on the boy's progress. 'If you look at Naseem's style, he's got a little bit of everybody and some of himself, but you can see he really learnt from Herol. He was fortunate he was in a good gym with a good trainer and mentor, with good people to look up to.' Throughout their time together, Herol and Naseem were regular sparring partners. The boy would chase the man around the ring, and the man would block, slip and duck but never fire back. 'People sometimes ask me, "Why does Naz fight like you?" and I say, "Well, we used to spar together all the time," and I mean *all* the time,' Graham says. 'He was only a little midget, so I used to do the running around. He got to know all my movements, and would try to nullify them. He would just chase me around and that's how he learnt.'

But Naseem was also fortunate to have been blessed with a variety of innate qualities which come under the heading of 'natural ability'. These include his rhythm, reflexes, metabolism, physical strength, hand–eye and time–distance co-ordination, wide peripheral vision, and an astonishing insensitivity to pain which, for instance, allows him to take extremes of heat and cold without flinching. From day one it was apparent that in addition to his dedication and the excellent tuition on offer, unlike his brothers, the boy arrived with tremendous gifts in terms of physical potential. It is also worth pointing out that Naseem is right-handed (with a propensity towards ambidexterity in certain areas) but like most of Ingle's best boxers, he favours a southpaw stance. The 200-year-old notion that a boxer should lead with his weaker hand and hold his stronger hand in reserve for knockout blows is one Ingle threw out of the St Thomas's Road gymnasium window. The logic behind this ancient orthodoxy was premised on the traditional style of boxing at an obtuse angle, seldom throwing hooks or working the inside. It became so entrenched in boxing that many fighters, including Joe Louis, were kept away from southpaws because they had no idea how to fathom their style. But in the modern game, when knockouts are more likely to come from a left hook than a right cross, and where the jab is used as an offensive weapon rather than just a points scorer, it makes sense to lead with your stronger hand rather than holding it in reserve. This becomes even more effective when the boxer has the ability to confuse his opponent, and rest his lead hand, by switching between stances. From early in his amateur career, Hamed developed the ability to 'switch' to orthodox with the same effortless grace that Herol Graham had displayed.

By the time Naseem started at middle school in September 1982, he had already been boxing intensively for over a year and had reached a point of considerable skill and technical proficiency. He was an established presence in the gym, still too young for formal competition but far too good and cocky to be ignored. 'I would say we *had* to work with Naseem, so we got used to him,' Nelson remembers. 'He progressed and got better and better and better, and after a while, one by one, a lot of people didn't want to spar with him, because it was like being hit by a bag of rice and not being able to hit back. He was so fast and skilful. He could talk a good fight, but he could back it up, and if you tried to grab him he was so fast you just couldn't catch him.'

He was to spend his next four years as one of 270 pupils at Concord Middle School, and the memories from his teachers' point of view were largely negative. While his sense of humour, vitality and 'untapped potential' are stressed, even more vividly recalled are the arrogance, laziness about school work, discipline problems and a predatory tendency that sometimes bordered on bullying. Concord's deputy head Mike Delaney, who was a senior teacher there during Naseem's time, says staff had plenty of problems with the young boxer.' He was arrogant and he was also a bit of a bully – well, I'm loath to say he was actually a bully because he didn't pick on one particular child, but a lot of children were in fear of him and I think he put a lot of pressure on them – emotional pressure, if you like – to get his own way, and he always got it because the kids knew that physically they couldn't match him.' When pressed on what the pressure was for, he says it may have been 'sweets and things.' He admits Naseem was not one of his favourite pupils and that he had some bad experiences with him: 'I go through all sorts of emotions when thinking of Naseem because he caused a lot of problems at school.' Particularly in Naseem's first year, he would get into fights, Delaney recalls: 'Initially it was a bit like the old cock of the school thing – the strongest person in the school had to prove himself and the young princes challenge now and then, and this happened with Naseem, and he could handle himself, alright. He was very wiry and was much stronger than he looked. The kids knew this and the parents were loath to challenge the family because they knew they'd have to use the shop, so they just told their kids to stay away. Most of the kids were in awe of him and we had to constantly keep an eye on him because of his relationships with other children. But we managed to keep him out of serious trouble.'

Naseem has a different view of his school years at this age and does not recognize the perception of himself as a bully or as a major league troublemaker. He claims he seldom had problems with the other children. 'I never really got into many fights at school because I had a reputation, so there was respect. They gathered that the small one was the effective one who was trained to fight, so I never got into trouble. They knew that if there were a fight, it wouldn't last very long – not even a minute, like they usually do. So nobody dared abuse me. I'd leave people alone and they'd leave me alone.' John Ingle agrees, saying the idea of Naseem as a bully is far-fetched. 'It's just not credible. He was weighing 60lbs when the average weight of guys his age was 85lbs.' Herol Graham recalls that Naseem was not one of those boys who would pick fights, and usually used his gift of the gab to avoid them. 'He used to get into some scuffles, but he was intelligent enough to get out of them. He had the speed of his legs and the wit of his mouth, and his sarcasm seemed to get him out of everything. But if he had to defend himself, he could defend himself, alright.'

With Sal spending long hours in the shop and with his community obligations, Caria raising the younger children, and neither being familiar with the British school system, it was usually Riath, as the oldest son, who was sent to the school to handle things. Riath was barely seventeen when Naseem finished at Concord but the staff were impressed by his maturity and remembered him as being academically inclined and responsible, so they were happy to accept this role. 'Anytime we had a problem, it was Riath who came to sort it out,' Delaney recalls. 'We never saw his parents, but they would always ask, through Riath, "How are the boys getting on?" – the boys, not the girls – and when his mum and dad went back to the Yemen for a holiday for several weeks once, he seemed to take on the role as head of the family, and we had no problem with that, because if there were problems with Naseem then he would come in and support us. If a note went home or a telephone call saying we had trouble, he came round straight away and whatever agreements were made, happened. Say if Naseem was to be grounded for any length of time, he sorted it, and we couldn't fault that.' Brendan also created a favourable impression, not only through his success in channelling Naseem's aggression, but also because of his occasional visits to the school to find out how his young protege was doing. 'I remember him coming to us a few times, and asking how Naseem was getting on, and I must say I was quite impressed with the guy,' says Delaney.

At the same time, however, Naseem's teachers felt that his obsession with boxing was detracting from his academic potential, though Ingle mentions that Naseem's daily Arabic lessons were also responsible. And aside from these time-consuming activities, Naseem was also expanding his array of other extra-mural interests, particularly in the sporting field. 'I was very good at football, good at table tennis and later I became good at snooker and basketball. I found I had some kind of natural ability at ball games,' he says. However, at school he seldom joined in the mass football games and did not have a large group of school friends, with the gym and the Yemeni community filling much of that need. Graham says the reason for this was that his classmates did not understand him. 'He had some school friends, but most were down at the gym. He was so big-mouthed then – nice with it, but big-mouthed – and at the school they didn't understand him because of his mouth. But everyone at the gym understood where he was coming from.'

The school recognized him as a boy with a good deal of unfulfilled academic potential who, overall, produced below average results despite spells of achievement. Naseem's intelligence was not reflected in his written work, Delaney says. 'He's got talent, alright, has Naseem. He certainly could have achieved more had been more focused, and there was always this unproved gut reaction on our part that he could do better than he did. But he had to work hard to be average and he was lazy about schoolwork and therefore struggled. We often find a particular boy will be brighter than some of the girls, but this doesn't manifest itself in their work. Naseem was like that – he had problems committing things to paper.' Again, Naseem takes a different perspective, stressing that he already knew he was going to be a professional boxer and therefore did not see much point in putting time and energy into schoolwork. 'I just couldn't wait for the last bell to ring so I could go down to the gym and train every day, so for me school was just a passing of the time, because from the age of seven I knew what I wanted in life, through and through.'

This tunnel vision is not something he has accredited to himself retrospectively. His friends say that right from the start boxing was his only real passion and he would regularly remind them of his glorious destiny. Some say he was so single-minded that he missed a great deal of what is taken for granted in a regular childhood, because every day after school and at weekends, he was in the gym. Even in class he would find ways of bringing his obsession into the arena. In one late Friday afternoon session in 1985, for example, each pupil was required to present a show-and-tell oral on his or her hobby. Naseem, then eleven-years old, played a hip-hop number on his ghetto blaster and proceeded to fill the time with a non-stop, high speed shadow-boxing exhibition which impressed his classmates no end. 'We had never seen anything like it,' one of them, Nick Jones, said. 'We were whispering to each other: "That were great." But we never let on to Naz. He already knew how good he was.'

But if some of his classmates were won over, from the school's perspective 1985 was the year when most of the problems with Naseem came to the fore, and it is no coincidence that this was a year of great frustration for the aspirant young fighter. Amateur regulations only allowed boys to begin boxing competitively when they reached the age of eleven, so Naseem presumed that after four years of learning his craft, he would at last be able to enter his first tournament and was devastated to discover he was still eight pounds too light to be allowed to compete in the lowest weight division. He was quite prepared to fight boys bigger than himself, but the regulations compelled him to compete within the accepted weight divisions and there were none light enough to accommodate him. He ended up having to wait a full year before he had grown large enough to enter his first competition, and even then, with some intensive eating under his belt, he couldn't quite make the four and a half stone required. At the time, Ingle had a simple, romantic explanation for this: 'It is very difficult to fatten a thoroughbred, and he is a thoroughbred.' But when he had finally made enough of a dent in the scales (with a couple of pounds help from little pieces of lead around his waist), Brendan was ready. The local press was tipped off that the next 'Bomber' Graham had arrived, his gym-mates were on hand to give him a rousing send-off, and the twelve-year-old had stars in his eyes and was burning to go.

There can be few pre-teens whose sporting debuts have received as much publicity as Naseem's. For the lads of the gym it must have been a bit like waiting for the American boxing authorities to allow Muhammad Ali back into the ring in 1970. Naseem had been at it for five years and was already the best junior in the gym, and, finally, on 24 February 1986, at the age of twelve years and twelve days, was allowed to prove himself – although he wasn't guaranteed a place on the bill. The result shows that the 58lb Hamed won a unanimous decision over Grantham's Peter Ironmonger, who outweighed him by five pounds, at a dinner show at Sheffield's Cutler's Hall. 'I remember it very well,' Hamed says. 'I went along as a spare on the night, just to see if there was an opponent for me, because I wasn't on the programme. Anyway, there was someone to fight and we boxed and I won in style – stole the show – and ended up being named the Fighter of the Night and winning the cup. It was my first fight and it was a good feeling, a good start, a great start.' Brendan heralded Naseem's entry by announcing to the audience that they were about to see a future world champion, prompting the boy to hide his head in a rare show of embarrassment. The trainer then watched the fight from the ringside seats, with his son John in the corner to keep the amateur officials happy. When Brendan tells the story he still glows with pride, because this first win proved all he had been saying about this young upstart. 'He was tiny, smaller than the other fella, but he boxed absolutely brilliantly. He dazzled this kid.' Ingle was immediately onto the local press, chirping Naseem's praises, with the result that the first, gauche printed words about Naseem appeared in the *Sheffield Telegraph* the next day: 'Bomber Graham look out – the schoolboy terror is after you!' The story went on to quote Ingle: 'This fella has got it all, just like the Bomber did, He's a natural.'

Three months later, Naseem fought in Hull against Vince Okenyi who was six months older and six inches taller. Hamed's team-mates thought he won, but a majority of the judges did not approve of his style and gave the other boy a split decision. Okenyi and Hamed never fought again, and his first conqueror was the only lad to stay one-up on him. Of that loss, Naseem has this to say: 'I beat him, but he got the decision and afterwards he looked at me all funny and I thought, "Why's he smiling when he knows he lost?" and I said to myself, "Is there any way we can get him into the ring again?" Then I knew what he was thinking, and I smiled back at him and walked out of the ring smiling, because that was the best thing to do – smile.' Okenyi's coach, Mick Bromby, says justice was done. 'It was a clear, fair decision – definitely no robbery. Vince won that fight comfortably. He was much taller and had much longer arms, and he was able to land straight, hard shots. It was a clean contest, but Vince's longer reach was the telling factor. After that, whenever Naseem saw me he'd say, "Where's that tall black boy I fought?" The last time, a few years ago, I said, "He still lives around here but he's twice your size now, Naz," and he laughed.' After this, Okenyi always fought in a higher weight division than Naseem and went on to win a senior national schoolboy title in 1989.

By the time he finished at Concord Naseem had been boxing competitively for six months and had already had several mentions in local newspapers. Delaney believes this had a positive effect on his behaviour. 'He was good at boxing and successful, he was getting a lot of praise for it and he was going away to tournaments and winning cups and medals and certificates and getting the odd line in the press – the old "Wincobank twelve-year-old wins away" sort of thing – and it became self-perpetuating: the more he was successful, the more energy he put into it, and we were pleased because it gave him a controlled outlet. Brendan Ingle had got him into a bit of a lifestyle, with a timetable, and he got a bit more control in his life.'

Naseem was spending less time with his family now that his entire focus was on boxing. However, his father, who had initially objected to his boy boxing competitively, began to see the positive side to his obsession, and this was reinforced when his son started winning tournaments. By then Naseem was in the gym six or seven days a week and none of his other interests – football, basketball, snooker, martial arts movies, even his religion – could compete. 'Boxing became easy for me,' he explained. 'It was just something you did, like getting up in the morning, going to the bathroom, doing what you had to do in the bathroom. I realized I was very, very good at it and that it was going to be my living.' Even within the home he was constantly shadow-boxing. His sister Noele, then nineteen, complained at the time of sore arms from his 'friendly' blows. 'He doesn't know his own strength.'

By the end of 1986 his record stood at ten wins in eleven bouts, and he still weighed only 63lb – 3lb under the minimum for competing in a schoolboy championships. For the South Yorkshire Schools championship Ingle put him on a four meals a day diet to get him up to weigh, yet he still had to weigh in with a metal bar in the back of his shorts. He eventually won the title by default, because no opponent his size could be found. Within the next six months he would win several more regional schoolboy titles and the local papers adopted him as a mascot, quoting every superlative Ingle threw their way – but still sometimes getting his name wrong. 'Nahim Ahmed is one of boxing's young prodigies,' wrote the *Sheffield Star*, 'a little terror of a scrapper with one problem. He cannot put on weight.'

British amateur boxing has three national structures at the junior level, each with its own competitions: the junior ABAs, the Schoolboys and the Boys Club championships. Soon after Naseem turned thirteen he won his first amateur national title when he outpointed the Kent boxer Michael Wright, in the 32kg (70.5lb) National Schoolboy Championship finals in Derby. As had become his custom by this stage, Naseem entered the ring by vaulting the ropes, wearing what he called his 'wicked gold gown' (complete with shoulder pads and tassels), danced around the ring, did an Ali shuffle, and put on a bit of a show for the crowd. The 4ft 6in, 66lb Hamed was clipped several times in the opening round by his 70.5lb, 4ft 11in opponent, but Naseem's speed allowed him to dominate the second half to win a split decision which he celebrated with his customary front flip. Several of the gym's leading boxers had travelled to Derby to cheer on their young mascot and by the time the fight was over Herol Graham had lost his voice. Naseem returned the compliment by stating that the 'Bomber' was his model. 'He's got all the style and all the moves, and that's how I want to fight. I don't like two people just knocking lumps out of one another.'

Brendan was ready to capitalize on his charge's success, expounding his virtues to everyone who would listen. This included politicians like local Labour MP Richard Caborn, local sports reporters, and businessmen like the Harrogate financier Nigel Burrows, who was shown a Naseem gym exhibition and taken to one of his fights. He was bowled over and in September 1987 announced that his company, Analysis Group, was sponsoring Naseem for £300 a year to pay for his training and travel needs until the age of twenty. This also helped secure a spate of fresh publicity, with the flow aided by the fact that whenever Herol Graham was interviewed, Ingle would ask a favour: 'Don't forget to mention the little Arab lad – he's gonna be the best of the lot.' The *Sheffield Star* ran a full-page spread on the thirteen-year-old, complete with a picture of his family, a wild claim that he was an A-student at school and a Naseem prediction that he would win an Olympic gold medal and a fortune in the professional game. He made it clear that no other occupation interested him. 'I know I can go on to make it as a professional boxer. These plans won't fall through, because I shall just train harder if things get tough. Doing anything else never occurs to me. Boxing is the only thing that matters.'

By this stage Naseem was also becoming a familiar face on the professional circuit, touring the country with his trainers to watch his older chums in action. One of those who got to know him was Des Gargano, a Manchester bantamweight who would go on to become one of Hamed's early professional opponents. 'He's one of those guys I feel I've always known, because he used to go to all the shows as a little kid, travelling around with Brendan, and he used to hang around the professionals,' Gargano recalls. 'I got to know him quite well and he was always telling us he was going to be a champion. Once he told me that one day he'd fight me, and I said, "You'll have to wait a while", but in the end it happened. I always liked him. He had a lot of spirit and he was really confident, but not cocky. He was great.'

At weekends, Brendan would have him over for videos of Sugar Ray Robinson, Kid Gavilan, Muhammad Ali, Ray Leonard, Roberto Duran and Marvin Hagler, and Naseem would watch spellbound and the next day become that 'legend' in the gym. One day he would be Robinson, boxing off his toes, firing off pinpoint hooks while in retreat. The next he would be Hagler, switching from southpaw to orthodox and back; or he'd get his squat little pubescent body up close and bang away, slipping the counters, like Duran, or wind up right and then sneak in a surprise bolo like Leonard. But most of all he was Ali. Anyone who watched the wide-eyed young heavyweight shouting 'I must be the greatest!' would recognize the root of Hamed's antics, even in the amateur ring. Everything about Ali appealed to the youngster: 'Sugar Ray Robinson was a great fighter, but he was way back, so for me the main one was Ali,' Naseem says. 'I watched all of the fights of the young Ali, as well as the Robinsons and Leonards, Haglers and Durans, and Ali was the best – the greatest fighter of all time. He was my idol and I loved everything about him: his style, his charisma, his showboating, the way he succeeded, his class, how he became a world figure. He was a credit to boxing and sport in general. He's made what our sport and all sport is today, especially when it comes to what we get paid. The ball really started rolling with Ali, and I wanted to be a legend like him – the new Ali – so that when I'm gone they'll say, "There'll never be another Naz."' Ali's ideas about life and his approach to his profession seemed to rub off on the impressionable young Naseem, even though 'The Greatest' was by then well into his retirement. When combined with the teaching from family members and Yemeni community activists, and the impact of some of his older stablemates, this contributed to Naseem's conception of himself as a black fighter and his pride in being a member of a broader black community. While he says he seldom experienced direct racism, it is something he is certainly not oblivious to: 'I fight like a black man, and at the end of the day, for a lot of white people here, a nigger's a nigger – don't matter if you're black or brown. I identify strongly with the black community here.'

Another source of inspiration was his love of martial arts movies, particularly those featuring the late Bruce Lee, who died the week Naseem was conceived. Ever since his teens Hamed could be seen pumping out high kicks with considerable dexterity, with some of the moves drawn directly from movies like *Enter the Dragon*. 'In my mind Bruce Lee was a legend,' Naseem says. 'He was a great fighter – the physique he had, the speed, the power, what he could do. I admired him a lot. Bruce Lee had it exactly.' Part of this inspiration related to the way Lee's celluloid creations overcame their diminutive stature to beat up bigger men. Like Lee, Hamed says he has always taken great pride in handling heavies. 'I've always sparred with cruiser-weights and heavyweights, and it don't matter to me how big they are. I could avoid a heavyweight all the way through a fight, but I like taking them out, you know. I like to give them quite a lot of pain and show them the little guy is even stronger.'

Some of Hamed's stablemates say the favourite son treatment he received from Ingle, and by proxy from the press and sponsors, meant that he never had to face up to the adversity other boxers experienced. As Daniel Teasedale, the light-heavy-weight who is the gym's current young amateur star, put it: 'Unlike, say, Johnny Nelson, and in fact most of us, Naz always had it easy in his home life, and in the way he was treated as a boxer. It seemed like he was born with a silver spoon in his mouth.' But although Naseem was Brendan's chosen one, his life on the amateur circuit wasn't always comfortable. Prior to the sponsorship deal he would box in trainers and had one pair of boxing shorts, while he would share a pair of gloves with his brother Nabeel. Because of Brendan's amateur ban, the job of ferrying them to tournaments fell on his son John, who had taken charge of the juniors, and his friend Dave Marriet. Anything up to twelve boxers would be packed into the back of a transit van and transported to working men's clubs, hotels, community halls and even pubs in the pit villages where the tournaments were held, after which they would be presented with a yellow ticket allowing them to claim a meal. Naseem loved the camaraderie and the adulation he received, but, like the others, he had to endure last-minute cancellations, bigger opponents, dubious decisions, pain and disappointment.

His second loss came against Paul Sweeting, in Derbyshire in May 1987. Charlie Grace, the coach of the thirteen-year-old Droylesden prospect, says his lad not only deserved the decision, but also dropped Hamed in the first round: 'The scoring was quite close, but I don't think the fight as a whole was close at all. My boy won quite easily.' John Ingle recalls a different fight. 'I think Charlie Grace must have very fond memories of his boy, because I was there and it was definitely a majority decision and there was definitely no knockdown. I thought Naz beat him easy, and he was never knocked down in any amateur fight.' Hamed and Sweeting fought again in December 1987 and this time Naseem won a unanimous decision, which Charlie Grace concedes was fair. Two years later they fought for a third time in the National Boys Clubs quarter-finals and Naseem won on a third round disqualification. 'Naz was great by that stage – really fast – but he hadn't yet developed his power and strength, so I told Paul the only way he could win was to rough him up,' Grace recalls. 'It was close and Paul was doing quite well, so I told him to try and finish Naz off, but instead he butted him and got disqualified.'

Hamed's third setback was even more controversial, this time against a Buxton boxer he had previously beaten, Vic Brumehead. John Ingle describes this as the worst of the lot. 'They robbed Naz blind. Naz just left the ring laughing, because there was no other way to react. It was total robbery.' Brumehead's trainer, John Taylor, saw things differently. 'Look, Naz was a better boxer than Vic, no doubt about that,' he concedes, 'but I had watched him carefully in their first fight and I told Vic, "You must wait for him to get to you and counter-punch," and he did just what I said. Vic fought very well that night. If Naz had attacked more it would have been different, but I thought it was a fair decision and I think John Ingle is being biased if he says otherwise.' Three months later, in March 1988, they fought once more and this time Naseem picked up an easy points win. 'Yes, I've got to admit Naz was somewhat special that time, and after that Vic didn't have a chance against him,' Taylor concedes.

A fourth loss for Naseem came in 1988 against another opponent he had previously beaten, a tough Darlington lad of travelling stock, Jacob Smith, who would later be jailed for culpable homicide. Once again the fight judges' decision incensed Naseem's people. 'There is absolutely no way Jacob Smith deserved it,' says John Ingle. 'Naz won by a mile, and in fact with each of those so-called losses we felt that he was a clear winner. But the Smith and the Brumehead losses were the worst.' However, Laurie Degnan, Smith's coach, says the verdict was fair. 'I thought it was clear-cut. Jacob forced the fight and got on top of him. He chased Naz around the ring and had him on the back foot, and he won clearly.' Smith, like Hamed, went on to win a national Boys Clubs title, and the pair of them fought twice more, with Naseem winning both comfortably, stopping him in 1989 and then breaking Smith's nose and beating him on a unanimous decision in 1990. 'Hamed had improved tremendously in the eighteen months or so since Jacob beat him,' Degnan recalls. 'By their last fight he was brilliant. The speed of his improvement was unbelievable.'

Naseem won his second national Schoolboys' title on 25 March 1989 in Derby, with a unanimous decision over Plymouth's two-time national champion Scott Dann in the 42kg (92.7lb) final. *Boxing News* described it as a 'blistering display, which revolved around a stiff jab thrown as Hamed moved left and right around the centre of the ring'. Two months later, however, he was to suffer his final defeat, to a tough pressure fighter, Dean Pithie. Naseem had outpointed him earlier that year in the national Schoolboy semi-finals in the Midlands, but they fought again in the 42kg division in the semi-finals of the junior ABA national tournament in Manchester on 23 May 1989. 'He really got robbed then,' says Brendan. 'I remember that fight well. Naz was very flashy and the judges thought he was arrogant, so they just didn't give him credit for how good he was, even though he landed more clean punches and avoided most of Pithie's blows. In fact, he never actually lost any fight. He just got robbed because of his flashiness.' To which his son, John, adds: 'It didn't look that close to me. I actually thought Naz beat him easier than the first time they fought.'

Once again, the opposite corner saw it differently. 'Both fights were fairly close,' says Ron Harkness, Pithie's amateur coach. 'In the first, I thought Dean's cleaner, harder punching may have clinched it, but I wouldn't argue with the decision because it was very tight. But in the second, Dean won every round. He was pressurizing Naz and didn't give him room to move. Naz was trying to wrestle and throw him down because he couldn't do much else. In those days, you see, he was still flicking his punches. The power only came later.' Pithie insists he deserved both decisions. 'I definitely thought I won the first, but I wouldn't complain – it was a majority decision and could've gone either way. But the second fight I beat him easy. It was a very convincing unanimous decision. I knew where he was coming from and I stayed on top of him, stepped on his toes and threw more punches. He was punching quite hard, but not nearly as hard as he would later.' They never had a rubber match because after this, Naseem competed in a heavier division. Pithie went on to win the senior ABA featherweight title, and the WBO inter-continental super featherweight title as a professional.

For Naseem, this defeat confirmed his already healthy cynicism about the inconsistencies in amateur scoring: 'None of those defeats were genuine. I didn't find the fighters who beat me were actually better than me. In my heart, I knew I never lost. I never got out of the ring feeling the opponent had been too strong or too good. Never.' He blames those decisions on the prejudices of the amateur officials: 'The judges in the amateur game didn't like the flash business. They didn't like me because I boxed different from any other boxer in Britain. So when I boxed in championships, I either had to stop my opponent or win very easily, because if I won a close one, they'd probably give it the other way. But I never actually lost.'

David Prior, the amateur administrator who covered Hamed's fights for *Boxing News*, agrees there was stylistic bias at work and that Ingle's 'anti-establishment' stance may also have been factored into the equation: 'They didn't like the hands down, floating round the ring type of thing. I queried it and asked, "Which rule is it contravening?" and no-one could say, but his approach certainly did not find favour.' Hamed regularly received warnings from the referees for his antics, and once, after doing a somersault in the Yorkshire finals, the referee told him, 'I will sling you out of the ring if you ever do that again.' Ray Black, a Humberside official who refereed several of Hamed's fights, said he had to warn him continually for 'intimidating' opponents, clowning and not keeping his hands up. 'What he was doing was showmanship, not boxing. In the rules, it says you have to defend yourself at all times, and that meant you couldn't dangle your hands at your side like he did. It was just a case of applying the rules. There was definitely no prejudice against him. In fact, I liked him – he was a real character.' Gordon Ibinson, a former amateur referee who became Billy Hardy's professional trainer, even gave Hamed a count for this reason: 'I refereed him three times when he boxed in Darlington and he won them all. He was just like he is now – cocky and flashy, but he wasn't knocking them out in those days. I gave him a count of eight once, for dropping his hands. He said, "Why? Why? Why?" and I said, "Because in the amateur rules, you've got to defend yourself at all times," and he had his hands at his sides. It's a different game from the professionals.'

This attitude prompted Brendan to reassess Naseem's style, and to teach him how to set himself for punches without sacrificing his speed. From then on, the 15-year-old Naseem went in search of knockouts. He began to plant his feet more firmly when punching, and having passed through puberty, his strength developed rapidly. The result was that within six months he turned from a relatively light-fisted, hit-and-move boxer, for whom an inside-the-distance win was a rarity, into a knockout specialist. The 1995 senior ABA featherweight champion David Burrows, who lost a majority decision to Hamed in 1989, noticed the difference in his power after seeing him in action again the following year. While Hamed was always strong and skilful, he says, 'it was only when he was fifteen or sixteen that he started to punch.' Larger gym-mates, who had previously described him merely as fast and elusive, became wary of getting into the ring with him because of his new-found power, and everyone there spoke of his remarkable improvement. Films of his fights during his late teens reveal a boxer who was extremely quick on his feet, moving around the ring with his hands low and darting in and out to land telling punches. He was so quick he seldom took a solid blow, and while he had nowhere near the power of his world championship years, he was already able to land far harder than any of his opponents.

By then he was doing serious sparring with professionals

like future British middleweight champion Neville Brown, future WBO light-middleweight champion Paul 'Silky' Jones and middleweight contender Shaun Cummings – and was sometimes getting the better of them. His brother Ali, who had been drifting in and out of boxing, remembers returning to the gym in 1990 and being amazed by Naseem's improvement when watching him sparring with a far larger professional. 'He absolutely destroyed him, he hammered him and was giving him a lot of abuse, and I thought to myself, "How can a sixteen-year-old do that?" And from then on I realized that Naz was going to be extraordinary, because I had never seen anyone like that.' Silky Jones is another who has vivid memories of those sparring sessions. 'The last time I sparred with him was probably 1991, and he was still a boy then, but obviously a hell of a fighter. He used to give me nightmares. There was no-one else in the gym I used to dread sparring with, apart from Naz.' Although Naseem never managed to give Herol Graham much trouble, the Bomber also noticed the sudden development of his friend's power at the age of sixteen. 'As a young kid he was nothing,' he recalls. 'He always had the boxing ability, but not the power. But all of a sudden, because he was getting more mature and stronger, and sparring with bigger guys, he started to punch hard. He was hitting them and hurting them and a lot of people became afraid of him.'

After the Pithie setback there were no more close fights and Hamed dominated every tournament he entered. Twice that year he represented England Schools against Wales, and by the end of the year many were calling him the best junior in Britain. When Naseem had time, he would help out in the shop, but usually he was working out in the gym or touring the country with Brendan or John, competing in tournaments or watching fight films at Brendan's. As a result, unlike his older brothers, he seldom got involved in looking out for his three younger siblings. Ali Hamed spent very little time with Naseem during these years because he was either away or in training. 'He's never been a big brother, to tell you the truth, and sometimes it was like I didn't have a brother called Naseem,' he said with a wry chuckle after Hamed won his first 'world' title. 'There's two older than him, so I never saw him like that, and he was so busy that it's not like we were very close. Even now we're not as close as we should be, because of all his dedication to his training.'

Naseem's single-minded focus had a mixed impact on his

secondary school career at Hinde House High, where he was one of 900 pupils. His academic performance suffered, although Naseem says he got on well with all his teachers and resents those who stress his arrogance and behavioural problems, putting this down to 'jealousy.' Graham Hicking, the deputy head teacher who taught Naseem, says that while there were never any major disciplinary problems, women teachers found difficulty in getting him to respond. 'If it was me or another male teacher then he would listen, but he would find it hard to listen if it was a young lady teacher telling him what to do. Perhaps it's a cultural thing.' He does not recall Naseem getting into many fights, and says that while he was always extremely self-confident and had a quick sense of humour, he usually preferred being a loner or sticking with one or two close friends, before shooting off to the gym after school. Another who taught Naseem, David Caratt, offered a slightly different emphasis, pointing out that in addition to being arrogant, Naseem had leadership qualities. 'He was very self-assured and a bit of a ring leader. He was cheeky, but appealing.' His teachers stressed the role played by Brendan in persuading him to toe the line. 'I was warned that he was a bit of a tearaway,' his former head teacher Graham Elliot said. 'He got into the occasional scrape, but nothing serious. If I ever had any reason to see him, I always said to him: "I can always ring up Brendan, you know."' This mild admonition seemed to work. Hicking believes that had it not been for Ingle, Naseem might not have followed the straight and narrow. 'He was the sort of boy who could have turned out differently if it hadn't been for the positive influence of people like Brendan. He had a certain arrogance, aloofness and a sort of supercilious manner that could get taken the wrong way by teachers and classmates. That arrogance could have turned into aggression if it hadn't been for Brendan.'

Naseem's attendance record and punctuality was good up until his final year, when he was frequently away on boxing tournaments, but his results were poor. He says he was entered for seven GCSE (national year 11) examinations but only completed and passed 'two or three' because of boxing. 'I did well at school. I took some qualifications and passed them, but the main thing I did was I turned up and never took time off school.' School records show he signed up for GCSE courses in art (painting and drawing), physical education, home economics, maths, English language, English literature and two science subjects, but only completed the courses in English (grade F) and art (grade G), along with an internal qualification in maths. Naseem says his aptitude should not be judged by his performance at school, because his focus was on boxing. 'I didn't really set my mind on getting qualifications or on being a clever chap in theory. I just couldn't wait for the last bell to ring so I could go down to the gym and train every day, so for me school was just a passing of time because I knew what I wanted out of life, through and through.' His May 1990 school leaving report describes him as a 'pleasant, well-mannered student ... extremely confident and outgoing with a good sense of humour.' It also calls him 'lively with a friendly personality' and notes that he 'socializes well with peers and enjoys discussions, both giving opinions and listening to others' and is 'keen to succeed.' However, it adds: 'He has been, on occasions, too confident but recently he has made a more consistent, serious attempt to improve upon his efforts.'

During final two amateur years – 1990 and 1991 – Naseem proved himself to be the outstanding flyweight in Britain, even though for most of that time he was not old enough to be allowed to compete against seniors. He started 1990 by stopping Bedfordshire's Richard Izzard in the second round to win the National Boys Clubs 48kg (105.8lb) finals in Basildon on 19 January. Izzard, an experienced, heavy fisted fighter, attacked from the start, but Naseem was nowhere to be found. After a minute of moving around the ring, he shifted stance and connected with a five-punch combination, prompting the first of two standing counts in the opening round. In the second, Naseem, his hands carried low, picked Izzard off with heavy shots, prompting calls of 'stop the fight' from the crowd. A final Hamed right cross persuaded the referee to step in after seventy seconds. 'Naseem turns on all his power,' announced the *Boxing News* page headline. 'Hamed now has the power to complement his style and gold-gown image,' wrote its correspondent Steve Bunce, who added that Naseem 'scored on the move with either hand, from either stance and was powerfully impressive when he set his feet fractionally closer and whipped in three or four shots of hurtful accuracy.' After this, the paper featured 'the golden boy Hamed' as the main attraction among the UK juniors.

Naseem and his close friend Ryan Rhodes pulled off what the

Yorkshire press called 'an historic triumph for Sheffield' by both winning National Schoolboy titles at 48kg in their age groups, in Derby on 31 March 1984. Hamed took 110 seconds to stop Darren Williams in his final. Williams was known as a banger and a mover, but he kept hitting air as Hamed picked him off with jabs and hooks while frequently shifting stance. He then stepped in with a short lead right hook to drop the Londoner, and when he put him down for the second time with an identical punch, the referee stepped in.

Hamed's fifth national final saw him up against his old rival Michael Wright. Naseem had taken a split decision in their first meeting in 1987 but won far more easily in the second in 1989. On 26 May 1990 they met for a third time in the national junior ABA finals at the York Hall in Bethnal Green, and early in the first round Naseem suffered his first serious injury when he landed a hard right on the top of his opponent's head, and then another on his elbow. For the rest of the fight Hamed was in agony and emerged with his right hand badly swollen, although X-rays later showed severe bruising rather than a break. For the remainder of the contest he used his right sparingly, while darting in and out with his left, using it as a cracking lead punch and then backing off and employing it as a defensive jab, but always moving with both hands below waist level, with plenty of clowning thrown in. In the third, Wright launched a sustained attack but seldom connected with anything serious. The East End crowd did not like what they saw and a section screamed abuse at Hamed throughout the fight. 'I was bashing him up,' Naseem recalls, 'and all I could hear from the crowd was: "He's only a dancer, the black bastard! Nigger!" It affected me by making me bash him up harder.' Naseem won a unanimous decision, but afterwards the capacity crowd booed him for several minutes, with the only dissenting voices being chums like Herol Graham and Johnny Nelson.

Naseem had just completed his schooling and was focused on turning professional after the 1992 Barcelona Olympics. 'I have not missed a day in the gym for nine years, I have five national titles and I am on my way up,' he said in an interview at the time. 'I am confident that there is almost no-one of my age who can beat me. I want to win the ABA title and the Olympic gold and then I will turn pro. I have no distractions.' Brendan, however, could see some of the potential obstacles and said that although Naseem

was Britain's best flyweight, he did not expect him to get picked
for the Olympic squad because of the 'politics of amateur boxing',
recalling that the same thing had happened to Graham in the
1970s. Instead, Ingle speculated that Naseem would represent the
Yemen. 'We know he will get picked and will win a gold medal;
we know he is the best in the world at his weight. A country just
united after twenty years of civil war would suddenly have a
sporting hero.'

While Sal Hamed had reservations about Brendan's
appropriation of his third son, and particularly resented an
invitation for Naseem to live in the Ingle home, the influence of
'Old Irish' remained considerable, extending not only to every
aspect of Hamed's boxing career but to most of his life choices.
Interviewed prior to the parting of ways between Naseem and
Brendan, Sheffield's Yemeni community leader Dr Abdul Shaif
said Ingle's impact on the young boxer's life had been parental in
its scope and implications: 'Brendan was not just his second
family, but as much his first family as his actual family. He's not
only been a carer for Naseem but an inspiration as well.
Brendan's trained him, given him everything he has, and Naseem
needs to relate to him just as much as he needs to relate to his
father. It's as simple as that. Brendan has been the dynamic force
behind Naseem's success, and Naseem owes a lot to him.' More
than anyone else, Ingle could see the potential in the youngster.
He had taken Graham and Nelson to the verge of being world
champions, only to see them falter at the summit, and he'd taken
numerous other boxers far further than their natural talent would
have suggested.

He knew Naseem had more innate ability than any of those,
but he had also seen scores of sixteen-year-olds rebel or slip
through indiscipline. One potential problem was the temptation
of drink and drugs, which Naseem's Islamic faith had kept him
away from, although Ingle had a certain caution with regard to
Islam, making it quite clear that, as he put it, 'the Muslims ruined
Ali's career.' Another was 'chasing' girls, something Naseem was
already showing an interest in. Ingle was also wary of his boxers
'hanging out with the wrong crowd' and getting into crime
through peer influence. Naseem, however, had kept his nose
clean, and aside from his disapproval of Naseem's sleeping and
waking hours and the quantities of chocolate and rich foods he
ate, Ingle was delighted with the way things were going. He

predicted his young charge would one day become world professional featherweight champion but also stressed some of the obstacles along the way. 'How good is Naseem?' he asked rhetorically at the time. 'If I could get Johnny Nelson winning a Lonsdale Belt and going into the world ring after an amateur career of three wins in thirteen, there is no limit to what this boy can do. But one thing we have drummed into him: we have told him if there was anything in drinking, smoking and going around with more than one woman at a time, we would all be doing it to better our lives. Naseem has the greatest talent for his age of anyone I have ever seen, but if he wants to be a champion he must live like a champion. He will win everything provided he can live for boxing in the next nine years the way he has lived for the last nine, and I know that will be difficult. From the age of seven he has knocked around with professional fighters. He has seen how champions are made and he has seen the pitfalls. If he is intelligent enough to choose his friends wisely, he has the greatest chance of anyone we have ever had in this gym.'

Naseem's school leaving report stated he wanted a job in the construction business 'to learn a trade with my hands', but instead he opted for the telephone business after Brendan persuaded Steve Strafford, a director of Ashford Communications, to sponsor him for a telephone engineer's apprenticeship at a starting wage of £90 per week. The idea was that Naseem would be able to take time off to box. 'This was Brendan's idea,' Strafford acknowledges. 'Naseem had to be committed to the gym and we agreed, even though he missed some excellent tuition in his apprenticeship course because of this commitment.' He was one of thirty apprentices and, according to Strafford, mixed easily with his workmates, participated in company activities like fun runs and football games, was keen to learn his trade and showed some dedication. 'He was held back from developing his technical skills by his boxing training, which always came first, but he could certainly have become a telecommunications engineer given the time, because Naz is someone who will make a success of whatever he does.' Eventually, the training scheme collapsed, but Hamed remained with the company until turning professional in 1992 and learnt enough to install new phone lines in his parents' house.

Strafford, who has known Naseem since his amateur debut, says they always had an easy relationship. 'You can't not like the lad. It's a shame, all the bravado on TV, because people don't see the other side of him.' Naseem, however, says he never intended to follow a career in this or any other industry. 'The reason I took this job was because he would give me time off whenever I wanted, give me great hours to train and pay me to watch boxing and to box, and though I still served my apprenticeship, and passed my exams and learnt something about the trade, I actually spent far more time in the gym than at work, so I owe Steve Strafford a lot. People would say to me, "If anything goes wrong with your boxing career, you can turn around and be a tradesman," and the only thing I'd say to them was, "You must be crazy – the reason I'm doing this for a while is because I know what I'm going to be and do and it won't change in the future, so get that silly statement out of your head, because I'll never fall back on any trade." '

Shortly after he started working, Naseem achieved his most impressive result when he outclassed the US international Dan Acevedo in a twelve-fight match-up between the American Olympic junior team and the English youth team at Heathrow on 12 July 1990. Naseem, the team captain, fought at 49kg (108lb). He landed at will with both hands and had the favoured New Yorker bewildered by his constant switches in stance and sudden attacks. After the unanimous decision was announced, Naseem did a triple somersault and received a prolonged cheer from the crowd. The only other English boxer to win was Dean Pithie.

Naseem was then chosen by Brendan to be part of the Herol Graham's 'camp' in the Bomber's preparations for his second 'world' middleweight title challenge – this time for the WBC title against Julian Jackson in Spain on 24 November 1990. Naseem spent eight days in Tenerife training with his older chum, specifically to sharpen his timing and improve Herol's mobility, which were seen as the key to beating the slow but thunderous punching Jamaican. 'Naseem had the reflexes and speed to help me because I was doing the running and he was doing the attacking,' says Graham, 'so he was making me move my head, because I wouldn't hit him back. He really made me work.' Naseem was convinced his buddy's extremely positive attitude and all round sharpness would secure him victory this time, after the disappointment of his rather lethargic, disputed loss to Mike McCallum eighteen months earlier. For three and a half rounds he toyed with Jackson, hitting him at will, closing his opponent's eye and taking little in return. But just as Graham moved in to apply the finishing touches and the referee was on the verge of halting the massacre, Jackson, one of the hardest punchers in the history of the division, connected with a trip-hammer right to end the fight. It's a lesson Naseem remembers well: 'That taught me never to lose concentration, not even for a fraction of a second.'

This was reinforced in a sparring session with a 6ft 4in, 225lb professional heavyweight, Adam Fogarty, who dropped Naseem for the first time in his life. 'That's his claim to fame – that he knocked a sixteen-year-old kid down when he was around 6ft 5in, 260lb,' he says, with some exaggeration and a touch of bitterness. 'But I got up and if you looked at his face and you looked at mine, you would have thought I had been the winner, which I was. He had a nose bleed and he took some good shots and some good punishment that night.' Brendan watched this incident from the far side of the gym with both horror and amazement: 'I was just coming in the door when Fogarty lifted him off the floor with a punch and put him on his backside, and then Naz backflipped off the floor and hit Adam on the chin and then bust his nose.' Fogarty himself has disputed this version, saying that he clipped Hamed accidentally and denying that Naseem hurt him, but Johnny Nelson, who was the time keeper, says this is not another piece of Brendan blarney. 'Naz was being his brash, fast self and he was really taunting and tormenting him, because Adam couldn't hit him. Naz was hitting him, then telling him what punch he was going to land next and each one went off, and Adam got frustrated – and as Naz went in, Adam closed his eyes and hoped for the best and he connected. As Naz went down he did a backwards somersault, springing straight back onto his feet again, jumped back in, hit him with a right cross and just nailed him. He broke Adam's nose and gave him two black eyes. Unless you saw it you would not believe it, but I was there, and it happened.'

Hamed ended 1990 by beating Michael Wright for a fourth time, to take his second junior ABA title and his sixth national amateur title, this time at 51kg (112.4lb). Boxing once again at Bethnal Green's York Hall, he gave a more lethargic performance but still won a wide unanimous decision. Two months later he turned seventeen, making him eligible at last to box seniors, though still classed as a junior in the international realm and in some of the national championships, including the ABA seniors.

As a result he had only a handful of fights in 1991. His senior debut took place in Sheffield on 15 April 1991 when he took a unanimous points win over Northampton's Chris Robson, after which he won the National Boys Clubs flyweight title in the seventeen-year-old age group at the Grosvenor Hotel in London, on 13 May 1991. Naseem was up against Colchester's Danny Adams, who, like him, was a former national schoolboy and ABA junior champion and England international. It was a harder fight than most of his others, with Adams landing several solid punches, but Hamed was far too fast for him and had a higher workrate. In the last round Adams was given a public warning for holding as Naseem rattled home rapid-fire combinations.

The final outing of Hamed's unpaid career came after a long period of inactivity. On 17 October 1991 he accepted a late call to box in Manchester and was given time off from work to make the trip. Together with John Ingle and the 'old man' of the St Thomas's gym, Jimmy Wood, he drove across the Snake Pass in stormy weather to face local favourite and Young England international Michael Brodie, a seventeen-year-old national junior ABA and national Boys Club champion. The event, hosted by the Ancoats and Miles Platting Lads Boxing Club, where Brodie was the star attraction, and held at the Manchester Club, drew a capacity crowd who booed 'Ahmed', as he was called in the programme. Before the fight the two stables had agreed that both boxers would make the flyweight limit, which meant Hamed had to sweat off a couple of pounds. He came in at 111 and was irritated when Brodie came in above the agreed weight, at 113 lbs. The seething Naseem was determined to end it quickly. Wood, a self-styled 'money lender' and 'half-millionaire' who, in his mid-fifties still trained and sparred every day, remembers the occasion vividly. 'Naz came out in his leopardskin shorts and did his vault over the ropes and the crowd went "Boo, boo," and some of them shouted racist slogans, and then Brodie climbed through the ropes and got a massive cheer. The bell went, Naz circled for a few seconds and then he landed a brilliant combination to the head and Brodie was counted out after thirty-two seconds, including the count, and there was silence, complete silence.' Brodie went on to win the British, and European Commonwealth super-bantamweight titles as a professional.

At seventeen years and eight months, Naseem Hamed's amateur career had effectively come to an end with an official record of 62 wins (18 stoppages) and five defeats (all on points), and with seven British junior titles to his name. Impressive though it might be, his record was deceptive. First, some who followed his career say his real tally should have been 67-0, and it is notable that he went unbeaten for the final two and a half years and twenty-three fights. Second, while his 27 per cent knockout ratio does not suggest much power, almost all of these stoppages occurred in the final stretch. Third, when he entered the professional ranks he was far more experienced than his record suggested. Although he had only competed for five and a half years, he had been active for over ten, two or three hours a day, six or seven days a week.

By this stage Naseem and Brendan had already decided he would turn professional as soon as British Boxing Board of Control (BBBC) regulations allowed: on his eighteenth birthday. Some in the amateur ranks resented this move, pointing out that for several years Hamed and Ingle had been predicting Olympic gold, only to abandon the ranks six months before the moment of truth. The fighter himself says the decision was motivated partly by his desire to earn 'real' money as quickly as possible, but also by the perception that he would not get picked. It was once even hinted to him by an amateur official that his image might not be right for the British team. 'There was a lot of politics in the amateur game,' he says with a still resentful tone. 'I would have been the best in the country and I could have made the team easily but they were always picking those English kids they favoured. It was like they were already picked. In the amateur game, if your face didn't fit then you wouldn't get in, and that's what it was like.' Ingle reinforces this point, stressing that the amateur establishment's long-standing 'hatred' of his club meant that the Olympic selection committee would find a way of bypassing Naseem. It is worth pointing out that at the time, there was a good deal of infighting in the amateur establishment and widespread allegations of financial mismanagement and maladministration as well as favouritism. 'The politics of the amateur game is such that we've always had problems,' says Ingle. 'He wouldn't have got picked, because of his style and because they knew where he was training.' And it is here that Ingle gets onto a point that his many amateur critics say smacks of paranoia. 'If you're the national coach, you're onto a good thing. You've got your whole system of training and if my kids lick yours, then my system has to better than yours, but you can't admit that to yourself. They felt humiliated.'

But there was more to it than that. Brendan was concerned about allowing the British national coaches to tamper with Naseem's winning style and was wary of attempts to poach Hamed by offering huge financial inducements after Barcelona. He also knew that Hamed's age counted against him, as he'd had little chance to prove himself as a senior in Britain, and that the Yemen option had faded because of the Olympic requirements regarding nationality. Today Brendan insists the decision to go professional immediately has proved to be the correct one. 'If he'd been picked for Barcelona, sure, he would have gone and won the gold medal, but in the end we proved our point. What is better, to be world champion and a millionaire at twenty-one or to be still fiddling around with the amateurs and have people messing you about?'

2

THE ARABIAN KNIGHT

Naseem Hamed's childhood amateur debut had been marked by remarkable fanfare; his teenage start in the professional game took this to new and unprecedented heights. However, it was a start which took longer than intended to materialize as he had to wait six extremely frustrating months without a fight. The gap was not supposed to be so wide, but a couple of amateur engagements fell through and his professional debut could only be arranged nine weeks after his eighteenth birthday.

But the time was not entirely wasted. Every day the young boxer would walk the 200 yards from his front door to the St Thomas's Boys Club hall and work out for three hours, and sometimes more than once a day. Having always trained with professionals, and with a style that was to prove so well-suited to the professional game, it took no great effort for Hamed to adapt. His routine therefore remained the same as before, just with more rounds – and anyone watching them could hardly fail to be impressed.

A favourite trick he and Brendan liked to show visitors to indicate just how fast and agile he was, involved a combination of thirty-eight punches, with up to eight different foot movements, in eight seconds – nearly five punches a second, with a shift in stance or a step backwards or forwards each second. He was once timed throwing fifty-four punches in twelve seconds and it was not just pit-a-pat stuff; the blur of fists included jabs, hooks, crosses and uppercuts. Another trick he used to torment sparring partners involved keeping his eyes fixed on their feet while telling them which punch he would hit them with next, and despite their best efforts it would land just as he'd promised and without him getting hit in return. Those who worked out with him at the time say his improvement was remarkable. He had by then reached his full height of 5ft 3in but as his body thickened out, so his strength and power continued to grow.

Johnny Nelson, who sometimes sparred with Naseem, said he destroyed the confidence of several good, large professionals at this stage, including Neville Brown, who went on to win the British middleweight title, and Shaun Cummings, a super-middleweight contender. 'Naz was sparring with these big men, adults of twelve and a half stone, when he was still a teenager, and he was slaughtering them. Neville didn't want to spar with him anymore because Naz was hurting him, and Neville couldn't touch him – and he's a decent fighter. Naz just destroyed him, and the same with Shaun. They both left. There were lots of guys who came here and wanted to join the gym and when they got in with Naz, he ridiculed and destroyed them.' Or as Brendan Ingle put it: 'Naz would stand in front of Neville and punch the hell out of him, and Neville just couldn't take it. Naz stood Neville on his head.' Brown himself was happy to sing the praises of the youngster: 'I've sparred with that guy and I cannot believe what he does sometimes in that ring. I had to be on my top form just to survive in there. He's dynamite. I'm pretty fast, but he's out of this world. He can bang *and* box, and he's also got the balance to come back with a combination you don't even see.'

For thirty years Brendan Ingle had been developing his unique style of tuition and for over a decade he had focused on Naseem as his star pupil. He was the basic inspiration for everything Hamed did in the ring, but over the years Naseem kept on adding to it and pushing its parameters, with boxers like Nelson and Herol Graham available to learn from. The period of intensive tuition between the end of his amateur career and his professional debut helped consolidate his skills. 'Brendan told me to be flash, tricky, on my toes,' Naseem said in an interview prior to his later kamikaze phase as world champion. 'He told me I was right to think that the point of boxing is to hit and not be hit. I never want to get hit. Who wants to get hit? It hurts. I've always wanted to be different. If you are a normal fighter, people can work out how to beat you. I wanted a style so unpredictable that no-one can work out what's going on, what I'm going to do next. I can switch and lead off with either hand, from either foot. When you can do that, you've got to be special. I wanted to be extraordinary. Extraordinary. I've always wanted to be extra-ordinary, exceptional, supreme.'

Meanwhile Ingle was busy looking for the best promotional options and lining up sponsors. At that stage Naseem had been receiving sponsorship from his employers, Ashford Communications, the businessman Nigel Burrows and later the Yorkshire sports outfitter Tim Sugg. For a seventeen-year-old who had never won a senior national title, nor any international competition, it was a vote of confidence that illustrated both Hamed's potential and Ingle's wiles.

Another group that readily came to Hamed's aid was the Yemeni Community Association, which, a few days after his last amateur fight, agreed to loan him £3,000 to buy boxing equipment. This later became the centre of a row within the association that spilled over into the local press, with the issue of contention being Sal Hamed's role as a member of the organization's management committee. In fact, Sal was opposed to his son's choice of profession, feeling it was not sufficiently respectable nor a particularly secure way to earn a living. Three weeks before the loan was granted, Sal was quoted as saying that he and Caria had hoped Naseem would retire as an amateur and that they could not bear to watch him in the ring. 'I wish he would give it up. I don't like him boxing but what can I do? It's his life and it's what he wants to do,' he said. It did not take long, however, for Sal to get with the programme and soon he was a familiar ringside presence at every Naseem fight, nervously puffing on his cigarettes and then shouting and gesticulating and smiling all over when the job was done, often climbing into the ring afterwards to give his son a hug. Caria, while still nervous about the risks of injury, has encouraged her son ever since he made his career decision. 'My mum feels something, just like any other mother with her son going in to fight and with the dangers in boxing,' says Naseem, 'but we sit down before a fight and she says, "Which round do you want to take your opponent out in?" and I say the second or the third round, and she turns to me and says, "It's done – you just keep training, get your mind on the job and you'll do it." '

But it was not just his family he had to convince. When he started telling people within boxing of his plan to fight for pay immediately after his eighteenth birthday, the reaction was largely negative, the main argument being that he needed a couple more years within the amateur ranks to mature physically. With his old-fashioned side-parted short back'nsides, his child-like face and slight, boyish body, Naseem looked a good two years younger than his age and the idea of him competing in the toughest male profession of the lot disturbed some of his followers. 'A lot of people thought I shouldn't have turned pro at eighteen, that I was a bit young,' Naseem recalls. 'They were saying, "You told us you would box in the Olympics and that you were going to do this and that." I was quite young looking at the time, and they were underestimating me by saying I was too small and too young, so I just couldn't wait to show my ability – that I was strong enough to out-box, out-think, out-punch and out-strength mature men.'

Ingle had worked with several promoters before, but it was decided that the Matchroom boss Barry Hearn had the right style, connections and vision to take Naseem's career forward. The Romford-based Hearn was and is the archetypal Essex Man. Tall and handsome, with his cropped grey hair, easy charm, flashy smile and sometimes flash temper, this chartered accountant was the born salesman, who had made his millions through a business empire that involved revolutionizing world snooker before settling on boxing, and then, in 1994, expanding to football. As with most major league boxing promoters, there were many who did not like the way his organization sometimes did business, the control he asserted over his fighters and some of his business connections, but at the time the deal was negotiated at the end of 1991, he was the most dynamic promotional force in professional boxing. Among the fighters contracted to Matchroom were several 'world' champions, including Chris Eubank and Nigel Benn. Hearn had established extremely cosy ties with the World Boxing Organization (WBO) hierarchy, with the result that his fighters seemed guaranteed of generous treatment by that organization. Perhaps more importantly, at that point Matchroom was putting on more major shows than any other group and Hearn's fighters were generally getting a better deal as far as media exposure was concerned.

Naseem's fights would be televised by the satellite channel Screensport, which would give him exposure in Europe, with the prospect of bigger things once he 'took off'. It was initially agreed that Ingle would not relinquish his rights as Naseem's manager and that Hearn's sole role would be promotional. As with all his professional fighters, Brendan would receive 25 per cent of Naseem's purses (£1,000 per fight for the first year) for his role as both manager and trainer, and 33⅓ per cent when Hamed boxed abroad – an arrangement that would break down, with considerable acrimony, a few years later.

Long before Naseem's first fight, Ingle's brain was ticking over about how he could boost publicity for his young star, and the idea emerged of making a splash out of the mundane business of Hamed signing his professional boxing forms. Ingle contacted his close friend Richard Caborn, the Labour MP for Sheffield Central, and it was agreed that Naseem would launch his pro career at the House of Commons. A veneer of credibility would be added to the occasion by a meeting between Ingle and Hearn and the multi-party parliamentary boxing group of MPs (formed by MPs who are supportive of the sport). Caborn was delighted to co-operate. For over a decade he had established a close friendship with Ingle, working with him on a number of projects and providing financial assistance to the gym. He had also built up firm connections with Sheffield's Yemeni community and in particular the community association. Caborn had first met Naseem when visiting the gym ten years earlier. 'I thought there is no doubt this is a very talented lad,' he recalls. 'He was a tough little cookie but he had dedication and his feet on the floor.' Hearn and the St Thomas's contingent met with the MPs on 4 March 1992 – three weeks after the boxer's eighteenth birthday – following which a pre-prepared, laudatory statement was issued, noting that the parliamentary group recognized 'the sterling work which Brendan Ingle, the supertrainer from Sheffield has achieved for the sport.' After that Naseem signed his forms in the House of Commons in front of the MPs and the press – creating the desired impact, at least in his home town.

Another boost came when George Zeleny, the editor of the British monthly magazine *Boxing Outlook*, made the brave choice of putting Naseem on his front cover and running a four page lead story on him, entitled 'Boy Wonder', which began: *'Boxing*

Outlook predicts that Naseem Hamed is Britain's new super-star in the making.' It added a quote from Steve Bunce, *Daily Telegraph* boxing correspondent that 'There's no danger of him not being a world champion.' Zeleny went on to note that 'his entry into the professional ranks could be the most important milestone British boxing has passed since the ever-popular Barry McGuigan surged to the WBA featherweight title six years ago. We believe that this son of an Arab immigrant will be something really special, the breath of fresh air that British boxing has long been looking for. ... We believe he's the goods, the next boxing phenomenon, the next Boy Wonder.'

Naseem, Brendan and John Ingle also began to work on creating a more defined image for the young fighter, to add to the rope vaulting, acrobatics and gold gown of his amateur days. It was only at this stage, for instance, that the words Prince and Naseem were inextricably linked; sometimes as 'Prince Naseem – the Arabian Knight', or just plain 'Prince Naseem Hamed', and later simply as 'The Prince'. The idea was that the name 'Prince' combined images of fistic royalty with those of succession – prince today, king tomorrow. By mixing this image of being heir to the throne with the not entirely consistent picture of the Arabian Knight, an air of mystique was consciously introduced. This name-association was to become an ad man and headline writer's dream, the kind of instant identity that created a strong, definable image and was easy to play with – the two favourites, which achieved cliché status, being 'The artist still known as Prince' (a reference to the singer) and 'The Prince born to be king'.

All that was left was to find the right debut opponent and the best bill to feature the fight on. The opening came at the Mansfield Leisure Centre on 14 April, headed by a fight featuring Hamed's heavyweight stablemate Clifton Mitchell. It was decided to make an instant impression by skipping the usual practice of moving from the three rounds of the unpaid ranks in those days to four rounds for novice professionals, and instead to going straight into a fight of six three minute rounds – a move commended by the serious fight press.

After the first six designated opponents found reasons to cry off, the final choice, Dagenham's Ricky Beard, was regarded as bit risky by some of Naseem's more cautious advisers. A former North East London senior ABA champion, the tall, tattooed Beard had been a professional for three years and was rated the number six British flyweight, although he did much of his fighting at bantamweight. He was five inches taller than Naseem, naturally bigger, eleven years older and had a reputation as a banger. His record showed a moderate two wins (both inside the distance), one draw and six losses, but most of the defeats had come against top-rated men. He always put up a good fight and had never been counted out, although the future WBO world bantamweight champion Robbie Regan beat him on a sixth round stoppage in 1990. Six weeks prior to the Hamed fight, Beard had given the former British champion Francis Ampofo a good run in an eight rounder and seemed to be improving (an impression confirmed by subsequent wins, including an eighth-round stoppage of former Commonwealth champion Darren Fifield three years later). Unlike most debut opponents for future 'stars', Beard fancied the job. 'I was supposed to be the hardest-hitting flyweight in Britain, I was a lot older than him, I'd been fighting for fifteen years and I was having my tenth professional fight, so I knew I had a big edge in experience,' he said. 'I thought he was just a flashy kid and I could go out, meet him head on and knock him out.'

Naseem was in a state of high excitement, filled with the sense that his destiny was about to be realised. 'I had a lot to prove that night. People were saying that I was taking on too much by boxing a grown and mature man who had twice gone the distance with the British champion, and that I was getting in the deep end a bit. I had watched Beard before, in his second fight against Ampofo, and he put up a good fight, so he was a great opponent for me. I had to make people realize I had the skill and the ability to go with my confidence, and I just couldn't wait to get into the ring and prove I was going to be a great professional.'

Brendan did his best to drum up interest in the occasion, making a special pitch to the Sheffield Yemeni community by announcing that Naseem would be wearing his ceremonial Arab dagger, shawl and head-dress for the fight. 'I wanted to add a bit of colour and flamboyance to his image,' he explained. 'The Yemenis of Sheffield have lost a great deal and he has given them something to be proud of.' For many fans and reporters, his ring entrance provided their first glimpse of Naseem – coming down the aisle with his torso covered by the Arab poncho but still looking tiny and juvenile next to the huge, sullen minders accompanying him, and then vaulting over the ropes and giving the crowd a front flip. As he stood to face Beard, the instant impression was of a little boy defiantly facing up to a hard man. They might have weighed the same (114lb) but Beard looked so much bigger and stronger than the skinny lad in his naff fake leopardskin shorts. The combination drew peals of spontaneous laughter from the crowd.

Naseem started out extremely quickly from the southpaw stance, darting in and out, bouncing up and down, twisting and turning to get out of the way of Beard's bombs, leaping forward and landing punches in combinations of five, six and seven. Beard attacked, but only managed to land two punches, both glancing right crosses that connected while Naseem was moving away. Halfway through the round Hamed put Beard down for a two-count with a left-right combination to the chin. 'I'd never before been caught in the first,' Beard recalls, 'but his speed and power were unbelievable. I was the number five contender but there was nothing I could do with him and he made me feel like an inexperienced novice.' Hamed's supporters were shouting, 'Come on, Nabby', 'Come on, Naz', but Beard used his experience to survive until the bell.

Between rounds, Ingle told Hamed to calm down and set himself more. Soon after the bell, Beard's nose bled from a flush Hamed punch. The older fighter kept his guard high and smiled, trying to draw Naseem towards him, but it had no effect and he soon took on the demoralized look of a man who knew his own execution could no longer be stayed. Hamed had the look of a boy extremely eager to pull the trigger as he rained punches from all angles on his unfortunate opponent, every now and then finding time for a little clowning gesture. 'I wanted to put on a show for three or four rounds but I thought, what the hell. He was laughing at me behind his guard, so I let the body shot go and I knew he wouldn't get up.' The final, casual-looking bolo punch did not look particularly heavy, but it was so well timed, fast, and accurately delivered that its effect was devastating. Beard still remembers the final moments before Naseem slotted the *coup de grâce* through his forearms. 'He backed me up and I stepped one way and at the same time he stepped the other, and he hit me in the solar plexus with a very good right. It was a perfect punch which could have dropped Frank Bruno and I doubled up, went down and was counted out for the first time before or since.'

Beard has always been a brave trooper and despite being winded, he made a serious attempt to get up, before collapsing forward again. When referee Thomas's count reached ten at the 2:36 mark, Naseem performed four celebratory somersaults and did a little jig before announcing: 'I am strong enough to be world champion before I'm twenty-one'. Beard had no cause to disagree. 'He was really very, very good. Everything he says he'll do, he'll do.'

Ingle was delighted with his charge's performance, despite Naseem's overexuberant first round: 'It was a boy against a man in there, but the boy became a man in the second round. I give him ten out of ten.' Later Naseem was to say that this victory should have revealed his full potential to the boxing world. He had, after all, given a far more convincing performance against Beard than had Regan or Ampofo. 'I carried it off really well, you know. I showed I had it all from day one, and people should have realized I weren't a flash in the pan.' In fact, he had nothing to complain about. The Yorkshire papers were ecstatic and *Boxing News* treated it as the main undercard fight, under the heading 'Sharp Nas is a class act', while other more established performers like Naseem's sometime stablemate Paul 'Silky' Jones and middleweight contender Martin Smith were given footnote reports. Naseem was now on his way to fulfilling his calling. He had leapfrogged the flyweight rankings and in his first fight had made a name for himself.

A delighted Barry Hearn moved quickly to establish a momentum by featuring Hamed on the undercard of a show in Manchester eleven days later, headed by Chris Eubank's defence of his WBO super-middleweight title against John Jarvis. Naseem's opponent was the twenty-two-year-old Leicester boxer Shaun Norman, a former Midlands ABA finalist, who had won one, drawn one and lost three (all on points, at bantamweight) in his six months as a professional. In his last fight he had drawn with former British amateur international Neil Armstrong and in December 1991 had taken the then undefeated Mickey Cantwell (who went on to win the WBC international and British flyweight titles) to a close verdict. Norman was not expected to beat Hamed but was thought to be cagey enough to last a few rounds.

Naseem, weighing in once again at 114lb (half a pound less than Norman), put on a bit of a show at the start and took three right crosses for his trouble, before getting down to work, dropping his opponent with a left cross from the southpaw stance for a count of three. Norman returned to the corner bleeding from a cut under the eye and looking like he'd rather be somewhere else. In the second, Hamed continued to play, doing an Ali shuffle, dancing around with his hands low, making constant shifts in stance and teasing Norman with exaggerated feints. A right hook to the jaw shook the Midlander, after which Naseem pinned him in a neutral corner and pounded him. As Norman tried to escape he took a right which put him down and though he wobbled up at the count of eight, referee Roy Snipe decided he had seen enough, fifty-five seconds into the round. Naseem did three somersaults across the ring to celebrate.

Once again the Sheffield youngster had got the job done far more impressively and decisively than the top British contenders, and had given the crowd what *Boxing News* described as 'an entertaining and arrogant display of boxing and showmanship which put Chris Eubank to shame.'

This second victory had an unintended spin-off in boosting Naseem's profile. Just as the stuffy amateur establishment had turned up their noses at his antics, so now the professional authorities began to get shirty. British Boxing Board of Control secretary John Morris gave Naseem an imperious ticking off about his backflips and other acrobatic stunts, warning him to 'cut it out' – just as he would do in rather more deferential terms after the Steve Robinson fight over three years later. At the same time, clips from Naseem's two fights were shown on ITV and its commentator, Reg Gutteridge, used the opportunity to castigate Naseem's behaviour, which prompted *Boxing News* editor Harry Mullan to weigh in with an editorial piece entitled 'Carry on Clowning' (complete with a picture of a somersaulting Naseem) in which he argued that Hamed was entertaining, the crowds loved him and it made for good TV. 'I see nothing wrong or offensive in what Naz is doing, any more than in Eubank's theatrical posturing and posing,' Mullan wrote. For a two-fight flyweight to be the subject of such a high-profile debate was the kind of bonus that made Hearn salivate and Ingle smile, and its only effect on Naseem was to prompt him to search for new angles to best display his wares. He had never been someone to shun controversy, but from then on he did his best to court it.

His third professional outing came against Andrew Bloomer, a Welsh featherweight of sub-journeyman pedigree, in Birmingham on 23 May 1992. After an amateur career which took him to the Welsh ABA bantamweight finals, the twenty-seven-year-old from Pontypridd had turned professional as a featherweight in May 1991 and had amassed a neat record of eleven fights and eleven losses (all on points). What made the match-up vaguely interesting was Bloomer's size and durability. He stood 5ft 9in and at 120lb had a six-pound weight advantage. Fighting against bigger men was something of a hobby for Naseem, and a much-beaten featherweight presented no fears for a fighter accustomed to going head-to-head with heavyweights, but Bloomer was a real survivor who had never been stopped and only once dropped, and had lasted the distance against several noted bangers. The test for Naseem was to see if he could go one better by winning inside the distance.

This Hamed achieved with ridiculous ease. His first punch was a cracking right hook which connected, followed ten seconds later by another which missed and sent himself tumbling in Bloomer's corner. After that minor embarrassment, Naseem toyed with the heavily tattooed Welshman, switching from south-paw to orthodox several times to confuse him, clowning in the centre of the ring and thumping home a lead left uppercut, which after this was to become his favourite knockout blow. It wobbled Bloomer and left him with a nosebleed. The skinny Welshman threw a few desperate shots at the start of the second, all of which missed, before Hamed stepped in with a right-left combination, followed by another solid left hook. Bloomer took refuge on the ropes but Naseem drummed home a barrage of heavy blows. The final punch, a heavy right hook, caused Bloomer to turn away, his legs slowly folding, and referee Jim Pridding jumped in to rescue him at the forty-six second mark, giving Hamed his third second-round stoppage in a row – a result he celebrated with his obligatory backflips, cartwheels and twirls, before helping the forlorn Bloomer out of the ring.

Ingle trumpeted to the press that his boy had 'stolen the show' from the main event featuring Nigel Benn winning an extremely dubious decision against Thulane 'Sugarboy' Malinga. After this fight, Naseem expressed his disdain for the potential opposition within his division and he would later say he regretted he never had the chance to beat up 'those old-timers' Robbie Regan, Francis Ampofu, Dave McAuley and Pat Clinton. This was typical of Hamed's mentality – he found it difficult to refrain from expressing as provocatively as possible his honestly held beliefs, and these included a conviction that his God-given talents were far superior to those of anyone else within his range – and he always had a strong inclination to needle potential major league opposition.

The mid-1992 Hamed was far from the finished article – he still did too much jumping around, and had yet to develop the strength and power he later showed – but he already had all the basic tools which would soon make him the finest fighter, pound for pound, in Britain and Ireland. It was not the results that counted, but the way he delivered them. Beard, Norman and Bloomer were hardly world-beaters, but Hamed was flattening them up in far more decisive and unequivocal way than anyone else. Even at that early point in his career, Naseem probably hit harder than any other flyweight in Britain, was certainly faster and more difficult to hit, and was accustomed to boxing up to twenty fast rounds in the gym without visible signs of fatigue. The way he handled bigger men in sparring suggested the idea of him taking the British title in his fourth or fifth fight would have been feasible.

Ingle therefore announced he would be pressing the case for the Boxing Board to waive its regulation that a boxer turn twenty-one before being allowed to challenge for a British title and give Hamed special permission to challenge Regan for the flyweight crown. Needless to say, permission was not forthcoming. Meanwhile Naseem's natural body growth, combined with his taste for chocolates, junk food and his mother's cooking, meant that over the next seven weeks he filled out by over five pounds. With the realization that the flyweight title option was a no-go, Ingle decided there was no point keeping his lad's maturing body within range of the 112lb limit, and Naseem stepped up to bantamweight (118lb).

His fourth opponent, exactly three months after his debut, was another B-list Welsh featherweight, Nicholas 'Miguel' Matthews of Ystalyfera. He was one of those British boxers who get plenty of work from promoters because they're always available at short notice, they know how to survive in the ring and there's little danger of them pulling off an upset. Matthews, at twenty-six, had amassed fifty-one fights in less than four years, with a paltry six wins (two inside the distance), eight draws and thirty-seven losses (four inside the distance). It was a deceptive record, however, and he was far better than his official tally suggested. Several of the draws and losses had been out-and-out robberies, with around half of them being by half-point or one-point margins, and his conquerors included some of the best in the business between bantamweight and lightweight, among them WBO 'world' champions Colin McMillan and Johnny Bredahl. Matthews was four inches taller than Hamed and, at 122lb, had a two and a half pound weight advantage.

Fighting in London at Mayfair's Grosvenor House on 4 July, in a benefit show for Michael Watson (crippled after his return fight with Chris Eubank ten months earlier), Naseem had another effortless ride (albeit after tripping over the top rope on his way into the ring, before repeating the exercise correctly). This time he let things last one round longer, explaining later that he liked to give the crowd a bit of a show. After a playful, feel-out first round, he got down to business late in the second, dropping Matthews with a heavy right to the side of the head for a five count just before the bell. In the third he poured on the punishment, with referee Roy Francis stepping in after sixty-five seconds as Matthews went down again. The gutsy Welshman, who by 1998 had raked up 105 fights with eighty official losses, was not particularly impressed by Hamed and still insists the stoppage was premature. 'I genuinely didn't rate Naseem. He certainly wasn't the best fighter I've met and it really annoys me that he's got a stoppage win over me. I'm a religious man – I wouldn't lie – but that knockdown was a push. Roy Francis never gave me a count,' he said, adding that the lad's approach irritated him. 'Hamed's had it easy. Perhaps I'm jealous. I like a showman – Ali and Eubank come across well – but Naseem's attitude just stinks.'

Afterwards Naseem was presented a trophy for the 'Outstanding Prospect of the Year' in the annual ProBox awards for Screensport fighters – the last time he would box for them because, to the astonishment of many within boxing, this fight was his final effort under Hearn's Matchroom umbrella. Six months after their high profile signing, Ingle decided to sever all ties with the Romford promoter and instead accepted an offer from rival promoter Mickey Duff for Hamed to fight under his National Promotions banner. It would be nearly seven years before Hamed and Hearn would work together again.

Hearn was incensed by this defection. Interviewed by *Boxing Monthly* a year later, he still claimed to be dismayed by Ingle's decision, calling it 'a mistake of colossal proportions'. He complained that he had built Hamed to the point where he was known all over Europe and was about to become a household name. 'I'm possibly the worst trainer in the world, so I don't train fighters. Brendan should take the same approach to his manager-ship,' he said. Several years later Hearn's anger had not abated. 'It's like everything with Ingle – a pound note is usually enough,' he remarked, his voice thick with bile. 'The major fall-out was because we were doing a lot of work together in co-promoting shows, but then Ingle sold his promotional rights in his stable to Mickey Duff without even discussing it with me, so that's the type of person he is. He's done it before and he'll do it again. I wasn't disappointed for Naseem, because obviously he's always been a quality fighter and he was always going to get there. I was disappointed that you have to do business at any time in your life with people like Brendan Ingle.' Hearn belittled the Irishman's managerial abilities and was not even prepared to recognize his prowess as a trainer. 'I prefer to acknowledge the old adage that great fighters make trainers great,' he said, before adding, with the self-deprecating wit that is part of his charm, 'It's also true that great fighters make promoters great.' He claims he had a 'fine relationship' with Naseem, and insists he knew better than anyone else how to channel his skills and personality. 'I had no problems with Naz at all. He's an outgoing young man and he's extremely talented and has the potential to be a phenomenon, and I would obviously have done a fantastic job on him,' he says, before catching himself again. 'But then what would you expect me to say? He was going to get there anyway and I think, to be honest with you, he made it in about the right time.'

Ingle sees things rather differently, arguing that Hearn's own predatory tendencies and desire for control were the cause of the breakdown in relations, and that the Essex man's sales pitch far exceeded his service. He mentions a string of incidents of dispute and claims that Hearn was pressurizing them to sign a contract in which Ingle would be forced to relinquish effective managerial control of Hamed. Ingle has long had wariness about other managers and promoters 'stealing' his fighters, having had to contend with several defections. He saw Hearn's acquisition of his super-welterweight prospect Paul 'Silky' Jones as a precursor to what the promoter was trying to do with Naseem. In fact, he was already extremely cautious on that score following several ill-conceived attempts to 'buy' Naseem, including one involving Hearn's other star, Chris Eubank. 'I'd had Silky Jones since he was a kid of fourteen, and I'd taught him everything he knew, and then I sent him down to work with one of Hearn's fighters and all of a sudden Silky leaves me and goes to Hearn,' Ingle says in a tone which matches Hearn's. 'And then with the contract that Hearn wanted me and Naz to sign, he would have had control of him, lock, stock and barrel, and there was far too much work gone into him for that. So we went to Mickey Duff.'

In his first three months as an active professional Naseem had completed four fights, which had lasted a total of less than nine rounds. But the changeover in promotional control meant that while contracts were being signed and options considered, the eager young fighter was not fighting, and it took three months before he fought again, a big gap by Naseem's standards at the time.

Duff was a known quantity for Brendan Ingle – a streetwise old wheeler-dealer who had fought his way up from the bottom, had done the business in every department and seldom missed a trick. They had worked together for many years, particularly with Herol Graham, and although there had been several fall-outs and disputes over financial issues, there always seemed to be a basic respect between the philosophically-inclined, yin and yang, white haired Irish ex-pug and the wily, witty, foul-mouthed Cockney hustler. Duff is an institution in British boxing – as a fighter, trainer, corner man and manager, and over several decades as Britain's pre-eminent matchmaker. For many years he and his partners Jarvis Astaire and Terry Lawless operated what his rivals regarded as a promotional closed shop, effectively restricting access to BBC Television. But in the early eighties, Frank Warren broke in and, through access to the ITV channel, smashed their hegemony. Ten years later, Hearn repeated the trick through the Sky satellite channels, before Warren and Frank Maloney pushed them both to the margins. However, in 1992 National Promotions was still a significant force. Among those fighting under their control at the time were several British, European and Commonwealth champions and world-rated boxers, with Frank Bruno the ace in their promotional pack.

The deal with Duff provided for Naseem's fights to be screened on the satellite channel Eurosport, and offered him a purse of £3,000 per fight and the promise of regular work on National

Promotions undercards with the hope of bigger things in the future. Once the contracts were signed, Duff and Ingle moved quickly to ensure the momentum was maintained and decided to put Hamed on a bill featuring Andy Holligan against Dwayne Swift in Sunderland on 7 October 1992. His opponent was the Manchester bantamweight Des Gargano, an old friend of Naseem's who came in as a late substitute at less than twenty-four hours' notice.

Gargano, then thirty-one, is known in the game as a 'runner' – a ducking and diving southpaw whose general modus operandi is to circle the perimeter of the ring, stay out of trouble, lose the decision, collect his pay cheque and go home to his wife and kids, or better still, go on a fishing trip. The Des Garganos and Miguel Matthews of this world are a feature of prizefighting – honest survivors, whose main role is to make up the numbers, to be available whenever they're called up and to make other men look good. They're seldom winners, and don't expect to be; they just hope that now and then someone will treat them right. When Gargano fought Hamed, his record stood at twenty-six wins (two stoppages), two draws and fifty-eight losses. He had been the distance with some of the best little men in Europe – Pat Clinton, Jimmi Bredahl, Bradley Stone and Joe Kelly – and now and then managed a short winning streak, although basically he was a tough, hard to hit, elusive loser. The challenge for Naseem was to put him away, a task assisted by the fact that the 5ft 5in Gargano, who weighed in at 120lb, one less than Naseem, was already weak in the legs, having trained the previous night before being given his call-up at 10.20pm.

Hamed, fighting in a pair of bright green satin trunks as a temporary change from the leopard spots, went straight into attack and soon had his man down for a six count. Although the Mancunian got on his trusty bicycle, he went down again from a push-punch combination shortly before the bell. 'He gave me a terrible first round,' Gargano recalls. 'He would stand in front of me with his head a few inches from mine, and I just couldn't find a way to catch him. He would fake and feint a lot and look at the canvas or at his corner and then catch me with a punch at the very same time, and he was hurting me with some really big body blows, and winded me a few times. I managed to cover up when he wound up for most of his big punches, but he would catch me with the little ones.' For the rest of the fight, Gargano fled and

Hamed pursued. In the second, Naseem leapt into the air to drop Gargano with a surprise punch, but he was up immediately. He was dropped again in the third and finally Naseem caught up with him for long enough to finish things in the fourth, pinning him in a corner and ending it with a thumping left to the solar plexus which felled the veteran and prompted referee Gerry Watson to call a halt at the 2:06 mark. 'I just doubled up and went down,' says Gargano, 'and when I struggled up, the referee could see from my face that I couldn't breathe – I just couldn't suck it in – and he stopped it.'

Having told Gargano seven years earlier that he would one day fight and beat him, Naseem had delivered just as he promised. Gargano, still boxing at the age of thirty-five, and with 120 fights to his name, was not a man to take a beating personally and was happy to acknowledge he was enormously impressed. 'I've boxed with a lot of champions and I thought I was indestructible,' he says. 'I take a lot of pride in going the distance and I'd never been knocked out, but Naseem was really classy. He was extremely difficult to hit, he had very quick reflexes, moved a lot and he hit really hard. And I've always liked him, too. He has a lot of spirit and I think what he's doing for boxing is just great.'

Hamed's sixth and last fight of 1992 featured him as the main undercard attraction on a poorly attended show at the Everton Sports Centre in Liverpool on 12 November. Naseem was given another awkward customer, Peter Buckley, his most difficult opponent yet. The twenty-three-year-old Birmingham spoiler was the Midlands super-featherweight champion, although he did most of his boxing at featherweight. He came in with a record of eighteen wins (three inside the distance), eighteen losses and five draws, though he was considered unlucky not to get the nod on several occasions. After making a hopeful start to his professional career, losing only two of his first eleven fights, he settled into the 'opponent' grade – good enough to beat the lesser tryers and to give a frustrating night to the champions; slippery, hard to hit and extremely adept at grabbing, holding and wriggling out of trouble, but lacking the power or ambition to do much more. The 5ft 8in Buckley weighed in at 122½ lb, three pounds more than Hamed, but looked several weights heavier when they stepped into the ring.

After taking a couple of stiff punches, the Birmingham boxer decided the only sane course was self-preservation. He tucked his chin behind his forearms, grabbed, held, ducked and dived, but threw very little in return. Naseem tried everything, shifting from southpaw to orthodox and back, throwing surprise punches from unusual angles, the Ali shuffle, dropping his hands and inviting his man in, and talking to Buckley and even to the ringside press, but nothing worked. He became frustrated, lost his gumshield in the second and third rounds, was warned for holding and hitting and finally descended into sloppiness. His only real moments of success came late in the third when he dropped Buckley for a two count and followed up with a combination of three right jabs and a left cross. Hamed also managed to wobble him with a solid left shortly before the final bell. Referee Phil Cowswill scored the fight 59½ to 58, indicating that Naseem won four rounds to Buckley's one, with one even. A clear win and a fair score, but by no means a flattering performance.

For the first time in his life, Naseem received bad press. *Boxing News* headed its report 'Not so princely this time, Hamed', noting that it was 'a contest that fell sadly short on entertainment value.' Naseem's own view is that Buckley was entirely to blame: 'Sure, he took me the distance, but I wouldn't say he was my toughest opponent. It's just that when you get in with a fighter who's not going to commit his self to fight, whose goal is to lose and to go the distance by holding, covering up, doing things he wouldn't use to win with, then obviously you're going to have a bit of a problem. If he wanted to win he would have to throw punches back, but he was just trying to make a name for his self by going the distance with me, even though he was taking a beating in every round. Now, to me, that's silly.' Buckley, however, does not share Hamed's egocentric view of his motives and believes he boxed sensibly. 'I wasn't intimidated by him and I think that's why it went the distance. He'd had only five fights and I'd had over forty, so he didn't really give me no problems. He wanted to dictate the pace but I was just messing him about, know what I mean? He was more of a showboater in those days – he's settled down a bit now – but I just tried to keep my chin down and to keep close to him. I've got a good defence and when he came close, I just tied him up. He won the fight alright, yeah, no complaints about the decision at all, but he didn't hurt me.' Despite this, however, Buckley came away with the impression that Naseem was a boxer of enormous potential. 'I'd been in with former world champions, but even then he was something special, and I could see he was going to go all the way. He might have been lacking in experience, but he had all the natural ability and I knew he would be a world champion.'

If the Buckley fight left a bitter-taste end to an otherwise successful year, 1993 started on an even more dismal note, although for once the reason was not of Naseem's own making. For the first seven years of his boxing career he had been the darling of the Sheffield business and political establishment and, more particularly, the Yorkshire press. Usually at Brendan Ingle's prompting, the *Sheffield Star* and *Sheffield Telegraph*, and some-times the *Yorkshire Post*, were only too happy to fill their pages with gushing reports on the young boxer's exploits. Naseem is not much of a reader, though he very occasionally makes his way through a pulp fiction novel (*Papillon* is his 'all-time favourite'), devours the fight magazines and skims the national and local press to find references to himself. Of all the papers it was the *Sheffield Star* which was most attentive, so it came as something of a shock, when he woke late in the morning on 4 January 1993 to find a three-page investigative spread with a decidedly different tone. 'Boxing star caught in row over £3,000 loan', ' "We need new probe" – critics', 'Yemeni cash row' and, to balance things a bit, 'The meteoric rise of the Arabian Knight'. The nub of the controversy concerned the £3,000 loan from the Yemeni Community Association to Naseem, to help him train and buy boxing equipment, at a time when his father, Sal, was a prominent office holder within the organization. A thousand pounds had been presented to Naseem shortly before he completed his amateur career in October 1991 (when Sal was sitting on the association's nine-person management committee) and the remaining £2,000 in May 1992, shortly after his professional career started (when Sal was its chairman).

One of the complaints from three prominent members of the association, including its vice-chairman and its education officer, was that the group's auditor had not been told that Naseem was Sal's son – a complaint dismissed as irrelevant by its spokesman Dr Abdul Shaif, who stressed that Sal had played no part in discussing or voting on the loan, and that the loan was made because it was felt that Naseem was an important symbol of the community and that it would identify him with the association. The suggestion from the complainants – who were subsequently expelled for making what the organization's hierarchy called 'baseless allegations' and for being 'disruptive' during a power struggle – was that there was favouritism at work and that the association's imprecise financial procedures allowed the loan to pass unnoticed. They mentioned, for instance, that the initial £1,000 was recorded under a hardship fund intended for disadvantaged Yemenis. Shaif responded that this was merely an 'administrative error' and stressed that in return for the loans, Naseem had agreed to pay back the £3,000 at 15 per cent interest and to allow the association to sell T-shirts bearing his name and picture – prompting Sal Hamed to comment that the purpose of the deal was to make profit for the community.

The background to this controversy involved the closure of the steel mills in the 1980s. Unemployment within the Yemeni community (which had taken on many on the hard, unhealthy jobs shunned by locals) had rocketed and there was evidence that Yemenis were suffering from a range of social problems, including racial discrimination, in their attempts to find fresh employment. The Sheffield City Council therefore made substantial annual grants to assist with the welfare dimensions of this problem. There were, however, persistent allegations that the money was not being properly accounted for, leading to several investigations and warnings from the council for the association to improve its accounting procedures. However, a December 1992 council report said that while there might be legitimate concerns about accountability, there was no evidence of mismanagement.

The affair was a reflection of the factional, personal and ideological struggles within the organization, with the trio opposing the loan being more conservative and traditional than the rest of the leadership. Shaif insists the complainants had 'their own axe to grind' – not because of opposition to Naseem, but because of his father's position within the association and within its internal conflicts and disputes. 'The way we perceive it,' Shaif says, 'is that this was a young man in need, who came to the community to say, "I need help," and it was an opportunity for the community to respond in a positive way by supporting him, because he had talents that would, hopefully, one day symbolize the whole community.' He argues that despite the brouhaha, it helped to cement the relations between Naseem and the organization. 'For us this was a very good investment, not necessarily in business terms but as an investment in confidence for the community. And I think we've got more than that back because

Naseem has not only been an inspiration to the Yemeni community here, but to Yemenis wherever they are in the world. Naseem will always remember the community supported him at a fundamental turning point in his life, when he was just an amateur turning professional. He'll never forget that.'

In fact, by this time Naseem was already returning the favours by making intermittent appearances at various Yemeni community projects, opening exhibitions, giving his name to fund-raising drives and allowing his merchandise to be sold for community fund-raising purposes. This role, combined with his success in the ring, established his reputation as an heroic and inspirational figure for Yemeni youth at a time when rising unemployment was exacerbating the social problems in the community. 'Our young people see him as their king, as doing something they would once have only dreamt of doing,' said Shaif. 'Now they don't have to dream; it can become reality because Naseem has done it. So when Naseem started making a name for himself, a lot of young people began channelling their energies into sport – energies which could otherwise be aggressive, or which would have been wasted playing cards in a cafe. He has given them an element of hope.'

Nevertheless the accusations continued to simmer for some time in the local press and inevitably were picked up elsewhere, and this had the effect of making Naseem more cautious with the press and more wary of their motive. From then on, those surrounding Naseem, and the boxer himself, became more overtly protective of his reputation, often requesting lists of questions from would-be interviewers, as well as copies of draft feature stories, and insisting that questions of a personal, religious or political nature not be asked. While Naseem often likened his public style to that of his hero Muhammad Ali, this was one of many areas which reflected poorly on him by comparison. Despite his love of public acclaim and attention, by 1993 Naseem had already become suspicious with the public and the press. Ali, in contrast, seldom refused an interview, a signature, a hug or a kiss.

But despite this diffidence and his occasional displays of 'Don't you know who I am?' petulance or 'Piss off, I'm busy' pique, Naseem was establishing a reputation for 'doing his bit' for Sheffield. From late 1992 he began to offer public backing to a wide range of civic, community and charity projects, prompted largely by Ingle's connections and the Irishman's activism on behalf of Sheffield's poor. It was standard practice for Ingle to involve as many of his boxers as possible in charitable projects, one of most enduring and endearing being the inmate versus team-mate sparring sessions at the sports centre in the nearby Doncaster Lindholme Prison which he organizes twice a year to raise money for charity. Ingle started this programme in 1991 after several years of doing a similar exercise with Herol Graham and other boxers in some of the local pubs and schools. Each time, he picks a few of his better boxers, who are put in with a team of prison boxing hopefuls for a round apiece, with the rest of the inmates (sometimes up to 600) paying £2 for the privilege of watching their pals try to land a glove on Brendan's boys. The rules, as Ingle explains it, are simple: 'My lads can't hit the prisoners, but if the prisoners hit them, the governor is supposed to give them £50; and if they knock any of my lads out, he gives them £100. There's great excitement and the prison fellas go mad, but after two minutes they're completely knackered.' Ingle's boxers seldom suffer the indignity of taking a solid punch during the two-minute sessions. As Ryan Rhodes put it: 'With our training, if you get caught, then it's your own fault. It does happen occasionally, but really it's a good laugh. They go wild and the other prisoners cheer for them, but they cheer for us as well.' Naseem did his prison duty several times and was never caught, and his presence made him a huge favourite with the inmates and screws, some of them ex-boxers. Around £1,000 a time is raised for charities for children, the disabled and cancer sufferers. The boxers are free to return home, while the prisoners return to their cells by a different gate, with the exercise serving as a lesson to both groups that this is not the place to be.

While Naseem's local charitable ventures may have been motivated partly by his image-massaging needs, he has always held genuine affection for his home town and can be exceedingly sensitive about any contrary impressions. He tolerates the tired phrase 'the Yemeni Yorkshireman', but stresses his identity is city-bound rather than regional and will tell you he does not know what it feels like to be a Yorkshireman but that he's truly proud to be a son of Sheffield. Even from these early professional days, he tried not to antagonize any section of the local population, right down to refusing to reveal his local football loyalties, despite regularly attending Sheffield

Wednesday's games. When pushed, all he offers is a wry smile and a vacuous answer: 'I support Sheffield Wednesday *and* Sheffield United, and the Sharks in basketball, the Steelers in ice hockey and the Eagles in rugby, because at the end of the day I support the whole of Sheffield and anything to do with Sheffield, because I'm born and bred in Sheffield.'

What was needed after the funding controversy and the Buckley disappointment was a quick return to action to re-establish momentum. Instead, however, he had to wait three and a half months before he was to step through the ropes again, a delay that would become part of a pattern over the next year. The consolation was that he was to appear at the Wembley Arena in London against an unbeaten opponent, and on a more substantial bill than the previous two. This time he was up against the twenty-four-year-old Newport bantamweight Alan Ley, on the undercard of a 24 February 1993 bill headed by the British lightweight title fight between Billy Schwer and Paul Burke. Ley, a former Welsh ABA flyweight champion, had turned professional in September 1991, compiling a record of four fights, four wins and no knockouts. He shared two opponents with Naseem – Andy Bloomer and Shaun Norman – and had outpointed both of them while Naseem had knocked them out. Ley was known as a skilled southpaw who was lacking in the power department.

The fight was made at the bantamweight limit (118lb), and with Naseem's inactivity and his habit of eating as he pleased, he struggled to make it. Two days before the fight he was surprised to find himself three pounds over the limit, prompting Brendan Ingle to give him a ticking off about his undisciplined diet. To help him shed the excess weight Ingle offered to join him for thirty-six hours of complete abstinence from food and water. When they arrived in London the night before the fight, Naseem was still two pounds over, and neither of them allowed the other to sneak even a sip of water. They went for a brisk walk before the weigh-in and Naseem made it by half a pound, while Ley came in on the button. Ingle, incidentally, was down to 163lb, five less than when the deal was done. 'The trouble with Naz,' he recalls, 'was that he was still growing but he was continuing to eat as he pleased, and the wrong foods, too. And let me tell you, this is a fella who could eat for England.'

The fight itself turned out to be far easier than expected and once again showed off the Sheffield teenager in the best possible light. From the opening bell he had his fellow southpaw in trouble, pumping out his right jab and firing home left leads and right hooks from unexpected angles without having to take anything in return. Midway through round one, after several changes in stance, he banged the Welshman over with a left-right combination. Ley was up at eight but soon after was dropped again, this time with bone-jarring right. He decided the best strategy was to grab and not let go, a move that kept him buoyant until the bell. In the second round Ley continued to hit and hold, but it was clear his legs had gone and Naseem dropped him twice more. After the fourth knockdown, Ley chose to remain on his knees for the full count, still conscious but too shaken and demoralized to rise.

Naseem had given his most impressive and polished performance since turning professional and did not waste the opportunity to let the London press know what he had in mind. 'I'm good enough to win the British bantamweight title right now,' he said, in what was the first of several public salvos directed at national champion Drew Docherty. And with Schwer having lost his title on cuts to Burke, Ingle did not lose the chance to press home to Duff his claim for a better billing for Hamed, announcing that his charge was the 'new star' and best bantamweight since the heyday of Alan Rudkin – a rare understatement by the effusive Irishman's standards.

Hamed, who had been vaulting the ropes ever since his junior amateur days, soon added another element to his expanding acrobatic repertoire: his trademark forward-somersault-over-the-ropes ring entrance. He did not invent it himself, however. That honour belongs to his friend Ryan Rhodes, then still an amateur. 'I first tried the frontflip over the ropes in the gym ring in about 1993,' Rhodes recalls. 'A few people seen it, and then a couple of guys tried it, and then Naz started doing it and he got really good at it, and then a little while later he started doing the flip in his fights. But I was the one who invented it.' Naseem, who scornfully claims that Chris Eubank borrowed his previous rope vault from him after visiting the St Thomas's gym in 1991, acknowledges his debt. 'I'll tell you the truth about that. The first time I saw that frontflip, it was Ryan who did it. I'll never tell a lie where I got something from. End of the day, when I get something from him, he should get the credit. I seen him doing it and I thought that was a wicked way to get into the ring.' His sideways vault had been risky enough (in one fight he fouled it up and had a near spill in the ring, before exiting and repeating it correctly), but with the frontflip there was little room for error. A poorly timed landing could result in a sprained ankle or worse, but so far there have been no mistakes.

1993, however, would not be the year Naseem's acrobatic skills and pugilistic talents were shown off in the way they deserved. Mickey Duff's vast promotional experience and network of contacts were proving to be less valuable than Ingle had hoped and the two men were starting to argue incessantly, with the trainer wanting more action and profile for his boxer and the promoters saying this depended on getting more security for their investment. It took over three months before Naseem's next fight, against yet another Welsh loser, Kevin Jenkins, on another Andy Holligan undercard at the Mansfield Leisure Centre on 26 May 1993. Jenkins, who was twenty-two, had started his professional career in 1989, picking up two wins and a draw in his first three outings, but after that he quickly settled into the 'hamburger' role, losing, usually on points, to bigger name prospects. The high point of his record of three wins, twelve losses and three draws had come when he shared the honours with the Commonwealth flyweight champion Darren Fifield three months earlier, and he had also been the distance several other champions. He possessed a firm chin, but hardly qualified as a stern test.

Eager to put on a show after so long out of the ring, Hamed made the most of his boogie down the aisle, his rope flip plus forward roll ring entrance and his eyeball stare-out of the Ammanford weekend warrior, who responded with a phlegmatic grin and later explained he had never heard of Naseem before the fight and knew nothing of his reputation. In the opening round Hamed (119 ½ lb) decided to put on an exhibition, dancing around, shooting from surprise angles, getting warned for slapping and then going into a breakdance routine which Jenkins attempted to imitate. In the second, Naseem decided the fun was over and fired hard punches through the tiny gaps left in his opponent's tight guard, hurting him on several occasions. Jenkins, a pound lighter, gallantly tried to fire back but towards the end of the round was trapped in a corner and hammered with a volley of very fast punches. As the bell rang for the third, Ingle said, 'This is the round.' A vicious left hook to the body felled Jenkins for a nine count. Seconds later Naseem was warned for a low blow, but the next punch – a sickening right to the solar plexus – knocked all the wind out of the Welshman and he collapsed in agony, prompting his corner to throw in the towel. The referee, Jim Pridding, kicked the towel out of the ring and ordered the boxers to fight on, but after one final punch, he called it off at one minute fifty-eight seconds.

When Jenkins had recovered he said he was unimpressed with his beating and that a previous opponent, Danny Porter, hit harder. Today, however, he sees things differently and acknowledges Hamed's brilliance. 'He was way too good for me and more or less beat me up, didn't he? He's a totally different kind of fighter, much better than any of the other top rated men I'd fought. I tried my hardest to hit him but I didn't connect once in four rounds,' he says, stubbornly insisting that he lasted until the fourth, rather than the third, when the fight actually did end. He tacitly acknowledges that his sour grapes, post-fight remarks were not entirely accurate, and that Naseem was by far the biggest hitter he'd faced. 'He's got immense power, more than anyone else I'd fought, and I'd been in with some strong featherweights before, so I didn't want to stay in there too long because I knew the score – that there was no point staying in there and getting hurt when there was no way I could win. I really thought he was something else.'

It took another four months before Naseem was featured again, and this time he was 'lent' to the new Irish promoter Brian Peters for his first ever show at Dublin's National Basketball Arena on 24 September. Ingle was delighted to show off his protege on his old stomping ground, even though Naseem had to face the mild indignity of appearing on the undercard of a bill headed by a fighter he was convinced he could beat, and who had turned professional exactly a year after he had. Wayne 'The Pocket Rocket' McCullough, the Ulster bantamweight, had won the silver medal at the Barcelona Olympics and, after seven months as a professional drew a capacity crowd for his Irish debut. Naseem, by contrast, was having his third, and last, fight of 1993, against the twenty-six-year-old Central featherweight champion, Chris Clarkson from Hull. Clarkson had been a fine amateur, twice winning national schoolboy titles, but had not cracked it in the professional ranks. By the time he fought Hamed, his record showed eighteen wins (two on stoppages), twenty-one losses (four on stoppages) and two draws. Over the previous three years he had beaten several middle-ranking fighters, including former Hamed opponents Gargano and Buckley, and also fought for the IBF Intercontinental bantamweight belt, while his conquerors included several of the best men his size in Britain, Europe and the world. But Naseem's aim was to outshine McCullough, and this is precisely what he pulled off.

Before the fight, Ingle used the opportunity to talk his fighter up as only he knew how – the best fighter he'd ever seen, the finest bantamweight in the world, and so on. And once Naseem had completed his rope leaping, gyrating, dancing and prancing, the crowd was captivated. Weighing in at the super-bantam-weight limit of 122lb, his heaviest yet, he was still two pounds lighter (and an inch shorter) than Clarkson, but from the first minute it clear this was of no consequence. Hamed demonstrated a few of his old tricks, and some new ones like looking at his opponent's feet while simultaneously hitting him on the chin, but for the most part his opening round was far more businesslike than usual. Clarkson remembers it well: 'From what I'd seen of him before, he was flashy and I thought I'd go out and give him one straight away, but he did none of that dancing around with me. He came out to do the job with a crouched-down style, face lowered, and he did the job. He slipped everything I threw with his head movement and then countered with a right jab through my guard which hurt, and straight away I thought, "What have we got here?" ' Things rapidly deteriorated for the Hull fighter and with just over a minute to go he was dropped with a left cross, over the top. 'I was badly dazed,' Clarkson remembers, 'but I somehow survived till the bell, and when I sat down in my corner I said, "Every time I move, he hits me," which was true because he can land from any angle.'

Early in the second Hamed was onto him again, dropping him with a perfectly timed right cross. Clarkson was back on his feet when referee Barney Wilson reached the count of eight, and he knew the end was near. From the safety of a few years' distance, he remembers his demise as a thing of beauty. 'Naseem got straight on top of me, worked me round to the corner without throwing a punch, and just as I heard my corner screaming "Out of the way!" he whacked a left hook right underneath my heart which was so hard that I don't remember the next few seconds, but as I started getting up I heard the referee counting ten. The man's a devastating puncher.' At one minute and fifty seconds, Naseem had scored his eighth stoppage in nine fights, and his fifth in the second round. The Irish crowd roared their approval.

Soon afterwards, McCullough gave a less spectacular 'home-coming' performance in beating Algeria's Boulem Belkif on a fifth round technical knockout and inevitably the comparisons were made. Clarkson, who had recovered sufficiently to watch 'The Pocket Rocket' in action, left in no doubt as to who would prevail: 'I watched Wayne very carefully and afterwards I thought Naz would tear him apart.'

Hamed and Ingle stayed for another couple of days in Dublin and found that their efforts had been worthwhile, with Naseem frequently being congratulated by well-wishers when walking in the city centre. 'When we arrived no-one had heard of him, but he stole the show, and I tell ya, they really loved him in Dublin,' Ingle says.

Naseem and Clarkson became firm friends after the fight, as so often happens in boxing. They were staying in the same Dublin hotel and for a couple of days had a fine time hanging out together, an experience which suggested to the Hull boxer that Hamed was not quite as egotistical as he had assumed. 'We really got to talking and when I got to know him, he wasn't like I expected at all,' he says. 'I've got two sons and he was talking about them all the time and was very interested to know more about them. He's not the big, upfront person everyone thinks he is. He's got a heart, and he's a funny guy as well, and basically he's a real nice kid.'

After this impressive outing Naseem's active career went from slow to halt, and when 1994 arrived he had been out of action for four months. By this stage McCullough had seen off eleven opponents in eleven months, while Naseem's record showed only nine victories in twenty-one months, with a paltry three outings in 1993. There were many excuses for the lulls, but one thing was clear: National Promotions was falling short on delivery. One reason was Duff's ongoing dispute with Ingle over the nature of their deal. He was holding out for a joint involve-ment in Hamed's management, arguing that their existing agreement provided insufficient protection in the promotional contract, because, as Duff put it, 'Otherwise the boxers can just tell you to fuck off after a while.' In effect, the group was not prepared to make a major league investment in Naseem unless a more advantageous contract could be secured, and Ingle was not prepared to budge. And the result was another parting of the ways.

Today both men are magnanimous about the dispute and there is little of the hard feeling associated with the Hearn bust-up. 'I wouldn't say they left me; I think parted is the better word,' Duff insists. 'We parted ways because Naseem had to go into another league, and at that particular time there were people who I was involved with – not me, but others – who weren't prepared to put up the funds necessary, and Frank Warren was in a position to sign a long-term contract and to guarantee larger amounts of money than I was.' Duff says he had a good business relationship with Ingle and a sound, though not particularly close, personal relationship with Hamed: 'Let me put it to you this way: nobody has a bigger opinion of Naseem than I. I always thought he was an exceptional fighter and nothing has changed my mind. I didn't get to know him that well at the time, and you don't need the fingers on two hands to count how often we met. In fact, since we parted I've probably met him more often than when we were together. I found him eccentric and quite jovial. There's nothing wrong with him, and we still get on reasonably well.'

At the time, Ingle said the main reason for the move to Frank Warren was the promise of live coverage through ITV. 'Mickey Duff was paying well but Naz wasn't getting the exposure he needs,' he explained. Today he still stresses that despite their disagreements, he respects Duff for having no hidden agenda: 'He may have tried to bully me a few times but to be honest with you, Mickey was very fair with us, and that's important. But the agreement ran out and he wanted to do another agreement, and Frank Warren offered us a better deal, so we went there.'

The year had not been entirely wasted, however. Naseem's progress in Britain may have been far too slow, but he was flourishing in the Middle East and particularly in the Yemen. For several years Brendan Ingle had been talking about promoting his young fighter in his parents' homeland, and had used the family connections to ensure the groundwork was well laid. In 1990, the year after the Republic of Yemen was established as a single unified state having previously been divided between the communist south and the Islamic north, Ingle started sending videos of Naseem's amateur fights, along with all his results and stories about his prowess, to the Yemen. So by the time Naseem turned professional he was already a figure of repute there, despite the fact that boxing had previously been virtually unknown to them. His fight films were shown on national television, a video of his life was produced, and the president, Ali Abdullah Salah, became a personal fan. Ingle had boned up on the country's geography and history, and reckoned the time was right for a high profile tour of the Five Cities, complete with several exhibition fights, all of them televised throughout the Gulf region. The Yemeni government was delighted to have acquired its own sporting hero and bent over backwards to facilitate and fund the trip, not only for Naseem, but also for Brendan, Alma, Sal, Riath, Nabeel and two sparring partners.

This was officially announced in a rather odd, full-page advertisement in *Boxing News*, publicly sponsored by the government of the Yemen, which provided details of the forthcoming tour and at the same time issued a public challenge to British bantamweight champion Drew Docherty: 'THE ARABIAN KNIGHT PRINCE NASEEM HAMED – Nine fights, Nine wins, Eight KOs – will be 20 in February. He sends out a challenge to: DREW DOCHERTY for a £5,000 sidestake to defend his British bantamweight title in Sheffield. Hamed's manager/trainer Brendan Ingle has backed the Prince to win *FOUR LONSDALE BELTS OUTRIGHT* within the next five years at weights from bantamweights to lightweight.' A week later Ingle himself made a public offer to bet £500 that Naseem would win four British titles, from bantam to super-feather. Needless to say, Docherty did not respond, no-one took up the wager, the fight never took place and Hamed never got his shot at any British title, let alone a clutch of Lonsdale belts.

For Naseem, the Yemen had previously been a place where vague childhood memories intermeshed with his parents' stories, and had taken on a distant and romantic hue. The two-week visit, starting on 26 November 1993, was his first since returning home at the age of four and he had little idea about what to expect. What he received was a reception that astounded him and the entire delegation. When he arrived he found himself mobbed by thousands of admirers who wanted to touch him and hug him, before being whisked off by heavily armed bodyguards for VIP treatment at the presidential palace, where, among other gifts, he was presented with a gold Rolex watch, subsequently valued at over £10,000, by the president.

Brendan Ingle thoroughly enjoyed himself, delighted in the knowledge that everything he had been saying about Naseem's support there had been proved, and more. 'Naz came there and it just absolutely took off,' he recalls. 'It was marvellous watching it. You get sixty thousand people out there to meet him, and all over the country we were mobbed by people and very well received. It was unbelievable.' He and Alma were happy to take a back seat and view the experience with a distance that was not available to Naseem, who had to make do in his rusty Arabic and constantly meet up to the colossal expectations he was confronted with. Ingle, however, has never been over-impressed by pomp and ceremony and finds it hard to ignore disparities in wealth and privilege, and it was the connection with the ordinary Yemenis that Brendan relished more than any other aspect of the trip. 'It gives you such a lift. It's a beautiful country and the people are lovely, but like everywhere else you got your problems,' he says with unaccustomed diplomatic understatement. 'It's a Third World country. Very, very poor and very, very rich.'

During this visit, crowds estimated at almost 10,000 turned up to watch one of Naseem's exhibitions, which was announced only the day before. Perhaps for the first time in his life, the young fighter felt a little overwhelmed: 'I was a bit surprised at first, but I had to get used to being mobbed by these massive crowds, and protected by these bodyguards. It was great in that you get the people out there basically admiring your skills and talent, and they think I have brought great things to their country and basically that I've put it on the map, but it was very hectic out there.'

The Yemeni government was delighted by the success of the venture and was eager to make their contact with the young fighter more regular, with the idea of having him back to fight there – a plan that has yet to materialize. Their attitude was that Naseem was an example to the youth and a unifying figure in a nation with a history of political conflict and division. 'Boxing is not much practised in Yemen but we are talking about an achievement by a young man who was reaching the top of his profession through hard work, strength of character and per-severance,' said the country's London embassy spokesman Mohamed Beshr. 'He's a good example to follow – not necessarily to become a boxer but as an example of what can be achievement through dedication. He became a role model to the people because of this, and there is universal admiration for him in Yemen. We regard him with pride and admiration and it is like he is a national hero.'

Ever since returning from that initial visit, Naseem has stressed the Yemeni connection more forcefully. He began fighting under both the British and Yemeni flags, and has always made a point of mentioning his Arab heritage and of being 'part of the Arab world', an oft-used phrase which no doubt endears him to the other Arab countries where his fights are screened. However, some of those within Sheffield's Yemeni community would like him to take a more distanced and critical perspective on the region, though given his continued excitement about his VIP treatment there and the official gifts – from a watch to a jewel-studded dagger, two cars and two houses – that have been coming his way, this is not likely to happen. Expressing his personal perspective, Dr Shaif drew a strong distinction between the country's political and military elite and its masses. 'Hopefully, Naseem will work for the people of the Yemen, not for its leaders, but he will need to be more politicized about what's going on there before he can present a strong view, because Yemen is a place of chronic political activity with a history of chronic instability, and there are certainly many problems, as well as a lot of positive things.' Naseem, however, has never been a political animal and has remained blissfully ignorant about the motions and method of politics, whether at home, in the Arab world or elsewhere. For example, he seemed genuinely surprised on hearing in 1997 that there was substantial anti-Arab prejudice in the United States, although this new piece of information prompted him to assume he could put the Americans right on the issue.

Despite his generally dismal year in terms of career progress, Naseem returned home elated and received a further boost when the London-based international magazine *Boxing Monthly* ran a perceptive four-page lead cover story hailing Naseem as boxing's finest prospect anywhere in the world – better than Oscar de la Hoya and Roy Jones – while offering strong criticism of his under-exposure from National Promotions. Among the quoted claims about his prowess was one by British middleweight champion Neville Brown, who said Hamed was 'the best thing to come out of this country, by far' – a bold prognosis for a nine-fight nineteen-year-old. The story served notice that Naseem was a major force to be taken into account and contributed to the explosion of interest from the national broadsheets and tabloids which followed in 1994, frequently being quoted or referred to.

Naseem was also making his mark in various fields outside the ring. Early in his amateur days he had declared his preference for the world of the night owl, arguing that 'body clock', like so many things about him, was tuned differently from other mortals, and that he was at his most alert and active deep into the night. As a teenager he liked to go to an out-of-town snooker hall, often until the early morning, and would spend many hours playing and invariably winning. Now and then he would also participate in various other ball games, but snooker has long been a passion that he spends many hours on during fallow periods. Naseem regularly watched major snooker tournaments and later struck up a friendship with snooker world champion Stephen Hendry. His best break is between thirty and forty and, as with boxing, he hated to lose and loved to demolish the opposition. As Brendan Ingle put it: 'If he plays you in snooker, you'll play ten games and he'll beat you nine in a row, and you'll tell him you've had enough. But you can't do that with him. He'll say, "You're still playing," and you'll have to wait for ten, and then, when he's beaten you for the tenth time, he'll commiserate with you. That's how he is.'

It was also in this period that Naseem started to become more vocal about another passion – fashion. This first received publicity when the women's editor of a local paper used him as an extremely willing clothes horse for a Sheffield boutique, and it did not take long before his views and tastes in menswear became a staple of just about every interview he granted. He would tell you his hobbies were 'shopping, shopping, looking *good* and shopping', and later began designing his own clothes.

After completing his schooling, and particularly after turning professional, he also established a reputation as a regular at various Sheffield nightclubs, and during the sparse Mickey Duff spell he started making frequent trips to London's West End clubland, attracted by the music, the women, the prestige and the late night excitement. Inevitably, given his size, his reputation as a cocksure professional fighter, and his sometimes vainglorious attitude to his growing fame, there were men tempted to have a go at him, although it was something Naseem preferred to underplay. 'I get a lot of respect out there. People realize I'm a boxer, that I can fight, and they leave me alone – even earlier in my career. I don't have no problems whatsoever, and anyway, I got friends around me all the time. But I've never had bodyguards except when I was in the Yemen. I think, who's going to bodyguard the bodyguard?' He pointed to himself with a knowing smile, prompting the response of, 'You!' 'Exactly, exactly,' he replied with a nod. Some of those around him are rather more equivocal on the subject, claiming that people leave him alone because on several occasions he's proved what he's capable of. Brendan Ingle made the point that Naseem usually managed to avoid trouble because from the start his lads were taught to walk away from insults. 'But, you know, it's very difficult because people see him on television, and the only crime you can't be punished for is envy and jealousy. You get a small element who get jealous, but he handles it well.'

There are several urban legends in Sheffield about what handling things well can mean – about large and aggressive drunks swinging at fresh air before getting their decisive come-uppance. There is even a much quoted tale, which seems to grow with each telling, of Naseem teasing two women (and in the more vivid versions, 'a pair of lesbians') having a scrap outside a Sheffield club, and getting pushed/punched/decked/knocked cold for his troubles. More credible is a story of an encounter with a large bully at a Sheffield disco when he was in his late teens. As an eyewitness put it: 'I was on the dance floor and this big bloke came flying past me. We all cleared out of the way and he got knocked right across the dance floor. I looked closely and I saw the guy who'd hit him was this little Pakistani boy, or at least I thought he was Pakistani. Everyone said it was Naseem Hamed, and that the big guy had started the fight. A little while later, when Hamed started getting his picture in the papers, I recognized him as the guy.' John Ingle, however, says most of these tales were apocryphal and counters with stories of how Hamed tries to avoid fights: 'Once we were playing five-a-side football and this guy from the other team went for him. Naz could have knocked him cold, but he just danced away and laughed. Another time, this kid went for me and Naz could have taken him out with one punch, but instead he just calmed the kid down.'

3

THE BIG
BREAKTHROUGH

Frank Warren has long been a betting man with an eye for the big
chance. In the 1980s he had used ITV to break the Mickey Duff-
BBC monopoly. In the early 1990s he'd shacked up with Don
King, and then with Sky to become the dominant force in British
boxing. But perhaps his most audacious gamble came in taking a
little bantamweight from Sheffield and turning him into one of
the richest sportsmen in the world – a move which eventually
aided his bid to drop King, link up with HBO and start his
attempt to conquer America.

Warren first watched Naseem on television a year after the boy
wonder turned professional, and felt he had seen the future of
British boxing: 'I just couldn't believe it. He came across with so
much confidence that I thought, this kid's going to be a star. He
was with Mickey Duff at the time and I was a little disappointed
because I thought to myself, well, I missed one here, but as things
turned out he saw the light and came over.' As soon as he heard
the Duff contract had expired, Warren invited Brendan and
Naseem to his Hertfordshire mansion for a long chat on Hamed's
future. The Sheffield pair did not need persuading that things
were not moving according to plan under Duff, and the offer put
forward by Warren and his Sports Network company was
enticing: a one-year or ten-fight contract (with the option of a

second year) and the promise of live ITV exposure, purses of an order neither Hearn nor Duff could contemplate, and the sweetener of a new car for Naseem thrown in for luck.

The subtext was particularly reassuring to the suspicious Ingle. 'The agreement was we'd work as a team – he is the promoter, I'm the manager and trainer, and my son John the co-trainer, and he said to us: "I won't steal him off you," ' Ingle says. Warren, in fact, stressed that he was not interested in Hamed's day-to-day business management – his contracts with sponsors, advertisers and his press relations – and later said he was delighted with the role played by Riath Hamed in this respect: 'I made it clear I didn't want to get involved with the commercial side of fighters. I just haven't got the time. If I can help them, I help them, but Riath and Naz have done some cracking deals that I'd be proud of doing, so good luck to them. It's nice to see that and it's good for boxing.'

The basis of the relationship, of course, was money. Through his partnership with King, and his contracts with Sky and later with HBO, Warren was in a position to deliver loads of the stuff. In addition, by the time they made their deal, he had already established his flair for spotting talent and exploiting it, his instinct for taking chances by putting his money on risky wagers, and his inclination towards imaginative and lateral thinking. But its survival was also cemented by Warren's tendency towards honest accounting with his partners. In any business, success has a great deal to do with trust, and whatever disquiet remained about some of Warren's past wheelings and dealings, the word from most boxers, managers, sponsors and fellow promoters was that this was a man who would cut you a fair deal: a hard-nosed, pitchforking bargainer, certainly, but also a straight talker in a bent business.

As boxing promoters go, Warren is forthright in appreciating the difference between self-interest and reality. He has had his convenient blind spots – Don King certainly was once one of them – but for the most part he communicates a disarming frankness about the world, his profession and himself. When you first set eyes on him, those almond-shaped eyes seem to contain a defensive wariness and a hard inner core – which is no more than you'd expect from a man who survived an assassin's bullet through the lung and a financial wipe-out that almost left him bankrupt, and who stoically re-emerged, Job-like, more powerful than ever before. Instant impressions, however, are seldom entirely accurate.

When you spend any time speaking to the forty-six-year-old promoter, one to one, he pushes a directness about his work and life well beyond the normal call of duty, giving opinions about his boxers, the sport's administration and sometimes his own motives which are unexpectedly forthright. He also communicates a love and passion for the sport and a knowledge of its history, which also is surprising in a businessman who has never himself laced on the gloves, and he combines this with a hint of conscience about its sometimes tragic consequences, which he has had to face up to. He is capable of bursts of pique, vanity and temper – his obvious pride after punching the exiled fraudster Roger Levitt in the face 1997 being one example – but his eyes smile a lot more than they do in public, his humour is sometimes self-deprecating and he is introspective enough to be able to discern when he is 'sounding hypocritical', as he sometimes confesses, and when his motives are base or merely pecuniary.

Warren was the product of a large, tightly knit, working class Islington family. He left school at fifteen and in his first job worked as a Smithfield meat market porter, before setting up his own business renting vending machines to pubs. He has always been a prodigious gambler and came into the boxing business after winning a £25,000 even-money bet on an unlicensed fight. 'It was all a bit of an accident really,' he says. 'A friend of mine was involved and he couldn't come up with the money, and I stepped in and got bitten by the bug.' He began promoting unlicensed shows – gloved competitions but with rather laxer rules than the licensed counterparts – and this put him on a war footing with the Boxing Board of Control and the rest of the sport's establishment. Soon, however, he ensured the medical dimensions were tightened up and in the late 1970s his organization narrowly missed being elected as the WBA's British representative at its Florida convention – a move which prompted the British Boxing Board to make its bed with the WBA as well as the WBC. Warren then realized the unlicensed universe was about to implode and decided to 'go legit' by taking out a promoter's license with the Board. Over the next decade he established himself as the country's busiest promoter, breaking Mickey Duff's promotional headlock through linking up with ITV, signing up many of

Britain's most successful fighters and promoting ten 'world' title
bills between 1985 and 1989.

He developed an image as the ultimate eighties high-flying
entrepreneur, setting up several companies, becoming the first
promoter to acquire a stock exchange listing, a big-time investor
in the Docklands Arena development with a 70 per cent stake in
the London Arena, and a man with an ostentatiously well-heeled
lifestyle – the Tudor mansion on 90 acres of prime Hertfordshire
real estate, the Rolls-Royce, the fur coats, the lot. He had the look
of someone who always landed on his feet. But on the last day of
November 1989, he discovered he had at least one potentially
mortal enemy. As Warren arrived at Barking's Broadway Theatre
in London's East End to attend one of his boxing shows, a man
with his face covered by a woollen hat stepped out of the
shadows, pumped four bullets through his chest and left him for
dead. Somehow Frank hung on and remained conscious,
knowing that if he didn't, he would never wake up. He underwent emergency surgery, keeping his life but losing half his lung.
And that was just the start of his troubles.

First, the man charged with his attempted murder, his first
'world' champion, Terry 'The Fighting Fireman' Marsh (the
Basildon light-welterweight who retired, undefeated, after one
defence of his IBF 'world' title), was acquitted at the Old Bailey.
The attempt on his life was the catalyst for a collapse of his
business empire, with investors and clients running scared after
hearing the news that there was a price on the main man's head.
With his broken ribs still aching, Warren discharged himself
from hospital after ten days in a bid to salvage the situation, but
failed. By 1991 the empire had collapsed and he was in debt to the
tune of £30 million, much of it from the ill-fated Docklands
venture and particularly the collapse of the London Arena
scheme.

Then in April 1993, when Warren was already down, Kelvin
McKenzie, then editor of the *Sun*, decided he was ripe for a
kicking and ran a story over nine days focusing on an extra-
marital affair. The paper broke the tale by driving Warren's
former mistress to his home for a doorstep set-to with his wife,
providing a blow-by-blow photo-story of the event. 'McKenzie
made it his mission in life to try and destroy me by writing about
my personal life. It was just an awful time, very difficult, and
what was of more concern to me was the effect on my wife and

family. I know it sounds hypocritical, and I had done some silly things, but I was deeply concerned,' he says, before adding for good measure: 'I hate that bastard Kelvin McKenzie.'

His marriage survived the strain, but with the threat of bankruptcy proceedings and eviction from the Hertfordshire mansion looming, he was struggling to keep afloat. 'I'd lost a helluva lot of money, my businesses, my health, my personal life, but I worked hard trying to get myself back in the game, and I've worked hard at keeping the family together, which I've managed to do.' He co-promoted a couple of 'world' title promotions with Barney Eastwood, used the profits to begin satisfying his creditors, and eventually settled his debts (although in February 1996 the High Court banned Warren from taking up a position as a company director for seven years, following a four-year Department of Trade and Industry investigation into the financial collapse of the London Arena).

What helped to pull him back from the brink was the spin-off from his relationship with Don King, who arrived in his life just at the right time. King was one of the first to wish him well after he was shot and until their 1997 break-up, Warren was one of the few to sing King's praises. He argued vociferously that the shock-haired former convict was not a bad man and that the antagonism to him from the 'white' press amounted to racism. 'When doing a deal with Don King, the negotiations are very tough and whatever the deal is, that's the deal you got,' he told me in late 1995. 'If you make money from it, great. If you don't make money from it, that's your problem.' But as Warren would later come to appreciate, this was only a small part of the truth about the enigmatic American. King may have been the greatest promoter in the history of the sport, but he also qualified as one of its least reputable human beings. It's easy enough to dismiss his links with organized crime as a thing of the past, as Warren did, or his criminal record as old hat, and to be bamboozled by his grandiose gestures, comical verbosity, sense of fun and undoubted charm, but behind the malapropisms there has also been a pattern of abuse of his fellow human beings, and most notably his boxers, which takes some hard swallowing, even for those who admire the Don's intelligence, chutzpah and flair.

For Warren this partnership happened partly by design and partly by being at the right place at the right time. Early in 1993, King, who was still in the cold as far as the heavyweight titles

were concerned, was taking a long-term view by trying to sew up
as many of the sport's other major fighters, divisions and control
bodies as possible. At the time, Warren was just beginning to
claw his way back by promoting Colin McMillan and Paul
Hodgkinson and had connections with Barry Hearn, through his
involvement with ITV, as well as with Barney Eastwood. King
wanted to extend his empire to Britain and Ireland and had
established a periodic working relationship with Warren since
1985. He saw in Warren a man he could deal with – well
connected, dependable and not sufficiently established in his
own right to offer much competition. Specifically, he asked
Warren to negotiate a British terrestrial television deal through
ITV. Warren jumped at the chance, secured a favourable TV deal
and established a close working relationship after which he
moved quickly on, signing up the best and brightest in British
boxing through offering higher purses, the ITV connection and all
the largesse that came from the King connection. At the end of
1993, when Warren made his offer to Brendan Ingle, his comeback
had succeeded and he was once again the most effective moving
force in British boxing.

Unlike the short-lived experiments with Hearn and Duff, the
relationship with Warren flourished, extending to several other
Ingle fighters and later to an extremely lucrative deal with Sky
television. By the start of 1999 the Ingle contract had reached its
sixth year, and all the parties professed still to be delighted with
the way it was evolving. 'Frank Warren has been as good as gold,'
says Ingle, a manager who is not averse to criticizing his
promoters even while his fighters are still under contract to
them. 'This is important, and I emphasize it: after we first sat
down together, everything he promised, he's done, so we've
had a good relationship. He's done for me things that Mickey
Duff and the rest would never have done, and what this
relationship has meant for my gym and my boxers has been
tremendous. It has given us the financial security which had
never existed previously, and on top of that I get on well with
him. So I genuinely have no complaints and nothing but
gratitude.'

Naseem, with his love of money, title belts and sparkling
displays of wealth (like the jeep he received after winning the
European title and the Cartier solid gold watch Warren gave him
after the Robinson fight, or the Aston Martin gift from Warren and

Sky in 1997), also remained an extremely happy camper, forever declaring his loyalty to his promoter and fiercely resisting any other claims to him while steadily upping the pressures for American delivery. The two had a close personal chemistry, with Warren sometimes playing a paternal role while giving the young fighter the respect he felt he deserved. They also seemed to enjoy each other's combative, competitive, take-no-prisoners attitude to the world. 'Yeah, he's the main man,' said a gushing Naseem in a British television interview. 'He's doing the business …He's the best promoter in the world, I reckon. Respect to Frank Warren! Respect, Frank – you're a badarse! Love it, Frank! Two-time Frank! Just get me another belt!'

So both the manager and the boxer were delighted with their mutual promotional fortune. However, it was at this point that the money began to put strains on the relationship. In fact the first signs of fissure could be detected early in 1993, when Naseem mocked Brendan in the gymnasium after hearing his mentor had backed down in an argument with Mickey Duff. For Brendan, the Duff incident was an example of nothing more than knowing when to pick your fights and when to avoid them, but for Naseem it was a sign of weakness, and he taunted Brendan for this. Nine months later, when they were driving home from their meeting with Warren, Naseem took his opportunity to exploit this perceived weakness. 'He told me he had something on his mind, and I knew what was coming,' said Brendan, who had long been warned by his wife that Naseem would make trouble, particularly over money. 'He said he wanted my 25 percent share only to include purse money, not anything outside of that like sponsorship, and that I shouldn't get $33\frac{1}{3}$ percent for fights outside the country. We argued the whole way back. I said to him, 'what are you doing to me, Naz – you can't be doing this to me. Remember I've been with you since you were seven and we always agreed on my 25 percent and one third for fights outside of Britain'. I reminded him that as his manager and trainer I was entitled to 35 percent, but he's clever when he needs to be, and dug his heels in, and in the end I felt I had no option but to accept it.'

The boy had taken on his proxy father, and won and from then on the relationship would change rapidly and substantially and finances would remain an issue of dispute. Many successful professional boxers harbour feelings that their managers are glorified pimps. As they earn more, and the managerial total increases accordingly, the resentment tends to grow and frequency leads to split-ups. For Naseem, this view came to fore as he moved out of his teens, and he began to regret his childhood promises that Brendan should receive a full quarter, no matter how much he earned. Part of Naseem's resentment was premised on the view that his talents were God-given, rather than Ingle-created. Brendan saw it differently. Without him, he argued Naseem would never have been a boxer. Without the thousands of hours he put into training Naseem for the ring and for life, he may never have succeeded. He believed what he imparted to the boy was unique; that no-one else could have done it, and to back it up he pointed to his stream of success stories from veterans like Herol Graham and Johnny Nelson to youngsters like Ryan Rhodes and the young amateur Daniel Teasedale. 'He seemed to think I was getting more than I deserved because he was the one putting in the punches, but he was forgetting all those years I put into him.'

Naseem's first fight under Warren was against his old *bête noire*, Peter Buckley, the only man to have taken him the distance. This was set for Cardiff on 2 January 1994, over four months after his previous outing. Fighting on the undercard of the Nicky Piper-Leeonzer Barber WBO light-heavyweight title bill, Naseem's task was to make a good impression on television and to do significantly better than first time around. In the fourteen months since their previous encounter, Buckley had fallen more squarely into the 'opponent' role. He had challenged Harald Geier for the WBO's vacant PentaContinental super-bantamweight title, and though he lost on points he did surprisingly well, even dropping Geier in the ninth round. After that, however, he lost nine in a row, although he lasted the distance each time and a couple of those defeats were disputed. This brought his tally to twenty-nine losses in fifty-two fights.

Naseem, who like Buckley weighed in at 122lb, approached his task with focused resolve this time, dispensing with the clowning and showing far more patience in his bid to take the Birmingham spoiler. He frequently changed stance and used every punch in his arsenal, including numerous thumping body blows, but Buckley was unmoved and remained in his shell, his head well covered. He seldom attempted anything meaningful in return despite Naseem's willingness to tempt him by hanging his chin well within Buckley's range, and most of what the Midlander attempted, missed (although Hamed's right eye was slightly grazed). Having won the first three rounds easily, Hamed piled on the punishment and at the end of the third, referee Mike Heatherwick asked Buckley if he was alright. 'I'm fine, but thanks for asking,' he replied. But at one minute forty-eight seconds in the fourth, after Buckley took seven unanswered blows ending with a right to the head which twisted his neck around, the referee decided he'd seen enough, bringing the fight to what the crowd and much of the press felt was a premature end. While Hamed was winning easily enough, Buckley did not seem to be in serious trouble and may even have had a chance of surviving the distance for a second time. Nobby Nobbs, his manager-trainer, was incensed. 'There's not a mark on him. God help you if you'd had to referee Galento–Louis,' he shouted.

Today Buckley acknowledges he was outclassed and that Hamed had improved considerably since their previous fight. 'He tried to stop me from the first bell and really tried to take my head off,' he recalls. 'He's very fast, so you don't see the punches and he throws them from really awkward angles, so you can't tell where they're coming from, and he uses plenty of tricks, like staring at your feet and then throwing a punch, but I wasn't really fooled. I even tried my own trick – treading on his toes – but he said to me, "I know that one," and he trod on *my* toes.' But it was only the second time he'd been stopped in his long career (which passed the 100-fight mark in 1997) and Buckley remains irritated about it: 'He's very hard to fight because no-one else fights like him, so you can't find anyone to spar with who'll really help you, but the longer the fight went, the easier I thought it was getting to avoid his punches and work out his style. I don't argue with the referee, but I was alright, I wasn't really hurt, and I think he stepped in too soon, with no good reason.'

Hamed and Ingle were both well satisfied with his effort. While it was not a spectacular performance, Naseem had shown marked improvement since their first encounter – more patience, less unnecessary movement and more effective punching, particularly to the body. Afterwards Warren claimed that he would have Naseem fighting for a world title before the end of the year, and shortly afterwards announced that his next encounter would be at Earl's Court in London four weeks later. This was a major opportunity for Naseem. His opponent was to be the former British featherweight champion Peter Harris, but more important, this bout would give Naseem the kind of British and international exposure he needed. The 26 February King-Warren co-promotion featured Nigel Benn's WBC super-middleweight title defence against Henry Wharton and Michael Nunn's WBA super-middleweight title defence against Steve Little – a combination which meant Naseem would be displayed before a full contingent of the capital's press as well as several of the major American boxing writers and commentators. But, for the first time in his professional career, he sustained a training injury, spraining an ankle on the eve of the fight, forcing Ingle to pull him out at the last moment and leaving Naseem extremely frustrated at the way his destiny kept on being interrupted.

When Naseem had recovered, Warren went on an opponent search for a new date at Mansfield on 9 April, finally coming up with a twenty-six-year-old Belgian of Sicilian extraction, John Miceli, who had a record of ten wins (four inside the distance), two losses and a draw. Miceli was known as a capable and aggressive fighter with a good chin (he'd never been stopped) but was lacking in power and fairly easy to hit. He lifted the Belgian featherweight title in June 1992 but after one defence had dropped down to bantamweight to challenge the world-rated Vincenzo Belcastro for the European bantamweight title, and though he lost a clearcut decision and was dropped in the sixth round, he put up a sound display and succeeded in cutting Belcastro. He had been ten or twelve rounds four times, while Hamed had never been beyond the sixth. 'He'll fall in six,' Naseem predicted, later changing that to eight on co-promoter Alma Ingle's advice.

Naseem made a strong impression before his live ITV audience and capacity crowd, treating them to a short and explosive rendition of his repertoire. Coming in again for the third time in a row at the super-bantamweight limit (1½ pounds more than his opponent), Hamed nailed the Belgian with a short right-hand counter soon after the start. Miceli was up immediately and attacked, but failed to land a single punch on the phantom in front of him. Twice Hamed stared at Miceli's feet and then fired a crisp combination into his face, and it was clear the visitor had little clue how to deal with his tormentor. Halfway through the round, a right hook to the top of the head put Miceli down again. He was up at eight, still wobbly, but launched another futile tilt at the wind, before the windmill began punching back with a vengeance, landing from astonishing angles and with impressive timing and precision. With twenty seconds to go, Naseem ended his night's work with a right hook to the body, right hook to the head and finally a massive southpaw left which somehow found its way through Miceli's high guard and deposited him face-first on the canvas, where referee John Coyle counted him out.

After performing his somersaults, Naseem wasn't about to let the moment slip. 'I'm going to be a legend, a legend,' he announced to his national TV audience. 'Let's forget the world title – three world titles, that'll do me, but I'm aiming to be a legend and I will be!' Frank Warren backed this up by saying Naseem would become 'the best fighter from this country' and comparing him favourably to the past decade's stars of his promotional stable. The performance won accolades in the Yorkshire press and boxing magazines, but, far more important, it introduced him to millions of ITV viewers. With this victory, Naseem Hamed had established himself as a star.

Ever since moving up from flyweight two years earlier, Naseem had set his heart on winning the British bantamweight title, and particularly on taking out the then unbeaten champion Drew Docherty. But ten days before Naseem's twentieth birthday, Docherty was outclassed by the rough, tough, cagey European champion Vincenzo Belcastro. Warren and Ingle gambled on their view that Naseem was ready for Docherty's conqueror and announced that he would challenge Belcastro at the Ponds Forge International Arena in Sheffield on 11 May, in a fight to share ITV live national viewing with Chris Pyatt's WBO middleweight title defence against Steve Collins. This decision caused consternation among some of Naseem's well-wishers, who argued that the Italian would be too experienced, strong and clever for a twenty-year-old novice. As Ingle recalls: 'We had an element in Sheffield, particularly, saying to me, "What are doing putting him in with Belcastro? He's had fourteen world title and European title fights." So I was a bit on edge and discussed it with Frank, but then Naz says, "What are you worrying about? I'm going to bash him up." '

At thirty-three, Belcastro was at the peak of his boxing career (as well as being at the start of an alternative one as a chartered accountant). His record showed twenty-eight wins (four on stoppages), six losses and three draws, but several of those setbacks were disputed and, more important, the quality of his opposition was of a league Naseem had yet to encounter. In addition to Docherty, he had outpointed and then drawn with Billy Hardy (Britain's former world title contender and European and Commonwealth featherweight champion), knocked out Fabrice Benichou (who went on to lift the IBF 'world' super-bantamweight title) and twice fought for IBF 'world' titles himself, being outpointed by Jose Sanabria for the bantamweight crown in 1988 and, more controversially, by Robert Quiroga for the super flyweight title in 1991. Moreover, he was enjoying a three-year winning streak which suggested that despite his age, he had improved – a view reinforced by his subsequent achievements, which saw him remaining at world class for another two years. At the time he fought Hamed, he was rated sixth in the world at bantamweight by the WBC and the July 1994 edition of *Ring* magazine rated him as one of the ten fighters in all weight divisions 'most likely to surprise the champs'. He was extremely hard to tag, had an impressively high workrate and an excellent chin (having never been stopped or even dropped), and was one of the strongest and dirtiest bantams in the world.

He was, indeed, a big risk for an eleven-fight twenty-year-old and Ingle was taking no chances. Naseem had not fought within the bantamweight limit since facing Alan Ley fifteen months earlier, and Brendan had not forgotten the final two days of thirst and starvation to make the weight. He feared they would have the same problem again unless he watched his charge, day and night. They set up camp at the Rotherham United Hoosten Roberts training ground, which Ingle said was ideal for their requirements, and got down to work three days after the Miceli blow-out. Today Ingle says Naseem has never since trained quite as hard or as consistently as he did for the Belcastro fight. He made the weight on the 118lb limit without much trouble, while Belcastro weighed 1¼ pounds under.

For Hamed it was a huge occasion: his first professional fight in his home town, his first title fight and his first outing against a world-rated opponent. He was to be paid the biggest purse of his career to date – £12,500, excluding perks and expenses. Arriving in his gold gown and a new pair of leopard-spotted trunks, he delivered a performance which, for all the controversy it generated, was one of dazzling brilliance and which completely eclipsed Collins's fifth round stoppage of Pyatt. There was barely a second in the fight where Naseem was not in absolute control, although he chose to squander some of this largesse by clowning his way through several rounds, and doing everything in his power to belittle and humiliate the Italian.

From the start of the first round – when, at the twenty-five second mark, he dropped Belcastro with a right jab and left cross combination – it looked as if he could end the contest any time he pleased, but had set his heart on proving his ability to box twelve fast rounds at a trot. Though it was obviously not quite as simple as that, it was certainly clear from the start that Belcastro was devoid of ideas on how to compete against the man-child in front of him. Towards the end of the first round, the Italian fired a purposeful jab which, like almost all his punches, missed, and suddenly, from what seemed like way out of range, Hamed was upon him with a heavy, looping southpaw left which hit the mark. The European champion looked utterly dismayed as to where this had come from, and how a boxer with a sixty-three-inch reach could find his face at such a distance. From then on the Italian's strategy was to make himself as small and tight a target as possible and fire his right cross at Hamed's inviting head. When that failed, Belcastro would use his own head at close quarters, fire short punches at Naseem's crotch when the Belgian referee Bob Logist was unsighted, and grab Hamed around the shoulders whenever he came close (though Naseem himself occasionally replied in kind – throwing the Italian down a couple of times, landing an elbow to the throat at one point, a back-hander at another, pulling Belcastro's head down and dropping his own occasionally). Naseem emerged with a graze under the right eye (courtesy of a headbutt in the second), a small cut on the side of the left eye (a butt in the seventh) and a slightly bruised groin from at least four dangerously low blows, as well as sore hands and an aching stomach. Other than these little triumphs, and a pair of right crosses to the chin in the ninth and tenth, the European champion had no success and a thoroughly miserable evening.

Naseem did exactly as he pleased – pouring it on, then easing off, here some pain, there a taunt, now fast, then slow. Every time he chose to open up, Belcastro was hurt. In the second, a left hook wobbled the European champion. In the fifth, another left hook caused him to lose his balance and go down, although it was ruled a slip. A round later Naseem concentrated on his body attack, firing off damaging hooks and bolo punches which thudded heavily home, and after that Ingle told him to pace himself. 'Relax it, you're trying too hard. Come off the jab,' he said, and Naseem more or less followed this instruction. In the ninth, after taking a right, Hamed cracked home a left hook that left the Italian's legs in pasta mode. He wobbled his opponent again with a right uppercut in the tenth and dropped him with a lead right cross-left hook combination from the orthodox stance in the eleventh. Belcastro rose wearily at the count of seven, nodding to acknowledge the legitimacy of Hamed's effort, after which Naseem opted to dance and display his amazing reflexes and uncanny ability to read an opponent's thoughts, anticipate his moves, and evaporate in the face of his attack.

In his corner at the end of the eleventh, Brendan said: 'Naz, you've done it. Go and enjoy yerself,' and Naseem pranced out, his hands in the air, then on his hips, then waving Belcastro in like a matador trying to coax a well-lanced bull into a final charge, and all the while pulling faces at the ITV cameraman and chatting away to Brendan. He was having plenty of fun at the other fellow's expense. In the final, fantastic minute of the fight – the most controversial of the contest – neither boxer landed a punch; Belcastro because he couldn't, Hamed because he wouldn't. As the new champion put it, echoing his mentor: 'I had done all the work and I wanted to enjoy myself.'

The unanimous decision was generous to Belcastro. Logist made it 120–109 (scoring two rounds even), Pentti Rautatnen of Finland scored it 120–107 (making just the last round even) and Walter Schall of Austria somehow found it within his heart to give the Italian the last round, scoring the fight 119–110. Afterwards Hamed gave cursory praise to his victim, and a great deal of praise to himself. As he was quick to point out: 'Belcastro never caught me with a flush punch all night. I could have stopped him, but now I know I can do twelve rounds in my sleep.'

Throughout the fight, sections of the crowd (including some in the press benches) shouted abuse at Hamed for his tactics. 'Fucking wanker,' was a frequent catcall, and the man from the *Irish Times* mumbled: 'It's fucking disgusting, I'd have him out of the ring.' In addition, ITV commentators Reg Gutteridge and Jim Watt, as well as many of the leading boxing writers, made it clear

they felt rather ambiguous about the morality and taste of this
display. The effect of this controversy was that Naseem gained
unprecedented exposure for a twelve-fight bantamweight. The
national broadsheets, not usually accustomed to giving European
title fights much more than a results footnote, devoted page leads
to pontificating about Hamed's tactics and talent. They castigated
him for his vulgar and sadistic humiliation of a worthy
champion, while at the same time acknowledging and praising
his brilliance. In a long feature on Naseem in the *Sunday Times*,
Hugh McIlvanney described him as 'a spectacular talent' and
noted that 'his effortless mastery of Belcastro ... was an
astonishing feat,' but at the same time he bemoaned Naseem's
'eagerness to treat his demoralized victim as if he were no better
than something you wipe off your shoe.' Other papers ran similar
critiques, and for several weeks *Boxing Monthly*'s mail was
packed with anti-Naz hate letters.

Ingle, who seemed perplexed that anyone should want to
criticize Naseem's showing, mounted several disparate defences.
He said variously that Naseem's tactics were his answer to those
who said Belcastro was too experienced; that it was Naz's
response to the many fouls committed by the Italian; that Naz
wasn't really Naz in that last round – he had put himself in the
shoes of the greats, and for this one he was Sugar Ray Leonard
out-hustling Marvin Hagler, or Muhammad Ali making a fool out
of George Foreman, and that he was 'still a baby of twenty years
old' and therefore should not be blamed for putting on a show;
and finally that Belcastro took it all in his stride (and in fact the
pair of them went out for a meal together afterwards).

Naseem listened with wide-eyed admiration for his trainer's
blarney, but offered no immediate excuses or apologies, instead
insisting he did not intend to humiliate Belcastro and that the
Italian's camp did not take offence. And when that was ignored,
he announced: 'I will not change my style for anybody,' and
suggested that the Sheffield and British public should be proud of
him. 'I showed him respect by letting him get in the ring with me,'
he asserted, with yet another extraordinary display of arrogance.
'I'm Mr Nice Guy outside the ropes. Inside the ring I've learnt an
art and mastered it. Either people want to see me win or lose.
Either way I don't mind, as long as people are buying tickets for
my fights. It was show time and at the end of the day, there are
things I have to do to put bums on seats.' A few months later,

however, in a rare display of contrition, he reluctantly acknowl-edged he had pushed things a bit: 'I'm sorry when people think badly about me. I'm not a bad person. I made a mistake against Belcastro. I know I went a little too far. If I could have that last round back, I'd do things a bit differently. I would do a lot of the same stuff again but I wouldn't push it as much as I did.'

With this fight Hamed had arrived as ITV's new young 'superstar', a boxer capable of attracting massive viewership figures, with his status as the channel's prime attraction con-firmed after Chris Eubank defected to Sky. Naz had become a point of discussion way beyond the confines of the sport's traditional debating chambers. Within Sheffield itself, where he was given a full civic reception by the City Council after his victory, he was now one of the town's most recognizable citizens. Nationally, he had established a significant youth and women's support base, attracted as much by his boyishly appealing looks (the alternatively flaring or doleful dark eyes, cruel but sensuous mouth, prominent nose and cheekbones, even the comical jug ears), as well as his limbo dancer's grace and acrobatic dexterity, his 'attitude', his taste in music and clothes and his exuberant love of life and self. It was noticeable that the average age of the spectators at Hamed's fights was considerably younger than that of most other bill-headers, making him an attractive commodity to advertisers, sponsors and magazine editors. The major national papers and radio stations, men's magazines like *GQ* and *Esquire*, sports magazines, teen fanzines and the international fight press were paying attention. And Naseem was loving it.

Growing up in the crowded house above the store in Newman Road, and watching the likes of Herol Graham acquire and then lose riches way beyond his reach, had made Naseem intensely aware of the connection between his two fists and the world of his dreams. 'Money equals freedom, and I want to be free,' he would say. For a long time before turning professional, Naseem had talked about becoming a millionaire, but now the figures needed reviving, and his love of money and the goodies it can buy became an overt and frequently cited motivational mantra. 'I'm very ambitious, so there's no knowing what I might do. I can't predict just how much money I'm going to make from this business, but I want to be financially secure and have a great standard of living for the rest of my life. I will make so much money my family will live like royalty.'

Asked what he wanted to do with all this lolly, he stressed he was a good saver and a careful custodian of money, before telling of dreams and habits that would put him close to the Chris Eubank level of extravagance: 'I'm interested in doing a lot of shopping, spending plenty of money on the right clothes, the right houses, and one day I want to have my own island in the sun, in the Middle East or the Caribbean, with a huge mansion, and a new house for my parents and a mansion of my own here in Sheffield, and a house to hire out to students. It's one of my main ambitions to be the richest sports person ever from Sheffield.' And just in case this wish list left you with any doubt on the matter, this shop owner's son from a socialist background pressed home the general point: 'I've always been completely confident I would be very rich. Wealth is part of success, and I love wealth.'

After the Belcastro fight he broke into the world rankings for the first time, making it to number ten in the WBC's list and number nine in the WBA's. Naseem, Ingle and Warren were confident he could fight for a world title before the end of the year. While Warren and Ingle were searching for appropriate morsels for their young fighting pup to devour, he returned to pasture for three months, which gave him a chance to pump up the self-publicity volume by slotting in scores of interviews and public appearances around the country, one of them being the Professional Boxers' Association dinner in London, where he won the Prospect of the Year award.

Warren and Ingle finally settled on the idea of getting the official European title obligation out of the way by defending against the mandatory contender, another Italian, Antonio Picardi, before making a bid for bigger things. After the full-house success of the Belcastro fight, they decided to use Sheffield as a base for his next couple of fights, this time picking the Hillsborough Leisure Centre, 200 yards from the football ground of his favourite team, Sheffield Wednesday.

Picardi, a thirty-one-year-old Neapolitan veteran, was no more than a filler opponent, with a record of twenty-four wins (five inside the distance) and ten losses in an eleven-year career which had taken him no further than the Italian title. He managed to outpoint Belcastro in June 1987, but was outscored by his fellow Italian in 1988 and then twice in 1993. Four of his losses had come inside the distance, but three of those were on cuts. He was rated

twenty-fifth in the world by the WBC and number one by the
European Boxing Union, and over the previous five years and
seventeen fights, only three boxers had bettered him: Belcastro,
former WBC world super-bantam champion Thierry Jacob, and
WBO junior-bantam champion Johnny Bredahl. Picardi was a
strong, durable fighter with an upright style and a fair array of
skills, but not much power and a tendency to cut.

Three weeks before the fight, Picardi suffered a twisted ankle
and the promoters had no option but to postpone for eighteen
days, until 17 August, a decision which adversely affected the live
gate and meant that for his second hometown fight Naseem had a
less than capacity hall, which irritated him. He could take some
consolation, however, in the fact that he attracted an ITV audience
of over seven million, his biggest yet and a remarkable figure for a
Wednesday night fight. Despite the delay, which upset Naseem's
training routine, he made the weight with ease, coming in at
117¾ lb, three-quarters of a pound more than Picardi and his
lightest in eighteen months.

Picardi said he had trained harder than usual and had come to
Britain to win, which is about as modest as pugilistic predictions
come. Naseem said he did not feel like going the full twelve
rounds again and announced: 'I would like it to be three – yes,
three rounds, that's my prediction. I have respect for my opponent but I'll knock him out.' And he tacitly acknowledged that
all the criticism of his antics in the Belcastro fight had affected
him, by reassuring everyone he would tone it down: 'I will have
to ease off. At the moment the public are thinking, "Are we going
to love him or hate him?" I want people to like me.' True to his
word, this time Naseem downplayed his vaudeville antics, although he found it impossible to dispense with them altogether.
He mothballed his gold, tasselled gown and his frontflip
entrance, this time arriving clad in nothing but his leopard-
spotted trunks and an orange turban around his head.

When the bell rang he moved out quickly, his thick legs, as
always, wide apart, and suddenly lunged in with one of his
speciality punches, the twisting lead uppercut, this time thrown
with the right. It missed and Picardi, fighting from behind a peek-
a-boo guard, tried to counter, but despite the fact that Naseem
was completely open and exposed, his magnificent reflexes
ensured the punch sailed harmlessly past. It did not take the
young champion long to find his range and he began whipping in

his surprise punches, shifting now and then to the orthodox position, and back again without missing a beat, and soon the Italian was on the canvas from a snappy right hook and left behind the head combination. He was up immediately without a count but was hurt again, with a left, seconds before the bell.

In the second, Naseem stepped up the punishment regime, using his right jab and hook effectively and then banging home with big southpaw lefts. One of these sent Picardi back and Hamed tripped him up as he looked like going down, causing referee Knud Jensen to rule it a slip. When Picardi rose, the young man in his face had changed his stance and was firing off fast left hooks, two to the body and one to the head landing in quick succession. He followed with another left to the body and a right hook which just seemed to nick the back of the head, and Picardi dropped to his knee and took a count, despite protesting that he had been pulled down. After taking another left uppercut, the Italian champion had his sole moment of success, landing a left hook, which prompted Naz to give a little bum wiggle in mock appreciation.

In the third, there seemed to be nothing Picardi could do to improve his predicament. Hamed swayed, twisted and gyrated away from his punches in a display of amazing elasticity, shifting stance time and again. The visitor went down from Hamed's momentum after avoiding a punch, then suffered a legitimate knockdown from a short, fast, southpaw left. Using the ropes, Picardi picked himself up at the count of four and Naseem pounced on him with an eight-punch combination, six of which landed, including a cracking right and three thudding left hooks. Picardi sunk to the canvas, and although he bravely dragged himself up again, referee Jensen waved it off at the 1:26 mark, while Naseem did his somersault.

'Didn't I predict the round would be the third?' he asked his millions of newfound television followers, before taking them through the final moments. 'Boom. See that? Oh, yeah! Baby, good shot ... He didn't want to know after that. Oh baby, you looked so good,' he said directly to the camera, and from there to seven million living rooms. ITV's Gary Newbon then asked his father Sal whether Naseem had always been like this. 'To be honest, yes,' the old man replied. Frank Warren looked on with an expression of total wonderment on his face. 'I genuinely believe he is the best fighter I have ever been involved with,' he enthused.

Even Mickey Duff was willing to share in this enthusiasm, noting that 'nobody could have done a better job on Picardi.'

Naseem was convinced he was already by far the best bantam-weight in the world, and after this victory his management and several of the country's leading boxing writers shared his confidence. He'd previously told everyone how easily he would be able to handle local rivals, but he was also absolutely adamant he could whip any of the four 'world' champions, including McCullough (who had lifted the WBC title) and one of the greats of the division, IBF champion Orlando Canizales, who was about to make his sixteenth title defence. Hamed's view was that the twenty-eight-year-old Canizales would provide him with some competition but, in the end, would be 'too old and slow' for him.

He had less respect for McCullough and at that point began a serious campaign to needle his Belfast rival. 'He's not in my class at all. He's hiding in Las Vegas, knowing that if he fights domestically he's going to come up against me and will get stopped. I missed boxing him as an amateur, but I would have knocked him spark out even then,' he told me at the time, an astonishing assertion considering that McCullough was a senior bantamweight who won an Olympic silver medal and Hamed was a flyweight in the junior ranks. Warming to his subject, he made the first of many predictions of the Ulsterman's demise: 'He's nothing, and all I can say is that it's going to make him a very rich man if he fights me, but he'll get beat convincingly. He won't be able to lay a glove on me and I'll carve him up, and I'll do it in his backyard in Belfast if he wants. He'll get stopped inside four rounds.'

But as Naseem was quickly to discover, the gap between wish and fulfilment can be wide, even for the best-connected players. For one thing, there was the question of tiptoeing through the minefield of international control bodies, which were run as private businesses – motivated by greed, party to special interest lobbying, open to manipulation and financial inducements, and seldom holding the best interests of the sport or its participants close to heart. Then there were also promotional alliances, control by rival television networks and regional and national fiefdoms to negotiate. Warren had, by then, become the most powerful promoter in Britain, but this did not change the fact that McCullough, Canizales and the rest were tied to rival promoters who knew that Hamed represented a considerable risk to their investments.

In December 1994 it was announced that Hamed's next defence would again be against his mandatory contender, the former WBO super-flyweight champion Johnny Bredahl, at The Point in Dublin on 4 March, after Frank Warren won the purse bid by putting up £285,000 (including £175,000 for Naseem). However, after some prevarication Hamed's team dropped the plan, feeling that a victory over Bredahl would bring them no closer to a world title challenge and that the more sensible option would be to allow Naseem to make the inevitable weight rise and start campaigning for a shot at the super-bantamweight title. As a result, Hamed relinquished his European bantamweight title even though Ingle felt that with the right combination of diet and discipline, the 118lb limit would still be feasible for several more months.

A week after beating Picardi, Naseem made one of his regular trips to London, which he began describing as his 'second home'. This time, however, the main purpose was for him to 'network' with Don King and the American fight crowd who were in town to see the Oliver McCall–Lennox Lewis fight. According to Ingle, the McCall camp were so impressed with the stories they heard of Naseem's talents that one night they woke up the future WBC heavyweight champion to show him what this cocky little buzzfly could do in the ring, and he came away enthralled.

Warren felt that Naseem's ability to dazzle inside and outside the ring, and his absence of youthful bashfulness, would serve him well on the American fight circuit, and the talk in his camp began to turn towards getting him major league exposure on the King-connected cable network, Showtime. Like many gullible boxers, Naseem developed a childlike admiration for King, calling him the 'best promoter in the world' and claiming his future lay with the larger-than-life American. 'I like to be different, I like to be unique. I like to be number one, the original article, a Don,' he said. Before returning home, King gave Naseem his seal of approval, and in so doing provided an early hint of proprietorial interest: 'This kid's so great he's gonna go all the way. We're taking him to America! Yessirree! The Prince is Vegas-bound!' To which Naseem responded: 'I'm the best bantamweight in the world. No one can touch me. I wanna get to America and show them Yanks how to kick ass.'

With this in mind Naseem made his first ever trip to the United States for a ringside seat at King's six world title bill at the MGM Grand in Las Vegas on 17 September 1994, headed by the Julio Cesar Chavez–Meldrick Taylor return. The idea behind the brief visit was to show Naseem off to the American boxing writers and fight personalities and get him acquainted with the US fight scene. Finding himself short of kudos or even recognition from the American fight fraternity, Naseem became increasingly eager to display his wares in the United States, believing he could be an even bigger 'hit' there than in Britain. It was later announced that Naseem would be fighting in the United States early in 1995, and would have a place on Mike Tyson's first comeback bill in Las Vegas in mid 1995, but like so many firm plans, this one too went awry, and the closest Hamed came to the Tyson comeback ring was another ringside seat as part of another PR and networking visit.

From the time he beat Belcastro, Naseem had his eye on Steve Robinson, believing that despite the size differential, the WBO featherweight champion had a style made for him. In June 1994, Robinson made the fourth defence of his title against Freddy Cruz, and though he won a unanimous decision, the Dominican took him the distance. Hamed naturally felt he could do considerably better and saw fighting Cruz as a way of needling Robinson, as well as being the quickest route to a title belt. The day after Naseem returned from Las Vegas, it was announced he would be fighting Cruz, once again at Sheffield's Ponds Forge Arena. At stake was the WBC's vacant International super-bantamweight title, a bauble of no significance.

Cruz came into the Hamed fight with an understated record of forty-four wins (fifteen inside the distance), six losses and six draws, but these stark figures told very little of the full story of his considerable ability. This Italian-based boxer from Santo Domingo turned professional in 1986 without knowing much about the game, and only managed to win three of his first ten fights. After that, however, he went thirty-nine fights without defeat before losing a dubious majority decision to the little Puerto Rican darling of the WBA, Wilfredo Vasquez, in his bid for that organization's super-bantamweight title. After that he won nine in a row before being outpointed by Robinson at a higher weight at ten days' notice. And although he was thirty-two years old and had been a professional for eight years, he had shown no sign of slowing down. He was a cagey customer – hard to hit, awkward, with a tight defence, a very firm chin (he had never been stopped) and a good workrate, especially when he was well-prepared, as he was for this one. He was not a huge puncher, but had stopped six of his previous thirteen victims.

Naseem put in only three and a half weeks of unbroken work for Cruz and as usual his regime was inconsistent, often relying on a late night whim to get back to the gym. For the first time in his career he openly defied Ingle when it came to preparation – refusing to run and training when *he* felt like it rather than when Brendan proposed. On most days he would get up after 10am and spend an hour in the gym after a light breakfast. His next two-hour session would start at around 4.30pm. For supper he would eat whatever his mother cooked, usually having two helpings. A sauna and a swim would often follow. At around 10pm he would train again and would go to bed whenever it suited him, usually well after midnight. After six months of trying to keep Naseem's weight down, Ingle was happy to let him eat virtually as he pleased, including traditional no-nos like chip butties, but he made the weight without any problem, coming in at half a pound under the 122lb limit (half a pound more than Cruz, although Hamed looked far smaller).

For anyone outside the strange world of professional boxing, and for everyone with a sense of the absurd, the shenanigans of 'head-to-head' press conferences and weigh-ins for major fights tend to come across as little more than comical theatrical farces, invariably full of melodramatic sound and fury, and signifying absolutely nothing. Ever since Muhammad Ali turned his pre-fight medical and weigh-in for his first Sonny Liston fight into a mad house, major promoters have cottoned on to the idea that getting the fighters to have a go at each other is bound to impress the punters. The boxers themselves, however, do not always see it this way.

For prizefighters, their choice of profession is seldom solely about money. Each fight is a test, not against some objective measure like a tape or clock, but against another man. It is partly a test of how well they have prepared. By weigh-in time, if they have done their job properly, they would have put in weeks of intense training and abstained from many of the pleasures and temptations of life. If they fight in the lighter divisions, they may be hungry and thirsty when they step on the scales. Their blood sugar level is therefore down and their irritation level up. It is also a test of a very traditional notion of masculinity, or at least that's the way it is often viewed by the fighting men. The weigh-in is the last occasion the two men will get to see each other before attempting to beat each other up. If you are a bill-heading boxer, even a rare one with a well-developed sense of irony, it is hard to take these theatrical occasions anything other than seriously – to see the man next to you as just another opponent rather than an enemy who will be trying to take away your earning power, your sense of self-worth and your manliness – which is why so many fighters say they hate their opponents before a fight, even though they may embrace them and say kind words to them afterwards.

For anyone outside the loop, the pre-fight set-to between Hamed and Cruz was one of those occasions where the promoters got their money's worth through a few neat sound-bites, fit for pre-fight packaging. Hamed began by predicting he would take Cruz out in four or five rounds. The Dominican smiled and patted him on the cheek: 'I thought I was coming to fight a man. I am not sure I can fight with a child. I don't want to end up in jail.' Naseem seethed. When you're a boyish 5ft 3in twenty-year-old and you believe you're the best fighter in the world, you do not take kindly to being demoted back to childhood. Naseem spoke to his audience, not to the out-of-line foreigner: 'When he gets in the ring, he's going to realize that it's a man punching him; a very strong man,' after which the insult-swapping descended to kindergarten levels. But for a boxer with a more inflated ego and a more defined sense of purpose than any other, Cruz's repartee represented a slight to be avenged. For the first time in his career, Naseem was upstaged and insulted.

With 'Prince' on the front of his trunks and 'To be King' on the back, Hamed made his usual pantomime entrance, with his cornermen adding some colour by arriving in their own top-to-toe leopardskin outfits, which Ingle dubbed their 'Fred Flintstone suits'. Brendan also made a point of handing out a few Flintstone ties.

Naseem moved straight in with a long southpaw right jab, which missed, but he soon started connecting. He changed his stance several times and the confusion in Cruz's reddening face was soon evident. He avoided several punches but was still getting hit hard and often. Midway through the opening round,

Hamed landed three thumping left hooks in a row, and then a right, and Cruz seemed hurt. The 5ft 8in Dominican succeeded in connecting with one solid left hook to the head, but Naseem was completely unperturbed. Later in the round, the home boy landed a left lead, followed by a five-punch combination which left Cruz looking wobbly.

At the bell, Cruz graciously held out his gloves as a gesture to acknowledge his opponent's superiority, as if to say, 'So, I accept you are a man after all.' His manager Rafael Guerrero asked him: 'Why aren't you throwing any punches?' To which Cruz replied: 'I don't know where he is. First I see him on the right. Then he's behind me on the left. What happened?' Implored by his mentor to attack, Cruz came out purposefully in the second, throwing a barrage of punches, but Naseem, crouching low, effortlessly swayed from side to side, and every one of Cruz's blows missed the mark. And then it was Hamed on the attack again and Cruz running for his life, trying to counter but missing. After pulling back from three consecutive jabs, Hamed dug in a pair of left hooks and a right hook at the end of the round.

The third was a less tidy affair. At one point Naseem threw a low blow and Cruz complained, at another he landed a big left and then effortlessly threw Cruz to the floor, as if to say, 'Look how strong I am, boy.' The veteran had some success, particularly with one right cross which landed flush, but by the end of the round Hamed was displaying his full repertoire and there was nothing in the visitor's long experience that had taught him how to cope with this lot.

In the fourth, Naseem did some clowning before cracking home a big right uppercut which caused Cruz to clutch for safety, though he managed to come back with a snappy left hook to the head and several body blows which the Englishman appeared not to notice. In one wonderful moment near the end of the fourth, Hamed's considerable momentum carried him forward and both men tumbled to the canvas in an undignified heap. For any other boxer this might have caused embarrassment, but not Naseem. He rose with a spectacular backward somersault, landed on his feet, and his home crowd roared their approval. The next round was slower, with Hamed concentrating on his strength-sapping body attack, those hefty hooks to the ribs, liver, kidneys and stomach. Cruz looked beyond the point of substantial resistance; his hands were dropping, he was gulping air

in through his mouth. He tried holding and hitting and was
warned by referee Larry O'Connell.

At the start of the sixth, Naseem picked his final weapon of
destruction: the lead right uppercut. This time it just grazed past,
but soon after he threw it again, feinting with a left while
dropping his right shoulder and starting from low as if about to
fire a jab to the body, and then bringing it up with a twisting
motion, impeccably timed and with all his weight behind it, to
connect perfectly just under Cruz's unguarded left cheek. It was
perhaps the best single punch Naseem had thrown during his
career – he later called it a 'pearl' – and it prompted former WBC
'world' lightweight champion Jim Watt to enthuse: 'Hamed
seems to have the ability to change the direction of a punch after
he starts to throw it. That looked as though it came out as a jab
and he just switched it into an uppercut bang on the chin. I've
never seen that done before.' Cruz was out on his feet and Hamed
launched a relentless attack to the head and body – a bit wild,
with several of his punches missing, but still compounding the
earlier damage. All Cruz could do was grab, but Naseem pushed
him hard in the face with both gloves and wobbled him with a
right and left hook. After a final right uppercut thudded home at
the 2:03 mark, O'Connell called it off. Brave to the last, Cruz
protested, but it was clear he was in no condition to continue. It
was the first time he had been beaten inside the distance in fifty-
seven fights.

Naseem, remembering the earlier slight to his maturity, was
quick to gloat. 'He called me a child. I showed him I'm a man
tonight. He's going home knowing that I'm going to become a
king. I'm the best featherweight, super-bantamweight and
bantamweight. I'm the best in the world.' And with Steve
Robinson at ringside, he was quick to let the WBO featherweight
champion know that soon he would be getting the treatment too.
Robinson acknowledged he was impressed, but insisted it would
be different when they met: 'It's a big move up to featherweight
and I will be too strong for Hamed.'

Again the victory helped to raise Naseem's profile, not only
through its success on ITV but also through the way both the
press dealt with it. This time it was the punches rather than the
antics that were the subject of focus. *The Observer*, for instance,
provided its readers with two diagrams of the decisive uppercut
along with a story focusing on that single blow. The difference

between Naseem's reception and that of Chris Eubank, who, three days later, was gifted yet another rubbish WBO decision against a low-rent opponent, was not lost on the Sky Television bosses. *Boxing News* also provided an apt comparison: 'Stunner and the Stinker,' their front page read, together with pictures of a triumphant Hamed and a struggling Eubank.

Frank Warren is a promoter who believes that in boxing, big is best – that the days of the small hall show are over, and that what works today is scale and quantity. He showed his confidence in Hamed's drawing power by placing him at the head of his biggest bill of the year at the Cardiff Ice Rink on 19 November 1994. Relegated to supporting status was a showdown for the British heavyweight title and fights for the British light-heavyweight and European flyweight titles featuring Welsh stars Nicky Piper and Robbie Regan. After several options fell through, the unbeaten Laureano Ramirez, who had been in constant training for the previous seven weeks, was chosen as Hamed's opponent.

Ramirez, at twenty-eight, had also just moved up from the bantamweight division, where he was listed as the number three contender in the IBF world ratings. Raised in the Dominican Republic and based in Spain, he came in with fine amateur and professional credentials. At the age of eighteen he reached the flyweight quarter-finals of the 1984 Olympics, but waited until 1990 to turn professional. His record showed seventeen wins and a draw (in his fourth fight in 1991). After seven wins in 1992 he went on to outpoint Indonesia's Junai Ramayana for the IBF intercontinental bantamweight belt early in 1993. Hamed was his third opponent of 1994, Ramirez having knocked out the other two. He was an elusive southpaw with quick hands and a tight defence.

Naseem's preparations were adversely affected when he went down with a severe bout of flu a week before the fight. Ingle considered withdrawing him, but this would have meant yet another setback to his progress. By the end of the week his temperature was back to normal, though he was still feeling a little weak from the effects of the virus. He made the weight bang on the super-bantam limit (while Ramirez was 2¼ pounds under) and was his usual confident, strutting self. To the boos of a signifi-cant section of the 4,000 strong, capacity Welsh crowd ('Fucking faggot' was one of several refrains questioning his sexual preference) he came in once again with orange turban, this time flashing a red, white and blue gum shield, then made his usual frontflip entrance, followed by his dancing and strutting routine. The torrent of boos and obscenities continued during the fight's three rounds, which were Naseem's least impressive since the first Buckley fight two years earlier.

Starting from the southpaw stance, Hamed barely landed a solid punch in the opening round, although he did not take one in return either. He pushed out his jab now and then, but Ramirez was fast and slippery and Naseem was struggling to find his rhythm and timing. Whenever the visitor tried something in return, Hamed would bend back, Ali-style, and sway out of range. They were like two ghosts firing blanks at each other. This unsatisfactory pattern continued in the second, with Ramirez attacking from behind his quick southpaw right jab, but still not getting home. Naseem would just stand in front of him, swaying rhythmically in slow motion, a bit like a Tai Chi master, occasionally attempting something himself but missing most of his punches.

Finally, in the third, he landed a solid left hook and then another ten seconds later, both of them catching Ramirez coming in, although a quick left counter clipped Hamed. He became frustrated when Ramirez held, pushing his opponent back with his forearm and then petulantly throwing him hard to the floor. Referee Mickey Vann – who deprived Pernell Whitaker of his richly deserved victory over Julio Cesar Chavez a year earlier – gave Naseem a stern, finger-wagging rebuke. Soon afterwards Hamed connected with a thumping lead right hook to the mouth, followed by a fast three punch combination, and Ramirez turned and walked to his corner in a 'No Mas' gesture. After a few seconds' delay, Vann waved him to fight on, and Ramirez ran. By this time Naseem had found his range and as his challenger was backpeddling, he connected with a short, devastating right hook high on the jaw, and Ramirez fell as if he'd taken a slug from an AK47. Somehow finding the courage that had been lacking fifteen seconds earlier, he dragged himself up at the count of eight, but Vann waved it off at 2:45 in the third.

'Oh baby, it hurts to be this good,' Naseem bubbled. 'I have the skills to be the greatest boxer this country has produced. I am another legend coming through.' It had been a decisive end to an otherwise off-colour performance. But even at his worst, Naseem was in a different stratosphere from a man who in 1995 would go on to outclass top British prospect Michael Alldis for the WBO intercontinental super-bantam title before losing on points against the highly regarded IBF 'world' super-bantamweight champion Vuyani Bungu, after being given only a week's notice.

When it emerged the press were not entirely satisfied with Naseem's showing, the fighter and his people displayed their irritation. 'How can you win in this game?' he asked in the tone of a boxer who had been robbed by the judges once too often. 'Everything went to plan, it was all correct. I made my prediction to win in three rounds and it happened. This man has never been stopped or beaten. He's number four in the ratings. I change my tactics for different fighters. If you don't, they soon realize what you are doing and you end up getting beat. From the first round onwards I went out and snapped my jab out coolly and calmly, and round three came and I did the business.' Ingle's conspiracy antenna was also up, and he castigated the press for missing the point: 'I'm supposed to be the Paddy, but you guys are making me look intelligent. He's in front of them, he makes them make mistakes and then he punishes them. You won't ever see anyone like him again for a long time, so you may as well enjoy him while you've got him.'

The fight drew over five million viewers for ITV, which delighted the network considering that it came at the same time as the BBC's inaugural coverage of the National Lottery, and outside the ring Hamed's fame and standing continued to grow. After the fight he made the first of his numerous non-sporting talk show television appearances, suffering a rare moment of embarrassment when a set-up in the audience tossed her knickers at him while he was being interviewed by Terry Christian on Channel 4's *The Word*. From then on he became a regular 'celebrity' television and radio guest. His attempts at humour or at retaining his 'cool' persona did not always come off, but he could usually be relied on to provide a spirited presence.

His rise to 'legendary' status had not happened as hoped in 1994, and it was a year filled with several setbacks and disappointments, ranging the injury-induced cancellation of the Harris fight early in the year to the failure to secure a world title fight in any division by the end of it. But in most other respects it had been a spectacular success. Under Frank Warren's promotional umbrella, Naseem had risen from a six-round preliminary fighter to a bill header capable of filling a hall and drawing several million television viewers. His six victories were all impressive and he was now ready to capitalize financially on his talent and fame. Even without that longed-for world title belt, The Prince had arrived.

4

THE YEMENI CONNECTION

Frank Warren had two parallel strategies to get Naseem a 'world' title shot in 1995: first, do everything possible to entice one of the champions into the ring; second, put him in with a regular diet of serious opponents to force his way into the mandatory contender's position. And when genuine contenders couldn't be found, there was always the alternative of using respected veterans who would provide a useful yardstick to measure his progress.

His next test was of the yardstick variety. It involved the thirty-one-year-old seasoned veteran Armando Castro, for a 21 January date at Glasgow's Scottish Exhibition Centre and once again Naseem was to head the bill. Castro was one of those perennials who always gave good service but never quite cracked it at the top. In thirteen years as a professional he had compiled a record of forty-two wins (thirty-six inside the distance), seventeen losses and three draws. After several years as a Mexican champion, he had fought for three 'world' titles. In December 1991 he challenged the formidable Khaosai Galaxy for the WBA super-flyweight title, knocking him down before losing a close decision. Then in December 1992 he travelled to Japan for a second shot at the WBA crown, this time being outpointed by Katsuya Onizuka, and ten months later he was outpointed by Alfred Kotey for the

WBO bantamweight title. Castro was extremely tough (never stopped in sixty-two fights) and hit hard. No-one anticipated an upset, but he was given a good shot at repeating Belcastro's success by going the distance. The challenge for Hamed was to become the first man to knock him out. 'He will not go beyond round five,' he predicted.

Hamed trained for five weeks, sparring 200 rounds, many with cruiserweight Johnny Nelson, and even breaking a habit of abstinence by doing some light running while on holiday in Tenerife. At one point – after taunting Brendan about how he had never even won an Area title in his day – he sparred six rounds with his trainer (while Ryan Rhodes did another six), leaving the old man with seriously bruised ribs and body pains that lasted over a week. He was on the weight limit over a week before the fight (later coming in at 121¾lb, a quarter of a pound less than the Mexican). When Naseem arrived in Glasgow he was concerned he would get the same kind of reception he had received in Cardiff two months earlier, but instead found himself being hailed on the streets and treated with respect by the Scottish press. Staying in the £175-a-night honeymoon suite at Glasgow's Marriott Hotel, he woke up at just after midday, showered, washed his hair and new goatee beard and moustache, and took his tea and toast in the bedroom. The afternoon was spent with Chris Saunders and John Ingle listening and dancing to music. Finally, at 5.30 he took a taxi to meet Frank Warren at another hotel and from there it was on to the arena.

A couple of hours before the fight he borrowed a new theme song, 'Here comes the Hot Stepper', from Ryan Rhodes, who was originally due to make his debut on the bill but was scratched at the last moment. 'I'd brought the "Hot Stepper" tape and was going to come out to it,' Rhodes recalls, 'but my opponent pulled out, so I gave it to Naz and he really loved it, and started using it for himself.' In his tiny dressing room at 10pm, Naseem was dancing with the ghetto blaster at somewhere near full volume, waiting, with his shades on and his greenish tartan kilt well fastened, his multi-coloured gumguard in place, for the call. Entering the ring, he looked like he was having a great deal of fun and instantly endeared himself to the 2,500 capacity Scottish crowd, who roared their approval and clapped to the beat of 'Hot Stepper'. Ingle once again came out in his Fred Flintsone outfit, after being advised by a ring steward not to wear the Irish green and white he favoured, as these were the Celtic football colours and it would upset the Rangers fans present. Castro, oblivious to such symbolism, knelt in his corner to pray and glowered when referee Mickey Vann patted him on the shoulder to let him know it was time to take his knocks.

Coming out from the southpaw stance, Naseem immediately got serious, banging in two long left hooks and then scoring at will with both hands, deliberately telegraphing some of his punches and somehow still landing them. Castro managed to connect with a solitary left hook in return but, soon after, a short right hook wobbled him and he wandered around with wooden legs, dazed for the next minute. From that moment Naseem looked like he could win any moment he chose, but instead opted to prolong the affair, put on a show and fulfil his prediction. A left hook sent the Mexican into the ropes. He beckoned Naseem in and another big Hamed right landed flush. Castro looked finished, but at that moment Mickey Vann decided it was time to remonstrate with the Mexican about why he shouldn't be beckoning Naseem. Vann's little chat lasted seventeen seconds, quite a conversation to have with someone who doesn't understand your language. Hamed lunged in wildly, missing with two hooks but landing several more, and Castro was saved by the bell.

In the second, Naseem started southpaw, switched to orthodox and smashed in an uppercut followed by a left hook and Castro went down. Referee Vann ruled this clear knockdown a slip. Fifteen seconds later a cracking southpaw left hook, right uppercut and push combination put the Mexican down again. Castro complained and Vann decided to warn Hamed about this, letting a further seven seconds pass. Naseem slotted in a right uppercut and then poured on the punishment, landing eleven unanswered punches, but the visitor, his face already marked up, bravely motioned Naseem in, jeering at him. Castro came out defiantly for the third and made a courageous attempt at an all-out attack, which Hamed treated with contempt, slip-sliding out of the way and throwing long, surprise punches in return, prompting the Mexican to beckon again. It was apparent Naseem was carrying his man, but he was doing it with such panache that no-one minded, and the packed arena responded warmly both to Hamed's brilliance and Castro's bottle.

In the fourth, Naseem moved out from the orthodox position with the obvious intention of ending the mismatch. He soon landed a stunning lead right cross which dumped Castro on the canvas for a count of four, and then performed a little jig, strutted about like a peacock and moved in with a jab. Moments later he began letting go with both hands, at one point twirling his right, Sugar Ray Leonard style, and still landing it on Castro's head. Switching to southpaw, he smashed home a hook-uppercut which deposited the challenger on the second strand of the ropes, allowing Naseem time to land two more huge hooks to Castro's jaw and face. Vann stepped in and it looked like it was all over. Hamed did a backward somersault to celebrate, but instead Vann gave the Mexican a count. With a dazed and confused look in his eyes and his gumguard half out, Castro made a final effort, but Naseem was all over him, missing more than he was landing but connecting with enough to put Castro in danger of being seriously hurt. Finally after a right cross and left hook combination thudded home, Vann decided he had seen enough and, at one minute and fifty-two seconds, called it off as Naseem gave the crowd another backflip.

Hamed again took his 6.5 million ITV audience through the final moments before telling them, in the Yorkshire-Yankee hybrid he cultivates for such occasions: 'He's gone. Goodnight viewers, because you *know* I'm champ. This was the man Alfred Kotey could do nothing with – he went twelve rounds. They said before, I'd be doing well if I could match his performance, but I beat him inside four. I was going to do it in five, but he was getting a bit too cheeky so I did it in four. He had no right to showboat like that if he couldn't back it up.'

Shortly before leaving Glasgow, Naseem displayed another side to his personal repertoire. He was told of an eighty-two-year-old blind pensioner who had been robbed of £1000 – her entire life's savings. His response on hearing this story was immediately to write out a cheque for the full amount and hand it over on the spot, a gesture which reflected his buoyant mood. He was so delighted by his reception from the Scottish crowd that, for once, he let his normally impenetrable hometown guard slip when, on 2 April, it was announced that his next fight would also be north of the border. 'I can't wait to get back to Scotland, because the Scottish people like their boxing,' he said. He should have left it there but could not resist adding: 'The Sheffield public is not a real fight crowd. I think only now the Sheffield people have realized what a fighter they have.'

Naseem was met by a barrage of criticism from the Sheffield public and papers. The editors of the *Sheffield Star*, his longest-standing and most faithful media backer, felt this insult deserved a back page editorial along with a 'What do you think?' invitation to readers. After praising his talents, they got down to business: 'What you may not expect to hear is Naz having a go at the Sheffield public. Perhaps you may think it's a blow below the belt,' it suggested, before going on to argue that despite its lack of a pugilistic tradition, Sheffield had been fulsome in its support for the Prince: 'The city wants Naz to succeed and when he fights here again, the Sheffield public would no doubt be happy to prove him wrong.' Stung by the response, Naseem tried to explain his remark away as a banal reference to his city's wide range of sporting choice. 'I am definitely committed to Sheffield. It is my home. I'm based here and I always will be. Those comments were taken out of context.' After this, however, he bent over backwards to make sure he never let an interview pass without putting in a good word about Sheffield and its people.

Before meeting Castro, he had signed his first major advertising contract with the German motor manufacturer Audi, for an initial fee of £10,000. But two weeks after the fight, there were fears that the deal would be scotched when Naseem was convicted in Sheffield Magistrates' Court of driving at 70mph in a 50mph zone, his third conviction for speeding in the past year. His solicitor pleaded that a driving ban would 'give him extreme hardship', by seriously jeopardizing the Audi deal, and would adversely affect his extensive charity commitments for the Sheffield Children's Hospital. The court, however, was un-impressed, banning him from driving for three months and fining him £150 with £20 costs. 'It was what I expected,' Naseem conceded afterwards. 'It will probably make things difficult while I'm banned, but I did not get six months.' The jeopardy level, however, had been overstated. A week later Naseem was back to his charity circuit, providing backing for an anti-crime drive in a local estate and further support for the children's hospital.

And far from dropping Naseem, Audi opted to use him more extensively, placing an advertisement in all the national news-papers and magazines with Naseem in his leopardskin trunks alongside their A4 model car, above the slogan: 'They're both the most powerful in their class.' Audi retained the rights to the picture until the end of 1995 and after Naseem drew nearly ten

million viewers for his next fight, the company offered to give
him one of the £21,000 cars he had become associated with, but he
turned them down, opting instead for payment in cash. In the
tradition of an Audi television advertisement of the time,
featuring a crass, aggressive yuppie city whizzkid, who says of
the Audi: 'It's not my style', Naseem publicly snubbed his
advertisers. 'I could have had an Audi but I didn't want it. But I
would have taken a Mercedes sports car' (which, in fact, he was
in the process of receiving from the Yemeni government). An
Audi representative made the best of the insult. 'We chose to use
him in the advert to show off the power of the new model. We
were not looking for him to drive around in the car. Like our TV
advert shows, our cars are for people who have made it but are
understated about it.'

Despite the fact that he was a mere featherweight who had yet
to win a world title, further sponsorship and advertising deals
poured in, many of them being turned down. He signed a long-
term contract with Joe Bloggs clothing, which later included
provision for Naseem's designer talents under the label 'The Nas
Collection'. There was also a £100,000 contract with Sony
Playstation and later his multi-million contract with adidas.
There were further deals with car manufacturers, fast food
chains, sunglass manufacturers and sports equipment companies, a ghosted column in the *News of the World*, regular fashion
shoots for a range of magazines, advertisements for Sky TV and a
spate of one-off commercials for the highest bidder, such as his
controversial Dime Bar ad which featured a sparsely clad
Naseem holding an 'erect' chocolate bar above his underpants.
Another involved a sixteen-hour filming session to make a Jetstar
records commercial for a cable television channel, advertising a
jungle music compilation album, after which he announced he
was reconsidering his plans to become an actor after retiring in
favour of a pop career. In August 1995 Polygram Videos released
the first of several Hamed videos, 'Natural Born Thriller', which
went straight to number one on the sports video sales list and
remained in the sports top ten for several months. At the same
time he was being besieged by radio stations, television companies, newspapers and sports, teen and men's magazines for
interviews and picture spreads, with his minders increasingly
careful to finesse the terms to ensure the image portrayed was the
'correct' one. For instance, after being with two 'babes' in a stretch

limo for the 'new lad' magazine, *loaded*, Naseem commented: 'That is the first and last time I will do anything like that. I can see how people might easily get the wrong impression.'

Forbes magazine estimated his earnings in 1995/6 at £12 million, including $9.5 million in purse money. This made him the twenty-second highest earning sportsman in the world, and the third biggest earner among the world's professional boxers. The speed of the change in Naseem's commercial fortunes, not to mention his lifestyle, prompted some of his associates to advise him to retain a London agency to handle his accounts and books, but he turned this down, resisting the idea of a pack of boxing-ignorant southerners telling him what they had booked him for. Instead he handed over this side of his affairs to his brother Riath. A team of solicitors and tax advisers and a young marketing expert, Frankie Burstin, who played a personal assistant role, backed him up. At the same time the Naseem Hamed Fan Club was launched under the direction of Nabeel Hamed, who also took over the merchandising of his products through the company Naseem Hamed Enterprises.

Even before that otherwise obnoxious aristocrat the Marquis of Queensberry had the good sense to put his name to a set of rules to 'civilize' the profession of prizefighting, authors and sports writers of varying calibres had been straining to have a go at the best and brightest the pugilistic profession could produce. Byron took lessons from the old bareknuckle champion Jack Broughton. Paul Gallico tried his luck against Jack Dempsey and survived to tell what it felt like to be knocked unconscious, and George Plimpton famously boxed three rounds with Archie Moore. But Broughton, Dempsey and Moore were big men. What about a big, young, well-conditioned former amateur boxer-cum-writer against a tiny professional? It was a question posed aloud by Claude Abrams of *Boxing News*, who had boxed for over four years in the amateur ranks as a welterweight in the early eighties, before growing into a light-heavyweight. Shortly after the Castro fight, when breakfasting with Naseem, Abrams provocatively put forward the view that there *must* be a fair degree of hyperbole in all those stories about this bantamweight standing heavy-weights on their head. Naseem invited him to try his luck and Abrams figured that at ten inches taller and fifty-odd pounds heavier, he would do fine. 'I just couldn't imagine that someone so much smaller than me could hurt me and I just assumed that those tales of him battering all these big professionals were greatly exaggerated.' They agreed on a session of 'body sparring' with 16oz pillow gloves for three two minute rounds – as mild a trial as you get, Abrams assumed.

The entire gym turned out to watch and just before Abrams made his way through the ropes, Ingle, who refereed, whispered: 'You know, Naz is a horrible bastard when he's in that ring.' And that, as Abrams remembers it, is exactly what he was. The first punch Naseem landed was a sickening left uppercut to the stomach, just to test the journalist's resolve, and after that Abrams got to feel first-hand a little of what Hamed's opponents experience in the ring: the constant side to side movement, the punches from angles outside of a normal human being's peripheral vision, the talent to anticipate your punches before you do – and disappear as you fire, only to reappear with a crunching counter a fraction of a second later. Abrams's body was aching and he was soon reduced to a crouch. As he put it: 'He chopped me down with body punches until I was at his level and then he let me have it with one or two to the head,' at which point blood started leaking from the writer's nose. 'We had agreed only to go for the body and I had to think, "Do I retaliate to the head?" But I realized straight away that if I tried anything like that, he could really do me damage.' After two and a half rounds, Ingle decided it had gone far enough and called 'time'. Hamed had a look of disgust and disappointment in his countenance, or as Abrams recalls it, 'He looked like a dog who's just had a piece of steak removed from his bowl before he was able to finish it.'

While Naseem continued sparring with the professionals, Abrams left the ring with his ribs, solar plexus and nose aching, full of relief and admiration. 'After that I was totally convinced. Each time he punches you, even if his feet aren't planted, he really hurts you. I was totally amazed by his power. It was quite incredible.' Hamed later apologized for going too far and consoled Abrams by telling him he'd had a hard day on his feet doing some serious shopping at the massive Meadowhall shopping centre. Abrams, however, came away with the view that whatever Naseem's mood, he was a fighter who was unable to take it easy once the gloves were on. 'The point is, he becomes a totally different person once he's in the ring. He really doesn't seem to know how to hold back.' Naseem sees things differently, stressing that he had a point to make that afternoon. 'The main thing that happened before we sparred is that Claude was definitely convinced he was a big, strong man and he just couldn't see a guy so small and young upsetting him. So I proved him wrong, and Claude knew from that time onwards that I was going to be great and achieve everything I said I would do.' Since then, Hamed has frequently referred to this incident, occasionally reminding journalists of what happened to Abrams or challenging them to have a try.

Naseem's next fight was not against a light heavyweight journalist, but a world-rated professional super-bantamweight at the Forum Centre in Livingston, Scotland on 4 March. The Argentinian Sergio Liendo, aged twenty-five, was rated eighth in the world by the WBC and had a record of forty-one wins (twenty stoppages), four losses and four draws. After a fine amateur career he turned professional in 1989 and went undefeated in his first twenty fights, taking his national title along the way. He went on to win the South American title and then the WBC international title. He had lost only one of his last twenty-three fights and had won his previous six. Liendo was a strong, awkward boxer, a fair puncher, and possessed a sound chin, having never been stopped.

A week before the fight Naseem was at ringside at the London Arena to watch Nigel Benn put up the finest performance of his career to knock out the favoured American Gerald McClellan in ten of the most brutal rounds of modern British boxing, to the short-lived delight of 13.1 million ITV viewers (the highest for any sporting event in Britain in 1995). McClellan underwent an emergency operation to remove a blood clot from his brain and remained in an induced coma for over a month. He was left blind, partially deaf and partially crippled, and in a state of permanent confusion and deep depression. Naseem stayed overnight at McClellan's bedside at the Royal London Hospital and was moved by the stricken American's plight. Afterwards he announced he was 'dedicating' his fight with Liendo to the McClellans. 'I was very concerned for Gerald and his family,' he said. 'I stayed in London especially so I could pay them my respects. It was a bad blow for him and the whole of the boxing world. I will have to blank all of that out of my mind before Saturday, but I do feel sorry for him and his family.'

But while the picture of the stricken McClellan was in his mind for several days before the Liendo fight, Hamed says he cut it completely from his thoughts once he got down to business. 'It was hard in a sense, but I'm a professional, that's the main thing,' he told me, 'and when you're a professional you should act like a professional and a champion. I looked at McClellan and it was sad and unfortunate for boxing, but I took it really well. I realize I have so much power for my weight, and this did enter my mind before the fight, but when I entered the ring I blanked it out and the only thing in my mind was to be victorious, because when I start to box I've always got a clear head and I don't think about anything else. I like to show people I've got craft and heart, but I don't think about hurting anybody. That's not what a boxer wants to be thinking about before a fight, and I'm aiming to be legend, so I can't let anything put me back.' Brendan Ingle, however, is a trainer who worries a great deal about the risks involved for those he trains, which is why he prefers body sparring and why he emphasizes the evasive techniques he has become known for. Having been the spit bucket man in McClellan's corner that night, he described it as 'the most fascinating, fantastic, unbelievable fight', he'd ever watched, but said that while it brought home to him the risks of the profession and the agonies he has when his own fighters take their bumps, it was not something that concerned him when Naseem was in the ring. 'I never worry about him and he tells me not to worry either,' he said. 'The only time I'm really confident in the ring is when he's in there with me.'

Despite the raw nerves and controversies stirred by the McClellan fight, Naseem was hardly subdued in his pre-fight boasts. While rounding off his training in Scotland, he remarked: 'I saw half a minute of Liendo on a video and that is all I need. He's a stand-up fighter, very strong, but I fancy the job. I can see myself doing something inside three.' And at the weigh-in (where he scaled 121lb 10oz, six ounces less than the Argentinian) he dismissed his opponent as 'a bum' – hardly the kind of remark to help counter the anti-boxing lobby.

Whatever the sensitivities, it had been decided there was to be nothing subdued or understated about Naseem's ring entrance, which had been planned several weeks before the McClellan tragedy. After the Castro outing, 'Team Naseem' had put their heads together to discuss gimmicks to further enhance the fighter's profile. Brendan mentioned a recent conversation he'd had with one of Hamed's female fans. 'She said to me: "You know, he doesn't show a lot of leg", and I thought to meself, women, what are they on about?' Naseem and Brendan's son John knew exactly what she meant and it was then that the now twenty-one-year-old fighter revealed his talent for fashion design, announcing to an amused John and a bemused Brendan that he had 'a great idea for a pair of shorts' and producing a design involving sixty strips of leopardskin material hanging from a waistband. One of the St Thomas's club regulars had a girlfriend fresh out of design school who had recently opened her own business, so off they went with Naseem's bizarre idea. Joanne Wragg was not convinced at first, but using an old pair of the fighter's size 28 trunks, she got down to work a few days before the Liendo fight, and five hours and £50 of material later she was surprised at the effect, noting that the finished version of Naseem's design worked far better than she had anticipated. After that she was commissioned to make new versions of the Flintstone suits for cornermen, and soon others in the stable adopted the Hamed-patterned trunks.

Coming in for the Liendo fight once again to the beat of 'Here comes the Hot Stepper', Naseem received a rapturous welcome from the 3,700 capacity Edinburgh arena crowd. The roar grew louder when he removed his kilt and sunglasses to reveal his hoola skirt. Even Ingle was won over: 'Women were ringing up from all over the place. "Marvellous", you know, "terrific" and "when he does that flip we were just wondering, has he got anything under the shorts?"'

Naseem glided out of his corner jabbing from the orthodox stance, before switching to southpaw. Liendo looked composed and connected with a right to the body and then two lefts and a right to Hamed's chin. With his head tucked in tight (and occasionally used as a weapon) the Argentinian made an elusive target and after the first minute he was looking like a serious test, but it was not to last. After switching back to orthodox, Naseem came in and missed with a left hook but found the mark with one of his speciality corkscrew right uppercuts. It was a jolting blow that persuaded Liendo to retreat into a defensive shell, only to be tagged again, this time with a right hook.

Hamed came out from a southpaw stance in the second, but soon switched to orthodox, after which Liendo managed to connect for the fifth time in the fight, with Naseem giving him a gracious nod of acknowledgement. The fight was beginning to look competitive until Hamed steadied his man with a left and followed through with the most devastating punch of his career to date. It was a perfectly timed, measured and executed left hook, thrown with his full body weight behind it and at blurring speed, and landing flush on the side of Liendo's jaw. The visitor's head swivelled ninety degrees to the left, his legs shuddered and dipped and his left glove brushed the canvas. Naseem started a little jig, but when, somehow, Liendo's legs straightened by reflex, Hamed shot in, before Liendo tumbled, with quick, hard right cross to the side of the head.

Liendo wobbled up at the count of six and was obviously in no condition to continue, but the Belgian referee, Daniel van de Wiele, seemed oblivious to his plight and after a cursory inspection, allowed Hamed in again to complete the duckshoot. The visitor gazed vacantly at his corner as Hamed exploded another crunching left hook to his head which spreadeagled him on his back.

Van de Wiele, to his limited credit, dispensed with the count and was quick to remove Liendo's gumguard and call the ringside physician through the ropes. The Argentinian's eyes opened and he was breathing, but he remained prone for three worrying minutes. Given the anti-boxing outcry after the McClellan tragedy, it was not a spectacle the sport needed and it was hardly helped by van de Wiele's pathetic attempt at justifying his lapse in judgement. 'It is easy to say I should have stopped it but when I went to him his eyes were clear, his hands were firm, and when I held his hands there was resistance, his arms and his legs were strong,' he said, despite the visual evidence to the contrary. 'I did not think I should stop it at that stage and the damage was done when Naseem landed that last punch. For a moment, when he was laying on the canvas, I thought the worst.'

Ingle did well to restrain Naseem's celebrations, and afterwards the young fighter agreed that Van de Wiele should have stepped in after the first left hook. 'I just went out and did my job, but I thought he would have stopped it there ... I just hope he's nice and safe and everything's great.'

Liendo eventually rose to his feet and truculently turned down Frank Warren's impassioned pleas to spend the night in hospital. The relieved crowd then proceeded to give Naseem a warm send-off with a throaty rendition of 'Flower of Scotland', after which he was allowed to give full vent to his self regard: 'I've proved I'm no flash in the pan. I've told you I am going to be a legend. I've a God-given gift and I'm going to use it. Spectacular, superior, extraordinary – those are the words I like.' The fight gave Britain its fifth highest sports ratings for 1995, attracting 9.4 million viewers, well ahead of the FA Cup Final with 8.7 million. Much of the press coverage inevitably focused on the referee's failure to stop the bout when Liendo's life seemed in danger rather than on the punches that put him in that position, but the superlatives came through nevertheless, and anyone who watched it was not likely to be in much doubt as to who was best super-bantam-weight in the world.

Immediately after the fight, a Republic of Yemen government representative, who had attended as part of a Yemeni VIP delegation, presented Naseem with a solid silver, jewel-studded ceremonial dagger to add to the gold watch and Mercedes sports car he had already collected from them. It had been sixteen months since Naseem's previous visit to the Yemen, and it was time to return the favours. Together with a delegation that included his father, Brendan Ingle, Johnny Nelson, light-middle-weight Kevin Adamson and writer Steve Bunce, Hamed spent nearly three weeks in the country in March and early April.

In the period between the two visits, Naseem had risen from being a promising prospect to a British celebrity, and the pomp and ceremony of his reception in the Yemen reflected this. While his agenda was similar to the previous trip, his profile was far higher this time, with even larger, more ecstatic crowds turning out to his exhibitions and whenever he appeared in the bazaars or on the streets. He travelled the country doing a series of exhibitions with Kevin Adamson, stopping over at the major cities and visiting his father's village.

Once again Naseem was astounded and a little overwhelmed by his reception. He discovered that the country's major football teams play for the Naseem Cup, named after him, and when he attended the final, a crowd of 80,000 rose to give him a standing ovation. There was a non-stop agenda of public engagements, ranging from visits to the presidential palace to visits with the troops, where he was once required to take the salute while holding a grenade launcher. He even led the country's elite troops in a march past, which he did in T-shirt and sunglasses to a swaggering dance step. He could see his face on school exercise books, tissue boxes, postage stamps, milk cartons and posters, and watch re-runs of his old fights on television. Mothers would approach him telling him they had named their sons after him and his sparring exhibitions were attended by crowds of up to 30,000 well-wishers. Everywhere he went he was mobbed by an instant throng, who would chant 'Naseem, Naseem, Naseem' or 'Haboob' (the loved one), and invariably the crowd would move forward to get a closer look or perhaps a touch of the great little man. 'I'd never seen anything like it before,' Adamson recalls. 'We was getting driven around and we had a lot of guards, and then we would go into a shop and the streets were empty, there was nobody around. Give it five minutes and you couldn't move. The street was blocked and you had to put the guards outside and they had to clear the streets when you came out of the shops. It was that bad.' 'It was like going to a football match and landing smack bang in the middle of the pitch,' Johnny Nelson added. Or as Frank Warren put it: 'It was a bit like what Beatlemania must have been like from the inside.'

There was considerable concern about Naseem's security, with fears not only of the crowds getting out of hand but also of an attempt on his life. Particularly in Sana'a, where, a few months before, a fresh outbreak of internal military conflict had seen a Scud missile landing in the capital, there was a round-the-clock security presence, both overt and covert. Whenever he was outside Naseem was guarded constantly by several eagle-eyed heavies, armed with Kalashnikov rifles, and even when inside the hotel he was watched by three suits, each with .45 automatic pistols at the ready. When he drove around he was led by a jeep with a mounted machine gun and a trio of soldiers. 'We were all treated like we were Michael Jackson,' says Nelson, 'army escort wherever we went.' After a while all the smothering attention and the constant watch got a little too much, even for the attention-loving Naseem, but he just had to put up with it. 'For the entire three weeks I was there, I couldn't really walk the streets freely because I would just get mobbed everywhere. People out there don't really want to hurt you or anything like that – they love you so much that they want to grab you and touch you and kiss you, which is why there are always these big old bodyguards with their big guns. It was all very controlled, and had to be, because it was very hectic out there. Once I walked into a shop to buy something for my mum and sisters and by the time I'd turned around, there were faces plastered all over the window, and soon we couldn't get out of the door because there were thousands of people outside. Then the army brought in a tank to make a path and there were soldiers firing machine-guns in the air to clear the way, and we had to wait ages until the police and army got us through.'

The delegation also travelled to Malah, his father's old village about three hours' drive from Sana'a, 'to see how my dad grew up'. The visit had several major spin-offs for the village. Prior to Naseem's arrival it had no running water or electricity. Naseem made a request to the president for this situation to be remedied and within two days there was running water and electricity, while new roads were being built. They arrived in a procession of five cars early in the morning, expecting a low key, family welcome. Instead they found every citizen from Malah and the surrounding villages waiting for their arrival. 'That was madness,' says Kevin Adamson. 'When we got to about a mile outside of the village, we was met by the villagers that had come to show us the way. When we got closer to the village, we couldn't move. They had a little reception tent, first, for the villagers to see him, but again it was mad there, you couldn't get through and there was guns going off, left right and centre. Everyone was firing guns, there was even machine guns.' Before he left, in fact, the gun-loving locals had also taught Naseem to shoot, and this kind of experience persuaded Brendan that this martial inheritance had been throught the gene pool: 'His father's village was full of marvellous people, but they all carry guns out there and they shoot, and the concentration and the accuracy and the determination to succeed, it's terrific – and Naz has got that too. I drove around there, and you could see the way the men there drive, and Naz boxes like that, with the same recklessness.'

Johnny Nelson, on the other hand, saw the visit to Naseem's parental village as an object lesson in the similarities in humanity throughout the world. Sal, Riath and Nabeel acted as informal interpreters for the rest of the delegation, who were a little surprised to discover how 'normal' the villagers were in their dreams, desires and attitudes, despite the appearance of chaos, guns and madness. 'You go to see where people's parents come from, and you find they're just like everyone else deep down inside. Whether they're from the Yemen, Jamaica or Sheffield, the backgrounds aren't that different. It proves that what got Naz to where is, is more his mentality and commitment than his heritage.' What impressed Naseem most about his trip to the village was how his own fame had rubbed off on his father. 'He's very big out there in the village now, obviously. In fact, they know him everywhere in the Yemen and wherever you walk, they know who is because they know his son.'

At least in terms of protocol, the highlight of the visit was the formal welcoming ceremony at the presidential residence in Sana'a, where General Ali Abdullah Salah, the president of the Yemen Republic, presented Naseem with the Order of Merit, First Class medal, the highest civilian decoration in the country, for his 'outstanding achievements'. After speaking informally to Naseem, the president addressed Frank Warren: 'Both the British and Yemeni people can be proud of Naseem. We want him to be a world champion and with your guidance he can be,' to which the promoter replied in glowing but guarded terms: 'It will take an almighty amount of work but with your support it's possible because I know Naseem wants to fight in the Yemen for a world title.' To which the Yemenis responded: *'Insha Allah'* (Allah willing). For some time, in fact, the government of the Yemen had been lobbying to secure a Hamed world title fight there. At a meeting at the Yemeni embassy in London with the then Foreign Secretary Douglas Hurd, the possibility of Naseem fighting in Sana'a was raised and the issue came up several times during the visit. For instance, the sports minister, Adul-Wahab Rawih, raised the matter with Warren because, he was quoted as saying, 'it is important for the Yemen and for Naseem to win the title here.' While Warren considered staging a Hamed–Wilfredo Vasquez in Sana'a's 80,000 seat football stadium in July 1995, this option never materialized, and since then there have been no concrete plans for a major fight there.

Nevertheless, the Yemeni connection has continued to be cultivated by both sides. After his second visit, the government presented Naseem and his parents with land and houses outside of Sana'a, while before every fight the president phones Naseem to wish him luck. 'I love going back there for visits,' Naseem says. 'The people there really love me, and it's great to be loved, but I don't think I would like to live there. I'll always live in Britain and in Sheffield.' His reputation has grown in the Yemen since his last visit, to the point where there can be very few of the country's eleven million citizens who do not know a good deal about him.

football match made the top five, while no rugby, cricket, tennis, athletics or golf broadcasts even came close. Now, suddenly, ITV were virtually boxer-less, and with the BBC having relegated itself to the low-rent margins of the sport, it seemed as though boxing and terrestrial television had parted ways. This provoked ripples of shock, and some indignation, in British boxing but Warren fired back that ITV 'couldn't deliver either financially or as a vehicle to develop young talent' and that there was frustration over the failure to secure good fights for regional TV, and more particularly to screen Don King fights. In contrast, he argued, the satellite deal secured the futures of many British boxers and Sky had made a firm financial commitment to the grassroots development of the sport while also giving priority to King's US promotions. He specifically rejected the accusation that the deal had lowered Hamed's profile, pointing to the supplementary publicity and income he was receiving from a number of sources, including a spate of new advertising deals and the continued requests for stories and interviews from newspapers, magazines, radio stations and the terrestrial television channels.

The background to all this was the disastrous deal conducted for Sky by Kelvin McKenzie, involving the promotion of eight Chris Eubank fights in one year, in addition to other Barry Hearn fighters. What McKenzie failed to grasp was that Eubank was a declining draw-card – and in any event, after three fights on Sky, he lost his WBO super-middleweight title to Steve Collins. With Eubank defeated and McKenzie ousted, Sky was able to strike again and this time chose Warren and the Frank Maloney-managed Panix Promotions (which handled Lennox Lewis). The result was that numerous top boxers previously tied to Hearn, Duff and others, found their way into these two rival promotional camps, thereby completing the changing of the guard within the sport.

However, the financial deal with Sky heralded further signs of discord between Naseem and Brendan. The 25 per cent scheme was something he had drummed into all his boxers from their early amateur days – that he would wipe their noses, dry their tears, cart them around the country and teach them to box, but if they ever chose to fight professional, he would get some of this investment back. Naseem, however, was never one for easily accepting the status quo. As Ingle remembers it: 'I used to inspire him by telling him he was fighting at Madison Square Garden and the like. I remember when he was about twelve years old and we were driving to a show, I says to him before one of his fights: "Naz, now remember, this one is the world title. If you win you'll get a purse of £400,000 and I'll take a quarter of that, one hundred grand." For once in his life Naz goes all quiet for a few seconds and then he tells me: "I'm not too sure about that, Brendan. One hundred grand is a lot of money." I thought, the greedy little bastard, and I told Alma, who said, "I think you may have a bit of bother with that little fella." Then a bit later, while we was in the gym together, he comes up to me and say: "It's very important – I must talk to you." So I says, "What is it, Naz?" and he tells me: "I've talked about this with my dad, Brendan, and you can have your one hundred grand."'

Ingle enjoyed this story, repeating it often, until soon after the Warren deal was done, when Alma Ingle's premonition seemed to come true. In mid 1994 Brendan had attempted to protect his investment by writing to the Boxing Board to enforce an anti-poaching rule enabling managers to unilaterally extend contracts with their boxers for two years after winning a major title. By then Brendan was wary of his protégé's intentions and attitudes to money. He viewed this 'change' in part as a consequence of earning too much too soon, and in part as a result of Riath's influence. 'Naz always told me he'd never be like Herol, but he is and worse. He said he'd never let money and fame go to his head, but he has. Part of it is that his brother, Riath, got to him.' Naseem was outraged, feeling it was an indication that Ingle didn't trust him. Ingle felt it was justified after their previous financial dispute. A year later it was Hamed's turn to strike back. With Warren having taken over much of Ingle's managerial role, he felt it was unfair for Brendan to continue receiving 25 per cent of his purse money, and decided to cut it to £600,000 of the £4 million he was promised in terms of the Sky deal which amounted to 15 per cent. Subsequently he also insisted that John Ingle's salary of £30,000 a year had to be paid out of Brendan's total. Once again Brendan was outraged; once again he concluded he had no option but to accept. If he refused he would have not only lost Hamed but may have put the relationship between the rest of his stable and Warren/Sky in jeopardy. But it did mark the end of the father-son dimension to the relationship. As had happened with Herol Graham earlier in his career, from then on it became primarily a business and boxing relationship of the Ali-Angelo Dundee kind, rather than an intimate partnership.

Meanwhile, after his defeat, Eubank followed Collins into the Warren fold, won a warm-up fight and then lost the return against Collins even more decisively, after which he temporarily retired. This series of setbacks for the former WBO champion, and his replacement by Naseem as the budding star of satellite television, prompted the young fighter into a fresh verbal onslaught against a former friend who was now down on his luck and out of the picture. Although it now seems hard to imagine, there was a time when the two biggest egos in British boxing managed to co-exist in harmony. Eubank had invited Naseem to his wedding and Hamed had admitted admiring the older boxer and being grateful for his offers of assistance. But it all broke down, according to Hamed and Ingle, after Eubank tried to 'nick' him from Ingle. After Naseem turned him down, he said Eubank became haughty and distanced. 'He even tried to belittle me once, when he said: "You can talk when you accumulate the kind of money I make,"' Naseem claimed. From then on, Hamed seldom missed an opportunity to undermine Eubank. He made a point of telling everyone who would listen that he was the one who taught the Brighton Lip his rope vault when Eubank visited the St Thomas's gym in 1989 as one of Herol Graham's sparring partners. He also claimed to have been the inspiration for some of Eubank's other antics, including his strutting and posing walk down the aisle on his way to the ring, and says that Eubank used to phone him regularly for advice and would study his fight videos. One of his favourite stories was that Eubank once phoned him on his mobile to give him a rather bizarre word of advice. '"Naz", he says, "I'm going to tell you something important now. You must listen!" All serious-like, he says, "Naz, you must learn to absorb punishment. One day someone is gonna hurt you, because it's a brutal trade. You must learn how to soak up punishment like I can." Jeez, can you believe that! I just said, "No, no, no, Chris – you got it all wrong. I'm not you! I'm the Prince. I'm different. I ain't taking punishment. I want to be doing the hitting – that's why I'm unbeatable and untouchable!"' Naseem was irritated – 'disgusted', as he put it – by Eubank's cavalier acknowledgement that he did not like boxing, and with the way he was 'taking advantage' of the boxing public. He liked to describe Eubank as 'a fourth division fighter who is just not producing the goods', as a 'failure' and, even less charitably, as 'a fake and a fraud who will end up in a mental home'. In 1994, when interviewed by the *Sun* while sitting between two models in a stretch limousine, Naseem descended to his lowest of vindictiveness. He was quoted as saying: 'Chris Eubank wouldn't have the guts to take on two girls at once. For one thing, he's far too ugly – his nostrils are much too wide apart.'

The one-horse town of Shepton Mallet, better known as an agricultural centre and as a stop-over point for visitors to the Glastonbury festival, is not where you'd expect a budding superstar to be displayed for his satellite debut, but Naseem had already proved his ability to pull the punters in droves almost wherever he landed (this was his twelfth town in eighteen fights). With Ross Hale from nearby Bristol heading the twelve-fight undercard, it was seen as a gamble worth taking and with 5,500 rowdy punters squeezing their way into the Royal Bath and West Showground agricultural hall on a sweltering night on 6 May, it certainly paid off. As one farmer who drove thirty-six miles for the privilege of seeing Naseem put it, 'You got to realize that around here, this is the only show worth seeing, and besides, none of us have Sky yet, so what the hell.'

Naseem's Mexican opponent, Enrique Angeles, was a 5ft 7½in southpaw with the kind of give-no-quarter background typical of so many fighters from his part of the world. He grew up in the slums of Mexico City, where, as one of a family of eight, he learnt to fight long before his first boxing lesson. His brother Martin started training at a local gym and Enrique followed him, winning thirty-six of his thirty-eight amateur fights before turning professional at the age of sixteen in 1989. Most of his early fights were in the intense daytime heat of Mexico City's Arena Coliseo, where so many of the best Latin fighters earned their spurs. He won his debut match but in 1990 lost a couple of decisions to more experienced fighters. By 1992, however, he was beginning to rise above the pack, showing a combination of boxing savvy and power that saw him through twelve wins in a row before he faced the heavy-handed Alejandro Landeros in an eliminator for the Mexican title. In the second round, Angeles's eyelid split open and the referee ruled it had been a punch, giving him his only stoppage loss. But he was soon back to his winning ways, knocking off a number of top Mexican fighters before being granted his return with Landeros in May 1994, this time reversing the result by pulverizing his rival in two rounds. After a couple more impressive victories, he lifted the vacant Mexican super-bantamweight title, but lost it on points to the world-rated Enrique Jupiter in his first defence (before winning it back in 1996). He was still eleven days short of his twenty-second birthday but already had a record of twenty-six wins (fifteen stoppages) and four losses and was rated thirteenth in the super-bantamweight division by the WBC. He was an awkward southpaw, with quick hands and a good punch, plenty of heart and a reliable chin, having never been knocked down. He was also an aggressive fighter and one who, when the moment required, was adept at counter-punching.

Naseem had trained with intense focus in the month between his return from the Yemen and fight time, his concentration broken only by advertising commitments. At the weigh-in, Angeles came in at 120lb while Naseem made the 122lb limit on the button. Hamed, who had been impressed with Angeles's counter-punching and movement after watching a video of his fights, once again showed his underlying disdain. 'I take every fight like a world title fight, it's as if I'm fighting for a world title. But I know I've already won. I only have to turn up. I'm very confident,' he said before parroting his familiar refrain. 'I may look arrogant, but I'm not. I'm a different person altogether outside the ring.' By fight time a large component of the crowd were happily well-oiled and ready to scream themselves into delirium at the sight of this tiny northerner who was about to grace their region with his presence. And when he gave them an entrance that made his previous antics look boringly tasteful by comparison, they roared. An eardrum-numbing explosion of fireworks and percussion launched a sound-and-light laser show which gave 'Here comes the Hot Stepper' new meaning. The jiving silhouette of Naseem emerged through a burning sheet covering a door high in the arena, smoke filled the air, the crowd clapped and chanted: 'Prince Naz, Prince Naz, Prince Naz' as he revealed once again his leopardskin tasselled trunks and frontflipped his way into the ring, followed by a team of bobby-soxers, the Union Jack and the Yemeni flag.

Angeles charged at Hamed when the bell tolled, launching hooks into the smoky night air. Naseem twisted and turned his way out of danger before snapping in a right hand of his own. The Mexican continued throwing haymakers, but the opposition was nowhere to be found. Hamed taunted for more, tapping his chin to suggest a target, before disappearing once again in the face of the onslaught and reappearing with a crunching combination. Angeles tried again, and this time Naseem leaned backwards at an exaggerated angle – a tactic the purists say you should never use, because it puts you off balance. In the final minute Naseem went to work, cracking home a pair of huge right hooks and then a quick, heavy left hook, each hitting the mark. Angeles emerged with blood seeping from a cut near his left eye as Naseem fired home several more painful rights which left the Mexican looking wobbly at the bell. Hamed started the second with another southpaw right that staggered the visitor, at which point it was time to put on a show. He walked away a few steps, gazed at Angeles's boots, and then popped in a jolting jab which landed smack on the Mexican's nose. Now it was time for the pay-off and as Angeles trundled forward, Hamed connected with a bomb of a right cross from a seemingly impossible angle, followed by a sweeping left hook, just for fun. Clenched leather connected with skin and bone and for the first time in his life, Angeles folded. He dragged himself to his knees at the count of six, then thought better of it and sat out referee Larry O'Connell's count. After three minutes and fifty-five seconds, his shot at the big time had come and gone. Afterwards he would admit he had never been hit so hard before in his life.

As soon as a microphone came near his face, Naseem gave his new television audience exactly the kind of thing he assumed they loved to hear: 'When I say I'm supreme, people just laugh. Now what they going say when I become world champion? That was a *beautiful* workout. Oh *baby*, I'm feeling *so* good.' This time, however, he was outdone by Frank Warren, who shook his head in amazement at the performance of little gold mine he had purchased. 'He's awesome. He's got so much juice, you not seen any of it yet. There is so much in reserve. No-one's put him under pressure – what's he gonna be like then? This kid is fantastic. He's the best fighter I've ever seen in my time in boxing and I include, you know, all the Tysons.' All the Tysons indeed.

Two weeks later Naseem was back in London where it was announced his next fight would be at the Royal Albert Hall on 1 July. He said he was becoming impatient for a world title shot, and though he would prefer a shot at a 122lb 'world' title, he would be happy to move up to featherweight to beat Cardiff's

WBO world champion Steve Robinson. 'I'm the best boxer in Britain, and the most entertaining,' he boasted, and once again predicted he would win world titles at five weight divisions, while Brendan claimed he was capable of going all the way up to middleweight. 'Let me just say this to you: The best fighter I'd ever seen was Ali,' he told me. 'At the moment, Naseem's as good as Ali. People ask me, "How can you say that?" Ali could only box orthodox. This fella can box southpaw, orthodox, he can switch. Ali could shuffle, he can shuffle, but he can also knock you out with either hand from any angle you want, and you can't touch him. I've watched all the great featherweights, the Henry Armstrongs, the Willie Peps, the Alexis Arguellos, and Naz is the best I've ever seen. In truth I've never seen anything like him.'

A week later Warren came up with an opponent: Colombia's Juan Polo-Perez, the thirty-one-year-old former IBF world super-flyweight champion who had been a professional for thirteen years, in which time he had raked up a record of thirty-six wins (twenty-two inside the distance), twelve losses and two draws. After a chequered early career, he hit a fourteen-fight unbeaten streak which included a win over former WBC flyweight champion Prudencio Cardona and a draw with former WBC super-flyweight champion Sugar Baby Rojas. He finally lifted the IBF title from Ellyas Pical in 1989, but lost it to Robert Quiroga six months later. He moved up to super-bantam in 1993, and a year later outpointed the former IBF world champion Jose Sanabria to get his title shot against WBA champion Wilfredo Vasquez of Puerto Rico in October 1994. Polo-Perez boxed out of his skin and seemed a very clear winner, with some independent observers giving Vasquez only the last two rounds. But the Puerto Rican was then one of the favourites of the WBA and the judges delivered a decision widely regarded as one of the most disgraceful in the association's dismal history. Then in May 1995, Polo-Perez lost a split decision to the world-rated South African super-bantam champion Lehlo Ledwaba, who went on to win the WBU world title. Three years later, the crafty, elusive and tenacious Colombian was still good enough to hold Wayne McCullough to a split decision.

Polo-Perez reasoned that because he had been sufficiently lively to 'beat' both Vasquez and Ledwaba, he could do the same with the younger, smaller and less experienced Hamed. Like so many boxers who had studied videos of Naseem's fights, this moustachioed Colombian, with his weary but unmarked face, thought he saw flaws he could exploit. 'I know he hits hard and is very fast. I've also heard he is a good showman, but what he does outside of the ring is of no interest to me. I'm here to fight and give him a hard time, not just to fill a place on the bill. I will win or lose by knockout. My plan is to make him run for three rounds and finish him in the fourth.' He went on to call Hamed a 'boy' and to predict he would break the youngster's nose. When the fight was announced, Hamed had predicted a knockout in four rounds. After Polo-Perez's forecast, however, he revised this to a two-round knockout. He later explained that his attitude was motivated by patriotism. 'Perez is a former world champion and everybody said before, "You gonna have to watch it because he beat Vasquez and he's a great fighter," and this and that. I looked at him at the press conference and he didn't impress me at all. They all come over to Britain and say they gonna beat me. No way! I'm not having that! I stare them in the eyes and they stare me back. I can't take them coming over and saying, "We gonna beat the British fighters like we done over the years," so basically I told him if he thinks he's gonna stop me in four rounds, I'm gonna stop him in two.'

With his cropped hair tinted with a light brown rinse, Naseem once again provided a pyrotechnic entry for the 5,000 mainly youthful-looking punters who packed the Royal Albert Hall. They reached out to him in adoration as he boogied his way down the long aisle before dancing on the ring apron and then frontflipping his way into the ring. Perez (at 120¾lbs – 1¼lb less than Hamed) looked on impassively, although his cornermen could not help smiling. Naseem viewed his opponent with contempt, moving around the ring and thrusting his face towards his, throwing combinations with the look of an axeman executioner practising his strokes.

He started more cautiously than usual, pawing with his jab and making regular shifts between southpaw and orthodox, as he probed for openings and weaknesses. All the time he carried his hands by his hips (and sometimes his knees) and glided around with his legs spaced widely apart. The Colombian fought behind a peek-a-boo guard, jabbing and missing and occasionally trying tentative right crosses. He only success came in making Hamed miss several times, once with a breezy uppercut which would have ended things if it had landed. Midway through the round,

Naseem suddenly switched from his playful mode and drove Polo-Perez into the ropes with a solid left, and when the counter-attack arrived he bent his body backwards at a ninety-degree angle and the punch flew harmlessly by. He then taunted his visitor to have a try at his chin. From then on, the pattern was that Perez would throw a punch and miss, and Hamed would land with his far harder counter. Eventually, Perez connected with a single left jab, which Hamed playfully acknowledged, but that was the Colombian's sole meaningful contribution to the opening round. At the end of it Naseem whacked home his corkscrew right uppercut and followed through with a left, before giving a little shoulder shrug of satisfaction and bouncing back to his stool.

In the second, it was time to fulfil his revised prediction and he fought with a confidence that suggested he could do it whenever he pleased. He punched in flurries, without absorbing anything in return. At one point he came forward with such momentum that Perez was bundled into the ropes. After taking a heavy right hook and several uppercuts, Perez freed himself and managed to catch Naseem flush on the chin with a solid right cross, which had no effect on the rampant twenty-one-year-old other than to increase his determination to end matters. Showing magnificent dexterity and timing, Hamed avoided a volley of Perez punches and then, as the Colombian moved in, fired off a devastating southpaw lead left which collided with Perez's mouth and nose and dumped him on his back, as his conqueror stood over him, the tassels of his trunks tickling the nose of the former world champion. Naseem then skipped off to his corner with a delighted little hip-shake. The dazed and confused visitor pushed himself back onto into a sitting position and wobbled up on toddler legs, his nose broken and his face showing pain and resignation. Referee Mickey Vann ignored his pleading eyes and Hamed moved in for the kill, firing a southpaw right hook which missed but landing with a big left, and then switching to orthodox and connecting with a right cross. Perez went careering into the ropes and collapsed on his forearms, conscious enough to get up but wise enough to stay down, despite Hamed's pleas to 'take some more'.

Hamed boasted that he had taken his man out with less than 50 per cent of his power and complained that Polo-Perez should indeed have risen to take some more. 'I'm not making a song and dance about it, but believe me, they just can't take the punishment, they can't take the power. The power's extra-ordinary, and I keep saying extraordinary. I'm blessed by God. What can I say? It's a gift.' He reiterated his desire to get into the ring with one of the super-bantamweight champions and to put on a show no-one would forget. 'I ain't shouting my mouth off anymore. I'm the best and everybody knows it. When I fight they going to get beat, just like the rest, and in style – early nights all the way. I ain't going for long twelve rounds – make it boring. People like excitement. People want to be entertained. I'm an entertainer, and a banger and a champion too. I'm not bragging or anything, but I'm *too* good.' Later, he indicated that just as had happened against Freddie Cruz, he had been stung by the derogatory references to his maturity. 'He said he was gonna break my nose and silly stuff like that. He got his nose broke and straight after the fight he had to go to hospital. It all happens on them who say it and can't back it up, they gonna get hurt. But if you can say it and you can back it up, then you got no fear. I walk through fear.'

It was originally announced Naseem would be fighting on Mike Tyson's comeback bill on 18 August, but by this stage the Steve Robinson fight had been set for Cardiff and Naseem's second American trip therefore involved no more than another waving, handshaking and getting-in-front-of-the-TV-cameras ringside appearance, plus a couple of interviews. He was disappointed with the lack of enraptured interest. All anyone talked about was Tyson and no-one was asking him the gushing questions he was accustomed to in Britain. 'They only seemed interested in their own boxers,' he complained, 'and to tell you the truth, they didn't really know me. If you haven't been on television there, they won't know about you, and until you get that kind of exposure people aren't interested.' His early views on the United States were therefore ambiguous (and remained so). On the one hand it was a country where his boxing talents would be appreciated to the full once he received the exposure he felt he deserved, but on the other, not a country he had much desire to live in, despite its palpable influence on his dress sense, musical taste and speech patterns, and his plans to buy property there. 'I like America in a way, but in another way the people can be kind of shallow,' he told me. 'Like, you go to a shopping mall and they have people saying to you, "Have a nice day sir, nice to see you, sir," and they don't have any idea who you are, and have never met you before. I find it a bit insincere, actually.' He particularly resented the jingoism of the American press and their reluctance to appreciate the talents of all but a handful of foreign fighters, although he had no doubt he would soon become one of the chosen few. 'I know I will go down well there when they see me fight,' he said. 'The Americans will love my style, they'll really appreciate it. You watch Muhammad Ali and Sugar Ray Leonard. The credit they got for winning the way they pleased and putting on a show was phenomenal, but you see they were in America. When you get a British fighter doing it, they don't like the sight of it, but the Americans are going to take to me well, because they will like what I do in the ring. I've got a great style for the Americans.'

One of the reasons why Hamed's American adventure remained elusive was because the relationship between Warren and King was becoming fraught, with Naseem inadvertently at the centre of the brewing troubles. Being billed as a Sports Network, rather than a Don King Promotions fighter meant that despite the contract between the two promoters, Hamed received less priority from King than British fighters in which the American had a controlling interest (such as Bruno, Henry Akinwande and Benn). King wanted more out of the deal before assisting Hamed, while Warren was not prepared to relinquish any promotional control on his top boxer, prompting the start of a rift that would eventually lead to a vituperative divorce, complicating the US plans for Hamed. As Warren euphemistically put it to me at the time: 'Naseem is definitely going to box in America in 1996. We are going to take him out, but you got to remember: while America is a great place for a boxer to get exposure, Naseem is the highest paid featherweight in the world by far, so America's got to come up with something extra special for us to take him from here, where we have guaranteed sell-outs, guaranteed big TV revenue, guaranteed sponsorship and the whole thing that goes with it.' From Ingle's side there was also much caution about handing over power to anyone else. 'We don't have a professional relationship with Don King, we're just with Frank Warren,' he stressed at the time, while privately making it clear he did not trust the former convict.

While the seeds of this impending conflict were being sown in the deep background, the details of Naseem's highly protected love

life were coming out in the public wash. Like all celebrities,
particularly those in Britain, Naseem could not avoid press interest
in his private affairs, and like many, he has done his best to avoid
this focus becoming too specific (ably assisted by his brother, Riath,
who would instruct interviewers that Naseem's love interest was a
no-go area, along with his political and religious views). Part of the
difficulty, however, was that the intense exposure to the attentions
of considerable numbers of 'available' women for any length of
time was a new phenomenon for him. Throughout his teenage
years he was accustomed to spending every day of the week in the
all-male environment of the gym, which meant his exposure to girls
outside of school hours was less extensive than many of his peers.
Herol Graham, for instance, says he can't recall Naseem having any
serious girlfriends as a teenager. 'Not that I knew of, anyway, and I
knew him very well. He might have secretly – I know I did – and
there could have been the odd girl around, but not many.' Even as a
young adult he continued to live at his parents' home until a few
months before his twenty-second birthday, and except for his
rented accommodation in Mayfair, his occasional jaunts overseas
and his out-of-town fights, that was where he spent most of his
nights. Even at nightclubs and public events he was usually
surrounded by close friends and family members who acted as
informal minders. In particular, his brothers Riath and Nabeel did
their best to watch his back, though not always with complete
success.

Naseem grew up in a household where his mother and four
sisters provided strong and assertive role models, but at the same
time traditional views about women's roles in society and the
home tended to prevail. He had to contend with his parents'
advice about eventually marrying a Muslim girl, and with
Brendan's frequent admonitions about the dangers of women to a
boxer's progress and well-being. As with most gyms, the
prevailing attitudes to women tended to be predatory, but
Brendan did his utmost to ensure that Naseem was regularly
reminded of the potential pitfalls of 'chasing' girls. He regularly
offered his boxers homilies on women, lust and sex. 'Ryan
Rhodes, come over here, will you?' he would say. 'Now tell me,
what are your two worst vices as a boxer?' And Rhodes would
dutifully reply: 'Women, and getting up late.' Brendan would
nod sagely: 'Right, watch them. Off you go now.' He would tell
his fighters story after story about young men from his gym

whose careers and lives were ruined by sex and lust – the fighter who loses control of his emotions in the ring because he thinks his girl is not treating him right; the talented prospect who enters the ring with a streaming cold and gets stopped, because he just couldn't resist the temptation to get laid behind the pub on a freezing pre-fight night; the talented sixteen-year-old who loses focus and direction when he 'puts his girl in a family way'; the stablemates who are fighting over one girl, and so on. He would preach to them, from the Bible, from his own experience. 'It's all been done before,' he'd say with a note of resignation. 'King David went with a top general's wife. It was against the religious law, against the state law. He put the top general in the front line, got him bumped off and then got his wife. Still happening today. The only thing that hasn't changed is human nature. You get a big breakdown in a marriage – I've seen it so many times in here – and two years later there's another partner and another kid, and then there's three partners involved, so all they're doing is making problems for themselves and for society; and I explain this to them.' He'd take on the tone of an Isaiah, doing his duty but knowing the minions would continue their sinful ways, before concluding that a little bit gets through. 'You might say, "How can you work in this atmosphere, with all this stealing and girlfriend stealing that goes on in this gym?" But that is life. What happens, by preaching and talking to them, is they start to improve, but jealousy, greed and lust are the biggest problems. Especially lust. I've seen the whole lot in my years in this gym, all the trials of life: births, deaths and the terrible things that people do to one another, and nice things, too.'

Early in his professional career Naseem would often stress he had learnt from the mistakes of other boxers, like Herol Graham, when it came to women and he would predict with confidence: 'You will never read about scandals involving me where women are concerned.' His response to questions on his love life tended to range from assertions of his fortitude – 'there are plenty temptations out there but I don't give in to them' – to coy hints about the implications of his robust masculinity – 'I've got female friends, let's put it like that, and it's great to have female friends because at the end of the day I'm only human, just like the rest.' When asked whether the Prince had himself a Princess, he would deflect the question with his stock rejoinder: 'There is just one woman in my life: my mum' – to which he would sometimes add, 'there used to be two before my grandmother died.' His other frequent recourse was to stress his single-minded approach to his priorities, while making certain that no-one should think for a single second that he was light on his feet anywhere other than in the ring (not that anyone outside of the Cardiff hecklers ever has). 'Don't get me wrong, I love girls,' he'd tell you. 'I'm cool in all them departments, but there are problems in being a household name, and my career comes first and always has.' At the same time, he cultivated a reputation as a ladies' man and a flirt, something that most social page and 'showbiz' writers were well aware of. Usually he was happy to be seen at fights and clubs with various beautiful women, and to offer a general picture of what he was looking for ('great personality – funny, you know. Top bod. Great bod, got to be really fit. Good looking.') as well as his reasons for avoiding long-term commitment until he was older. But having continually placed himself in the public eye, it was not possible to prevent the emergence of sources of information or misinformation about his personal affairs.

Early in 1995 he met the dark-haired, Soho-based model Kadamba Simmons during a night out at the Emporium club and seemed intoxicated by her. Soon after, they began a brief relationship, seeing each other for the next five months on an on-off basis. She would accompany him to various public events, including boxing matches and he took her on a holiday trip to Ibiza. Simmons, a smoker, drinker and drug-taker, had previously had relationships with Liam Gallagher of Oasis and Nellee Hooper (Madonna's former record producer and Naomi Campbell's former beau), and was starting to make a name for herself as a prominent young party animal, bit-part actress and friend of the stars. It was therefore unlikely that their relationship would escape public scrutiny. Nevertheless, Naseem was caught off guard by the form of the exposure. He woke up on 14 August 1995 to be confronted with the headline 'GLOVESTRUCK!' in the *Daily Mirror*, with a story and picture focusing on, and exaggerating, his relationship with Simmons. The *Mirror*'s account went that Naseem had 'wooed' her away from Gallagher and then 'whisked' her off to Ibiza, and that he had helped her get over the 'heartbreak' of her break-up with Hooper. All this had prompted her to convert to Islam so that she and Naseem could become 'closer spiritually'. Simmons, then twenty-one, was quoted discussing her relationships with all three men, claiming that her life with the young boxer was 'pure' and 'real', that their love was 'unconditional' and that Naseem made her 'feel like a woman again'. The next day, Naseem's family was confronted by the *Sheffield Star*'s take on this tale, which came with the banner headline: 'I'm not in love!' In this version, Naseem was 'secretly' dating Simmons and their island holiday was also of the 'secret' variety. In response Naseem was quoted as saying: 'It's a load of rubbish. Just paper talk.' The journalist who wrote the *Star* story, Jan Vass, later said Hamed seemed extremely irritated by the whole saga. 'He was very dismissive and annoyed, but because it was Naseem we ran it anyway,' he said.

Later, however, when approached on the subject by the *Mirror*, Naseem moderated his response. 'Kadamba is a nice girl,' he was quoted as saying, 'but it's not going anywhere. She's not the love of my life and she has overstated the relationship. I'm living my life and she's living hers.' And to this he added the more general point that 'no-one would blame me if I was not 100 per cent', stressing that his actions had to be viewed by taking his age into account: 'I think like any other twenty-one-year-old man. I'm only human. God put us here for a purpose and that is to procreate.' The former *Mirror* columnist responsible for the original story, Kate Thornton, acknowledged there may have been some hyperbole in her main source's account, but insisted that the main details were correct. 'Look, Kadamba Simmons is a bit of a publicity seeker but we had proof that Naseem had a relationship with her, took her to Ibiza and later dumped her.' When I caught up with Simmons in 1996, she acknowledged she had a relationship with Hamed, but professed to be extremely unhappy with the way the stories were used, describing Thornton as a 'nasty journalist' and the *Sheffield Star* story as 'all fantasy and rubbish, absolute fantasy', to which she added, 'Let's face it, eighty per cent of what is written in the papers is complete invention anyway.' This story, however, has a tragic ending. In June 1998, nearly three years after their break-up police discovered the naked body of the 24 year old Simmons in the shower of a borrowed flat in Islington, North London. There was a ligature around her neck. A 22-year-old Israeli man, Yaniv Malka, whom she met two months previously while on holiday in the Indian region of Goa, later threatened to throw himself from the top of a nearby block of flats. He gave himself up after two hours of negotiations and needed hospital treatment for knife wounds to his wrist and neck. He was subsequently arrested and charged with her murder.

After the affair with Simmons was 'exposed', Naseem became even more cautious about discussing his private life, and more suspicious in the way he conducted his casual liaisons. He also became more intensely aware of the way, as he saw it in his chauvinistic frame of reference, Mike Tyson had been 'set up' with his rape conviction, and considered this a vital lesson to be learnt. 'Being twenty-one is hard – you have to keep women at arm's length,' he said at the time. 'Basically, you don't want to fall into the same trap as Tyson. But come on, are you really expected to believe that girl went to his bedroom at two in the morning because she wanted to have a picture of Tyson to give to her dad? If she had come to my hotel bedroom at two in the morning, well ... but then I am a bit more on the ball. I have my head screwed on. No girl will ever rip me off or pull any strokes. Women are so devious, it's untrue. That's why I cannot commit myself to any girl right now. My commitment is to my sport.' He stressed his disappointment and bewilderment about the way he was treated. 'I meet girls, but there's some girls when I meet them, I think to myself, well, obviously I've got to keep her at arm's length because she might be a bit tricky. I mean, you know when you meet girls nowadays, and they can say hello in a public place and basically they can go away and make up some kind of stupid story and sell it to the papers, and obviously you look in the paper and think to yourself, "What is this? Is this with me? How come it's happened to me? Why has it happened to me?" You do get some kind of girls that are tricky, and you can get set up in life.'

Right from the start of 1995, the prime aim of the Naseem Hamed project was to get him a shot at a world title – any world title – as soon as it could be arranged. Having reluctantly scotched the original idea to start with a bantamweight crown, Naseem moved up in weight and Warren put his feelers out to the various holders of 'world' super-bantamweight titles. The immediate problem Hamed's handlers faced came in their access to the champions and to those behind them pulling the strings. They needed to cultivate the right channels in the various international control bodies to improve his world rating, and also to find a manager of one of the champions who was prepared to take the risk for the biggest purse of their fighter's lives. All this proved to be more difficult than anyone anticipated.

For anyone counting themselves as a serious follower of boxing, the most depressing aspect of the sport – one that frequently drives bedrock fans to the point of despair – is the venality, corruption and maladministration of the organizations which have appointed themselves to the task of controlling the sport at an international level, and the way these alphabet bodies have mutated over the last two decades to the point where one can no longer talk about a 'world' champion except within inverted commas. This does not imply a sentimental desire for a return to the sport's 'golden age', whenever that might have been (each generation of boxing writers tends to put it at the time they were children). In fact, the good old days were pretty bad old days for many fighters. In the United States, organized crime had a lockhold on the sport, to the point where even some of the 'legends' had their mob protectors and sponsors. Fights were regularly fixed and many fighters were given little option but to take a dive or take a hike (and sometimes even a bullet). Also, with only one world title for each of the eight divisions, some of the finest fighters were frozen out because they were the wrong colour, did not have the right mob or managerial connections or were too good for their own good, or because they were not American. Today fights are still sometimes fixed, but less frequently (and usually by bribing the referees and judges rather than blackmailing or bribing the boxers). Racism is less prominent and there is a far wider international spread of champions. The role of organized crime has significantly diminished. Fewer boxers are squeezed out of title shots, partly because there are more titles to go around. And, mainly because of television, boxers are paid better and certainly have a good deal more power than in the pre-Ali days, when they were not expected to speak or think for themselves. The medical controls over the sport have also improved.

But where things are undoubtedly much worse is in terms of the spread of the organizations that manufacture world titles. The 'world' title prospects of top boxers rest more than ever on the relationship their promoters have with the various bosses of these organizations. These self-serving cartels appoint friendly officials who know their next foreign freebie and attendant perks may be conditional on rendering the desired verdict if the fight is close (and sometimes, even if it's not). Their world ratings have little to do with who's beaten whom or who is best at each weight, and everything to do with who is paying whom. They freeze out fighters whose managers or promoters they don't like and promote those who pay homage. They obstruct unification fights that result in them losing money. They play politics with the lives of men who risk their health and existence for the sport. They create phoney titles to spread the largesse further. They charge exorbitant fees for the honour of fighting for, promoting and holding their titles. They have devalued the notion of a world champion to the point where it now means very little at all, and whatever halfway democratic structures exist on paper are invariably ignored or manipulated by those in executive control, unless the courts force them to follow due procedure. Basically, these organizations exist to provide jobs, perks and kickbacks for the boys, which is why they continue to proliferate – it's a fine way to print money. While this might change as a result of the federal controls contained in the Muhammad Ali Boxing Control Act (aimed at tightening federal controls over American professional boxing), for the moment boxing's international control bodies bear no resemblance to those in other sports. They function as businesses that serve their clients and partners if the price is right.

As a result, even a relatively honest promoter has no option but to deal with one or more of these bodies if he wants his boxers to progress beyond a certain point. Warren has dealt with them all at one stage or another. While the WBC, WBA and IBF had committed sins aplenty – most notably through their overly cosy relations with Don King, among others – none could quite match the level of outright corruption, maladministration and greed of the WBO during its short history. Formed in 1988 with the shadowy Puerto Rican Pepe Cordero as the power calling the shots, it initially relied on the strong backing of the apartheid South Africans who had been squeezed out of the WBA when their presence became uncomfortable. While a powerless president, Jose Torres, played the frontman role, Cordero pulled the strings, taking bribes more openly and on a larger scale than he had done in his days as the WBA's playmaker. By the mid 1990s, Britain's Barry Hearn had established himself as the WBO's premier promoter, with the result that he and his boxers received favourite son treatment from the organization. The WBO became increasingly reliant on Hearn, particularly after its other major European promoter Morgans Palle, among others, cut links with them. Warren, who in October 1994 described the WBO as 'a bunch of guys you just can't trust and can't work with', also kept his distance for a while. By then the WBO had no recognition to speak of in the United States and, for the most part, had a crop of champions markedly inferior to those of the other organizations. Its bid to be included in the hallowed circle of the 'majors' seemed to have failed. This changed, however, in 1995. Cordero died and two of the other leading lights, Ed Levine and Mark Schechner, resigned, while Torres was ousted from the presidency to be replaced by Francisco Valcarcel, assisted by his own Puerto Rican cabal. They started to clean up their act. Rumours of kickbacks ceased to be heard, purse bids were judged more honestly and their stock of champions improved, even though some of the old problems remained.

Throughout 1995 Warren made serious offers to entice the champions of the WBC, WBA and IBF into the ring with Hamed but could not reach agreements with their managers and promoters. The only other option at super-bantamweight was the WBO title, which Warren was initially reluctant to pursue because it was widely regarded as the weakest and least prestigious of the alphabet bodies. This changed in the course of the year as the WBO won brownie points, and, more importantly, when the formidable Mexican Marco Antonio Barrera lifted its super-bantamweight title. Warren had no doubt that Naseem could stop Barrerra, but because of the Mexican's promotional ties it was not an easy fight to make, despite Naseem being granted the number one contender spot in the WBO super-bantamweight rankings early in 1995. It was also felt that it would make more financial sense to build this one up over a year or so, to make it the eventual super-fight of the division in late 1996. Meanwhile, Naseem himself was becoming frustrated with Warren's failure to provide him with the chance to get his hands on a title belt, and therefore the option of putting him in with the featherweight Steve Robinson became attractive. Originally this had been seen as a fight to be held further down the line, after Naseem had picked up one or more of the super-bantam titles – but he could not wait any longer. With Robinson under contract to Sports Network, it was felt negotiations would be less complicated than with any of the other champions, even though it would inevitably result in one of Warren's major attractions being devalued by defeat. What this meant was that Warren needed to strengthen his ties with the WBO, which he proceeded to do with spectacular results. Suddenly Hamed, a boxer who had never before ventured into the featherweight division, was made the number one contender for Robinson's title, meaning the Welshman had no option but to fight him or be stripped of his crown (a step the WBO threatened to take when the Robinson camp wriggled). The promoter insisted he made no representations to this effect, that the decision to challenge Robinson was made by Hamed and Ingle alone, and that the move to make Hamed the mandatory contender was the WBO's alone. It is certainly not beyond the realms of possibility that the WBO, seeing a chance to further upgrade its championship stock, took this expedient decision unilaterally. At the same time, it hardly needs pointing out that had Warren not made efforts to improve relations with the WBO hierarchy, they would have had little interest in accommodating Hamed with such a gratuitous display of generosity.

Warren later said that despite the appearance of hypocrisy on his part, his change in attitude about the WBO was entirely a consequence of the overhaul in the organization's modus operandi and the removal of various office bearers he regarded as particularly loathsome. 'I thought the old regime in the WBO was awful,' he told me. 'I had some real run-ins with their people and I was sick to death with the expenses being loaded onto us. I'd won every purse bid I put to them, and twice they knocked back successful winning bids and we had to threaten them with legal action, and they were bending over backwards towards Barry Hearn.' But when he talked about the post-1995 WBO, he was fulsome in his praise, calling the changes a 'revolution' and, with even a larger dose of hyperbole, portraying the all-Puerto Rican regime as an angelic host. 'The new people at the top have cleaned it up and have nothing but my admiration, because what they are doing is right,' he said, with no hint of a tongue anywhere near a cheek. 'They cleared away all the old dead wood and they're giving everybody a fair crack at the whip, which means that the boxers, the managers, the promoters, everyone does well, and that's what I'm happy with.' From then on, in fact, Warren replaced Hearn as the organization's favourite promoter and the favours followed accordingly.

Naseem could not have cared less about any of this. All he wanted was a title belt to strap around his waist, and when Warren told him it would be Steve Robinson's, he was delighted. He'd been needling 'Stevo' ever since the Belcastro fight, he owed the Cardiff crowd for the Ramirez fight, and now it was payback time. He knew the Welshman's style was made for him, he liked the idea of proving himself against a bigger man and he loved the idea of humiliating the yahoos who had spat at him and chanted obscene and sometimes racist slogans. As he saw it, the title was his from the moment the fight was announced.

5

A RAINY NIGHT IN CARDIFF

Try to imagine what it's like being inside Naseem Hamed's skin just before the ring steward says it's time to walk down the aisle to fight for a world title. Ever since first lacing on a pair of sparring mitts in a sweaty church hall fourteen years earlier, you've known with absolute certainty that you have been chosen for greatness; that you are someone very special; that God has given you this immeasurable talent and that your destiny is to be the greatest fighter ever to walk this earth (and to win a handful of world titles, earn millions of pounds, achieve fame across the world, attract the most beautiful women and do your people, your city and your religion proud). It's not something you thought *might* be, or that you've gradually come to appreciate; from the start, you've just known it and nothing that has happened since has given you the slightest moment of doubt. Now the laughing and joking and dancing in the dressing-room are over and it's time to focus, to shut out the distractions and taste the next hour. And it feels good. A few minutes more to wait and then, at last, after a year of frustration, it will be time to deliver and time to collect. You'll strut your stuff, perform, jive to your song and smile at his, somersault over those ropes. They'll boo and hiss, spit and throw things and then, when the bell rings, you'll make those bastards eat dirt. You'll compel the doubters to pay homage. You'll force old 'Stevo' to submit to your will. You'll make him miss and make him pay and then finish him in four. You'll prove to the world that you are Allah's own fighter – the finest on the planet. And when it's done, your month of abstinence will be over and you'll hit the highway and then dance the night away. It's time for the fun to begin.

For Naseem Hamed, boxing is all about exhilaration. Yes, of course, there are also the dimensions of achievement, competition, domination, vindication, the glorification of self and God, money, status, power, sex and a whole lot more, but most of all it's a thing of pleasure. Like no other boxer since Muhammad Ali in his prime, here is a young man who just adores the thrill of the ride, and for Hamed, unlike Ali or any other boxer, this enjoyment is seldom tempered by even the slightest element of fear. That is one of the many things unique about this fighter: he seems genuinely fearless. It's his idea of fun – vindictive, cruel fun, but fun nevertheless – and that is a major dimension of what makes him such a compelling figure.

Before every fight, but particularly the big ones, he carries within him a mixture of the anticipation of a long-withheld present, like a child who has had to wait almost a year for his birthday to arrive and wishes those last days would hurry up, and a spot of irritation with those who've been trying to get in the way of destiny. Naseem holds glittery baubles like world title belts in inordinately high regard, but he'd had a frustrating year trying to get one, being given the runaround by the champions in his weight class. He could have lifted a world bantamweight crown in 1994 if he'd been given a shot, or the super-bantamweight title at any time since, but politics and business and other fighters' fear of defeat got in the way. His people finally had to pull strings to get a shot at a bigger champion from a lesser international control body, who just happened to be from the same promotional group. Four days before the encounter, which was billed, none too provocatively, 'A Bridge Too Far?', the young Prince arrived in the Principality – and it soon becomes volubly apparent that this whole town of Cardiff was dying for him take a fall. This was great, marvellous, as Brendan put it. There's nothing better to get those fighting juices flowing than the prospect of making those enemies grovel. As the entourage travelled by van from Newport to Cardiff for the final, pre-fight, 'head to head' press conference, this is what Brendan and Naseem had in mind.

For a long time Hamed knew he would one day do business with Robinson, and although he would have preferred to pick up a couple of other titles first, it was a prospect he'd long relished. 'I basically knew he was there to be taken,' he said. 'I watched him box five times and I saw through his style and knew he was perfect, he was made for me.' And he showed no compunction about letting Robinson know this, as part of a long psychological battle he waged against this potential rival. Naseem views the war of wits in the run-up to a fight as being of crucial importance to breaking down an opponent's confidence, but more pertinently, it's just his way. Anyone who emerges as a potential rival is an object fit for needling and taunting and derision. His opening jab came after he beat Belcastro seventeen months earlier. Robinson praised his effort; Naseem cheekily retorted that he too would one day be getting the treatment, and after that he never lost an opportunity to denigrate his potential rival, calling him 'boring', 'ordinary', a 'fourth division fighter' and the like. When Naseem last fought in Cardiff, ten months previously, he was booed and jeered and the crowd called him a faggot. And whenever he went back to cause mischief at Robinson's fights, he got more of the same, and revelled in it. It made the whole thing more personal, more of a vendetta, more fun. Robinson and his people countered weakly that Steve was the strongest featherweight in the world – far too big, strong and experienced, too manly, for this irritating upstart. For goodness' sakes, he'd whipped three former world champions; who the hell had Hamed fought? A bunch of undersized has-beens, that's who. But their words lacked the resonance of Naseem's insults and achieved no more than to provide the challenger with an excuse to further humiliate the champion – to feed his lust for vengeance and his sense that he had something to prove.

When the Team Naseem van arrived in Cardiff for the pre-fight press conference, they were already playing out their battle plan. As usual they kept the press and the champion waiting by arriving over twenty minutes late at the Cardiff International Arena (which the locals call the CIA, with straight faces). Naseem positioned his leopard-spotted, wraparound, oval-shaped shades, and as soon as he spotted the cameras he gave them the walk and the look that made everyone aware that even though he might be the smallest fellow in the house, he owned the place. Then he unzipped his tracksuit jacket to reveal the logo on his black T-shirt: PRINCE Naseem Hamed WORLD CHAMPION. The taut, irritated countenances in the WBO champion's camp, and the red-faced resentment of some in the Cardiff press contingent, betrayed what some of them were thinking. There was nice, good Stevo, the Cinderella man who took his chances, grabbed a world title and outgutted some of the finest feather-weights in the world. It was bad enough he'd been 'messed around' by his English promoter, forced into this fight at short notice and short change. But then in came this arrogant, cocky, conceited man-child, who topped it all by taking over, with the London lackey press in his wake, treating this proud son of Cardiff like garbage. This little fucker was in Stevo's town, fighting for Stevo's world title, and he was already playing the king.

Next thing for Naseem was to give them all a sucker punch: draw them with a conciliatory feint and then swat 'em, just like he was planning for fight night. He started with a backhanded compliment, patronizing the champion gently: 'You are ob-viously the best boxer I will have fought, because I haven't met a world champion before … You've always been a polite kind of guy and you've got a lot of pride.' He told them all the *bragadaccio* of the past months was really no more than a touch of garnish for the ticket sales. 'Fights have to be built up. You can't have two guys being nice to each other. There's got to be a bit of a grudge, a bit of controversy.' Then, just when everyone thought they were getting a rare taste of a hype-free, Naz-lite, he came in with the old one-two. 'If a fighter doesn't know how to build up a fight, he might as well step down and leave it to a twenty-one-year-old who is a prince destined to be the king.' He pointed to the logo on his T-shirt then glared at Robinson. 'When you are flash and can back it up, no problem. You can wear what you want and say what you like. I'm flash because I can back it up. I'm just so glad you are going to turn up for me to take this title.' He raised his head haughtily, backtracked for a second by telling Steve he was not underestimating him, and then closed in: 'That doesn't mean I'm not going to kick your backside and take you out in four rounds.' As he said this, his lip curled and his eyes flared, and his contempt for the opposition shone through. He was puffed up now and could not resist overstaying his welcome. 'I can take a man out with one shot. I can move. I can switch from southpaw to orthodox. I have handspeed and accuracy. I'm the complete package,' he chanted, jabbing his finger at his chest. 'You will enter the ring a champion but you'll be an ex-champ when you leave.' And on and on, and all Robinson could do was look stoic and dignified and try his best to sound convincing. By the end, the entire Welsh press contingent and assorted hangers-on had broken any pretence of impartiality and were cheering for their countryman, and Naseem was loving it.

But not everyone in the challenger's camp viewed things from quite the same angle. Frank Warren was concerned his little earner was getting too far up the noses of the locals. After all, Frank was supposed the represent the promotional interests of both men, even though everyone knew whose side he was on, and he might want to do business in Cardiff again. So he announced that Naseem had agreed to donate £1,000 of his purse to a fund to build a statue of the 'legendary Jim Driscoll' who died of pneumonia in Cardiff seventy years earlier. You could see from Hamed's facial expression that he couldn't quite recall making any such commitment, and who the hell was Jim Driscoll anyway? A local reporter caught his blank look and asked him what he knew of Driscoll. Then he dimly remembered: a useful featherweight called Driscoll was the only man to knock Robinson down and went on to fight for the WBO title. 'I hear he's a real good fighter,' Naseem hesitantly replied. Problem was, this fellow was called Tim Driscoll and he was eighty years out of time. The local press chuckled smugly and put it in their columns the next day. Brendan and Frank winced. Naseem seemed oblivious to the dimensions of his mistake. Jim Driscoll, Tim Driscoll, what's the difference? Could beat 'em both in the same night. And though Frank Warren, who has on his office wall an eighty-five-year-old canvas poster advertising a Driscoll fight, wouldn't say it in this company, he agreed. 'Naseem's reflexes, his handspeed, his unorthodoxness, his strength – I can't see any featherweight beating him. Not even Jim Driscoll.'

The Driscoll *faux pas* was one for Robinson to take home in his black woolly cap after his verbal battering, but it was small consolation for a likeable twenty-six-year-old who had not had things his own way for a while. First, his previous promoter, Barry Hearn, sued him for breach of contract, and by fight time the case had cost him around £140,000. Then he was 'forced' into a mandatory defence against Hamed, a fighter who had never before even ventured into the featherweight division but who had mysteriously been granted the WBO's number one ranking. This meant that despite the best attempts of his lawyers, Robinson had no option but to take the fight at a month's notice and at a gross purse of just under £200,000, his highest ever, yet far lower than if he'd been in a position to play hardball for a while, and, more significantly, considerably less than the half a million-plus Naseem was getting. Warren would say there was no injustice here – it was Hamed and Ingle's decision to make the challenge and the WBO's to accept it. He'd also provide the figures to prove that under his Sports Network promotions, Robinson had become by far the highest-paid featherweight in the world. 'I was the guy who made sure Steve had all his defences in Cardiff, including the Hamed fight,' Warren protested indignantly. 'Eight world title defences in his home town. Never had to travel. I never lost a purse bid and he didn't have a mandatory challenge for eighteen months. I like Wales and I've been involved with all the good fighters down there, and I've always paid them well, and the only complaint I've ever had was from one man, Robinson, and I think he's an ungrateful bastard,' he said soon after their fight. He acknowledged that Hamed was receiving significantly more money. Fighters are products who get paid according to their market rate and their relative bargaining power. 'Of course. Naz is the attraction,' Warren said in an irritated tone. 'Steve's two fights prior to this, we struggled with. Wherever Naz boxed, we sold out, and when he boxed on ITV he drew ratings of ten million, and not in world title fights. Robinson's last couple of world title fights on ITV delivered just over three million.' But it was hard to convince a Robinson fan that Warren was doing anything other than sacrificing one of his fighters for the good of another, and for the good of his own pocket. As Warren acknowledged: 'There was no way I was going to win them over. They were all pissed off because there was a campaign down there in the newspapers.'

Both fighters put in just under four weeks' training, which for Robinson was three less than normal and for Hamed two less than his maximum. Steve stayed at home with his new wife Angela and their children, and worked quietly and determinedly in and around Cardiff. His sparring (principally with the southpaw Commonwealth super-bantam champion Neil Swain)

Early days: Naseem Hamed and Brendan Ingle first met in 1981 and hit it off immediately. *(John Marshall)*

Posing at the St Thomas's Boys' Club gym. *(John Marshall)*

From his early amateur days Naseem sparred with far bigger boys and men. *(David Muscroft)*

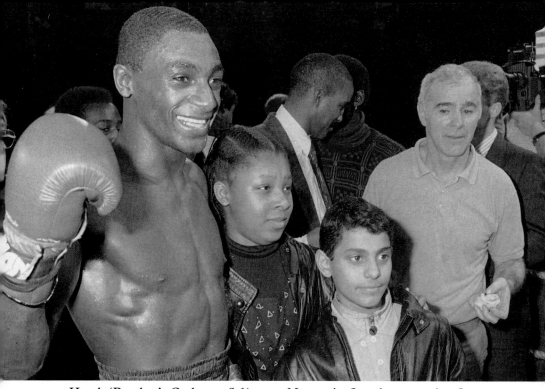

Herol 'Bomber' Graham *(left)* was Naseem's first hero at the St Thomas's Boys' Club gym. Here he is seen with his daughter, Natasha, Naseem and Brendan. *(David Muscroft)*

The 18-year-old Hamed soon after his professional début. *(David Muscroft)*

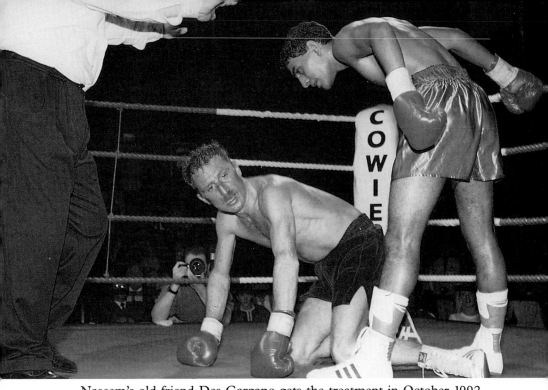

Naseem's old friend Des Gargano gets the treatment in October 1992.
(Nick Potts/Action Images)

A victorious Naz. Behind him are *(left to right)* the BBBC's John Morris, promoter Frank Warren, Brendan Ingle (in the 'Flintstones' shirt) and, far right, Sal Hamed. *(David Muscroft)*

Naseem taunts and teases his way to a shutout against Vincenzo Belcastro to lift the European bantamweight title in May 1994. *(Action Images)*

Hamed pumps a lead right into the face of Freddy Cruz, shortly before stopping him in the sixth round to lift the WBC International super bantamweight title in October 1994. *(Action Images)*

Naseem walks away from the prone Sergio Liendo after their March 1995 fight was allowed to continue several potentially damaging punches too long. *(Action Images)*

A snarling, sneering Hamed pours it on to the wounded Steve Robinson in the final round of their September 1995 WBO featherweight title bout. *(Action Images)*

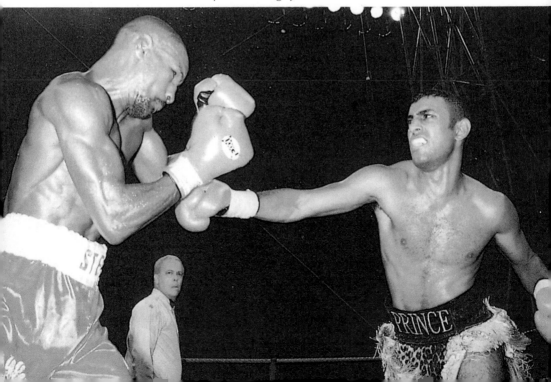

Naseem with Kevin Kelley prior to the fight in December 1997.
(Action Images)

Naseem and Kelley in the ring. *(Action Images)*

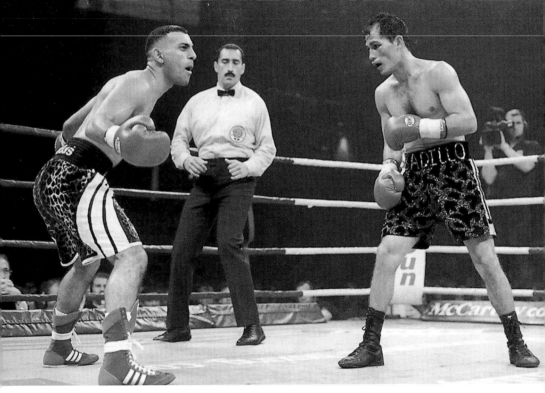

Naseem taunts Jose Badillo during his WBO Featherweight victory in October 1997. *(Action Images)*

Naseem and Badillo get into a tangle. *(Action Images)*

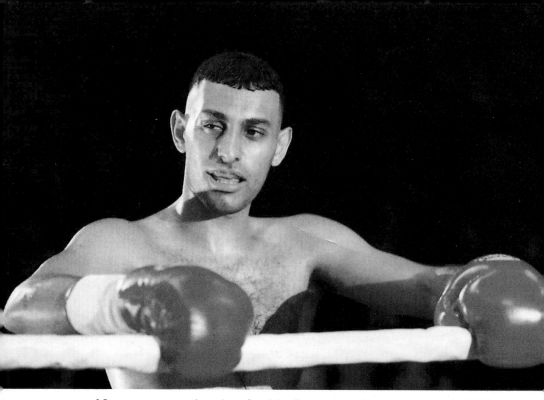

Naseem enters the ring for his fight with Vasquez in April 1998.
(Action Images)

Naseem raises his arms after stopping Vasquez in the seventh round.
(Action Images)

was done in his manager Dai Gardiner's new gym in Cwmcarn because Gardiner's Fleur-de-Lys gym had burnt to cinders a month earlier, while the pad work and ground work and their strategizing took place in Ronnie Rush's living room in the low-rent district of Ely, not far from Steve's own home. Before the fight, Robinson told me he was in excellent nick. 'I'm feeling very good, very strong, just fine. I've been training solidly for four weeks, so no problems. My conditioning is excellent and my mind is so focused on the fight that I won't let any of the problems get in the way. There are things about this build-up which have angered me and I'm ready to explode. I've just got to make sure it's a controlled explosion.' And his mum Yvonne confirmed this self-diagnosis. 'Steven said to me, "Mam, I'll fight him for nothing in the gutter." I've never seen him so determined. Steven's not a rude boy, he'd never put anyone down. He's very quiet. But he came in the other day and said: "Mam, I'm frightened. Frightened that I'm going to really hurt him, because he's getting me so mad. You haven't seen the best of me yet," he said.' After it was over, however, Steve told me there were problems a-plenty he'd had to cope with. 'I was training, sure, but I just wasn't 100 per cent. Things weren't right and I kept asking questions about the money because I got the short end of the purse, and the court cases, and the problems with Frank Warren. It was in the back of my mind. I wasn't psychologically right and I didn't have long enough to prepare. I had just come back from my honeymoon and had only three and a half weeks to prepare. Lloyd Honeyghan told me before the fight I needed eight weeks of training, so obviously my stamina wasn't right.'

By the time the Hamed camp arrived in Wales, early on the Wednesday evening before the fight, Naseem's training was completed and all that was left was to keep him sharp with light workouts and plenty of stretching. They took over an entire floor of the Celtic Manor Hotel in Newport, a venue they chose to keep secret, partly for security reasons because the anti-Naseem feeling in Cardiff was strong and growing. However, there were whispers in his camp about a dissipation of energies, with some of his gym-mates saying he had started serious training too late – only after returning from London where he played the cheerleader role for Frank Bruno in his WBC title winning effort against Oliver McCall. They added that he had missed the odd training session and that discipline and routine had become 'a bit of a problem'. Brendan Ingle acknowledged that Hamed did not train as hard as he had for the Belcastro fight, but his son John insisted Naseem was doing enough. 'I think Naz is still training hard. He hasn't really slackened off. The nightclubs are nothing new – when he was younger he used to go to a snooker place out of time until 2am. Sure, he doesn't sleep much at night and then gets up at 11am, but it's always been like that. He doesn't drink, smoke or do drugs, and he's always in shape.' What was apparent was that whenever Naseem did train, it was fast and frenetic and extraordinarily impressive in a madcap way. He defied several of the shibboleths of boxing conditioning: going to bed well after midnight, sometimes as late as 4am, and rising whenever it suited him; refusing to do roadwork (though he put in a few short sprints and swims); seldom skipping and never using weights. He did do some flexibility exercises, ground work, pull-ups and work on the heavy bag, speedball and pearball, but his sessions were usually framed around intensive sparring, as well as pad work with John Ingle and shadow-boxing. Hamed explained his unorthodox regime in terms of what was necessary for him to excel. 'My training is all based around sparring, and I train excessively hard. That's where I get my fitness and my strength and my strong mind from. I spar with heavy opponents and I push them back, and I get stronger and stronger.'

He was quick to debunk the conventional wisdom about fight preparation. 'Some people say you must get early nights and get up at five in the morning to go for a run, but if you're not like that, don't do it. It's rubbish. I'm not the kind of guy to get up in the morning to go running. Running is for runners and I like to stay in my bed in the morning, but I can spar two hours with any boxer from flyweight to heavyweight and I train any time I get the urge. I do what is necessary to win and when I step into that ring I'm fit enough to do twelve rounds, easily, and then twelve more.' He also claimed he had nothing new to learn and had revolutionized the sport with his innovations – that he was the boxer of the future. 'I have mastered the art of boxing, I know what it takes to be a great fighter. Well before the age of twenty-one I knew a massive amount, so much that you could never say I'm going to fight like this or that against you, because I change my style all the time to beat a particular opponent with his particular style on a particular day. I have sparred with all the different kinds of fighters, including champions – different styles and weights – since I was seven. I've gone through every move and manoeuvre, every way of boxing and surviving and punching. '

One sign above the ring in the Ingle gym ordered boxers to wear their headgear and never to spar without supervision. Another warned: 'Boxing can damage your health.' With this in mind, Ingle usually insisted that sparring sessions involved body work only. Underneath the ring canvas was an extra half-inch of padding to slow the boxers down. That way, said Ingle, 'when they get into a fight, they just glide around the ring.' The emphasis was always on defence – slipping, ducking, parrying, riding punches, moving out of the way, confusing the opposition, switching stance and developing speed, rather than on hurting the sparring partner. With Naseem, however, things were a little different. Whoever he was in the ring with, flyweight or heavyweight, he went all out. He seemed incapable of holding back, or at least unwilling to try, and now and then his punches would 'stray' to the head, or he would ask to waive the 'body only' rule. Anyone doubting the ability of this 5ft 3in youth needed only to watch him in training for Robinson, holding his own with far bigger men like the 6ft 3in, 200lb Johnny Nelson, to appreciate his prowess. He was effectively ambidextrous, possessed with a contortionist's flexibility and blessed with an antenna from God which allowed him to evaporate in the face of an onslaught and pump home his own rapid-fire combinations from impossible angles, or land perfectly placed bombs while gazing at the other unfortunate's feet. He surrounded his opponents, always a step or two ahead of them, being everywhere and nowhere at the same time, moving with such grace and speed that he seemed to be operating to different laws of motion. Nelson put it like this: 'When I spar with him, I've got to go full out. I've got to. There were a lot of guys who came down here and wanted to join the gym and when they got in with Naz, he ridiculed and destroyed them. They left because Naz was so powerful and fast and confident and they could not deal with him. So you've got to go full out no matter how big you are, because he takes no prisoners. Anybody who gets into the ring with him, no matter how good friends they are, or what they've done, or what they can do, or how big they are, has to go full out to survive. It's very hard because he is so fast and you've got to wait twenty rounds before he gets a little tired.'

Another regular was the former British welterweight champion Chris Saunders. 'I weigh 150lb and he weighs 125, but that doesn't mean a thing because he punches as hard as just about any welterweight. Me and Naz, we'd go full out against each other and not just body sparring – we did some head sparring as well – and we really had a go at each other. Even when he was eighteen he would give me a run for my money, and he's helped me a great deal because it's sharpened me up and made me a lot quicker and taught me new moves. I tell you, he's phenomenal.' Also assisting Naseem's preparations for Robinson was his middleweight friend Ryan Rhodes: 'We sparred together all the time and had really good spars. We're fairly evenly matched, but he's quicker and everything and he hits like a middleweight or a super-middleweight. I can hold my own with him, but I certainly don't need to hold back at all.'

The two men honoured with the task of becoming Hamed's chief sparring partners for Robinson were Kevin Adamson, a fast Walthamstow light-middleweight, and Jonathan Thaxton, a tough, hard-hitting light-welterweight and former European kick-boxing champion. Both were then rated within the top twelve in their divisions in Britain, with Adamson going on to fight for the Commonwealth title and Thaxton later winning the WBO intercontinental title. Ingle watched more carefully than normal, seldom turning away to chat as is his custom, out of fear that somebody might get seriously hurt. Watching Thaxton, who travelled from Norwich to Sheffield twice a week for three weeks for the privilege of getting beaten up, you got the distinct impression that even if he was allowed to use his feet, his head and no gloves, he would still receive a hiding. Naseem would enter the gym, always late, and everyone turned to have a look, to give and maybe get a nod of acknowledgement. He always made sure *his* music was playing – rap, techno and jungle – and warned everyone not to touch it and then got to work on Thaxton's 140lb body. Sometimes he played and danced, but mostly he was ripping in the punches without any hint of mercy. Several times Ingle called his charge off, telling the former kick-boxer he could do eight rounds rather than ten, but Thaxton bravely stayed the distance. Naseem was simply too quick, too elusive and hit too hard for the bigger man, and he was hurting him. After nine rounds the tape stopped and Naseem ordered a bystander to turn it over. One round later Thaxton's day was mercifully over, but

Naseem continued to pound away at the pads, worn, as usual, by John Ingle.

'I'm telling you now, he hits like a middleweight,' Thaxton gushed. 'I've sparred with Saunders, Adamson, and his power matches them, nooo problem. You think of two cars: if they're moving together at 10 mph, they not gonna do too much damage, but if they're going at 100 mph, different story. The thing with Naz is, he punches so fast and accurate and hard. He's a strong, strong fella. And I've only done body sparring with him, and that was bad enough. What it would be like with open sparring, I wouldn't like to find out.' Every one of those forty-eight rounds he had with Hamed had been an honour and an education, he said. 'I rate him with Roy Jones as one of the two best fighters, pound for pound, in the world. Yeah, Naz, Roy Jones, they're two of a kind. He thinks he'll beat anyone and in my opinion, he will. He's a once in a lifetime fighter. One in a lifetime.' Adamson also had a rough time, despite size advantages of ten inches and thirty pounds. He was a fleet-footed, jab-and-move man, but he struggled to keep away from the little fellow in front of him. Unlike Thaxton, Adamson did the occasional open sparring round, as well as the usual body work. 'The power he has is phenomenal for his weight,' he said. 'He hits like a strong light-welterweight, easy, and he's very strong for his size. He throws some beautiful body shots and they really hurt. For full sparring he is a lot more tricky on his feet and if you make a mistake he can drop you, no matter about the weight. You have to be 100 per cent aware and your punches have to keep flowing to keep him off, and with him I wouldn't hold back one bit because when he's coming on full strong, full speed, I can't afford to. If I hold back, I just get an onslaught of punches.'

When you watched all this and then thought of Robinson, you wondered how the hell he could survive. The fact that the tautly-muscled WBO featherweight champion had a walk around weight of 138lb (meaning he was naturally ten pounds heavier than his challenger, as well as four and a half inches taller), and had the benefit of three extra years of professional experience and eight world title fights, did not count for much. He was up against Naseem Hamed. Enough said. It is worth stressing, however, that this proud Welshman was a fighting man of considerable skills and enormous resolve, whose career had followed a remarkable trajectory for which the cliché 'fairy tale' seemed, for once, almost apt – almost, if only nasty little Naseem hadn't entered the plot. When Robinson turned professional in 1989, he was marked with the epithet 'journeyman' – just another willing Welshman at a time when Welsh boxing was going nowhere. Whenever a fight was close, the decision went against him and by early 1993 his record showed thirteen wins and nine losses, even though several of the negatives should have been positives. But under the tutelage of the canny Trinidadian trainer Ronnie Rush, he had acquired a dedication and resolve that had been absent earlier in his career. He gave up his £52-a-week day job as a storeman, increased his training regime and things suddenly turned around. The WBO featherweight champion Ruben Palacio tested HIV-positive and was stripped of his crown, and with forty-eight hours' notice Robinson, who was already in training, was called in as a replacement against England's John Davison for the now vacant throne. He fought his heart out, won the title and held it for two and a half years. Several times he started out the underdog and prevailed. Among others, he out-worked and out-punched the slick former WBO champion Colin McMillan. Then, even more impressively, it was the turn of the hard-hitting Merseysider Paul Hodkinson, the former WBC kingpin, who was out-boxed, out-muscled and knocked out in the final round. Next, the former three-weight 'world' champion Duke McKenzie was stopped with a sickening hook to the body in the ninth round. Robinson had developed into a formidable, world-class featherweight with an impressive winning streak, carrying with him a varied arsenal: a tight defence, a firm chin, an impressive array of hard punches, superb conditioning, great strength and a high workrate as well as the determination to prevail against the odds. He played the leading role in the revival of professional boxing in Wales, was enjoying a growing international reputation and was determined to unify the world title.

The weigh-in, twenty-eight hours before the first bell, was a chaotic, theatrical occasion. Over 100 Robinson followers managed to worm their way into an already cramped room at the CIA. Naseem, dressed in a mustard-yellow tracksuit, made an uncharacteristically understated entry, but when the television cameras and long microphones pointed in his direction his demeanour changed and he started bouncing around, joking, teasing and playing. His whole camp had been kitted out by two of his sponsors, Joe Bloggs and adidas, with Naseem designing several of his own creations. One of his cousins whispered to me, 'You know he trained last night until 2am and he'll be up even later tonight,' but the rest of his words were drowned out by Robinson's late arrival which was greeted with cheers and whoops and peals of raucous laughter, to laddish barks of 'Bring on the princess' and 'Send back the boy'. Then Mike Goodall, the announcer, boomed: 'Will you please welcome to the scales, Prince ... ', but was beaten to the punch by a joker who slipped in the syllable 'cess', which prompted a general round of hilarity and a chant of 'Prin-CESS, Prin-CESS' followed by 'Send him back to Yemenese'. This was a Cardiff crowd and Steve was one of their true-born sons, and the little fellow from Sheffield, or 'Yemenese' or whatever, was just an infuriating impostor to be insulted. Naseem seemed completely unfazed by all this, and later said he cut out all those comments. 'Even if I did hear, I would just think they were being childish. They don't know the score. For mature men to come out with silly stuff like that, well, it doesn't cross your mind to get mad or angry.' His own tactic was to make Robinson angry. For a couple of minutes he chatted quietly but provocatively to the champion, telling him, in effect: you say you will win; you're unhappy that I'm getting paid much more than you; how about a winner-takes-all deal? Steve was unsettled and muttered something about leaving this to his manager. 'Hamed was going on at me about the purse money, that he was getting more than me,' he said later. 'It was getting to me at the back of my mind and I was so angry, which I shouldn't have been.' For Naseem, Robinson's mumbled response was another sign that he had his man beat.

When the boxers stepped onto the scales, Robinson lost another psychological battle. Hamed made the weight first time with three-quarters of a pound to spare and then took a long, ostentatious drink from his water bottle. Robinson was four ounces over the limit and had to wait a while longer to wet his parched lips. After a brief workout, he returned to make it by a quarter of a pound and made light of this little embarrassment. 'I had no problems making the weight, really. I mean, what's four ounces? I just took off some clothes and made it easy the second time.' Two months later, however, he admitted it wasn't that easy. 'I'm a natural featherweight, but they usually give me eight weeks to train for a fight, and I am down to the weight about three or four days before the fight. This time I had four weeks and I only made the weight on the day of the weigh-in, and the last few days were a bit hard. I made it in the end, but it could have made me a bit sluggish.'

Steve Robinson had one more humiliation to endure. With scores of his chums begging for tickets, he asked Warren's press man Andy Ayling for his twenty ringside passes and was extremely peeved to receive only ten. A lengthy altercation followed but Ayling held his ground truculently, telling Steve in an offhand tone that was all he was getting. 'That definitely irritated me,' Robinson later acknowledged. 'They only gave me half what they promised. It was all psychological.' But when I caught up with him in the passages of the CIA after the weigh-in, Robinson did his best to sound upbeat and recited all the advantages Ronnie Rush had been stressing. 'I'll be too big for him, too strong, and hit too hard. I've improved with every fight. I'm definitely hitting harder and I'm actually getting bigger, just look at my shoulders,' he said, tapping his triceps. 'He's never fought anyone in my league but I've beaten the best. McMillan, McKenzie, Hodkinson – everyone predicted I'd lose to them and I whipped them easily. Can he take my power? I don't think so. And I'm not worried about his style. I've been sparring with southpaws and guys who fight like him and I know just what to do. I might stop him, but I don't like to make predictions. I'll just say I'm very confident of still being world champion tomorrow night.'

Hamed, however, had a faith of a different order, a total conviction he could not lose. 'There is no way I would look into Steve's eyes and say to myself, "Can I beat him?" ' he told me. 'I had it in my mind that he's gonna get beat and beat well, and there was nothing he had that made me think, "I'm gonna struggle here." There was never any doubt in my mind. To tell you the truth, I've never, ever sat down and said to myself, "What if you lose? What if you do actually get beat? What if a better fighter beats you?" Because my mind is so positive that I can't get beat. I've got so much self-belief in what God has given me, so I know, definitely, that I am blessed with a gift and I know, basically, that when I enter that ring God is on my side.'

After the weigh-in Naseem and his team drove back to their hotel. Eventually, at about 4am – after watching videos of Muhammad Ali and Sugar Ray Leonard – the boxer went to bed and slept until midday. 'I wouldn't say late nights in itself is a pitfall – it's how you control them,' he explained afterwards. 'I've stayed up till six in the morning and boxed that same night and knocked my opponent out. In one fight I stayed up all morning and all night without sleep – I was with my mates, chilling out. The main pitfalls are drinking, mixing with people who are a bad influence, and girls. You've got to pick the right girl. I've seen loads of fighters who have picked a girlfriend and it's gone totally wrong for them, but with me, my feet are on the ground. I don't drink, smoke or take drugs. There are plenty of temptations out there, but I don't give in to them, and it's very important for me to be religious and believe in God – this helps keep my life so clean.'

The day of a fight is a killer for many boxers. It is often when the real fear starts to kick in; fear of defeat, fear of the financial implications of losing, fear of humiliation, fear of failure, fear of looking bad and fear of pain. Invariably, however, these fears mesh into one general sense of foreboding, expressed through irritability with everyone around. You won't find many fighters focusing too specifically on, for example, the pain of body blows in their quiet moments, but if the task ahead seems too formidable, if the fighter has been roughed up too much in the pre-fight shenanigans, if his hidden aches and minor injuries from training are niggling too incessantly, if he's still shaking off the effects of that cold or bout of flu, if his bowels aren't working right, and he dwells too long on these anxieties, a mood of defeatism creeps in and the fight is often lost well before he's made his way to the ring. But if that fear is contained, its by-product is adrenaline and a more focused mental approach. This can be a major factor in victory. It is one of the old truisms of the game that every fighter feels some fear, and those who say they don't are liars or in a state of self-denial. But Naseem genuinely appears to be an exception. When you watch him in the countdown before a fight, it is clear that fear, at least as the word is generally understood, is not part of his condition. Certainly, he experiences the thrill of anticipating the ride to come – and there's a good deal of adrenaline production there – but such is his absolute self-assurance that defeat, pain and looking bad seldom seem to enter even his sub-conscious mental processes. They are not things he dreams about at night. What he feels in the-hour-by hour countdown before a fight is an overwhelming desire to start performing. 'I love boxing. It's in me, it's part of me and I think about it all the time, and I rise to every occasion I find. I just treat one bout the same as any other, and I'm just raring to go. A lot of boxers do say they have fear, but I don't. I've never been frightened before a fight, totally the opposite.'

His priority is to find things to do around the hotel which keep his low boredom threshold at bay. In the ten hours before facing Steve Robinson, Naseem used the swimming pool, joked and played around with his friends, watched videos and listened and danced to hours of rap, jungle, ragga, hip hop, house and garage music. His main pre-fight, early afternoon meal was pasta, seafood and salad. He also got in a quick read of the newspapers, and what he saw in Cardiff was satisfyingly plentiful and largely positive. Among the items in the *Sun*, which co-sponsored the event, was a Hamed fashion spread, while all the national papers predicted a Hamed knockout. Most of the former boxing champions also plumped for Hamed, though Barry McGuigan hedged his bet, noting, 'We've still got to see what Hamed is like under pressure, what's he going to be like when he takes some punishment,' while a patriotic Howard Winstone cautiously predicted a Welsh triumph, arguing that Naseem 'throws punches off the wrong foot all the time and does stupid things.'

From my own vox-pop Cardiff survey, the view in the street was fervently pro-Robinson in sentiment, though rather less strongly in faith, with Hamed's derision of their home boy providing an edge to the affection the locals held for Robinson, and to the desperate hope that he'd pull it off. They all loved their champion. Everyone knew how he'd toiled and sweated and prevailed against prohibitive odds. Yet there would be no statues built for good old Stevo. For that you have to be a Welsh fighter of spectacular accomplishment like Peerless Jim, or a political hero like Nye Bevan, or you should have brought in a whack of money like John, Marquess of Bute, an arrogant, eccentric Scot who refurbished the Cardiff Castle in high-kitsch, neo-gothic style 100 years earlier. Hamed, who paid his homage to the castle shortly before the fight, was also regarded as an arrogant, colourful and eccentric outsider whose presence was good for business, despite all the resentment it inspired. He was therefore regarded as worthy of a flutter, with the Welsh bookmakers Jack Brown saying they were receiving a flood of money from punters. The odds they offered on Hamed – the best in the country – were 2-5 compared with the London rate of 1-4.

Naseem's seven-man entourage joined him in his changing-room before the fight, including Riath and Nabeel, with his father Sal popping in to wish him luck. Naseem had instructed his mother and sisters to steer clear of Cardiff – this was man's work. Steve's mum Yvonne, also stayed at home with her cigarettes and a glass of vodka to babysit for her grandchildren, and listened on the radio because she didn't own a Sky dish. The mood was one you would expect from an after-party. Naseem's prayers had been said earlier in the evening, or so he claimed, but now it was time to get the juices flowing. There was music pumping out of a portable sound system. Naseem was teasing Adamson about being the token southerner in a northern party and imitating Thaxton's Norwich vowels, and there was much laughing and giggling and weak jokes. A Naseem sample: 'There's a rabbit and a bear sitting in the woods and the bear looks down at the rabbit and says, "Rabbit, do you ever have problems with shit sticking to your fur?" The rabbit says, "Not I," so the bear lifts up the rabbit and wipes his arse with him.' To his sparring partners, who expected a tenser mood for such a major league occasion, it all had a surreal feel to it. 'I wouldn't say I'm the most relaxed person when it's time for me to box,' said Adamson, 'but Naz is different. He likes people around him and his music on, so he can get the same sort of atmosphere from the gym, and for the Robinson fight he was unbelievably relaxed. All seven of us in that changing room were just dancing, having a laugh and enjoying ourselves, and you think the guy is about to have his first world title fight at a weight above what he boxes at. I just couldn't believe it.' 'Yeah, I'd never seen anything like it in my life,' Thaxton agreed. 'I know how I'm like in the changing-rooms, but he was dancing and singing and he had no worries, and outside there were 16,000 people disliking him a lot, and he was just loving it.'

Behind the laughter, however, was savage intent. Everybody had to be sure of his tasks. Naseem removed his fawn jumper and black tracksuit trousers and assembled his fighting gear. Brendan and John wrapped the bandages and tape, and made sure every detail was sorted: his boots correctly laced, his groin protector fastened right, his body oiled. How are you feeling? Have you been to the toilet? Does that feel comfortable? Naz finally pulled on his short, white towelling gown and climbed into his new, heavy-looking, Joe Bloggs-designed leopardskin, tasselled 'skort' trunks. 'They feel *good*! Wicked!' He was the only one in the room who looked completely at ease with his surroundings. Once he was gloved-up and ready, he started shadow-boxing with Brendan, then left the changing room and shadow-boxed in the inside parking section of the stadium. In the past, before his fights, he'd imagined he was one of the sport's 'legends' doing his thing: Sugar Ray Leonard finessing Marvin Hagler or humiliating Roberto Duran, Muhammad Ali crucifying Ernie Terrell or annihilating Cleveland Williams. But this time he was imagining he was Prince Naseem Hamed, legend in the making, and the taunts, feints and punches in his head were all aimed at a man called Steve.

Outside, under the arc-lights, it was pouring with rain. The Cardiff Rugby Football Club stadium seated 14,000 and despite the weather, the predicted sell-out had easily been achieved. The chants of 'Stevo, Stevo, Stevo', started at 7.30pm and never stopped. Finally, after two hours of this, it was time for the big one and the Welsh voices really came into their own. 'Oleee, Ole, Ole, Ole, Stevooo, Stevo', and 'Ha-med, Ha-med, who the fuck is Hamed?', over and over again. Then there's a burst of techno music, followed by the display of the Welsh flag and a par-ticularly defiant rendition of the Welsh anthem – the only anthem played, as the promoters wisely opted not to chance the embarrassment of 'God Save the Queen' being hissed and heckled. At this point a section of the crowd surged forward, climbing over barriers and blocking entrances. An anxious Frank Warren stepped into the ring to tell them there would be no fight until they moved. Finally, when calm was temporarily restored, Naseem was given the signal that his time had arrived. 'As soon as they tell me, "Television's ready – you're on," that's it. I become a different person,' he later explained to me. 'All the guys get around me and I just blank out everything else. I'm ready to walk out there to my music and do the business. I feel so calm, cool and collected, and I just can't wait to get into that ring and start fighting.'

From the back of the stadium a silhouette of a caped, dancing figure appears, striking an outrageously camp pose. It's the sort of high-kitsch display that made old salties like Henry Cooper despair for the fight game, but which helped deliver the ratings that keep the promoter's Roller running. A falsetto voice chanted: 'I am ready, I am ready' and exploded into the rapid beat, at near-numbing decibels, of 'I Believe'. Hamed said: 'It's a really good garage-housey track which I picked because I believed I was going to win the world title. The music is very important 'cause it's got to give me a buzz. It's got to hit me that it's the right time to fight, that the energy and adrenaline are there.' Surrounded by the eight security guards hired by the promoters, his cornermen and sparring partners, Naseem danced towards the ring, but from outside that huddle all you see is his canary-coloured gloves occasionally reaching for the stars. A large section of the crowd was booing, shouting obscenities and spitting at him. Some were jostling the minders and throwing things. Moments before Naseem reached the ring, a coin hit him. He stopped for a moment and picked it up – a memento to keep. Finally, he mounted the steps, placed his hands on the middle of the top rope and did the frontflip. His leopardskin trunks obeyed gravity, prompting a few pressmen to query whether he'd left his knickers at home. He landed neatly, straightened his gown, stood to attention and glared at the crowd defiantly. Soon the entire Hamed vanguard had joined him in the ring: Riath cheekily hoisting the WBC international super- bantamweight title belt above his head (much to the chagrin of the WBO officials, who told him to remove it), Nabeel holding the Yemeni flag, Johnny Nelson the Union flag, and Brendan and his helpers bustling around in their leopardskin uniforms.

There was another burst of pyrotechnics and the outline of a red Welsh dragon appeared in neon, followed by a roar and a cloud of smoke which covered the stadium and had the asthma sufferers reaching for their inhalers. Robinson had chosen a reggae number, 'Natural Mystic Blowing', and as he approached the ring the crowd erupted. More ululating as Steve, Ronnie Rush and Dai Gardiner made their entrance. Wearing his usual red trunks with 'Stevo' on the front, the champion raised aloft the WBO title belt. Meanwhile, Naseem was still dancing and smiling, clearly having a wonderful time. 'When have you seen a guy of the age of twenty-one, fighting for his first world title, coming down the aisle dancing to his music, getting into it, doing a flip into the ring, still dancing, and then dancing to his opponent's music?' he asked me later. 'I didn't expect to enjoy Steve's music, but I did. That's how confident I was. I knew I was going to win that world title and it showed in that smile on my face.'

By 9.45 the introductions were over and the rain was driving into the ring. For a few seconds while they sized each other up during the pre-fight instructions, Robinson looked like a winner. It was an image enhanced when Naseem's corner removed his top and the boxers touched gloves. From the waist up, Steve seemed several divisions bigger. Not only was he half a head taller, but he had far broader shoulders, a tighter and more defined musculature and a bigger head. His body was a ripped, powerful-looking, 5ft 7½in and 135lb by fight time. Hamed, at 5ft 3in and by then 128lb, had a body which was harder to define. Once he got moving it was clear everything was in perfect proportion, but from below he seemed to have a carriage which belonged, simultaneously, in three divisions: The head of a straw-weight, upper body of a bantam and legs of a middleweight – almost elephantine in comparison with Steve's spindly feather-weight pins. With most boxers in the lighter weights, a low centre of gravity and heavy legs are a seen as a drawback, the idea being that height is an absolute advantage and weight is most usefully situated in the upper body. With Hamed, however, this con-ventional wisdom does not apply. His entire platform is based on that solid undercarriage – his strength, his speed, balance, flexibility and ability to take a punch. But more than his legs, it was his eyes which told the story of what was to come. This was supposed to be the moment of truth, when the heart and adrenaline pumps overtime and the head feverishly anticipates the opening moves. Robinson's eyes glistened with pride, indignation and intense concentration, but Naseem's were unnervingly calm – completely focused, brimming with sneering contempt, but still calm. It was a look of absolute self-confidence.

The bell clanged and a southpaw Naseem attacked. Steve plodded forward cautiously, his head tucked behind his arms and gloves. Hamed opened with a body punch while Steve missed twice with rights, one of them brushing a cheek, which prompted a skinhead contingent in the crowd to let loose with a 'Hamed, Hamed, who the fuck is Hamed?' Hamed let them know by landing a cracking right uppercut after switching to orthodox. Halfway through the round, he paused to glance at the press rows and gave a withering look to a Welsh journalist, as if to say 'Told you so, arsehole' before sticking his chin out and smirking, dropping his hands to his sides, trying to draw the champion out of his fortress and into his own web. 'Come on, hit me,' he offered, letting Steve lead, making him miss, but seldom reaching anything more promising than Steve's liver. From the start, Hamed's extraordinary elasticity was apparent. At times he bent so far backwards to avoid the oncoming traffic that he gave the appearance of 'double-jointedness', yet his feet were squarely planted and he was never off balance. It was a sparse round in terms of scoring punches, but one where the challenger asserted his superiority. When Hamed returned to his corner, he asked Brendan: 'Did I do alright?' To which his trainer replied. 'You did great, marvellous.'

A southpaw Hamed opened with a crisp three-punch combination in round two, but soon started clowning again, trying to draw the champion out of his shell. He made Robinson miss by disconcertingly wide margins, on one occasion executing a neat side-step and waving Steve past as the Welshman's momentum carried him forward. During a brief, Robinson-instigated clinch at the halfway mark, Naseem tossed Steve to the canvas as if he were a tiny, leg-rutting pooch – earning a caution, but making a point. The champion's strength was one of his aces, and now it seemed to have been taken away from him: it was clear Hamed had no problem pushing Robinson around and was the stronger of the two. Naseem was quick to capitalize, reminding Steve with curled lips and contemptuous eyes: 'You told me you were the strongest.' Later he explained the significance of this moment: 'Before the fight, he and everyone else was telling me he was the strongest featherweight in the world. I said I was stronger. They said I was crazy, I was only twenty-one, I was not strong enough, not mature enough. I proved a lot of people wrong. I threw him around, broke him down mentally and took him out.' Steve also admitted to being taken by surprise. 'He was stronger than I thought – really quite strong, and he's elusive at the same time, but I still don't think he's as strong as me.' After this moment, Naseem momentarily shook Steve with a well-timed right uppercut, then gave a little bum-wiggle and an underhand wave to mark the harmless passing of yet another Robinson punch. He stood square-on, his hands again at his sides, challenging the champion to take a potshot at his chin, but Steve kept his own poker-set features tucked behind those yellow mitts and did not respond. Eventually, Hamed connected with a long left to the face which somehow found a way through the burglar bars. Robinson responded with a charge but his tormentor ducked low and squirmed out of the way, firing off solid counters in retreat. With forty seconds to go, Hamed connected with a right uppercut which slithered through a crack in Robinson's defences. The champion's legs did a momentary stutter, prompting another Naseem hip-shake and a grim smile from the Welshman just before the bell.

Hamed came out in the orthodox stance for round three, and retained it for most of the remaining rounds. Robinson tried to take advantage by leading with a big right, which missed by a millimetre. The crowd whooped, however, thinking their man had finally registered. But this illusionary moment of respite could not last. After thirty seconds, Naseem opened up with a tattoo of crisp blows, raising a swelling around Steve's right eye, although the champion managed to reply with a solid right to the head. Naseem grinned contemptuously, did yet another bum-shake and made Robinson miss with five consecutive punches before snapping in his own right uppercut. Robinson was looking downhearted but continued to press forward doggedly and had a moment of success when he made Naseem miss with a huge right uppercut. They exchanged blows after the bell and once again the yahoos chanted: 'Hamed, Hamed, who the fuck is Hamed?' For anyone other than the security guards, whose eyes were glued to the crowd, it was another clear Hamed round. Anyone, that is, except the American ringside judge Walter Calavieri, who decided that Robinson's single solid punch was worth more then thirty of Hamed's.

The fourth was the round Naseem had been saying for months he would use to end the fight, and he therefore came out more purposefully with the express intention of fulfilling his prediction. Robinson, however, made Hamed miss with four consecutive punches, though soon after he absorbed a vicious left-right combination to his body and then a right hook-left combination when cornered. Halfway through the round, Hamed began taunting again – 'Go on, try to hit me' – and even made a point of smoothing down his own tightly cropped hair, before offering a showy shuffle and poking out a series of light, probing punches. Robinson grabbed him and tried to pull him in, but the youngster wriggled loose and made the champion miss again. Steve pressed forward and briefly trapped Hamed, but again the challenger slipped effortlessly into the open water. At the bell Naseem raised his arms and laughed in Robinson's increasingly puffy face, despite having failed to fulfil his prediction. Later, however, he would pay tribute to Steve for this achievement. 'Full credit to him. Great champion. He went over the round I said I was going to do him in, so the credit's there. I went for the fourth round, but he wasn't there to be took out. He was strong, he stood his ground. I don't think I could have stopped him earlier. I tried to go for my prediction, but at the end of the day what happened, happened.' During the minute's break, Brendan implored Naseem to step it up a bit and use the jab more, to which the lad replied: 'Shut up and let me do the fighting'. The Irishman gave his stock reply: 'Marvellous.'

As Robinson rose it was clear the swelling around his right eye had spread, and Hamed moved to exacerbate the damage. He invited Steve to have a go at his body – 'Come on, try to hit me there' – but missed with his own combination. He moved in a rhythmic, Tai Chi slow motion, probing with feeler punches, beckoning his opponent, boxing orthodox and then switching effortlessly to southpaw and once again offering a target. Then, for a moment, the fight seemed about to change direction. Hamed fired a right hook to the body and at that moment Steve countered with his best punch of the fight, a fast, solid left hook which landed square and hard on Hamed's jaw. Then he connected again, but Hamed showed no sign of physical hurt, instead offering an exaggerated little booty-wiggle with a smirk on his face. Later Robinson remarked on this moment of success: 'I don't think I caught him clean. It was more of a glancing blow. He took it and pulled a face, but I think I hurt him – he admitted that after the fight, and if I had caught him with a few more shots then, I would have had him.' Hamed saw things very differently: 'I took a good left hook and I took it very well, and people have found out I have a great chin to go with all the ability. They now know I haven't got a glass jaw and that I can take a punch from a real, strong featherweight. He caught me with some good shots, but didn't hurt me.' After this Naseem taunted Steve, pointing again to his own body before countering with single, hard right jabs and a left which knocked Robinson back. With a sneer on his face, Hamed moved in to land a scintillating four-punch combination – a long left hook to the chin, right hook half-blocked by Steve's gloves, a left jab to the face and a fast, solid right uppercut which landed flush under the champion's chin. Robinson dropped for the second time in his career, his legs flailing in the air. He clambered up at the count of four and returned to his defensive shell. Hamed fired off a torrent of blows, pinning Robinson to the ropes, but the champion wisely clasped him in a vice-like clinch. Naseem threw him to the floor again, receiving a warning from referee Ismael 'Wiso' Fernandez. He then came in with a three-uppercut combination, followed by a right cross, and again pinned the champion to the ropes. As the bell rang, Robinson's legs still appeared wobbly and he looked exhausted. Hamed also seemed a bit puffed but returned to his corner with a wide grin on his face as his ecstatic father rose from his ringside seat, shouted and waved in delight.

In the champion's corner there was a flurry of feverish activity and advice. 'He caught you with a good shot, okay,' said a frantically focused Ronnie Rush. 'Now listen to me: you're packing up, you're packing up. You gotta start unloading shots when you get close. You hear?' He took stock for a second. 'Take your time,' he said, and the bell for round six clanged. Naseem returned to where he had left off, landing big with both fists and making Robinson miss by over a foot on the rare occasions he attempted anything. Steve covered up even tighter than before, fighting out of a pronounced crouch. Where he had looked so much bigger before the first bell, he had shrunk, and Hamed now looked like the fighter with the perfect physique – the advanced model, built for speed, agility, power and comfort. Steve shuffled forward mechanically, but without purpose, doing his best to cover up in the face of the onslaught. The crowd tried to lift his flagging spirits: 'Robinson, Robinson, Robinson,' they chanted, but Hamed spoiled the moment for him by joining in the chorus, mouthing the words with the added indignity of going through this ritual with his head a few, tantalizing inches from the champion's. It was an extraordinary moment, which perhaps more than any other revealed the level of Naseem's superiority and the extent of his arrogance. At times boxing is as much a mind game as it is a body game, but with this gesture Naseem took the art of 'mindfucking' to new levels. Afterwards he would come in for plenty of press and Control Board criticism for his taunting tactics, but he insisted it is an effective psychological ploy. 'Obviously there's method behind it. You watch Muhammad Ali doing it, you watch Sugar Ray Leonard doing it – the credit they got was phenomenal, but they were in America. When you get a British fighter doing, they just don't like it.' While this claim was not entirely correct – the fifteen rounds of verbal and physical torture Ali subjected Ernie Terrell to certainly came in for months of sustained public criticism – Hamed had a point when it came to psychological effectiveness, as Robinson later admitted. 'He was putting me off by pulling faces and stuff, and he upset my concentration. My mind wasn't 100 per cent. If it had been right I would have ignored his making fun and got on with the job like I usually do, but on the night I just switched off. He's the type of fighter who gets you.' Halfway through the round, however, Steve had another flash of success, landing a decent right cross to Hamed's chin, but the lad showed no sign of being deterred. He dropped his hands again and then suddenly launched an attack, bashing Robinson from post to post and landing nineteen hard punches without reply. Naseem was grinning and smirking, completely relaxed and loose. Steve was sucking in air; wounded and exhausted, the blood spraying from his mouth with each blow he soaked up.

Naseem opened with a heavy, orthodox left hook in the seventh, and then went strutting slowly in, completely disdainful of the champion and continually making him miss by margins that would usually be embarrassing, except that Steve was way past that point. Forty seconds into the round, Robinson threw a purposeful combination in the direction of Hamed's body and the boy wonder simply raised his arms, bringing them down again to parry the blows, and then landed a hefty left hook to the body. He then side-stepped Steve's lunge so that the champion flew into the ropes. A minute into the round, Robinson pressed forward with another attack, but Hamed slipped effortlessly out of range, ridiculing his efforts: 'Steve, Steve, this is me, this is me. I told you I was the champion, Steve.' Robinson stoically pumped out another combination, which fell short, and Hamed imitated his effort with a look of disdain. What we were watching was a ritual of humiliation, just another dimension of the cruel and unusual punishment a good man had to absorb. Naseem was working at a slower pace by this time, conserving his strength and taking a breather, but although he was tired he was landing at will, smiling and talking continually. He ended the round with a crunching left hook followed by a combination, an effort that left him panting heavily in his corner between rounds. But Ingle realized that the turkey was well cooked and tender enough for the knife. 'He's ready now,' he said.

Robinson, his right eye almost shut, was having trouble getting Hamed in focus by the eighth. The crowd gave him one more song to stir him on to the impossible, but there was nothing he could do about this jack-hammered phantom in front of him. His tormentor was landing from seemingly impossible angles, gliding around the canvas, slipping and blocking everything that came his way, bending and twisting and then firing unexpectedly. With his hands by his knees and still in the southpaw stance, Naseem followed the retreating Robinson around the ring, had a little stretch, jabbed twice, changed stance and probed with a left jab. The champion momentarily dropped his tight guard to try something and Naseem unleashed a perfectly timed left hook lead that connected flush on Steve's chin. His legs did a little involuntary jig before he collapsed backwards, hitting the deck and then falling forwards onto his face in Naseem's corner. He clambered bravely to his knees, but, at last, the none too wise Wiso Fernandez woke up and decided he'd seen enough. At one minute forty-eight seconds of the eighth round it was all over and Naseem Hamed was champion. Of the finale, Naseem had this to say: 'I was breaking him up mentally, and physically it was happening at the same time, and he just fell to pieces at the end. I caught him with a brilliant left hook. He fell for it. He dropped his hands and BAM! I caught him, and the shot was so perfectly timed that his legs just gave away. I picked the exact right time and it was the perfect ending.' Robinson, however, was reluctant to acknowledge the beauty of his own execution. 'He's quite a hard puncher but I took his best shots. It's just that I just took too many and when it went to the later rounds, I couldn't take it anymore. But I still managed to last eight rounds with him. Just imagine what could have happened if I had been 100 per cent.'

When it was over, Hamed raised his gloves in triumph then yelled and gave what looked like an obscene gesticulation at one of the Welsh reporters. The adrenaline subsided and he ambled over to embrace the stricken former champion, saying: 'Steve, you was a great champion. You was stronger than I thought and you really did well. I didn't think you was going to last how you did, but you did great.' Robinson's only words of reply were: 'You're a very hard puncher.' Naseem raised Steve's hand and paraded him around the ring, a move that brought a muted cheer from the crowd, though a small contingent shouted: 'Fuck off, fuck off, Moor.' The former champion appreciated Hamed's gesture: 'He's very arrogant, but after the fight he wasn't too bad – like, he said, "good fight" and everything. I don't hate him. I don't love the guy, but I don't hate him. He's alright.'

From his ringside seat, Sal Hamed, his eyes glistening with tears of joy, stepped through the ropes and hugged his son, followed by the rest of the Hamed's camp. In the Yemen and the rest of the Arab world, where MBC television claimed 'up to' 100 million watched Naseem's coronation, there was an eruption of spontaneous jubilation. In Sana'a, people poured out of their houses and into the markets and streets to party all night. In Lindholme prison near Doncaster, where Naseem had been doing exhibitions for years, every one of the 600 prisoners and half the screws were among the five million Sky viewers who watched the spectacle – the second highest rating for all satellite programmes in 1995. For several minutes they jumped up and down, high-fived each other to celebrate the fact that their home boy had done what he said he would. At home in her living room in Ely, Cardiff, Yvonne Robinson switched off her radio and went to bed.

After the fighters had left the ring, a woman from the crowd climbed over the perimeter fence screaming: 'Warren! Warren! How does it feel to stitch one of your boxers up? It's a disgrace! Three weeks' training!' This prompted the yahoos to get going once again. 'You're just a fuckin wanker, just a fuckin' wanker,' and 'Warren is a wanker, Warren is a wanker'. Meanwhile, Brendan Ingle was grinning and shaking his head as he slowly made his way back, his worries over for the moment. 'I tell ya,' he told me, 'Naz coulda beaten anyone tonight. I've been saying since he was a little kid that he was somethin' special, that he would be great. I've always said Ali and Sugar Ray Robinson were the greatest, but this kid can go on to be better. He was having his first fight at the weight and he outclassed an outstanding world champion. Didn't lose a single round. It was an awesome display. His level of skill is unbelievable. What can I say? He did great, marvellous, but that Steve Robinson has a heart as big as you get. His corner should've pulled him out earlier, but I tell ya, he's got a heart. Typical Welsh do-or-die effort. All power to him. It's been fifteen years, seven days a week, and I don't know where the time has gone. Yeah, I'm over the moon.'

An hour after the fight Naseem minced in, freshly laundered and not a mark on his face. 'It feels good! It feels good!' he began, and bubbled over with superlatives about his own performance, spiced up with barbed digs at the Welsh press for giving Robinson a chance. Colin Hart of the *Sun* asked why he goaded Robinson, and Naseem showed the fight had not quite left him. 'Aaah, don't say I taunted him or I ridiculed him. At the end of the day that's *your* opinion, Colin Hart. You can say what you *want*! At the end of the day it was *psychological* what I did in that ring. What I had to do to win, I did!' But he was quickly back in bubbly mode, praising everyone in sight.

Steve Robinson had been too hurt and upset to make the post-fight press conference. Instead he left the arena on foot with a clutch of family members and friends to comfort him. Later, this proud man, with his lugubrious blue eyes, admitted the manner of his loss was devastating to his self-esteem. 'It used to be nice to be stopped in the street and get recognized all the time. Being world champion was amazing, a fantastic feeling and I miss it, but what really hurt was losing to Hamed in front of that huge crowd in Cardiff.' But quickly he changed tack and his determination shone through. 'He's unorthodox. He throws punches from different angles and I found him quite elusive and strong and he's a hard puncher, but I think I could have beaten him. I know I took his best shots in the fight but I just didn't have the resistance to fire back. I just didn't go forward enough and fire. I'm very confident I can put up a good fight and beat him. He's a good fighter, but I can do it. Yeah, definitely. I'd out-work him and I think I could stop him in the very late rounds, because I found he was going down towards the seventh or eighth, and if I knew I'd had the fitness I would have kept on going and he would have gone. I can't see him keeping up the pressure, the way he was fighting. I would upset his rhythm, not give him time, pick up the workrate, back him up and be more elusive. I'll just go for it.'

Hamed made his exit at midnight. He was at the wheel of his new £100,000 blue V12 Mercedes sports car, his girl of the night beside him, still beaming with self-satisfaction. As he roared off for a long night of clubbing and carousing, it was difficult to contemplate a scenario where he would depart as anything other than a triumphant victor. In eight rounds of boxing, in his maiden world title fight, he had dished out a merciless beating and had only taken a handful of punches for his trouble. Perhaps not even Peerless Jim Driscoll could have lived with Naseem in that rainswept Cardiff ring, and the impertinent thought occurred that Naseem Hamed might become the finest featherweight of them all. Then a second thought occurred: as Brendan often put it, 'The only man who can beat Naseem is Naseem himself.'

6

DECLINING AND FALLING

When Naseem woke up in the afternoon of 1 October 1995, he had a smile on his face that pushed the minor aches and stiffness from the night before far to the back of his mind. He was the *WORLD* champion – no inverted commas there, not for him anyway – and the fact that the world of the WBO was a low-rent and parochial one did not interest him. He had arrived. 'I've always wanted to be world champion so bad,' he said. 'Everybody had put faith in me – God, my family, the people behind me, all my supporters – and they'd seen me since I was a little child, growing up, and I'd been telling them it was gonna happen because I knew in my heart that I was going to beat Robinson. And then I went out and did it and it was an absolutely unbelievable feeling.'

He returned home to a family who felt both ecstatic and, some of them at least, a little overwhelmed by the experience. They all expected him to beat Robinson, but when the moment arrived it took a while for it to sink in that it had actually happened – that their little son or sibling had become the most famous Yemeni in the world, the toast of Sheffield, the champion of the *world*. As fifteen-year-old Sabba, Naseem's youngest sister, put it: 'He's been training hard for all of my life, ever since I can remember, not just for this fight but for all his fights, and he just sort of pops up out of nowhere and suddenly he's famous. He's been great, really great.' Ali, who turned eighteen a month before the fight, was the family member with the most intimate feel for the game, being a talented amateur and he'd been reassuring some of the more nervous members of his clan that Naseem would win handsomely. But even he admitted some surprise at how easily it happened, and it brought home to him the speed with which his older brother had gone from being just a normal member of the family to an international celebrity. 'We never thought he would succeed this well and basically, it's been a bit of a shock,' he said. 'Really, his success has gone beyond our wildest imaginations. He's always expected it but not everybody else, in my opinion – and for the rest of the family as well, because they're not really into the boxing game like I am, so whatever I think, their opinion is like mine. But once it happened, once he knocked Robinson out, it was unbelievable. The feeling was overwhelming. He was just fantastic, and I felt very, very proud of him.'

And for Naseem this was only the start. Each taste of fame and fortune made him hunger for more and more. More victories, more title belts – that was most important – more money, more cars, more houses, more clothes, more women, more recognition, more public adoration, more family love. He couldn't wait. When I caught up with him again at the Dorchester Hotel in London, a fortnight after his title triumph, he made his entrance in his brand new Porsche Carrera 4 ('Oh no, *not* the Porsche, not the *Porsche*, he's never even driven it before, let alone in London,' his brother, Riath, complained later) with a couple of days' stubble, exhausted after two weeks of partying.

By his standards his mood was introspective. He felt like talking quietly. We were later to discover that during our time together, the young boxer James Murray's life was ebbing away while drunken yahoos were throwing chairs, cutlery and bottles at his conqueror Drew Docherty, the man who had so adeptly avoided Naseem's challenges two years earlier. Though we had no knowledge of what was happening in that out-of-control Glasgow dinner show, we soon got onto the subjects of mortality and immortality, and more mundanely, of the risks of Naseem's chosen profession. He told me the boxers most in danger of brain damage or worse were those who had not adequately mastered the art of self-defence, and those whose trainers insisted they had real wars in sparring, with plenty of hard head-blows to prepare them for the real thing. 'If you take a lot of stick and hammering in the gym in training, it's not going to be very good for you when you box, which is why we spar mainly to the body,' he said, and went on to insist that in any event, in his case, the dangers were minimal: 'I know how to box, how to survive, how to punch. I just know a massive amount about boxing, and I know the risks. You know, in my whole time in this sport – fourteen years – I haven't even had a proper black eye yet, so I can't see myself getting hurt.' But what about the men who were on the other end of his punches? Did he feel sorry for them ever? Steve Robinson, perhaps? He laughed at the idea because it struck him as absurd that he should ever feel sorry for the consequences of doing his job. 'You can't think compassion,' he said, chuckling some more, 'you can't think sympathy or anything like that for your opponent. Your mind is on something totally different altogether. Your mind is on winning and you have to be so single-minded and straightforward in your thoughts. What you want is there in front of you and you've got to take it, and you got to take it in the time you have, because if you don't, you may miss the boat and then it's over.' And how would he feel if an opponent was seriously injured, or died? Again, that incredulous look. 'If that happened – if I seriously hurt someone – I'd just have to blank it out of my mind and keep on going. It all comes down to knowing that what is written for a man is written.'

Even in his quieter moments it does not take much for Naseem to get onto his idea of what is written for him. And at that moment, he had so many plans and he wanted to fulfil them all at once. To 'chill out' in Barbados for a while, travel around the United States, tour the whole of the Middle East 'to meet the main men everywhere', more time to resample the night life of London, a giant shopping spree, new car, dream house in Sheffield, a flat in London, an island in the Caribbean ('You got to have your own island'), more clothes, houses for his parents, the works. Oh, yes, and some hard training for his next fight on 9 December, and make that for another world title, Mr Warren, and then a *big* fight in America, and some more champions to beat, maybe even Oscar de la Hoya one day. As it turned out, he got the cars, the houses, the time out in London and four days in Qatar, but for several months that was about it. The best laid plans of the best fighter fizzled one by one, and from the highest moment of his life followed six months of the lowest. No Bahamas holiday, no US tour, no more title belts (just a lot of hassle about his first one), no island. Instead a broken hand, a postponed fight, a re-injured hand, a cancelled fight, and reams of bad press and negative publicity. To be sure, there were plenty of laughs; it's just that it was meant to be so, so much better and bigger, so much sooner.

Three days later I met up with him again at the garishly expensive Mayfair apartment block where he was renting a bachelor flat. As usual Naseem was over an hour late, but when he was ready he brought out something to show: his pride and joy, the WBO title belt, which he draped over his shoulders, then around his waist and then handed to me to hold. Trouble was, this particular belt actually belonged to Steve Robinson (Naseem's hadn't arrived yet) and according to Robinson's manager Dai Gardiner, Hamed was only supposed to borrow it overnight for publicity pictures and then return it the day after the fight. Instead, ten days later, the new champion took it to Qatar, where he had an audience with the Emir and, naturally, needed the belt to show him and to parade around during his public appearances, finally handing it back to Frank Warren after returning home. Robinson, however, was extremely distressed about his missing token of past glory, as was his manager who called the whole thing 'disgusting and unprofessional' and threatened to call the police. Eventually, six weeks after their fight, it was returned to Robinson's solicitors, but the incident caused a spate of bad publicity in Sheffield and Wales, the first of several that were to plague the new champion over the next few months.

At the same time another little controversy was bubbling away. After his victory over Robinson, the secretary of the British Boxing Board of Control, John Morris, admonished Naseem for his antics in the ring. A month later the Board requested him to stop humiliating the man in front of him. In response, Naseem made it clear no changes were envisaged: 'I'm not holding back for anything …My style's not changing for no man. My style suits me. It's a great formula, a winning formula.' But although the Board backed off, Naseem's media detractors continued to plug away. There were stories saying he was behaving like a 'prat', criticising his post-fight gesticulations (which Brendan claimed were really nothing but a 'Yemeni sign') and, most particularly, his behaviour in the ring. For instance, ITV commentator and *Boxing News* columnist Reg Gutteridge condemned Naseem for his 'strut, his jungle boy shorts and demeaning an opponent.' And he went on to write: 'Okay, the punters love it, they say. The

Board has frequently blown in his ear. I know a referee ... who threatened to "throw you over the ropes if you do it again". That's telling him. Try that intangible thing called class, Naz, it works. You rarely get hit, which suggests you can last the course and keep on winning. You don't need an act and beware the bright lights.'

Henry Cooper, the popular former British, European and Commonwealth heavyweight champion, went further, announcing that the 'crazy hype' of modern boxing, exemplified by tactics like Naseem's, made him disillusioned with the sport and he was therefore retiring as BBC radio's ringside inter-round summarizer. He objected most strongly to the way Hamed 'humiliates and taunts his opponents'. Hamed and Ingle replied that the old heavyweight was, indeed, way out of time. The crowds loved the razzmatazz, which was necessary in an era where television was everything, and in any event Cooper should consider himself lucky that he twice had a chance to fight Muhammad Ali, the man who started it all in the early sixties. To which the tired Cooper responded: 'Ali was different. He did it with some wit for a start, and he knew that you knew his antics were just his way of scoring a psychological point. He always did it with a little twinkle in his eye. You could always see his tongue in his cheek, and he meant you to.' In fact, as Hamed's supporters replied, Ali did not always have a twinkle in his eye (look at the way he gleefully tortured Ernie Terrell), some of his psychological tactics had a hard edge of verbal bullying (the way he portrayed Joe Frazier as an Uncle Tom and a gorilla), and unlike pedestrian tryers like Cooper, the Alis and Hameds should be allowed more leeway because of their exceptional flair. They set themselves up with outrageous claims and then deliver by making good. As long as they could walk that wire, and continue to pull the punters, the room for complaint was limited.

After his return from Qatar, Naseem was inundated with scores of other requests for public appearances, interviews and endorsements, and at the same time Brendan was telling him it was time to return to the gym for a 9 December date with an opponent still to be announced. Aside from these obligations, there was his dedicated late-night clubbing and he also squeezed in as many charitable ventures as he could before Brendan won the day: joining Sheffield Wednesday in backing a major anti-racism rally in Manchester organized by the Trades Union

Congress, perhaps his most overtly political public action to date; enthusiastically participating in an anti-graffiti, littering and vandalism drive in the poverty stricken Brightside area; and helping to raise funds for the Yemeni Community Centre by giving them Hamed-designed, multi-coloured tracksuits for auction (at around £2,000 a shot). Together with Joe Bloggs, he also launched his own range of clothes. 'He has real talent and could make a living as a designer,' said the managing director, Shami Ahmed.

While Naseem lusted for more and more fame, he was starting to discover the drawbacks of the unwanted attention which arrived in its wake. Wherever he appeared, people came up to him to slap his back or high-five him, give him unwanted advice, criticize some aspect of his behaviour or his performance, demand his autograph with a dud pen, ask for their photograph to be taken with their Polaroid and then tell him, 'I never realized you were so short,' or give him the 'Put it here, old son' routine when they'd never met him before. Sometimes, when he was out with a girlfriend wanting to be left alone, he snapped. He was also developing a reputation for giving people the 'Don't you know who I am?' routine at nightclubs (without any hint of self-parody) and there were tales of well-wishers and autograph hunters, journalists even would-be friends who had been given the cold shoulder or humiliated. 'There's times when you like it and times when you don't,' he said soon after winning the title. 'There's times when you want to go out and you don't want to be hassled at all, you don't even want to be spotted, but obviously a lot of people like boxing, so I do get spotted nearly everywhere I go. But I'm holding it down and when people come up, I try to treat them in the best way.' What really grated were the casual acquaintances from way back who sucked up to celebrity and presumed a friendship that did not exist. It was something he had had to put up with ever since he first got his name and picture in the paper as a twelve-year-old and discovered that the classmates who a few years earlier had called him 'chocolate drop' and 'Paki' were suddenly treating him like a long lost mate. 'I know who my real friends are though, the people I've known for ages,' he said. 'You can't just let anybody on the bandwagon, but I'm not overly suspicious because of my great sixth sense. I'm a good judge of character.'

With the weight of public intrusion and press criticism steadily growing, there was some relief in the Hamed camp when the due date for Naseem's return to the gym finally arrived: 2 November, five weeks before his next fight, set for the London Arena on 9 December. After over a month of searching in vain for an appropriate opponent, Warren settled on the flashy, twenty-four-year-old, unbeaten Los Angeles-based Mexican Arnulfo Castillo, who had won all his nineteen professional fights, eleven of them inside the distance. The gym view was that Naseem would miss his first day, but he confounded the doubters by arriving on time. He chatted a bit to his buddies – Ryan, Johnny, Chris Saunders – and pulled on his leopardskin skirt and Muhammad Ali T-shirt, did a few rounds of shadow boxing for a television company, wrapped and taped his own hands, fitted his 'Prince' gumguard and then proceeded to do eight, fast rounds of light sparring with three boxers – a flyweight, a welterweight and a nifty little junior. Occasionally he would whack in a few heavy body shots with the adults, but mostly he was concentrating on speed, defence and co-ordination. He looked fast and sharp and at the end of eight rounds he was still fresh. When it was over he did a quick television interview, showered and drove off into the sunset. Over the next four days he gradually stepped up his workrate, then disaster struck. He was working on the pads with John Ingle and fired a heavy right cross which landed at the wrong angle. A shock of intense pain went through the hand and up the arm and Hamed knew immediately that something was wrong. It was the same feeling he'd had, in the same hand, when he outpointed Michael Wright for the junior ABA title in 1990. The X-rays confirmed the worst suspicions: a metacarpal bone fracture and the specialist insisted the only solution was at least two months' rest for the bones to heal. The Castillo fight therefore had to be postponed until 10 February. In early 1994 his fight with Peter Harris had been cancelled after he twisted an ankle, but that was a relatively minor fight and he was back in action less than six weeks later. This time there was far more at stake, not just for Naseem himself but for Warren, Sky and his sponsors. It meant that the momentum he had established of regular action and constant challenges had been broken.

To make matters worse, he had to contend with a series of rumours about how the injury had occurred. One version had it that it was the result of an altercation at the Pine Grove Country Club in Sheffield. Naseem was said to have moved the ball of a former bare-knuckle boxer, who, in turn, became so incensed he swung at him with his pool cue and Hamed instinctively blocked the blow, injuring his hand, before quickly getting out of the way. There was also a view that, in line with an established boxing tradition, 'hand injury' was a euphemism for some other problem or perhaps just for a lack of preparedness. It got to the point where Naseem, Brendan and Frank had to make a specific point of scotching these stories at a press conference to announce the new date.

The effect of this setback was to send Naseem back to London for a fresh wave of celebrity turns, more nightclubbing, dancing, snooker playing and an intense schedule of newspaper and magazine interviews, television and radio appearances and advertising endorsements, as well as a couple of overseas trips, a rap project with the Lancashire Asian group Kaliphz and a string of sporting awards. A positive spin-off was that the additional free time helped to spread his image even further. He made a series of celebrity guest television appearances and there was hardly a men's, sports, health, teen or trends magazine in Britain that, by the beginning of 1996, had not featured him prominently. It was not always successful, however. In particular, he did not respond well to Frank Skinner and David Baddiel's jibes on their *Fantasy Football* programme, coming back with customary aggression to the point where he looked like he might go for them. 'That's probably the only time I've ever felt a bit uncomfortable,' he later explained. 'Them guys are just out there to get a laugh at other people's expense. They're just prats. I wasn't really gonna flatten them, I just made it that way to keep them in check.' This experience prompted an even more cautious, suspicious, and carefully stage-managed attitude when dealing with the media, usually resulting in Hamed getting his own way with the kind of short, adulatory exchanges which pass for interviews.

But trouble continued to follow him. In December 1995, a new Hamed video was released, 'Prince Naseem – The Making of a Legend', focusing on his amateur days and his first professional fight. It prompted a storm of unwanted publicity because it included a Naseem voice-over, taped when he was only sixteen years old, with a statement some regarded as reflecting anti-Asian sentiments: 'I'm looking forward to become known as a British, Arab and a Muslim, but I'm definitely British. You hear my accent. It's like the normal, Yorkshire white kid. When the Pakistanis talk, they always got an accent. Most of the Arabs have got a normal, Yorkshire accent like me.' This did not go down well among many British Asians, and the comment was seen by some as playing into existing tensions between sections of Yorkshire's Arab and Pakistani communities. Most of his detractors did not seem to realize he was a teenager when he made this remark, which reflected no more than a desire by a young, first-generation Englishman to identify with his country, region and his parents' origins. But the debate prompted an obviously shaken Naseem to reply, at the *Boxing Monthly* editor's invitation, to readers' complaints on this issue: 'I am sorry if any remark on the video caused offence to anyone, but please understand that what I was attempting to put across is that while I am proud to be both British and Yemeni, my accent belongs to the part of the world I was raised in. I meant no offence to anyone and I certainly have nothing against Pakistanis or any other race. I view myself as a symbol of multi-cultural success. A champion of all people, a true champion of the world.'

Shortly before the Robinson fight Naseem met the young woman who was to become the love of his life, Eleasha Elphinstone, a pretty, friendly, blonde hairdresser from the nearby Yorkshire town of Wakefield, who was a couple of inches taller than him and several months older. For the previous year she had been dating a £200-a-week builder, Jason Batty, but as Batty put it to a local newspaper: 'What chance did I have against a millionaire fighter? I was travelling by bus because I hadn't got a car and living in a rented house. He had a Porsche, a Mercedes and a half-million-pound mansion. How could I compete with that? He set out to win my girl, and just like all his fights, he won.' Batty said 'everything was going fine until the end of the summer when she came home after a night out with some girlfriends and said, "Guess who I met last night?" ' After trying to 'chat her up' at a country pub in the Yorkshire town of Wakefield, Naseem began pursuing her, phoning her home and inviting her to join him on a trip to America. She refused, but soon after broke up with Batty. By the end of the year Naseem had started spending nights at her home in Crofton, not always to the approval of her neighbours. As one put it: 'He's not particularly well-liked. He's as cocky in person as he is on TV, and he parks his Porsche or Mercedes outside but hardly bothers to say anything to anyone. Even when local children stop him for his autograph, he ignores them.'

Eleasha soon became a dominant fixture of Naseem's life and early in the New Year moved in with him. As a 'traditional' male, Naseem did not want his girlfriend to be financially independent, so at his prompting she gave up work. As he later explained it: 'I'm the man out there – going out to train hard seven days a week, three times a day, and nobody sees that. I didn't want her to work. I wanted to take care of her and she has a lot to do now, cleaning a big house and cooking and all.' She also fitted into the irregular motions of his life, often driving him around (because of his one-year driving ban), always accompanying him to boxing matches and other public events, joining him in his passion for shopping in London or New York, or on holidays in Miami and the Caribbean, and doing her best to fit in with his large family, some of whom strongly disapproved of his live-in relationship with an older, non-Yemeni, non-Muslim woman. This cultural and religious gap was to be a cause of their break-ups in mid 1996 and again in early 1997, before their reconciliation and their pregnancy induced marriage in 1998.

Brendan Ingle, however, was delighted by his boxer's choice. As he viewed it, the 'wrong' women had driven many of his best boxers from the straight and narrow, but he took an immediately liking to Eleasha, describing her as a 'lovely girl who is the best thing for Naz'. He viewed her as a strong stabilizing influence, able to curtail some of Hamed's excesses outside the ring, and felt that while she was around he was more settled and calm about his career and his life in general. Naseem seemed devoted to her. It was his first long-term, relatively stable relationship and for the first time in his public life, he dropped his reticence about the private side of his existence and seemed proud to talk about her. 'She's a great girl. She'd do anything for me and I'd do anything for her. She's a lucky woman. I'm a lucky man. God must be looking on.'

Naseem had reached a position by this stage where he was assiduously avoided by many top boxers with a great deal to lose by fighting him, even when confronted with career-highest purse offers, but at the same time he was constantly courted and challenged by lesser fighters with a great deal to gain. This was particularly the case with British boxers, who saw in Naseem the kind of pay day that would set them up for life. As a result, all the best British-based boxers his size wanted to have a go. As Brendan Ingle put it: 'They're the men with the knives and forks and Naz has got the steak.' Knowing that none of these would-be opponents were anything near his class, and resenting being challenged on his own turf, Naseem loved nothing better than deriding them and this caused a genuine edge to emerge in some of these intended rivalries – perhaps none more so than in the case of the quick, stylish but fragile and light-fisted former WBO featherweight champion Colin McMillan. Several years earlier, when Hamed was at the end of his amateur career, the pair of them had sparred together, and unlike most of the Sheffield teenager's celebrity spar-mates from that period, McMillan insisted he had Hamed's measure. 'He really didn't give me any problems then. He was not used to men who could match his speed and I was able to make him box to my pattern,' he said. Less realistically, McMillan felt he could do it again if they ever met for real, but instead he had to face being derided by this fellow eight years younger than himself who now held his old title, and the anger and frustration felt by this intelligent and gentlemanly boxer led to another 'incident', this time in the Hanover Grand nightclub in London. This became the subject of a great deal of public rumour and press conjecture, with talk of a major row, even a brawl. In fact, it was no more than an animated conversation. As McMillan relates it: 'He had been going around saying that he was going to knock me out and put me in retirement. Usually I'm easy going about that sort of nonsense, but the way he did it made me a bit angry, so I went up to him at the nightclub and confronted him. I said, "You've been saying all these things, so when we gonna get it on?" and he said he was willing to fight me any time, but he wasn't aggressive about it – he was fine. We talked and there was definitely no scuffle. I don't know where that came from.' A year later, McMillan retired after losing his British title to Paul Ingle.

At the start of the New Year, Naseem resumed light training, but as soon as he threw the right, the sharp pain was back and the hand swelled once again. It was clear there was still much healing to be done and he returned to the Harley Street specialists. This time the Castillo fight was cancelled. At a press conference in London, a dejected Frank Warren said that three of the meta-carpal bones had 'fused together' and that Naseem would face keyhole surgery, although in fact there was no fusion and the doctors told Hamed that surgery was not a necessity. They suggested the alternative of intensive physiotherapy plus cortisone injections and complete rest to reduce the swellings. A thoroughly dispirited Naseem took the latter option, joking that 'operations are too sore'. After the first postponement, the revised post-Castillo plans had included a challenge for Vuyani Bungu's IBF super-bantamweight title, followed by a move to super-featherweight to take on the WBC champion Azumah Nelson, with fights against Barrera and McCullough later in the year. Don King was also keen to promote Naseem on the Tyson–Bruno undercard – and Warren was about to announce a major US television deal with Showtime – but all this fell away and the best they could hope for was a late March comeback against a softer option opponent, after six months of enforced inactivity.

For the next month Naseem was banned from the gym and decided his best option was to get away from it all for a few days by making a trip to Cannes with Eleasha, but even this led to trouble. He came close to being arrested and banned from the flight after yet another 'incident', this one of his own making. Checking in at Manchester airport on 23 January, he tried to take two items of hand luggage onto the plane. A British Airways clerk, Helen Russel, told him only one bag was permitted and that his other bag, which contained his personal stereo system, was over the 20kg limit, after which he handed it over to go into the baggage compartment with some reluctance, having previously seen Brendan's electronic scales damaged after being taken apart by inspectors. According to Russel, what followed was a statement made in all seriousness. According to Naseem and Nabeel, who was with him, it was just an example of the young boxer's off-the-wall sense of fun, which anyone with a humorous bone in their body would have laughed at. What is not in dispute is the content of Naseem's message: 'If my bag doesn't get to where it's supposed to be, I'll come back and find you, and sort you out with a shotgun,' or words to that effect. Russel burst into tears, later saying that no-one had ever addressed her in this way in her nine years in the job. Naseem, however, compounded the damage by refusing to answer standard security questions about the contents of his luggage, after which she contacted her supervisor, who immediately confiscated his ticket and boarding card, called the airport police and warned Naseem that he might be refused permission to travel. The police, aware of Naseem's reputation, found the tallest, toughest-looking constable on duty, who gave the boxer a 'talking to' in which he was 'advised about his behaviour'. After this, he apologized to Russel, explaining that it was all a misunderstanding and that the remark about the shotgun was made in jest. He was eventually allowed to proceed with his journey.

Naseem's management, assisted by Nabeel, was left to handle the damage control, explaining that he had only realized after the event that the check-in clerk did not share his sense of humour. 'It was a complete joke and everybody in the queue knew that. Naz said one or two things but the woman checking him in was so dry that she just didn't laugh,' Nabeel said. To which Naseem added: 'That was totally blown out of all proportion. She was just being so *funny*. We were just rapping some tune that had "shotgun" in it, having a laugh. Then she made out that I had threatened her with one. But not at all, load of rubbish. As if I'm gonna carry a shotgun or have anything to do with a shotgun. Totally silly, but one of those things you have to put up with when you're famous.' While the remark about the shotgun is certainly consistent with Naseem's sense of fun, the incident, which was splashed in all the national newspapers, seemed to confirm for many the stories about the young celebrity's arrogance and impetuousness.

At the beginning of February, his hand was deemed to have recovered sufficiently to allow him to resume training. The fighter and his management knew he was chancing it, but the months were passing by, his weight had risen to 135lb and the inaction was becoming intolerable. He tried the right out on the heavy bag and then on the pads again, and said he experienced no pain or psychological barriers when throwing it, though it took another two weeks before he could throw it with evil intent in sparring. Once his hand was cleared for action, it was announced he would fight again 16 March, the same date as the Tyson-Bruno bout, but six hours earlier at the Scottish Exhibition Centre, the site of two of his finest triumphs. Having been keen to fight in Las Vegas, Naseem was far from delighted with this news but put the best face on it: 'I like to be the main attraction, although it would have been good to be on the Tyson bill, but there will be loads of people watching me,' he said.

His opponent was the twenty-six-year-old Austrian-based Nigerian southpaw Said Lawal, qualified as little more than a warm body. His number-four featherweight ranking with the WBO was a reflection of that organization's capricious generosity towards its promotional friends rather than Lawal's standing. He had never beaten anyone of note and had never even fought outside of Austria as a professional, but, on paper, he seemed like a decent opponent to test Hamed's hand after such a long lay-off. The Lagos-raised Lawal started boxing as a fourteen-year-old and won thirty-six of his forty amateur bouts before shifting base to Vienna in 1991. He opened his professional account in March 1992 with a points win over the Romanian prospect Stan Mihaly, but it was a year before he would fight again. After that, however, his career got moving and by September 1994, when he faced Naseem's old victim Freddy Cruz, he had raked up ten wins in a row and held the Austrian title. But Cruz was too crafty and experienced and out-boxed him over eight rounds. Nine months and three victories later he met Cruz again and this time Lawal was given a draw, an indication of improvement. A further move into the outer fringes of the world scene was suggested by his victory over Zambian champion Paul Kaoma for the WBC international featherweight title and his successful first defence against the Dominican bantamweight champion Luis Sosa, both on points. His record stood at seventeen wins (seven inside the distance), one loss and one draw. He was known as a reasonably skilled boxer and a solid body puncher, an impression confirmed after the Hamed fight when he returned to his winning ways.

What was clear was that he did not have the tools to trouble Naseem, whose approach was nonchalant. He looked at Lawal's record and realized he had little to worry about. As he put it: 'I knew I'd win because he couldn't look after Cruz. I gave that man six rounds of punishment and left him crying like a woman, so this was always going to go my way.' He also watched a video of Lawal in action, but soon switched it off, satisfied he had seen enough. 'I watched the guy box for one minute, like I normally do – put the tape in, watch a couple of moves, turn it off. That's all I have to see. I saw that he was a good fighter. He looked very strong and quite tall on tape, and I saw that he was a southpaw, so I knew what shot to throw and I knew I was going to knock him out early.' Though the right hand lead is the classic answer to a southpaw, Hamed, in fact, told everyone for weeks that he was going to knock Lawal out with the left. 'I'm going to take him out with a perfect, cracking left hook in the second minute of the second round,' he predicted. 'For the first round, I'm going to box to the best of my ability and chill a bit, in a smooth way, take my time, flow around the ring. In the second, I'm throwing an awesome, timing-perfect left hook, and I'm not saying *if* it connects, I'm saying *when* it connects, I'm taking him out.' His training seemed to confirm the preference for the left, and some caution about using the damaged right, and when he said his hand was 'almost 100 per cent', most took that to mean 'still not in full working order'. While he trained for five weeks, he had, in fact, put in less sparring for this fight than for any other in his professional career, and it was notable that for many of these sessions he was holding back with the right. Instead, he did more work on the speedball, in shadow-boxing, ground exercises and skipping than usual, as well as hundreds of rounds on the pads to get his timing and speed back.

When they arrived in Glasgow on the Wednesday night, three days before the fight, his trainers expected the usual quiet wind-down after over a month's work, but Naseem had other ideas. As Brendan put it: 'Immediately after we arrived he insisted on training and he done fourteen rounds on the pads and skipping and shadow-boxing, and then on the Thursday night he done eight rounds of high-movement speed work, and his timing and his rhythm were so spot on I thought to meself, "I can't see it going longer than two rounds." ' But while his entourage was insisting that everything was hunky-dory, not everyone was convinced. Barry McGuigan, who had examined the hand shortly before the fight, was one of several to express concern, noting that it 'didn't look great' and adding: 'I think there's a lot more trouble with the hand than they're suggesting in the Brendan Ingle camp.' This kind of comment, as well as press reports suggesting that Naseem's career was on the line and that he should lay off for a year to give his hand a rest, infuriated the young champion and added to the frustration that had been building over the months. In the changing-room prior to the fight he announced to Brendan, John and the rest that his first punch of the fight would be a lead right, and that if this connected and hurt Lawal, he would end things then and there. 'What I read before the fight was un-believable,' he said afterwards. ' "Naz's career is on the ropes" and stupid stuff like that. Everybody thought I was going to make it a left hook, but I wanted to prove that the right hand was perfect and that there was no problem with it whatsoever.'

Paying up to £100 for the privilege of seeing him in action on a rainy, cold night, 6000 punters poured into the Scottish Exhibition and Conference Centre, known to the locals as the 'Big Red Shed'

– a graceless, prefabricated venue equally adept at housing concerts for ageing rockers or evangelical revivalists as it is for accommodating beery, potentially belligerent fight crowds. Lawal made his entrance under the Nigerian flag to the familiar chorus of sustained booing. Before the fight he had been saying with apparent confidence that he would be taking Hamed's title belt back to Vienna and the like, but when he stepped through the ropes he had the look of a deer caught in the headlights. The crowd began chanting 'Na-zeem, Na-zeem, Na-zeem' and the letters N-A-S-E-E-M appeared in fireworks above the stands before the theme from *The Omen* moaned ominously from the speakers. Then in a sudden Hamed-like change of pace and direction, the heavy choral tones made way for the thumping beat of the new rap single Hamed had collaborated on, 'Walk like a Champion'. As Hamed appeared, the words reverberated: 'Prince is in the House … Walk like a champion, Talk like a champion,' and the champion made his way to the ring wearing a new creation: a pair of long imitation leopardskin trunks decorated with six horizontal rows of feathery white fluff, giving the impression of a kind of sheepskin skirt until the wind lifted the tassels. The champion flipped the ropes, did a little swagger and fist-roll and then brushed past Lawal, giving him a mocking wide-eyed stare as he went by.

Naseem looked reasonably trim at 125lb 12 oz – the heaviest of his career – as he moved around the ring, grinning approvingly when he was introduced as 'the incredible, the unbelievable Prince Naseem Hamed'. Lawal, two inches taller and 12oz lighter, avoided all eye contact and shuffled about in nervous, jerky movements. At the bell, Hamed strolled out in a squarish south-paw stance, with that familiar contemptuous look on his face, pumping his arms in an almost playful gesture. Three seconds into the round he let loose a right hook with the hint of an uppercut in it, which landed squarely on Lawal's chin as he was coming in. The Nigerian collapsed to the canvas. He wobbled up at the count of six, a completely vacant look on his face, his legs barely able to hold his 125lb. Wiso Fernandez, the WBO's barely competent house referee, quite clearly should have stopped it then, but such precise judgement would have been too much to expect from the Puerto Rican and Hamed was allowed one more claw and bite at the wounded deer in front of him. He measured his man with a right jab, feinted twice, and then unleashed a long, casual-looking right uppercut which smashed home into Lawal's nose and mouth at the precise point his head was coming forward. The impact whiplashed his head against the back of his shoulders and he collapsed on his face, rising by instinct but without conviction or even consciousness at the count of four. At the thirty-five second mark Fernandez waved it off, giving Hamed the fifth fastest 'world' title knockout in boxing history.

It had been a magnificent thirty-five seconds – three punches timed and delivered to perfection and with such unrealistic force from one so small. The crowd was stunned for a moment and from the back of the bleachers there was some confusion, but when Naseem leapt onto the ropes and pumped his hands in the air, they realized that their evening's entertainment was over. For many it seemed a very brief bit of pleasure for a fair whack of cash, and to the tune of 'Bread of Heaven' they began singing: 'What a fucking, what a fucking, what a fucking load of crap,' before breaking into a sustained chorus of boos. Lawal, the prime target of this derision, looked like a fellow who had dropped one cap of acid too many. He had no idea what was going on or where he was, and had no recollection of the knockdowns or why he had been stopped. He asked his corner when he was fighting and then wept a little. Naseem could not resist a hint of derision about his unfortunate victim's state. 'I don't think he remembers much. He still thinks he's fighting later on. He was arguing with his corner [about] why he had not boxed. I seen it myself, him arguing with his corner, but, end of the day, what can I do about it? I done my job and I couldn't wait to get out. That was a cool, cool ending, you know. The right hand is perfect. You see, I don't tell lies. I would have loved to do him in the second round because I predicted it. End of the day, it hit him so hard, that first shot, I timed it so precise, that it put him down. So he was going, he had to go. All I needed to do is plant every shot correctly and hit him in the right place. I waited exactly for the shots I wanted to throw and I threw them and the fight was over, so I can't be more pleased with the way I boxed.' By the time he had showered and changed, however, he realized that the people of Scotland, or at least the Glaswegians who had paid to see him in action, were a little put out. 'I apologize to the fans, but it was going to be an early night anyway, so what the hell. I just apologize that it was over so early. I'll be back in Scotland definitely and giving an even better performance than that,' he said, adding, with a display of post-modern sensibility, 'but them shots were great for television.'

Half an hour later a stretch limo disgorged the Hamed clan at the Marriott Hotel, a mile away, for an all-night after party where Naseem led the revellers shouting the odds for Frank Bruno. When he finally retired upstairs at 6am, Bruno was an ex-champion and the twenty-two-year-old featherweight had reached the pinnacle of the Warren pile. With Nigel Benn having been whipped by Sugarboy Malinga, it had been a bad month for British boxing but, all in all, a good one for Britain's best boxer. In retrospect, however, the ease of his victory may have been the worst thing for Naseem at that stage of his career. It seemed to confirm his self-perception of God-inspired invincibility, and particularly the notion that a mere touch from the master would leave the other fellow in a crumpled heap. In short, he fell in love with his own power, neglected his defence and short-changed himself when it came to training. In the ring it soon became apparent that while the 'new Naz' was stronger and hitting harder than ever before, he was also getting hit like never before. Outside the ring the situation was even more worrying for many of those who had his interests at heart, because despite all his promises that he would learn the lessons of Herol Graham's failures, that he would be unaffected by fame and fortune, the opposite was proving to be true. The stress of constant public exposure was creating a more diffident and sometimes obnoxious public persona, given to bouts of pique, aggression and all-too-frequent 'off the ball' incidents. His love life became complicated; his relations with Brendan and some of his stablemates deterio-rated; he was losing his sense of perspective on the relationship between fame, fortune and reality; and around him a fortress mentality was developing among some family members, designed to shield him from criticism.

His second defence was against the WBO's number one contender Daniel Alicea in Newcastle on 8 June. Although the unbeaten Puerto Rican was by no means the most dangerous man in the division, there was much at stake in this fight. It would be Naseem's first television exposure in the United States – a delayed relay on the Showtime network – and it was therefore imperative that he made the kind of impression that would catch the notice of American cable viewers, with their customary myopia about anything which didn't hail from the land of the free.

It was also the first contest to fall under his new ten-fight, multi-million dollar deal with adidas, and several of the company's executives took their places at ringside to see what their new investment was capable of. The deal would see Naseem being promoted assiduously by the sportswear company, with his face appearing on billboards all over Britain and later in a television commercial (costing them £300,000 for US and UK distribution) showing him 'conquering' New York. His side of the deal was to wear the sportswear company's boots and garments wherever possible and to do his bit to promote the brand. (At times his enthusiasm for this role bordered on the absurd. A while later, for instance, in a television chat show hosted by the Nike-backed footballer Ian Wright, he got into a weirdly post-modern debate on the merits of their sponsors. 'Hey, what's that adidas doin' in my face?' asked Wright. 'You gotta respec' adidas,' said the indignant Naz. 'No, respec' to Nike,' said Wright – and so on.)

Alicea was not a fighter to attract brand-name endorsement, but he was a serious contender. He established a sound amateur pedigree, winning the 106lb gold medal at the World Junior championship in Peru in October 1990, by which stage he had won forty-six out of forty-seven bouts. He turned professional in New York in May 1992 before returning to San Juan, and in 1995 was recruited under Warren's banner. He was having his fourth fight in Britain and his professional record stood at fifteen wins, with no losses and fourteen stoppages. However, the only boxer of note on his record was the Arizona-Mexican Roberto Villareal, a former fringe contender whom he outpointed in 1995. In his last bout, nine weeks earlier, he had returned to Puerto Rico for a two-round warm-up knockout. He was quick, well-skilled and had a hard right cross, but the word in the gyms was that he was a bit on the chinny side. Nevertheless, many regarded him as Hamed's most dangerous opponent to date. In the lead-up to the Newcastle encounter, Alicea, who trained for two months and sparred 120 rounds, certainly gave a convincing impression of genuine confidence. 'Hamed is a good boxer, but he has his faults and I intend to expose them,' he offered. 'His style is designed towards unsettling the other boxer, but I am prepared mentally and it won't affect me. Every fighter has to lose some time and this could be the moment for him. I think I'll knock him out early. It won't go beyond eight rounds.'

Meanwhile the whisperings around the Sheffield gym were

growing louder – that Naseem wasn't training as hard as before, that he was too taken up with his celebrity lifestyle, that he wasn't approaching his job with the same fire. The professionals were guarded in their opinions, but some of the youngsters were saying that over the past year he had reduced his training load – that he used to work out two or three times every single day for six weeks but that by the time of the Robinson fight he had cut this to four weeks, was regularly missing gym sessions and was no longer working out between fights. In partial mitigation, some of his more loyal mates claimed he no longer needed to train for the same length of time, that his body clicked into the routine faster than before and it took less work for him to reach his peak. Others felt he was tempting fate. Brendan Ingle was saying what he had always said – 'The only man who can beat Naz is Naz himself' – but this time there was a hint of resignation in his voice and a slight, knowing smile.

What was clear was that his trainers were allowing him more indulgence – after the way he destroyed Robinson and Lawal, and with the money he was making for them, they could hardly do otherwise – but it was hard to escape the impression that there was a strong collective longing for the old, mad, bad, carefree Naz who just couldn't stay out of the gym and was always good for a laugh. Some gym regulars claimed he had indeed changed for the worse, by becoming more abrasive and rude and by lording it over the lesser fighters. However, his closer chums insisted he was indeed the same fellow. Ryan Rhodes said their friendship remained strong despite the fact that they did not see each other as much as before: 'Before he became world champion he was flashy Naz, and now he's still the same flashy Naz as what he used to be, so in my eyes he hasn't changed. Not to me, he hasn't. Not really, not *really*.' Jonathan Thaxton, who had known him for over five years, also insisted he noticed no change in their friendship after Hamed won the title: 'I know him very well and he's a real nice fella, a real genuine fella, a *nice* fella. He's got a bit of slagging in the press, but you got to look at all the pressure he's under. I wouldn't describe him as arrogant outside the ring, not at all. Sure, he's all arrogant when he gets *in* the ring, but it's a show, that's his party piece, his image – it's what puts bums on seats. But he still speaks to everyone in the gym and that, so I'd say he hasn't changed at all since winning the title. Well, not in my company he hasn't.' Naseem's own view was that the carping of his critics was all a load of nonsense and that nothing substantial had changed: 'Success has not changed me in any way. My feet are firmly on the ground, my goals are there and my mind's set on what I'm going to get. When it comes to training, I'll always be prepared and ready for anything I've got to take, and I take things with two hands and I make sure. When I get to fight I have hit a certain peak because I have always trained hard, and that's why my balance, my timing, my co-ordination is totally perfect. So there's no slackness whatsoever.'

The fact remained that he had been in full training for less than four weeks after only thirty-five seconds of the real thing in the previous eight and a half months. Naseem's featherweight stablemate, Paul Griffin, put in 14 rounds of sparring with Aliciea in Newcastle and returned to the gym to report that the challenger was nothing to worry about. Naseem took the message on board with the result that there was a casualness about his approach which had never previously been in evidence to such an extent, so it was hardly surprising that when he squared up to his opponent, his body appeared softer than before. Alicea entered the ring in his Puerto Rican colours, pounding his fists together, chanting slogans in Spanish, oblivious to the boos of the 9,000-strong Geordie crowd. Before the fight, Alicea's manager, Joe Fernandez, said that while his 5ft 7in boxer was a natural featherweight who sometimes fought at super-feather, Naseem was a natural super-bantam. That was certainly the way it looked when they stripped down, with Alicea taller, broader shouldered and more tautly muscled. Despite this, Hamed showed no sign of concern before the fight: 'I'm not one of them guys what thinks about this and that before a fight. I'm not a thinker, know what I mean? I just feel I'm totally cool all the way to the fight, the entrance, everything, just let it flow and go out and do what I have to do.' By his own retrospective admission, however, his entrance this time was a mistake. He arrived on a giant, gold-coloured throne carried by his six Nubian minders, accompanied by two near-naked ladies scattering petals to the crowd. He would later place some of the blame for his performance on this form of arrival, explaining that he needs to 'feel my feet on the ground, dance through the crowd. That's what they want and that's the best thing for me too.' Once in the ring, he waved to the audience, gave referee Raul Caiz a good- natured tap during the anthems, bent down to touch fists with his father and then approached his opponent's corner, pointing to a spot on the floor where he suggested Alicea would fall.

The challenger came out with purposeful aggression, attacking with his jab while ducking, slipping or leaning away from Hamed's ill-timed, out-of-range efforts. Hamed showed frustration at his misses and began showboating, dangling his gloves low, sticking his chin high, doing his limbo-dancer routine and switching restlessly from southpaw to orthodox, but soon was caught by a fast, hard jab from the unfazed Alicea. Naseem then tapped the right side of his body, suggesting a target, but the Puerto Rican was boxing sensibly behind his high, tight guard, taking no chances. His punches were shooting out quickly and returning with equal speed and his balance was excellent. Soon he caught Hamed with a stiff, short right, which prompted the champion to abandon an embarrassed clowning effort and get serious, but most of the lunging, heavy lead lefts and right uppercuts he threw were falling short. He attempted a quick one-two, which Alicea blocked, and then, the most testing moment of Hamed's career arrived. Alicea shot out a fast, long right cross that clipped Hamed's chin. He then landed flush a second, heavier right that twisted Naseem's head around. The champion bent low, twisted from left to right and tried a right from the orthodox stance which Alicea countered with a third, shorter right, this time thrown downwards and connecting with Hamed's chin. Being off-balance from his attempt at evasion, and with his legs unsteady from the first two punches, the third did the trick and Hamed pawed out his right as he toppled onto the seat of his sartorially eclectic adidas trunks. He had never been hit so hard and cleanly in his career. The blows were of the kind which had stopped all but one of Alicea's previous opponents, but Hamed sprung up in a flash, shaking his head in disgust as he took the standing eight count. His legs looked firm as he waved Alicea in, but he spent the last twenty seconds of the round on the defensive, jabbing and moving sensibly until the bell.

Hamed says that before most fights, he dreams of what will happen: 'It's uncanny. I have dreamt many times about certain punches and combinations in fights and I can see myself winning. That is how I have been able to predict correctly when my fights end so many times.' While taking a nap during the afternoon of this fight, he claimed to have dreamed of seeing the referee counting above him, while knowing that he was going to get up to win.

If this was true, his swaggering nonchalance in the first two and a half minutes of the fight was even more curious. Still, he seemed to have been shocked by what happened and later admitted he'd been caught cleanly. 'The first two rights were much harder than the blow which put me down,' he said, adding that, 'I shouldn't have been hit. I could have performed better.' When he reached his corner Naseem looked at Brendan and asked, 'What do I do now?' Brendan talked calmly, told Naseem not to worry: he was fine and would stop Aliciea in the next round. All he had to do was box behind his jab, keep his hands up and use combinations.

The visitor, however, was intent on capitalizing on his advantage and stabbed out his jab aggressively. This time Hamed was more careful, holding his hands higher with a look of absolute focus in his eyes and prodding out tentative southpaw jabs. He was soon rewarded for his concentration when he connected with a right cross followed by a looping left uppercut which grazed Alicea's face, leaving a red reminder of Hamed's power. Alicea continued to plough forward, while Hamed kept out of range before crowding in close and twisting to avoid the challenger's efforts, and then, just to show him who he was dealing with, Naseem pointed to his chin with his right glove and then switched to orthodox and landed another solid right. He had now found his range and was ready to move in. A minute into the round he delivered an impeccably timed right-hand lead to the side of Alicea's head. For a moment the visitor wobbled, frozen from the impact of the blow, and then fell backwards as it rippled through his body. A left hook helped him down. The feel of the canvas on his back brought him around and he was up quickly, with a confused look. He shuffled backwards into a neutral corner and propped his arms on the ropes during the count. Naseem was onto him with another right and Alicea grabbed in desperation, but lacked the strength to hold on as Hamed wrenched himself loose, landing some long and heavy blows but still missing frequently. When Hamed got through one of his rare body blows, Alicea countered with his last effort of the night, a left hook that connected, but this one had no effect. Naseem stalked patiently and just as the Puerto Rican was showing signs of recovery, he chose the moment for his payload – a left uppercut, followed by a right and a left hook, all thrown from long range, with the final hook connecting squarely and with full power. Alicea fell flat on his back and referee Caiz immediately waved it off and made him stay down for his own safety, while Hamed raised his arms and performed his obligatory somersault.

Afterwards there was an air of depression in his dressing room. For once the music was off, the party was over and there was not much to be said. When he had given it some thought, Hamed's usual swaggering bravado was mixed with a touch of humility. 'I went down, as you do, I'm only human. I never thought I would go down,' he said, forgetting for the moment about his dream, 'but that's boxing. He's a terrific fighter – strong, young, ambitious and I wish him the best in life.' But that was as far as his magnanimity would stretch and he was soon back to form. 'I got floored, tested the canvas for him and got back up, but at the end of the day, I took his and he couldn't take mine. If I hit any fighter my weight, I will put him down.' Asked whether he was worried or embarrassed after being floored, he was indignant. 'Worried? Did I look worried? No, not at all. I got straight back up and got on with it. I'd prefer to get hit with his shots than my shots. The power's awesome, I promise. It comes from God. I've been blessed with a gift. I can't see anyway that God will ever let me lose. Embarrassed? Never. I boxed a good kid, he was strong, he'd never been beat, he didn't know that feeling until tonight. You press that button, you get knocked down, you get back up. Even Mike Tyson got knocked down. Now who would have believed that? But if you're strong, you've got the heart there and you believe in Allah, you're cool.'

Former world light-heavyweight and cruiserweight champion Bobby Czyz, who was doing ringside colour analysis for Showtime, gave a mixed review in his accurate summary of proceedings: 'He has terrific speed, like Roy Jones. Kinda freaky, but he also leaps in with his punches, which creates power. He's certainly a great puncher and he's got an elusive defence – it's uncanny how he can jump out of the way of punches. But he got hit by a fighter that's not Azumah Nelson. He was hurt and he was down. Even though it was a flash knockdown, he got hit by three good right hands from a fighter who doesn't have the right hand, the power or the tools of a Nelson, or a Tom Johnson or a Wilfredo Vasquez. But this was a test for him – he got off the floor to show his championship qualities.'

As a spectacle, the fight had done Naseem no harm in terms of his American exposure, even if their first glimpse of Naseem did not show his best face. The second round had revealed the full extent of his powers, but the first had suggested a potential vulnerability which British audiences had never before witnessed. For the Brits, the aura of invincibility had been shattered. For the Americans, Hamed was revealed as a thrilling, risk-taking fighter with astonishing power, but one who was defensively inconsistent and who could be hurt. It was an impression that was to be to confirmed over the next two years.

There was to be no quick return to the basics for Naseem, as the pattern of taking a complete break from training between fights became set. But his activities outside the ring kept him in the focus of an increasingly prying media, and where hard facts were lacking, conjecture took their place. Two reports in particular had a compromising effect on his declining public image.

On a Sunday morning three weeks after the Alicea fight, Naseem found himself splashed across two pages of a national tabloid, the *People* under the banner headline: 'NASEEM WAS A PASSION KILLER ... HE MADE ME WATCH A VIDEO OF HIMSELF!' with the sub-head reading: 'He may call himself Prince but his crown jewels don't pack a punch.' The story, which was repeated in several other papers, was told by 'sexy blonde model' Lisa Thorpe (pictured in her underwear), who described a night at Naseem's Mayfair flat where she ended up after a nightclub party. Thorpe, a twenty-four-year-old presenter on the soft porn satellite station the Adult Channel, proceeded with a florid description of their time together, castigating him for his self-centred arrogance and describing his performance in bed in derisory terms. 'The only good thing I can say about him is he smells nice,' she concluded.

For Naseem, this was another example of venal tabloid muck-raking. He complains of 'girls selling their stories when they don't even know you, probably never even seen you before. There are some sick people out there. People who do that are just low-lifes. It'll all come back on them some day.' In this particular case it emerged that far from this being a recent fling, it had allegedly occurred soon after he won the WBO title, nine months prior to publication. Thorpe said she first met Hamed when they were both staying in the Celtic Manor Hotel before the Robinson fight. She was employed as one of the inter-round girls and claimed, unrealistically, he had 'given her the eye' between rounds and later unsuccessfully propositioned her at the post-fight party before getting his way at the London party a week later.

Worse was to come, however. Four days later, Naseem was hit by another allegation that was splashed across the country's newspapers and reported on national television. An eleven-year-old, Dale Boulding, who was one of Ingle's amateurs, claimed Hamed had assaulted him after he had made a cheeky remark. Boulding said he was playing football near the gym and 'when I took a shot at goal and missed, Naz said, "that was rubbish", so I said, "What, like you?" and he ran over to me and dragged me down. He bent my fingers right back and told me I shouldn't speak to the prince of the world like that. Then he hit me in the chest.' His mother said the boy returned home crying and looked 'as white as a ghost'. She reported the alleged incident to the police, who described it as a 'serious allegation' and interviewed Hamed, the boy and various witnesses before declining to charge him. Naseem described the story as 'a total load of rubish, a *total* load of rubbish. I would never hit an eleven-year-old. It's just low-lifes trying to make some money.' Brendan Ingle backed up his denial: 'To say Naz would assault an eleven-year-old boy is laughable. It was just a bit of harmless horseplay. Dale had shouted a racist remark at Naz who chased him in fun. He held the lad around the waist and told him to behave himself and get back to football, but Dale turned on the tears.'

There was much relief in the Hamed camp when his next fight was announced for The Point in Dublin on 31 August 1996. It was only Hamed's second fight outside of Britain and he was up against Manuel Medina, a well-respected former two-time world champion with a reputation as a skilled and awkward campaigner. Hamed had been stung by the press criticism that had followed his display against Alicea and it was hoped this would have the effect of returning him to the training regime of previous years. Naseem had also been hurt by the comparisons in the sports press with Oscar de la Hoya, who had just carved up Mexico's Julio Cesar Chavez. 'They don't know what they're talking about. Complete rubbish,' he told *Boxing Monthly*. 'De la Hoya beat an old man on cuts, but I knocked out a young, hungry fighter. You wait: two to three years down the line, I'll fight de la Hoya and then I'll show them what a legend looks like.' He predicted his usual second round knockout over Medina: 'He's good, I know that, but he doesn't belong in the same ring as me and he's going to find that out.'

The 5ft 9in Mexican was a boxer at, or near, the peak of his powers. He was only twenty-five years old but had already acquired a record of fifty-two wins (twenty-three on stoppages) and eight defeats. He had turned professional at the age of fourteen and ever since his third fight had fought at feather-weight or super-featherweight. He won the IBF featherweight title by outpointing America's Troy Dorcey in 1991, then, after four defences, moved up in weight to lose a decision to John-John Molina in a bid for the super-feather crown, and then lost his title to Tom Johnson in 1995. A week before Hamed beat Robinson, Medina pulled off a major upset by outpointing his fellow Mexican Alejandro Gonzalez for the WBC title, but lost it on a narrow decision to Luisito Espinosa three months later. Eighteen months after fighting Hamed he would win his third world title, outpointing Hector Lizarraga for the IBF title (which, by then, Hamed had won and then vacated). Medina was light and quick on his feet, had excellent defensive skills and a sound chin, and after ten world title fights seemed completely unfazed by the idea of tangling with 'The Prince'. All that was lacking in his arsenal was the hand-speed or heavy knockout punch of a modern great. Always modest, Medina displayed an understated confidence in the way he went about his business. 'I feel pretty good and, like Naseem, I'm hoping to win,' he said before the fight. 'I want to win just as much as he does.'

Once again this was a high-stakes fight, not only because of Medina's international status but also because this was viewed by Warren as an important advance in preparing the American market. Once again it would be screened on Showtime, which required a scintillating performance to build Hamed as a bill-header attraction. The adidas men were also doing their best to squeeze maximum advantage from their pricey investment, sending along four of their executives while providing four writers from youth and style magazines with all-expenses paid trips to Dublin to survey proceedings. With ticket sales flagging, in the week before the fight Brendan Ingle was driven around his old Dublin stomping ground, shouting the odds through a megaphone from an open-topped bus in an attempt to drum up interest. But the real excitement there was about the prospect of a showdown between Hamed and Wayne McCullough, who got into a heated exchange. McCullough claimed Hamed had made derogatory remarks about his wife, which Naseem denied. Warren said the Ulsterman started the trouble. 'Wayne turned up uninvited and he was far from affable and started to taunt and make derogatory comments to Hamed in front of the public and the Irish press,' he claimed. He stepped between the two boxers and said that if Wayne wanted to fight Hamed, he could do so. McCullough claimed the Hamed camp was ducking him, so Warren asked him how much he wanted to fight Hamed. McCullough replied that a million dollars would do it and asked for a contract. 'Obviously I did not have a contract with me,' said Warren, 'but I asked for a page from a notebook and wrote that I would guarantee him $1 million for the fight in Ireland before the end of the year. McCullough accepted the terms and said he would inform his manager.'

While this was going on, Medina was ignored and no-one in the British or Irish press gave him any hope of success. Had they known what was really happening behind the scenes, they might have been more cautious. Naseem arrived in Ireland five days before the fight and the following day contracted a cold that spread to his chest. He turned down Brendan Ingle and Frank Warren's offers to postpone the fight for two weeks, and instead tried to overcome the problem by putting his face over a steam bowl and covering his head with a towel several times a day. He then went to see an Irish fight doctor, who warned him against taking a particular medication as it contained banned substances. By fight time his condition had further deteriorated and he would later admit he made a terrible mistake in going ahead with the engagement. 'I felt so ill. Most people in that condition wouldn't have got out of bed to go to work, let alone put a world boxing championship on the line, but I didn't want to give anybody the chance to criticize me for pulling out. I knew they'd be saying, "He's meeting a two-time world champion, a Mexican who has never been stopped and now he has pulled out." ' In the three days before the fight, he worked on the pads for a few rounds with John Ingle and concluded he was well enough to get it on, convinced that Medina would not last longer than two rounds.

In the hotel room before the fight his spirits were revived: 'I always make sure I've got the right people around me before a fight: my family, of course, and my close friends – a whole lot of people who make me relaxed. I want a big laugh the whole way from the hotel to the training sessions and this time, as always, I had such a laugh, such a big laugh. You have a laugh about everything, whoever's in the room. Getting the right people there, that's the main thing.' At 5.30pm they were transported in a white limousine to the stadium and the party continued in the changing-room, as he enjoyed the camaraderie of Johnny Nelson, Ryan Rhodes, Clifton Mitchell, Kevin Adamson, Anas Oweida, Nabeel, Ali, and in particular the lightweight who had become his closest friend, Thomas Bradley. While Warren was pressing for significant cuts in Hamed's growing entourage, Naseem was reluctant to accede. 'Frank likes it to be a little more professional, with less people in the changing-rooms. I want exactly who I want to create the buzz I want. That's what counts at the end of the day, what I want and not what anyone else wants. If I want to have a laugh, I do.' With this motley crew behind him, by the time he made his Oasis-assisted entrance he felt something close to his cocky self again and was ready, as he put it, 'to do the business'. He paraded around the ring and conducted the 7,000 crowd in its mix of cheers and boos.

Medina, who had bounded into the ring waving an Irish tricolour and wearing shorts seemingly inspired in their feathery tassels by Naseem's, made his mark from the opening bell, making Hamed miss more often than he was accustomed and returning fire with light, short, accurate combination counters before gliding out of range again. In the second, it seemed as if normal service had been resumed. Hamed was switching stances frequently in a bid to confuse the Mexican and finally, towards the end of the round, found an opening. He took first blood with a long right to the nose followed by a left hook, then landed several hard jabs, a short right and a big left hook that floored Medina heavily, with the momentum causing Hamed to follow. The challenger was up at six and seemed seriously hurt, but was given several extra seconds of recovery by the referee Gino Rodriguez, leaving Hamed no time to finish him off. Had it not been for the bell, the fight would have ended according to script and the public would have been none the wiser as to Hamed's true condition. Instead, Medina regrouped while Hamed made the mistake of trying to take him out with single, leaping bombs that were easily evaded. Medina shook Naseem with a quick, long right cross, followed by a left hook, and towards the end of the third got home with a solid right hook. Naseem beat his chest in a derisory gesture, but it was becoming clear that it would not be another easy night.

In the fourth, Hamed began to tire and his efforts were strangely devoid of ambition. Medina forced the pace, catching him with several hooks and a quick right to the face. At the end of the round Naseem told Ingle: 'The power just isn't there.' Medina won the fifth as well with some proficient jabbing, and once again it was apparent that Hamed's attempts to gain advantage by switching stance were having no effect. When the bell rang, Ingle implored him to settle down, warning him that the fight was slipping from his grasp. Naseem was more aggressive in the opening minute, but Medina was more confident now and caught the champion off balance with a long right cross. Hamed came back with a solid right uppercut, and seemed to be spurred on when blood began oozing from the challenger's right eyelid. The referee led the Mexican to the ropes for the ringside doctor to inspect and he was permitted to continue.

Early in the seventh, Hamed's frustration was evident. He even tried a backhander; drawing an admonition from Rodriguez, but soon after, one of his desperate lunges – this time a wide right hook – connected. Medina responded with a series of jabs but Naseem was able to catch him with a left uppercut, followed by a pair of right uppercuts. Still Medina stayed up and fired back with a right-left hook combination before being wobbled by a heavy left hook. Again the bell came to the Mexican's aid, but in the eighth he turned the fight around for a second time, catching Hamed frequently and successfully drawing him onto his punches. His best moment of the fight was a well-timed right cross which caught Hamed flush on the jaw as he was coming in. His gumshield went flying, his legs wobbled and he looked ready to go, before Rodriguez stepped in to get the gumshield replaced – an operation Brendan Ingle took his time about to allow Naseem's head to clear. This move prompted prolonged booing from the crowd. It had been by far the worst round of Hamed's career, including the first against Alicea – and it brought him close to defeat for the first time in his career.

But Naseem seemed revived by the break and came out aggressively in the ninth, catching Medina with a big right hook which dropped the Mexican on the seat of his trunks. He pulled himself up at eight, but looked shaky and wisely held on when Hamed moved in. The champion's momentum bowled him over again and soon after another right hook dropped him once more. Medina clung on desperately for survival and when the bell rang,

Naseem grinned menacingly at him. One of Medina's seconds tried to stop the fight during the break but was overruled. The Mexican had his last moments of success in the tenth, but by now Naseem had found his range and even though he was throwing single punches, he was hurting the bleeding challenger every time he connected. The beating became even more painfully one-sided in the eleventh, with Hamed piling on the punishment, throwing heavy hooks that drove Medina back. The round ended with Hamed blasting away in the opposition corner and it seemed unlikely Medina would survive another three minutes. Wisely, his team retired him before he reached his corner, deciding their man was in no condition to continue. Naseem led on all three cards at the time.

Hamed's Irish troubles that night made me recall the words of the former world welterweight champion Lloyd Honeyghan nearly a year earlier. A few hours after Naseem's brilliant victory over Steve Robinson, I was rather surprised to find him offering me a sombre prognosis of Hamed's future, with his main criticism reserved for Naseem's supposed defensive short-comings. 'Naz has everything else, but no defence. He's got fantastic ability but he's got no defence. You need defence and the point is, he's got *no* defence, and he'll have to improve his defence, because when you get into the ring with a good fighter who can punch back, what's he going to do? How's he going to defend his self? The thing I'm looking at is his defence. He's got no defence.' At the time I put it down to the confused resentments of a yesterday's hero who had taken a few punches too many, but later, after viewing Hamed's shortcomings against Medina, I realized that in Honeyghan's emphatic repetition there were the germs of good sense. Hamed's defence, like Ali's, rested largely on his astonishing reflexes, hand-eye co-ordination, peripheral vision, speed and perfect sense of timing. That was how he got away with traditionalist sins like leaning away from punches, leaping forward with his lead hand and dangling his hands by his sides. But when that timing was off, when the reflexes were jaded by chest infections or inadequate preparation, then he could be easy to catch. It was a defensive system, which, while brilliant when it worked, required consistent preparation. He needed to be in perfect tune by fight time. Against Alicea part of the problem related to the imperfections in his preparation. Against Medina he had trained harder, but there was a viral problem. On both occasions this defensive genius was found to be defensively wanting, something that had never happened to him before. It certainly left a firm impression in American minds – that once again the Brits had oversold one of their own.

Immediately after the fight, Naseem announced his predicament, praised Medina and then praised himself even more effusively, saying he had displayed the 'heart of a champion' and that 'they will have to kill me to take my belt away from me.' He then went straight to bed and took another week to recover from his infection. Later, however, he gave a fuller explanation of his illness: 'I risked my whole career there. I'll never do that again. I don't care what anybody might say in the years ahead, if I'm not right, I won't fight. I never want to endure that sort of agony again. I was gasping for breath with the chest infection and never realized how tired and drained I was. It's the worst state I've ever been in for a fight. I had a temperature, my lips were going blue and the rest of my face was like a sickly mask and my body ached. It doesn't matter how good a boxer you are, you can't afford to take a chance like that. I wasn't even fifty per cent and I couldn't have imagined how exhausting it was going to be. I have nothing from my past fifteen years in the sport to compare with it. My timing was off, my speed was off, everything was off. My mind was working but my body couldn't react. I couldn't inhale through my nose, only my mouth. I dread to think what I would have been like if I hadn't done my training. I'll never step into the ring in that condition again. It was just too much, but in a way I'm glad I suffered the experience, because now I know what is at stake I won't even consider doing anything similar. It is definitely not worth it.'

For Naseem the barrage of criticism he received from the press and sections of the public was infuriating. Despite the viral excuse, his relatively poor showing was widely viewed as further indication of decline. He was therefore determined to get back into the ring as soon as possible, against a legitimate opponent. He was becoming frustrated with the fact that the big name fighters within his range – Marco Antonio Barrera, Wayne McCullough, Tom Johnson, Azumah Nelson, Luisito Espinosa, Wilfredo Vasquez – were eluding him and with Warren's failure to promote him in the United States. In each case, it appeared, a mixture of promotional politics, greed, fiduciary good sense and perhaps even fear got in the way. Nelson, for example, turned down Warren's million-dollar offer preferring to take on lesser men for smaller amounts. Johnson was playing hard to get. Barrera was due to fight America's Junior Jones. Vasquez and Espinosa were proving elusive partly because they were promoted by King, who was holding out for a greater stake in Hamed, using the United States and Showtime as bait. By then King was becoming loudly critical of the level of Hamed's opposition and using every opportunity to push the idea of a US debut, with the understanding that he would be the dominant partner in this venture, something Warren was not prepared to accept. As King put it at the time: 'Naseem is world-wide, he's international. He's world-renowned. Frank and I must get together and get him the kind of opponents which will catapult him toward what is his.'

For the local market the tastiest and certainly the easiest option was McCullough, who had vocally accepted Warren's million dollar Irish offer at the weigh-in, only to prevaricate immediately after the fight, prompting another exchange between the two. 'The reason I was angry,' Warren explained, 'was because McCullough tried to say I offered him £1 million, which is not true – he got what he asked for. Now McCullough has come back and asked for $1,750,000 and said that the fight must be at super-bantam. One thing is for sure: McCullough is not a $1.75 million fighter and would not be getting a $1 million offer if it was not for the fact that he would be fighting Naseem, who means far more in box office than McCullough.' Although Hamed always seemed an exceptionally small featherweight – even when taking into account his elephantine legs – Warren insisted he would not be able to drop four pounds to super-bantamweight, or even to the 123lb that McCullough's manager Mat Tinley proposed, along with purses of $2 million apiece. 'Naz can't make super-bantam,' Warren said. 'He even struggles to make featherweight and the medical dangers of him forcing himself down are obvious. If he could make super-bantamweight, I would have got him a fight with IBF champion Vuyani Bungu with a phone call.' However, Brendan Ingle had a different perspective on the weight issue. A year later, in December 1997, he told me Hamed had not grown out of the super-bantam range: 'Naz can make 122lb, no problem – but only if he really wants to.' The question was whether Hamed had the discipline to make the weight once again. It would mean training harder and longer, not allowing his weight to rise between bouts and cutting down on his addiction to fast food and chocolate, which Naseem said was his worst vice: 'I can't resist it and when you're trying to watch your weight, that's not ideal.'

So with McCullough reluctant to move up to featherweight, Hamed reluctant to move down and no agreement on the purse money, the Irish option collapsed only to be successfully revived, with the same purse offer, two years later. Negotiations with Tom Johnson were still at a sticky stage, and so, reluctantly, Warren had to settle for the far cheaper and considerably inferior option of Remigio Molina on a bill at Manchester's Nynex Arena headed by the return between Steve Collins and Nigel Benn. The 5ft 4in, twenty-six-year-old Argentinian had made it to the Olympic quarter-finals as a bantamweight in 1992 and had raked up twenty-seven straight wins as a professional. This looked impressive on paper until it was borne in mind that all of these fights had been at super-bantamweight, that he had never beaten a world-rated contender and that with only eleven stoppages to his name, he was not much of a puncher. Even his status as the number five super-bantamweight contender said more about the WBO than it did about him. By Hamed standards he was bum-of-the-month fare, something the Englishman reiterated by giving the Argentinian his usual contemptuous treatment. At one point he handed Molina a video of his greatest hits and warned the visitor not to withdraw after viewing it.

The towel-headed Molina (125¼lb, half a pound lighter than Hamed) chose his own personal stereo for his entrance in order to block out the noise and focus his mind and his nerves – a wise move considering that the Manchester crowd gave him the normal British reception reserved for foreigners, a sustained bout of booing. Naseem's entrance to a rap beat saw him jiving towards the ropes shrouded in a 'cage' of laser light bars, aided by the roar and image of a leopard, just so we got the picture. His cruel grin displayed a lemon green, day-glo gumshield, and he eyeballed his opponent with an 'I'm having you tonight, baby' leer. At the bell, Naseem charged out, feinted with a jab and tried to take Molina's head off with his right in the Said Lawal style, but this visitor side-stepped and started pecking away with his southpaw jab before switching to orthodox and back again. However, he lacked the hand-speed, skill, guile or power to trouble Naseem and nothing he threw connected meaningfully, though a pair of glancing rights early in the round grazed the champion. Naseem's own timing, however, was a little off in the first and although he landed with several hard single shots including a head-snapping right uppercut near the end of the round, he also twice missed by embarrassingly wide margins. At the bell, he grinned and gave a knowing little nod to the challenger's corner before strutting back to his people.

In the second, the predicted round, Hamed moved in purposefully, opening up with a series of measured head blows, including two uppercuts thrown, as usual, from the 'wrong' foot. A quick combination drove a wobbly Molina to a corner, where he was battered with a right-left combination. The Argentinian was a brave soul, however, and did his limited best to fight back, but Hamed had him and wasn't letting him go. A right hook/uppercut connected with Molina's chin, followed by a southpaw straight left which caught him on the mouth. The challenger dropped heavily and the champion preened triumphantly above him, raised his gloves and then sauntered to the neutral corner. When the American referee, Roberto Ramirez, reached the count of seven, Molina rose unsteadily and the attack dog was loosed once more on his bleeding quarry. Bravely, he flailed back in blind desperation, his years of training telling him to fight on rather than surrender as Nigel Benn would do in the next bout. Hamed was onto him, found his range with three punches and then landed an impeccably timed, full-power underhand jab which wobbled Molina again. A mix of blood and spit leaked past his gumshield, he tottered back for five steps and Ramirez decided it was enough for one night.

'Beautiful!' was Hamed's verdict. 'Beautiful, correct punches. Look at the punching power. I'm just *so* good. It was a brilliant performance. I proved the chest infection against Medina was no excuse (sic) and business was done as usual. Molina did really well and caught me with a couple of good shots,' he added with the kind of overstated generosity which is really saying something very different, 'but I knew when I came out for the second – when I felt those rocket launchers go – he was going to be out of there. This was a close to perfect performance. This boy came to fight and took some great shots but, at the end of the day, he wasn't good enough. People can criticise me, but I can live with it. I'll take the criticism and keep knocking them out. You're looking at a legend to be. I'm not going to let Britain and the Arab world down.'

While Hamed's perfunctory dismissal of the overmatched Molina was hard to criticize, not everyone was bowled over. Freddie Roach, the American trainer of the victorious Steve Collins, noted: 'He'll never be a legend if he just keeps beating stiffs.' The vanquished Nigel Benn reinforced the point with bitter vitriol. 'He needs to test his wicked punching power on the best Americans before running his mouth off,' he said. 'You can talk when you've gone across the big pond and done it there.' And that is precisely what Naseem was pressurizing Warren to do. He was, in fact, demanding Tom Johnson, whatever the price, with Barrera to follow. And with Don King spinning his sticky web in the near background, Warren knew he had to deliver. Johnson knew it too, and as an astute businessman and a realist, he was therefore upping his price accordingly. But as the year drew to a close, this was looking like the menu: first Johnson, then Barrera.

With this in mind, Hamed was despatched to Florida to make a presence at the undefeated Barrera's routine defence against the fragile-chinned Junior 'Poison' Jones on 22 November. While Hamed was at ringside, lapping up the attention of a palm reading from a resident magician, one of Jones's handlers approached him to come and visit the American in his changing-room. When Naseem returned a quarter of an hour later, he said: 'I told him to be confident, believe in himself.' Later, he would claim his advice had turned the corner in Jones's career, and that even though he wanted to fight Barrera, he knew the American would prevail – which, in one of the upsets of the year, is what happened. Although the official outcome was a fifth-round dis-qualification as a result of Barrera's cornermen entering the ring before the round was over, Jones had, in fact, stopped Barrera. Afterwards Hamed, who also had a pushing, threatening little encounter with the leading American featherweight Derick Gainer, expressed bitter disappointment that he had not been the one doing the job: 'I feel sick. That's £5 million down the drain. I can't believe it's happened before I got there. I've been saying for two years that he couldn't get out of the way of a right hand. I told them what I would do to Barrera,' he said. 'He isn't fast enough and he is far too easy to hit.'

When he returned home, his disappointment was eased by the news that his title unification bout against IBF champion Tom

Johnson was set for the London Arena on 8 February but at the personal level his life had once again hit a difficult patch. Despite his continued relishing of early morning clubbing with his mates, Naseem always seemed happiest and most focused when his relationship with Eleasha was going smoothly. However, he was under strong pressure to marry a Muslim girl and at that stage Eleasha had no intention of converting. This was causing conflict within his family circle, particularly among its older members. Naseem and Eleasha tried to resolve this tension during a holiday in St Lucia – 'great place to take your girl, but not really my type of thing, lying on the beach all day' – but this was not to be. Partly as a result of family pressures, in December they had their first split up, which, his friends said, left him tense and visibly unhappy. Eleasha moved out his £400,000 mansion to be temporarily replaced by his close friend and sometime chauffeur Thomas Bradley, a former fruit and vegetable seller who was training to be a journalist as well as being a light- welterweight of moderate ambition and talent. Bradley had known Naseem for fifteen years and was his regular pool hall partner, a friend who kept Naseem amused with his banter while providing little in the way of threatening competition to his prickly ego. But even this friendship had its difficulties. Ali Hamed, for example, seemed to resent Tom's presence, and on the eve of the Johnson fight, they had a fiery hotel room altercation which might have gone beyond the verbal had Brendan not intervened. However, at this stage, at least, Tom was Naseem's lifeline. 'All my friends at the gym make me laugh, but especially Thomas,' Hamed said. 'He's my mate and so funny.'

But there was not much to laugh about. What was clear by the end of the year was that fifteen months as a 'world' champion had massively increased Naseem's personal fortune and that of his family, but it had not brought him the kind of international success he thirsted for, nor the personal happiness he desired. Inside the ropes he had managed two emphatic blow-outs of vastly inferior opposition and had struggled against two better opponents. In the process he had seemed to confirm American suspicions that he was a deeply flawed piece of Britannia and his dream of unifying world titles and displaying his talents across the pond was still unfulfilled. Outside the ring his reputation had been significantly diminished within his home town and more widely, among the boxing public and the masses at large. A steady stream of letters to the boxing press about what was viewed as contemptuous treatment of fans sometimes gave the impression of a weary misanthrope lurking beneath the mantle of a people's champion. The relentless pursuit from the tabloid press had produced its share of kiss-and-tell results – some of them (like a girl who claimed to a Sunday rag that he made love to her with his boxing gloves on) clearly nonsense and others evidently exaggerated, but this had made him more wary of the press, more prickly about journalistic criticism and less willing to tolerate balanced questioning of his behaviour. And now his relationship with the woman he loved was in trouble, with his own desires pulling against those of his family.

7

WANNA BE IN AMERICA

After a Christmas break in the United States, Naseem returned to Sheffield to prepare to face the first American opponent of his career, the IBF world featherweight champion Tom 'Boom Boom' Johnson, in a title unification bout. Soon after, his relationship with Eleasha was rekindled, much to the relief of his mates and to the disappointment of some family members. They had been apart for over five months, and friends observed he was irritable and restless during this period, but became far happier when they 'got it together again'. The relative stability and contentment the relationship engendered offered him the focus he needed for this next assignment. As Ingle had impressed on him, he not only had to win, but had to do it so emphatically that the Americans would recognize him as one of the finest fighters in the world.

Johnson was generally regarded as holding the top slot in the world's featherweight pecking order, for good reason. His record showed forty-four wins, two losses and two draws, with twenty-five stoppages and he had not been beaten in his past nineteen fights, his last defeat coming on a disputed technical decision to Manuel Medina in 1991. In the February 1993 return, fighting with both hands broken, Johnston outpointed Medina to lift the IBF title, and defended it eleven times against some of the best featherweights in the world. There was some evidence, however, that he was in decline, having struggled to beat several challengers over the previous year. As he acknowledged before the fight: 'If Naseem beats me, there are those who will say, "Johnson was a great champion but at thirty-two he was getting old and on his way down," ' though he added, 'If I beat Naseem, I must be prepared to hear, "You beat a guy who was inexperienced and wasn't what everyone made him out to be." I think it will be a great fight but I also see a lot of questions still being asked afterwards.' His other drawback was, as his friend Kevin Kelley put it: 'Tom's a fine fighter but he just doesn't know how to cope with a southpaw.' This was revealed most graphically when he fought Colombia's Ever Beleno in Newcastle a year earlier. Although he eventually prevailed on a twelfth-round stoppage, he was dropped three times by southpaw lefts and rocked frequently.

Johnson was a highly respected veteran who had paid his dues, but despite his record of twelve 'world' title defences, he had never risen to the status of a pay-per-view bill-header and advertising magnet. To get a white-collar pay cheque, he needed to face the only man in the lighter weight divisions who qualified as a white-collar fighter: Naseem Hamed. As a result, for the previous year Johnson had been angling for the fight, while at the same time playing hard to get, and had been steadily raising his purse demands. Part of his strategy was to belittle his rival's achievements. For example, in April 1997, shortly after beating Beleno, he offered a downbeat assessment of his rival's talents. 'Naz is a good fighter but he's still a baby in the game. To boast about beating Steve Robinson is nothing. Robinson has a 50–50 record. If I'd fought him after twenty fights, I'd have knocked him out too. You can't take anything away from Naz, but if a guy is standing in front of me with his hands down, he's gonna get hit. There's no way you can go through your career with your hands down and walk out with your sanity. The guy is stupid to do this. It's a danger for him. Yeah, it's fun and it looks good, but he's gonna get hurt.'

This kind of statement riled Naseem and spurred his fiercely competitive instincts, with the result that he put pressure on Frank Warren to make the fight whatever the cost. And with Don King manoeuvring for a larger share in Naseem's career, Warren did not relish the prospect of his number one little earner turning into a dissatisfied customer. In the end, he swallowed hard and did the deal. 'It wasn't easy,' said Warren. 'Money was the stumbling block.' He admitted, in fact, that he had paid the American rather more than he was worth in terms of market value, which was one of the reasons why this became the first Hamed-headed show to be screened on a pay-per-view basis in Britain. Warren's total bill for the event was £6 million, of which he paid $1 million to Don King Promotions, which in turn paid Johnson. Not that 'Boom Boom' received anything like that amount. As part of his promotional agreement with King (which extended for another two fights), he was managed by Don's daughter Debbie and his stepson Carl – a situation he was told he had to accept if he wanted the Hamed fight. At one stage, he said, he 'considered pulling out of the fight' as a result of King's prevarication on the finances of the deal, but eventually decided to resolve the dispute after the fight. In a sworn affidavit in 1997, he said he ended up with a cheque for $200,000, and gave details of deductions amounting to $480,000 out of the original million which went to King or companies he controlled.

In the build-up to the fight, Johnson revealed himself as a wily man, and he consistently outwitted Hamed when it came to repartee. At the press conference to announce the fight, for example, he made his point by informing his young rival that 'no-one likes a man who is rude' and then stating that 'a lesson is going to be taught to somebody, and I'm the teacher, not a student. I'll go to Naseem's house, knock on the front door, move his living room table out of the way and meet him there.' He walked over while Hamed was pontificating, placed his hands on his rival's shoulder and said with a knowing tone: 'You know, sometimes you're good to listen to, but sometimes you're not,' and casually walked off, after which he flew to the United States to begin serious training at Gleason's Gym in Brooklyn. His sparring partners included top prospects like Quentin Fortune and Zab Judah, against whom Johnson looked sharper and more elusive than he had done for some time. 'I have never been punching so hard. This fight could be over within three rounds,' he said three weeks before the fight. 'You are going to see the old Boom Boom.'

But Johnson was up against a Hamed who had worked more intensely than for any fight since he befuddled Belcastro three years earlier. He put in over five consecutive weeks in the gym and for the first time since 1994 he included running in his routine, with Tom Bradley waking him at five o'clock every morning for around three miles a day (or at least that is what both of them swore to). 'I want to make sure I've done everything possible,' Hamed explained, though he said the rest of his regime had not changed substantially. 'I don't feel any different. I'm still training the same in the gym and I've even started taking vitamins.' Every morning he would get to the gym at 11.30 for a two-hour workout with another at 4.30pm. On some days he would put in three shorter sessions. It was clear that while he no longer had the speed of his bantamweight days, he was hitting harder than ever. After one session on the pads, Brendan Ingle had swollen fingers and spent the next day in bed recuperating, while Hamed's sparring partners were also taking a vicious pounding. 'The hardest part is on the pads because he can break your hands, so most of the time I just call the times out and John does the padwork,' Brendan said. 'There's just the odd little thing I'll spot and have a quiet word about. People think he's all self-centred, but he listens to me and takes it in. He has cut corners in the past, but he's in phenomenal shape this time. This is the big one and he knows it. He's never punched harder and he's never looked better.' Hamed seemed delighted with his condition. 'I'm in the best shape of my life,' he said. 'Even Brendan says he's never seen me looking better, and this is how I'll be training from now until the end of my career.'

As the fight grew closer, Hamed's response to the dignified American's gentle jibes took on a less savoury edge. A week before the fight he predicted a three-round victory because that was what his mother had envisaged, adding: 'You would then be in even worse trouble than if you were knocked out in the first ... You could be in the graveyard. This is a war man – Britain versus the USA.' He then rounded on Barry McGuigan and said: 'I would have knocked the boy spark out if we had been around at the same time.' Under pressure, Hamed withdrew the 'graveyard' remark and therefore escaped disciplinary action from the Boxing Board. Johnson, however, seemed unfazed: 'Grow up, kid. You don't need to hype this one. We are both world champions determined to win a second belt. It's not an easy fight for either of us.'

It was only at the weigh-in, twenty-four hours before hostilities commenced, that Naseem finally unsettled Johnson. When Hamed muttered a few choice insults in his ear, the American grew visibly irritated and had to be blocked by his own handlers as he moved threateningly towards his opponent. 'Go on, get mad,' Naseem taunted. Afterwards he said this was a job well done. 'It was wicked! He got so riled. It was beautiful.' After their fight, Johnson admitted Hamed had got to him: 'It put me off my game plan.' Still, he walked away well satisfied that he had made the weight – by half a pound – at his first attempt, something he had struggled to do in several recent fights. As usual, Hamed also made it first time and right on the limit. He looked harder and more defined than he had done for several fights. The American, however, looked far larger when stripped off – a couple of inches taller, far broader around the shoulders and back, with bigger, more muscular arms, a thicker neck and larger head. As always, Hamed had the edge only when it came to his sturdy legs, which were one of the keys to his power. As his friend and former sparring partner, British middleweight champion Neville Brown, put it, 'His ability to manoeuvre opponents into position with great body strength is part of his secret, and it comes from his powerful thighs.'

A capacity crowd of 12,500 filled the London Arena and went delirious when Hamed made his entrance, heralded by flames, via a descending platform, onto the ground, and then with a lengthy dance-step routine into the ring. While this was going on, Johnson, having been booed into the ring, dropped to one knee for a quick prayer and then reached out with his glove to Sal Hamed. During the introductions the boxers stared into each other's eyes in the now traditional pugilistic display of nerve and search for weakness, before returning to their corners, Johnson impassive, Hamed grinning.

When the bell rang, Johnson came out like a pecking snakebird, flicking out his jabs with his guard high. Hamed, the snake, swayed rhythmically, looking for the opening and moment to strike. Before the first was over, he had found his mark while avoiding an American advance. He connected with a lunging lead left hook that grazed Johnson's face and then a short left that landed squarely, sending the slightly dazed IBF champion into the ropes. Johnson recuperated quickly and kept on pecking away, while Hamed kept his distance. At one point Naseem lunged and missed, and then held Johnson's head in his armpit and marched him to the neutral corner, drawing an angry response. Hamed struggled to get through Johnson's tight guard in the second, but managed to land with one solid right to the head. He switched stance for a while and got closer, but was still out of range, although shortly before the bell he got home with several combinations, which prompted him to smile at his adversary.

The third was the round of Johnson's predicted demise and Hamed came out in the orthodox stance, with gloves uncharacteristically high and a more focused look in his eyes. Johnson, however, had the early success, landing several jabs and then a short right to the body and a left hook to the head after making Hamed miss. In the final minute, however, Naseem cracked home a big left followed by several decent uppercuts, and it was becoming apparent that his punches were far harder than the American's. Johnson held to clear his head, but Hamed was onto him with a series of combinations that caused his prey to topple forwards for the first knockdown of the fight. Naseem went in hard, but Johnson showed his experience in avoiding the onslaught and as the bell sounded he banged home his best punch of the fight, a right cross which twisted Hamed's head around, bent his legs and caused him to touch down with his left glove. Technically it should have been counted as a knockdown, but was not registered as such. Naseem smiled while returning to his corner, but Brendan looked concerned as he leapt to his fighter's aid. Naseem opened the fourth with a heavy straight left that connected cleanly and sent Johnson's legs into spasms. The American held tight and looked ready to go, but managed to stay erect until they wrestled each other to the floor. When they rose, Hamed taunted his man with a little leg wobble, and then circled in while Johnson got back to his jabbing ways, catching Naseem cleanly again, then clinching while raking several short cuffs to the body. Hamed, looking irritated, cracked home several punches, although he had to take a right to the head in return.

The sixth was the IBF champion's finest. He re-established his formation, moving on his toes to the left, bobbing and weaving, using his jab intelligently and countering Hamed's attacks with accurate rights. In particular, a hard right cross late in the round seemed to shake Naseem momentarily, prompting a dismayed expression, and it looked as if the fight's fortunes might be changing. The impression was briefly reinforced early in the seventh when Johnson delivered a firm right cross to Naseem's mouth. Johnson worked away from a safe distance, firing quick combinations. Naseem, in contrast, was throwing single punches and occasional two punch combinations, and looked like his sole goal was a one-punch knockout. Late in the round he made his point, delivering a short, heavy left as he fell into a clinch, and then knocking his man into the ropes with another. By now he was firing his big guns, most missing the target but enough connecting to put Johnson in desperate trouble.

Hamed resumed his haymaker strategy in the eighth, missing big and landing big. A quick right-left combination to the head rocked Johnson again and opened a cut under his right eye. Two minutes into the round Hamed struck again, with yet another short left. The end had come and Naseem's clinical finish was one of the finest of his career. He pursued his wounded adversary, caught him with a right and then slammed in a huge left. Johnson somehow kept his feet, but Hamed manoeuvred him onto the ropes and chopped in with a short right-left-right combination that sent his opponent stumbling backwards. Naseem, by now in the orthodox stance, stepped back, waited for Johnson's instinctive forward motion, and let loose with a perfectly timed right uppercut which connected flush on the side of the jaw. The IBF champion collapsed onto his side, unconscious, his legs rigid. Twice he tried to rise and then, the third time, succeeded and in a pathetically triumphal moment rose slowly at the count of eight, but it was evident he had nothing left other than pride and courage. Referee Rudy Battle wisely waved it off at the two minute twenty-seven second mark, as Hamed lifted his gloves to the heavens to start his prolonged celebrations.

At the time, Naseem was well ahead on all three judges' cards, having lost only the sixth. New Jersey's Al DeVito scored it 69-66, Mexico's Victor Salomon 69–65, while Michael Benitez of Puerto Rico had it 69–64. This indicated the extent of Naseem's dominance, and yet, for those of us who had seen him on his way up, it was a case of a perfect finish after an imperfect start. One dimension, of course, was Johnson's quality as an opponent, but it was impossible to escape the impression that Hamed was slower than he had been two years earlier, that he was taking too many punches as a result of a defensive decline and that his one-punch-at-a-time head hunting was detracting from the rest of his boxing skills. Once again he had taken a spill, albeit unofficially; he had shown signs of frustration when his opponent failed to fall on cue, and he had taken unnecessary risks in his bid for a quicker finish. For Brendan Ingle, the result was pleasing but he acknowledged the road had been fraught: 'Naz did a job on him, but we're going to have to go back to the gym and work on his technique, as we did before. If he does that then he'll be amazing.' The gracious ex-champion, however, had no complaints, recognizing that he had never fought anyone quite so good. 'Naseem is everything he says he is – a fine fighter. He did what he said he would do. I hope and pray he respects his titles, because they are harder to keep than to win.' He then added a hopeful little remember-me plug: 'I was a little too composed, but I gave everything. I think I deserve a rematch.'

Naseem, naturally, went along with his opponent's praise, but his main focus was on his perceived American audience: 'I see a big year ahead. I want to prove to the Americans that I really am the best. They love power, skill and excitement, and that's what I will give them. No-one can argue now, having beaten a superb champion in Tom Johnson.' Later, however, he offered a more self-critical perspective, admitting he tried too hard for a knockout. 'I couldn't throw my right uppercut because Johnson was too good. He would turn his elbows in and keep popping out his fast jab. There were no body shots, none at all. I just wanted to take him out. I got caught, too, and I know I can't afford to, but you are going to get hit now and then.' But Hamed's American connection, Jay Larkin of Showtime, was delighted, claiming unrealistically that ten million of his countrymen had watched the fight (compared with 344,000 for Sky pay-per-view punters in Britain). 'Boy am I a happy bunny,' Larkin gushed. 'We saw the making of a true star tonight – a great performer. American audiences are going to love this kid. He's not just a boxer, he is a great entertainer – the kind of sporting hero that everybody is willing to pay money to watch.'

But among the 250 or so million Americans who failed to tune in, the event made little impression, despite an invitation the following day for Hamed to appear on the David Letterman chat show. The boxing week had been dominated by the previous night's show in Las Vegas, which saw a blubbering Oliver McCall surrender to Lennox Lewis. The Hamed-Johnson result was not registered in most of the American newspapers, although the American fight press gave a collective nod of approval, with *Ring* magazine leading the way under its front-page headline: 'Naseem Hamed Proves He's For Real!' A few weeks earlier the

American praise-singer had announced to America via the adidas advertisement: 'You will fall before him. You will listen to what he has to say.' And as Naseem vaulted over the rails of an immigrant ship, he continued: 'It's too late. He is here.' But Naseem was not there, and wouldn't be for another ten, frustrating months, and so far there were not many outside the US boxing community actually hearing his many words of auto-praise. At home, however, Hamed had reached the zenith of his public acclaim and no other British sportsman was receiving quite so many column inches or so much television exposure. His own sense of significance was further boosted by meetings with the then British prime minister John Major and, a week after the Johnson fight, the Queen (along with 400 other British sports personalities).

In the three months before his next fight, Hamed had plenty of other diversions to fill his time with – Eleasha, holiday travel, clubbing, snooker, shopping sprees, 'chilling out' with his mates, exercising his growing fleet of cars which reverted to his personal use after his license suspension ended in April, and the numerous media and charity appearances which had been put on hold during the Johnson preamble. The gym reverted to its status as a casual acquaintance, to be renewed now and then, but not with the same regularity or commitment of his pre-championship years. Part of the motivational problem related to the next choice of opponent. Naseem wanted another world title unification bout, preferably against Vazquez or Espinosa, but Warren was unable to secure their services, with the result that Hamed's camp had to settle for the number one contender, Billy Hardy, who had little to offer in terms of international status, despite his claims that Naseem was avoiding him. The fight was eventually set for 3 May 1997 at Manchester's Nynex Arena.

The open secret within the Wincobank gym – that Naseem was off the boil when it came to training – began to leak out and become public knowledge. As Claude Abrams wrote in *Boxing News*: 'The champion's visits to the St Thomas's gym have reportedly been less frequent than against Johnson, though Hamed claims his training schedule has been equally as gruelling. I am not convinced – and if Hamed eventually gets nailed and defeated, he will have only himself to blame. He will argue until his face is as red as his gloves that it will never happen, but there has been a decline in the quality of his performances which goes beyond the explanation that it is attributed to the increasing standard of opposition ... Complacency stems from over-confidence – if Hamed had the devotion of Holyfeld or even the Los Angeles Golden Boy (Oscar de la Hoya), he would be unstoppable. But it seems apparent that he does not.'

However, Hardy was doing his best to relieve Naseem of his complacency. For several months he had been taunting and coaxing Hamed to accept the fight, and once it came his way, he tried to find every possible advantage he could dream of – even training in Sheffield, in a gym owned by former Ingle protégé Glyn Rhodes and used by Herol Graham. Both men provided 'insider' advice to Billy, prompting Brendan to describe them as 'a pair of snakes'. Hardy, however, was not finished and kept on trying to needle his man, throwing in tasteless, Naz-like remarks such as: 'Hamed might enter the ring on a chariot, but he'll leave it on a stretcher.' Three weeks before the fight Naseem stepped up his training programme, perhaps egged on by Hardy's impertinence, and during the last few days he looked in shape and his power was certainly well up to scratch. 'He's punching harder than ever. I needed to lie in the bath for an hour to recover,' Brendan pronounced after their final session on the pads. With six days to go, Naseem went along to Rhodes's gym to watch his would-be rival in action and, naturally, announced himself to be unimpressed. 'I want to see something more exciting than that – come on, Billy, hit it harder,' he said while watching Hardy on the heavy bag. He predicted it would be over in one or two rounds. Hardy, himself no stranger to the contemptuous gesture as a way of getting to his opponent, simply smiled, highly satisfied with his own condition, not to mention a purse which would be the biggest of his long career.

Some fighting men are driven by the desperation of shame, poverty and fear; others are pulled by the allure of love, neon lights and new wheels. Little Billy was a boxer who'd had his share of push and pull, but most of all he'd had his ears. Cruel, ninety-degree, stick-out jugs to make him the butt of every bully's taunts. 'Yeah, I had protruding ears and I think that's what kept me in boxing all them years, because I used to get name-called and everything else,' he confided to me before the fight. 'It does give you an edge.' Eventually, what was left of the money earned from boxing (after a divorce and alimony payments for three children) allowed him to have them pinned back, and everyone forgot about Billy's ears – except Naseem, who, despite his own pair of protuders, was never one to miss an opening, arriving at the weigh-in with his mates, all of them sporting pairs of plastic ears. 'He looked like he was trying to make a mockery of boxing, not me,' Billy complained. 'He and all the other lads all looked fools.' For most of the build-up, however, Hamed was low key with his insults, resorting to gentler digs about 'old Ginga's' flaming red hair.

Hardy, however, always remembered what had driven him at the outset. 'I should have had them done when I was a kid, but obviously my mum didn't really give a damn.' Obviously, because his mum had fourteen children and a husband to feed, clothe and keep off the back streets of Sunderland: 'I had a hard upbringing, to be quite truthful, but maybe not as hard as some.' At the age of six he had found solace from an unkind world in a boxing gym run by Gordon Ibinson, who helped give him the self-esteem lacking in his early childhood. From 1983, at the age of nineteen, Hardy worked his professional apprenticeship all over Britain and Europe, having to cope with dubious decisions, cut-rate purses, injury and inactivity, until in 1990, as British bantamweight champion, he took on the formidable Orlando Canizales for the IBF world title and lost a split verdict: 'I felt I won – everyone did – and to lose by half a point in your home town is terrible, but that's boxing.' In the return, in the scorching Texas summer heat, he was stopped in eight and they said he was finished. Instead, he moved up two weights and pressed on, flying to Johannesburg before each fight to spend a month in the gym with Richard Smith, a retired South African bantamweight: 'He was a great trainer and like a brother to me, and for five years we lived together as a family.' In 1994, however, Smith was murdered by an AK-47-wielding carjacker. 'I remember getting that phone call at three in the morning. Obviously, I flew out the next day, but it's still bitter in my mind. I still feel, like – emptiness.'

He returned to the solace of the ageing Ibinson while continuing his day job as a sports goods sales manger and pressed on, adding the European featherweight title to his Commonwealth honours. He finally clinched the WBO's top spot with a points win over a ring-rusty Steve Robinson to take his record to thirty-six wins (seventeen inside the distance), seven losses and two draws. However, in the six years since losing to Canizales he had suffered only one, disputed points loss, and was unbeaten since 1993, reflecting his status as the top featherweight in Britain, Europe and the Commonwealth (other than Hamed), despite the fact that he said he could still make the super-bantamweight limit. Although he lacked concussive punching power, the thirty-two-year-old veteran was a gritty boxer, with an upright British style incorporating sound defensive skills, a high workrate, plenty of pesky aggression, a solid chin and buckets of guts, determination and experience. He seemed to believe he had it within his power to pull off an upset: 'Naseem Hamed's got two arms and two legs, and I'm going out there to do a professional job on him. If he comes forward, I will come forward. If he runs away, I will run away. If he wants to coming running at me, I will run at him too, because that's the way I am – I've still got that edge. Inside me there's a furnace growing. My will to win cannot be diminished.'

With Hamed being quoted at 1–12 to win, only the most wishful Hardy backer was accepting his prognosis, with the result that the arena was less than two-thirds full and a pay-per-view flop. As Warren later admitted, it 'lost a lot of money'. A couple of busloads of Sunderland fans made the trip to Manchester after their football team's victory over Everton but they were outnumbered by Hamed's Mancunian supporters, who booed Hardy's understated entrance. The challenger then sat in his corner, his body covered by a red gown and his head nestling between his red gloves as he listened to his personal stereo for inspiration or desperate relaxation, before stripping down to reveal his taut, frail, 5ft 6in body and his red and white Sunderland FC shorts. Naseem's five-minute arrival was backed by a giant neon boxing cartoon background, a light show and Byron Stingily dance number, 'Get Up'. He looked softer than against Johnson, a result of his leaving-it-late training, but despite his three-inch height disadvantage, for once he did not appear the smaller man. Billy suddenly looked scared, as though he was momentarily regretting his prior bravado and was struggling to steel himself for what was to come. He shook his head nervously and then wound his arms backward in a windmill-style warm-up action, while Naseem strutted around the ring. Seconds before the bell, Hamed smiled at Hardy, this time without visible malice but rather in the conscienceless manner of a kitten readying itself to leap on a grasshopper. He was clearly enjoying the moment immensely and knew he was about to have plenty more fun.

He missed with his opening southpaw left hook and a right, but Hardy backed off hastily, realizing that if something like that happened to land, his night would be over. They clinched and on the break Hardy came forward with surprising aggression and had his first and last moment of success, grazing Hamed a short and snappy left hook. He backed off again, boxing off his back foot behind a defensive jab, while Hamed, who had switched to orthodox, stalked him, pawing his jab as a range-finder before returning to southpaw. When he spotted the gap, he launched his weight forward into a massive lead right which connected with the side of Billy's cheek and nose. The challenger was hurled back by its force, his eyes and mouth betraying a mixture of shock, bewilderment and pain. He clambered up at seven and backed off, but Naseem found his range, landing a left, a crunching right and then the pay-off punch, a left jab which collided with Hardy's nose, dropping him again. As Hamed did a jig in the neutral corner, Billy bravely rose at six, but referee Paul Thomas mercifully called it off at the one minute thirty-three second mark.

Brave Billy sank to his knees, crying about his abject failure on the biggest night of his fourteen-year career. His nose was broken, his jaw badly swollen, but later he would claim: 'I wanted to continue, my mind was clear even after the two knockdowns, but my pupils weren't focused and that's why he stopped the bout.' However, he was full of reluctant praise for his conqueror: 'Naz is always on about his explosive power, but until you experience it yourself you don't realize he is a devastating puncher. I haven't been hit like that in my life, and I've been in with some big blokes. The first shot he hit me with, I honestly felt my nose crack. I was all numb around my teeth. He's got a kick like a mule and I feel in my heart of hearts that he's going to be the four-time champion, because he's got that knockout punch.'

Naseem was full of magnanimity for his opponent and stressed his performance was the consequence of a gift from God, adding that his mum and dad were praying for him and that he 'truly believed' this made the difference. And then, for the first, time, he introduced his leopardskin-shirted woman to the crowd, saying, 'Respect to my girlfriend, Eleasha,' after which he turned on the critics who had questioned his training methods. 'They're so silly making these rumours up. I was well conditioned for the fight. You saw it for yourself. I was so fast, so accurate.' Later he would add to the picture, saying that Billy's 'mouthing off' before the fight had made him determined to end it emphatically: 'I purely wanted to make out how great I was. I wanted to take him out in one round. When you see the shot when Billy got hit, you can actually see the pain in his face and him telling himself, "That really, really hurt." '

The opponent he wanted next was WBC champion Luisito Espinosa: 'I'd say he is the man to beat, a good name and the WBC belt probably has a bit more prestige, but I'm not really bothered.' At ringside, Joe Koizumi, Espinosa's manager, was perhaps a little too impressed. 'Naz looked awesome,' he declared. 'If we agree to fight him, we will have to work out some form of special strategy. He's such a great puncher, so dangerous.' After this fight, in fact, all attempts to entice Espinosa into a unification bout failed. Among the other rave reviews was one from Britain's new sports minister, the former amateur boxer Tony Banks, who became a regular ringsider at Hamed events. 'Seeing Naseem Hamed box is almost like poetry,' he said. Showtime's Jay Larkin was also mightily impressed, but this time offered a note of caution. 'Naz is not as well known in America as he should be,' he said, before once again upping the pressure for Warren to come to an agreement with King to export his little product. 'If we can do a deal for his next fight, he could top the bill in the States. Nothing is certain, but a Naz fight in America must happen.'

In effect Warren's hands were being tied. He wanted Hamed to top a major bill on his US debut, but in terms of his contractual agreement with King that would be impossible without his partner's consent. And King wasn't giving anything without getting something bigger in return. In short, he wanted a controlling slice of Hamed, which Warren was unwilling to cede. The alternative was to keep Naseem at home, where the Sky pay-per-view agreement guaranteed big purses. But without King's backing, the services of top league featherweights like Espinosa and Vazquez were going to be even more difficult to secure, while their more popular American rivals, such as Kevin Kelley, Junior Jones, and in the super-featherweight division Arturo Gatti, were out of range because of their links with other promoters and with Showtime's more powerful rival, HBO. Warren's water-treading plan was to keep Hamed busy on a diet of inexpensive opponents while quietly making his move for a break with both King and Showtime. Naseem, who seemed oblivious to the intricacies of promotional and televisual politics, and impatient with their consequences, was upping the ante for Warren to act. He was becoming increasingly frustrated watching Oscar de la Hoya marching through the weight divisions taking on the best men available while he was left with the likes of Billy Hardy to feed on.

With Showtime not delivering, Warren cut a deal with ABC to get Hamed's next fight screened live to a mass audience in America. The money could not match that of the cable station, but the exposure would be useful. The date was set for 19 July at London's Wembley Arena, with the unbeaten (35–0) Argentinian Pastor Maurin chosen as suitable fodder. Warren was doing his best to keep Naseem contented while plotting his break with King, but he had another little ball to keep in the air. On 19 June his business premises in Hertfordshire and Essex were raided and searched by Customs and Excise officers investigating alleged VAT evasion. Later that day they announced they had removed 'a quantity of documents'. Warren and his partner Chris Roberts were detained for eight hours for questioning before being released, and had to return for a further interview two months later. They insisted on their innocence but over the next two years the interest of the Inland Revenue remained a headache for Britain's leading promoter.

Naseem, meanwhile, was running into problems of a different nature. Ever since winning the WBO title in 1995, his popularity within his home town had been showing signs of falling. Certainly the impression gained from conversations in pubs, shops and with taxi drivers, and within the boxing community, was that while Hamed's prowess in the ring was well respected, his extra-mural antics had created a barrier of antipathy with his fellow Sheffield residents. One of the reasons related to the expressions of his conspicuous consumption. For Naseem the consumer, a man's relation to the corporeal world was always a significant dimension of his self-worth. Displaying this relation was therefore an essential element of proving how well he had done and how far he had come, and this required ostentatious reminders to the rest of the world, through clothes, household goods, and most particularly, through cars. 'I'm always getting recognized. There aren't that many big cars in Sheffield, so I suppose I probably do stand out a bit,' he noted.

As a teenager he started out with a little Metro 1100, but by 1998 he was the proud owner of a fleet of luxury vehicles including an Aston Martin Vantage, a Ferrari 355 convertible, several Porsches, a Lamborghini Roadster, a Bentley Azure convertible, a pair of Mercedes, a Cherokee Jeep, a Wrangler and a fleet of company cars – most of them with personalized number plates such as 'P2 NAS', which he said, 'speak for themselves.' Like Mr Toad, he loved his cars and adored showing them off, telling you how quickly they moved, driving them extremely fast and, as it happened, sometimes badly. While this may have delighted some of his friends (particularly Tom Bradley, who would occasionally be seen driving to his journalism school in one of Hamed's £80,000 Porsches), it did not endear him to many of his fellow townspeople, who constantly complained about where he would park his various vehicles. Shortly before the Johnson fight, for example, he received a bout of bad press when his Porsche was found in a disabled bay belonging to a rheumatoid arthritis sufferer – his second admonition for disabled bay parking.

This kind of expose, and the public resentment it tapped into, was behind a series of events which nearly led to Naseem joining the likes of James Dean in boy racer heaven. Soon after the proposed Maurin fight was announced, Naseem's silver, £200,000 Aston Martin, which had been a joint gift from Warren and Sky, had its paintwork scalded by a vandal – an act of malice which, incidentally, would be repeated three months later. He sent the car to be resprayed and borrowed a £100,000 Ferrari Berlineetta for an extended test drive. 'I'd had the car for a few days and I just loved it – I felt so safe,' he said, though he claimed to have had a 'gut feeling' that something was going to go wrong.

At 2am on 23 June 1997, when he was driving along a rain-swept M18 outside Doncaster, while approaching a roundabout at a speed which he claimed was not more than 50mph, he lost control of the Ferrari after swerving to avoid a fox in the road (or so he said). He skidded and tried to steer out of the skid, but the back end of the car went over the kerb and bumped against the crash barrier, after which the vehicle spun around, this time with the front end hitting the barrier. 'I shouldn't have done anything so silly in such weather,' he later admitted. 'It had been raining for three days solidly. The conditions weren't on my side at all.' The impact was such that the front end caved in, the right back end was smashed, the wheels were buckled and the driver's door wedged shut, but somehow Naseem was unhurt and, he said, completely calm: 'I don't know what it is about me, but I am like that. Whatever is happening, I just don't panic. It's part of my make up.' He squeezed past the passenger seat and clambered out, before waving down four friends who had been doing their best to keep up with him in their Vauxhall Nova. He climbed into the back, but seconds later, while the Nova was reversing at speed in the mouth of the junction, a transit van smashed into it, severely damaging its back end. A few minutes later, a man driving a Ford Sierra stopped and drove them back to Sheffield where they reported the crash to the police and returned home at 6am. The following day Naseem was back at the gym, showing no sign of any injury, and soon after he became the owner of a blue Ferrari F355 Spyder – one of only three in the world, he would boast.

Afterwards he claimed to have learnt his lesson: 'When I realized I was about to be in a second crash I thought to myself, "What have I done wrong?" I think it was God telling me to calm myself down, but I wasn't even speeding. When you look at the state of the Ferrari it's hard to believe I didn't hurt a hair on my head. God obviously knows what he's doing.' However, Hamed's car troubles continued. Seven months later, for example, he was caught driving at 50mph in a 30mph zone in Sheffield, and was fined £300 and had three penalty points deducted from his licence.

His spate of driving misdemeanours had another negative spin-off – it meant that his family became the subject of ongoing harassment by traffic officers. For instance, during Naseem's driving ban, Nabeel said he was sometimes stopped twice a week while Riath kept a record of being stopped fifteen times. Later that year Nabeel was timed driving his BMW 750 at over 130mph, though he said he was driving at under 70mph and that they had stopped the wrong car. He claimed the 'racist bully' police constable who stopped him had inquired: 'Are you Naz? I love doing people like you.' After being fined with a licence suspension, Nabeel complained, 'In my opinion, there is no justice. There is institutionalized racism in the force.' The family lodged a complaint against the police constable, but dropped it six weeks later.

Cars, however, were not the major issue upsetting Naseem's equilibrium. Shortly before his next fight, he and Eleasha split up again and once more he found himself living alone. His friends said the reason related to pressure from his family to go out with a Muslim girl. Others said the final catalyst was his reluctance to let her join him on a nightclub jaunt. At the time, Naseem noted: 'I don't believe in arranged marriages at all, but I'll marry a Muslim girl.' Eleasha's mother, Liz Crilley confirmed this view when she was quoted by a local paper as saying: 'I think the subject of marriage came up at her brother's wedding. He's a Muslim and she's not, and she won't become one. He just said, "I won't marry you. I have to marry a Muslim." This is two years after they met and Eleasha just decided to leave. It is quite amicable but it looks permanent now. They will probably still be friends. Eleasha's quite happy – she's not upset.' Naseem, however, *was* upset, although he did his best not to show it. His stablemates said he became restless and bad-tempered and would sometimes drop everything to drive past her house. As one put it: 'He clearly missed her enormously. She was very good for him, and without her, he felt at a bit of a loss and wasn't always easy to be around.'

His troubles were further exacerbated when Pastor Maurin was cut in training, forcing Warren to go on a frantic search for a replacement. Six days before the fight, Juan Gerardo Cabrera, an Argentinian butcher and cobbler who doubled as a boxer, was drafted in. There was palpable relief in the Sports Network office that the show was still on and that ABC would remain on board, with Sky also screening the bout in its normal sports schedule – the pay-per-view failure of the Hardy fight having taught them a lesson. Cabrera had a respectable record of twenty-four wins (twenty inside the distance, seventeen on clean knockouts) and two losses (one a disqualification when he was well ahead), but he had never beaten anyone of note and, most ominously, was dropped and well behind on points when losing to Eduardo Barrios on a seventh-round technical decision, having been unable to cope with the Colombian champion's southpaw style. In the two months since, the twenty-two-year-old visitor had managed another win, and gave the impression of confidence: 'I am not frightened. I can hit as hard as Hamed and I'm as strong as he is. I believe I will knock him out in six rounds.' But there was nothing in his resumé to suggest anything approaching serious opposition, let alone success.

Everyone knew what was going to happen and therefore, in contrast to his previous London engagement, against Tom

Johnson, the occasion failed to attract sufficient punters to come close to filling the venue, with over a quarter of the seats empty. The brown-haired, 5ft 6in-pink-skinned Cabrera looked more like an insurance salesman in drag than a professional boxer as he was booed in to the sound of 'Don't Cry for me Argentina'. Naseem, who had struggled to make the weight, once again showing a softness around the gills that spoke of a less than fulsome commitment to preparations, arrived ten minutes later amid smoke, fire and giant sparklers. Cabrera danced to the champion's music, the garage club anthem 'Free', receiving a further deluge of boos. Once he had completed his rope leap, Naseem brushed past his man menacingly and then did a little crotch-wiggle, before patting his protector and grinning.

He missed with his opening swing but three seconds later drove a hard left into Cabrera's face. The Argentinian looked tense and moved around jerkily, his guard high, and when he attempted a right cross it missed, allowing Naseem time to counter with a sickening right uppercut which jolted his opponent's head back, causing his legs to wobble. Hamed then switched to orthodox and back to southpaw, taking his time, missing now and then, but looking like he could end the fight any moment he chose. His next casual assault came through a pair of big southpaw lefts. Cabrera fired again, but his left hook was way off the mark. Shortly before the bell, Hamed landed again with his left cross, which sent Cabrera staggering backwards. In the second, as ever Hamed's chosen round, he got down to business. Each punch was full of serious intent. Right jabs, left crosses, hooks and lead uppercuts crunched home. Within seconds Cabrera was cut over his left eye, his face was blotchy and his nose seemed to have been spread wider than before. After each onslaught, Naseem would stand back to admire his handiwork, before moving in with another vicious combination. Somehow, the Argentinian remained erect, but the physical abuse he was absorbing was becoming ugly. Hamed's final punches were two huge lefts and a right brought up from the champion's waistband. Cabrera wobbled and referee Lou Moret stepped in, examined him for a moment, and then waved it off at the two minutes seventeen seconds mark.

'Now the Americans will know the best featherweight in the world is a British Arab from Sheffield,' Naseem announced, but as the ABC network commentator Alex Wallau put it: 'Hamed can't be considered great until he beats someone great.' Later Naseem raised the pressure on his promoter to get him a US date. 'I can't wait to go over to America to show them my ability, my style and sell out a few venues. I'd love to sell out the MGM Grand and to box at Madison Square Garden.'

ABC's Bob Yalen claimed that eight million Americans watched this fight (while Sky's audited figures revealed an 831,000 viewership in Britain), but Hamed's performance had proved nothing and afterwards the press were pushing Warren for evidence of some more inspirational matchmaking. Naseem seemed to have been stung by these comments, reminding him of his own concerns, and his mood became ugly. A reporter from the London *Evening Standard*, no doubt wary of having his head chewed off, asked a suitably fawning question: 'Are you the best fighter, pound for pound, in the world?' Naseem responded: 'What kind of question is that? I *know* it! I *know* it. I make them take the pain.' Then, looking at the none too intrepid reporter, he saw something that set him off and the bully emerged in its undisguised glory: 'I'd like to see you get in the ring with me. I'd give you a right beating. I'd *like* to give you a right beating, a right beating,' and he looked up at the rest of us and added, 'all of you.' Frank Warren, who was also having a go at the 'negative', 'missing the point' press, tried to change the subject, but Naseem wasn't finished. 'Let me go, Frank. Let me give him a beating.' While Hamed always liked having a go at journalists who failed to appreciate his majesty, this time his tone encapsulated all the pent-up resentment against the media, the intrusive public, the stalled progress of his career, his break-up with Eleasha, his car crash and his still unrealized American dream. It was bitter, nasty, petulant, thin-skinned and as much part of the *real* Naseem as the fighter who palpably enjoyed delivering messages of pain to other, lesser men, or for that matter as the son who lavished expensive gifts on his parents, the boy racer who gave up time for charity and the lover who missed his woman terribly.

8

THE GARDEN PARTY

Naseem's bitter tone after the Cabrera fight impressed on Frank
Warren the need to act quickly in securing something meatier for
his impatient young meal-ticket. Naseem wanted to fight the
Americans, in America, and in New York if possible. But Warren
was facing even starker pressures from a different angle – his
partner Don King, who was making his move to assume greater
control over the British fighter's destiny and purse strings.

The immediate shape came in the form of the IBF mandatory
contender, Hector Lizarraga. This much-improved thirty-year-
old Californian was a good, hard-hitting veteran who had not
been beaten in over five years and seventeen fights (after an early
career record which included eight losses and five draws), but his
status as the IBF's number one contender owed far more to his
promotional contract with King than his own achievements.
Under King's influence, the IBF were insisting that unless Hamed
fought him by 8 August, they would strip him of his title. Warren
protested long and hard that Lizarraga was not worthy and the
fight wouldn't sell. 'It is a terrible match. I, as a promoter, do not
feel comfortable in selling it, yet I am being forced into it. For the
good of boxing we are asking all the organizations to let us try to
unify the titles. Let's get all the politics and all the rubbish out of
the way and see who is the best featherweight in the world,' he
protested. In truth, Lizarraga was far more worthy than Said
Lawal, Remigio Molina, Billy Hardy or Juan Cabrera. Even

Warren later admitted he was 'better than his record suggested'. The real pickle was of a different nature: money, power and promotional rivalry. If Hamed went ahead with the mandatory, Lizarraga's management, at King's prompting, would refuse Warren's offers and the IBF would review purse bids, which, in all likelihood, King would win. This would mean Warren's partner and would-be rival for Hamed's hand would be in a position to launch Naseem's American debut on his own terms. He would also be in a position to whisper sweet nothings into Hamed's ear in a bid to exploit his dissatisfaction with the standard of recent opponents.

The alternative was to take the opposite approach to the stated goal of unifying the titles and ditch the IBF belt. The problem was that Naseem was extremely unhappy with this course. He was set on unification and had a great deal more respect for the belts than they deserved. He also knew that the IBF title had more kudos than the WBO version. In the end, Warren had to inform him that there was no alternative – that this was not a situation of his own making, that King and the IBF were not playing straight, and that he would make it worthwhile and not just in the long term, but very soon. Hamed was forced to accept this, albeit with considerable reluctance and a good deal of resentment, and on 28 August it was announced he had vacated the IBF title (which was won by Lizarraga, who stopped Welcome Ncita in ten rounds before losing it to Hamed's former victim Manuel Medina – a result which had a satisfactory symmetry for Naseem). Warren later acknowledged the decision to vacate had its drawbacks. 'In some ways it was not a good idea to give up the IBF title, but in other ways it was a good decision. King was telling us what to do.'

In any event, their relationship had been in decline, ever since the 1995 Bruno-McCall fight when they fell out over monies owed. For over two years King had been trying to make moves on Naseem, and Warren had been resolutely resisting, but now his hand had been forced and he had to move quickly and decisively. While a break-up would have huge legal costs and would cut Warren off from access to King's empire and to Showtime, the time seemed right. For one thing, King's stock had been declining for some time, although he remained extremely powerful. He was facing a debilitating retrial for insurance fraud (which he subsequently won); he had lost ground in the heavyweight division, partly as a result of the US courts imposing the rule of law on the international control bodies, partly through Lennox Lewis's success and particularly through Mike Tyson's demise (and subsequent defection), and he had lost ground to other promoters, including a resurgent Bob Arum and the recovering Duva dynasty. Another dimension was the prospect that freedom from King offered to Warren in terms of access to HBO, a larger and more powerful cable network than Showtime. Most importantly, Warren was now big enough to survive on his own and perhaps to make it as one of the world's top four or five boxing promoters. This meant he had to bite the hand that had once fed him and had since been feeding off him. What was clear was that it meant war with King and Warren proceeded to put the pieces into place.

The putative catalyst was Warren's decision to end his relationship with Showtime and deliver Hamed to HBO, which meant he would have access to the most marketable little men in America. For several months HBO had been trying to entice Hamed and Warren and finally, in August 1997, the promoter began exploratory talks, then serious negotiations, with HBO vice-president Lou DiBella, who heads their boxing programme, with the idea of Naseem making his HBO debut at Madison Square Garden on 19 December. Kevin Kelley was earmarked as the opponent and negotiations were launched with Cedric Kushner, promoter of the Flushing star.

In the meantime, while this deal was being put together, Warren had to find a 'livewire' opponent for Naseem for what was being billed as 'the biggest British show in history', later to be dubbed 'The Full Monty', at Sheffield on 11 October – eventually featuring Chris Eubank versus Joe Calzaghe for the vacant WBO super-middleweight title. Once again this was to be a pay-per-view show but there was a collective groan in the sport when it was announced that the man to face Naseem would be the Colombian Victor Llerena, who had been soundly thrashed by Vuyani Bungu for the IBF super-bantamweight title in 1995. A week later, there was a change of plan – Llerena was paid off and a new and far more formidable opponent was announced, Jose Badillo. All Hamed had to do to unlock his and Warren's American dreams was to triumph over a twenty-seven-year-old Puerto Rican southpaw who had once knocked out the top-rated Mexican bantamweight Adan Vargas in front of a 130,000 crowd in Mexico City. Badillo's only setback had come in losing a disputed decision to Tom Johnson in 1995. He dropped Johnson twice and had him on the verge of a knockout defeat in the eleventh round before losing a majority verdict, and had since won three in a row to take his record to twenty wins (fifteen stoppages) and one loss. The Johnson fight showed he had trouble with boxers who moved a lot and could be out-boxed, but he was strong, a big puncher with a good chin and sound all-round skills.

But there were other problems for the champion. Naseem and Ingle were in the midst of a bitter dispute which threatened the survival of the relationship. One dimension was financial, with Naseem and his brother, Riath, offering him £30,000 out of the boxer's £750,000 purse. But there were other issues too. While Ingle was still fiercely loyal in public, privately he complained that Hamed was treating him, his stablemates and his public, with contempt, that he would only tolerate yes-men around him, that he was impervious to criticism and lacked respect for anyone outside his immediate family, and that, once again, his commitment to training had dissipated. He felt Hamed's negative influence was affecting the atmosphere in the gym and that he was setting a bad example to the other boxers. He could understand why Naseem no longer treated him as a father figure, but after 16 years together he resented being treated as no better than the hired help. As he put it: 'For those past three or four years my life had been terrible because of all the trouble he was giving me. They made me financially secure, but he put me through hell and I just thought it wasn't worth it.' On September 2 1997, shortly after the press conference to announce his next fight (to which Hamed arrived almost an hour late), Ingle informed Naseem that he'd had enough, and was resigning as his trainer. Later that day Warren and Riath joined them at a Sheffield restaurant where they discussed Ingle's problems. They eventually agreed to test the waters by staying together for at least the Badillo fight. Brendan would get £45,000; Naseem would re-commit himself to training and they would take it from there.

After this, Naseem found the inspiration he needed in the prospect of his American debut against Kelley and therefore trained harder for the Badillo fight than he had for Hardy or Cabrera. After watching a video of the Puerto Rican in action, he realized he was up against something serious and, particularly over the last two weeks, threw himself into his gymwork with something approaching the absolutist focus of old. 'In my eyes, this kid has never lost a fight,' Hamed said. 'I watched the Tom Johnson fight and I didn't think Badillo lost it.' Llerena he knew he could blow away with contemptible ease; Badillo he knew would take a bit more work, even though he predicted a third-round knockout. By fight time, his body was firmer and his mind more focused than it had been for a long time. The night before the fight, Naseem, as usual, stayed up watching a football game and a movie and listening to music in his hotel, only switching the lights off after the sun rose. He eventually had to be woken to go to the arena and still seemed tetchy when gloving up. In fact the tensions in the camp were still apparent in the final moments before the fight.

Steve Holdsworth, a former professional boxer who became a boxing journalist and the Eurosport TV commentator, and who has known Naseem since the boxer was ten, recalls Hamed's mood before the fight. 'I was in the changing room, interviewing Ryan Rhodes after he'd knocked out Yuri Episantsev and before Hamed's fight with Badillo, when Naz stormed up, pulled out a TV cable and screamed, "Everybody fuck off. *I'm* the fucking star here, so the rest of you can fuck off." I couldn't believe the language he was using given his religious protestations, and I didn't understand his motivation, but I went to one side and he came over and threw a karate kick at me which stopped just short of my nose, and then said, "Hi, Steve, my mate." But by then I was absolutely livid. I don't like the way he treats people.'

But once Hamed's show got moving, his mood improved. Badillo, who had been given the traditional British booing treatment, was kept waiting for several minutes until there was a fireworks explosion at the back of the hall, beginning the neon show which, eventually, led to Naseem's entrance. A 13,000 capacity crowd rose to its feet and chanted his name, and given the criticism he had received in his home town over the previous year, he seemed touched by their response. Badillo danced to Hamed's music and had a more confident look in his eyes than most recent opponents. Like Naseem he had a sturdy pair of legs, but he was the taller man by two inches. He had been in training for another fight when the call-up came twelve days earlier, and from his well-defined musculature he looked in excellent shape. He had insisted on bringing one of his own sparring partners from California and had also made use of several Hamed tapes to try to find a way of getting through his new opponent.

Before the fight, Brendan had impressed upon Naseem the necessity for more caution than usual. His early priorities included avoiding Badillo's bombs and using his jab to keep him off balance and in the early rounds landing single punches from confusing angles, rather than combinations. Naseem started by slamming home his heavy jabs while keeping a safe distance. His challenger, however, knew what he was doing, moving fluidly and snapping out his punches. What he lacked was the speed to get to Hamed frequently or to catch him by surprise.

From the first bell Naseem elected to box behind his jab, frequently making Badillo miss before countering and sliding out of range. Several right-hand leads and a thumping jab found their mark within the first minute, but Badillo managed to catch Naseem with a decent, glancing left hook which prompted the champion to move into reverse. By the end of the round, the Puerto Rican's nose was bleeding and his face was starting to show the signs of the heavy punches it was absorbing. Hamed was regularly beating his opponent to the punch and easily avoiding the counters. In the second, Badillo attempted a wide, wild left hook but Hamed easily evaded it and then pointed to his chin to suggest to his challenger where to aim in future. Late in the round Naseem landed a heavy right and it was looking like another early night.

In the third (the predicted victory round) the visitor had a rare moment of success, landing a heavy left cross as the champion came forward. Naseem's response was to smile in appreciation and then hurt his man with a quick left hook. As the round ended he was landing at will, ending with a right hook and a left upper-cut. Badillo was proceeding with extreme caution because his offensive efforts had had painful results. He was therefore doing most of his boxing off the back foot, but even there he could not hope to win the battle of the jabbers. There was a measure of desperation in his work and his attempts at counter punching were becoming wild and purposeless. Naseem was still biding his time, breaking Badillo down with hard, single punches that were reaching his opponent's face with sickening regularity. Late in the fourth, Hamed landed his first combination, a left-right which drove his opponent towards the ropes. Early in the fifth round he mixed a vicious attack with some wrestling, throwing Badillo to the canvas. He then added a spot of 'clowning'. He began to mock Badillo mercilessly, mimicking his opponent's dismal but brave exertions, smirking at selected ringsiders, raising his arms, dancing, and then conducting the 13,000 to applaud his antics. Later he charged at Badillo with his right cocked but found himself getting tangled on the ropes.

In his corner Brendan tried lecturing Naseem on his tactics, but the champion rose from his stool, shouting abusively at his trainer that he would do what suited him. Badillo plugged on defiantly, his face badly marked up, with nicks under both eyes and a cut to his left eyelid. Now and then he would have a hopeful moment. In the sixth it was a pair of solid left hooks and a right, but his punches had little effect on Naseem, beyond prompting a slight defensive adjustment which saw him raising his guard for a while. As the round ended, Hamed landed a heavy right which found its way through Badillo's tight guard. It had become apparent that the fight was almost over. Badillo landed one final right in the seventh, but from then on Naseem broke him up, wobbling him with heavy, accurate, well-timed punches. Finally Badillo was caught in his own corner, with nothing left to offer, and it was a source of considerable relief when his cornermen jumped in to rescue him at the one minute thirty-seven second mark. Hamed then went over to congratulate the man he had humiliated. The scorecards justifiably had him winning every one of the six completed rounds, two of the judges scoring it by 60–54 and the third 60–53. The punch statistics showed Badillo had landed a total of twenty-seven punches – an average of fewer than four a round.

After telling the people of Sheffield how much he loved them, Hamed apologized for failing to finish things in the third. He then engaged in some impromptu banter with Kevin Kelley, who was at ringside. 'Kevin Kelley has seen the skill and the speed of the Prince, oh gosh!' he said, before turning to his next opponent: 'I am going to knock you spark out. I can't wait.' Kelley, older, wiser and more mature, told his rival to calm down and then condescended to join in the banter. Some time later, however, Kelley would remark on how exasperated he was after this experience. 'He talks brash and doesn't impress me. I was sick to my stomach and it is hard to irritate me.' After the bout, Naseem offered a more considered opinion of his performance: 'Badillo is a very, very good, strong, clever fighter and yet he got a pasting. He was confident and he thought he was going to win and he took my shots, but he took a beating and got beaten by a better man. Maybe he was even better than Kevin Kelley, but I can beat any featherweight in the world.' Asked about the fact that once again he was hit more often than in his early days, Naseem replied indignantly: 'If I didn't want to get hit, I wouldn't have got hit. I could have boxed him, but you've got to take risks.'

Ingle was also pleased, describing it as Naseem's must complete performance to date. There was some truth in this view, in that Hamed had shown that the sound boxing skills of the past had not deserted him. His jab was heavier than ever and faultlessly accurate. He did not go wild, picked his punches carefully, and gradually broke down the resistance of one of the better featherweights in the world. In these areas it was certainly a more polished performance than he had delivered against Tom Johnson. Yet there was still a sense that some of the positive elements of his early days were missing. He ignored the body and lacked the evasive timing that had characterized his rise. Nevertheless, it revealed beyond reasonable doubt that when he put his mind to it, Naseem was able to resist the temptation to go for broke, that he had not forgotten the fundamentals and that he was still capable of sustained spells of beautiful boxing as well as demolition punching.

After a ten-day break in Sheffield, Naseem departed for the United States to promote the Kelley fight. However, at Heathrow airport he was involved in another of the off-the-ball incidents which had dogged his career, although on this occasion he had a lesser share of the blame. Once again the spat concerned Chris Eubank, the boxer Hamed had made a regular point of insulting for several years. This time the altercation became physical, with Eubank instigating the rough stuff but coming off worse in the end. Although the conflict had a five-year history, this particular round began in the run-up to the Badillo fight when Hamed seemed to resent the joint top billing and primary press attention given to Eubank's second coming against Joe Calzaghe. Before they left for the arena, however, Naseem made an attempt to patch things up, now that they were both fighting under the same promotional banner. He knocked on Eubank's hotel room door with the apparent intention of wishing him well, but was rudely rebuffed. 'He offered to make peace with me but I told him, "Go away – you two-faced little git," and shut the door in his face. He was always asking my advice when he was a kid and now he never stops slandering me,' said Eubank.

This set the tone for the airport showdown eleven days later, when both boxers crossed each other's paths near the Virgin counter (Eubank had gone there to discuss business with Warren). Heathrow workers said it started when well-wishers were going up to Eubank and asking for his autograph. As one put it: 'Naseem wasn't getting any attention and didn't like it, so he said to Eubank in a loud, goading voice, "You haven't got any belts like me." Then he got his belts out and waved them in front of Eubank.' At that point Eubank lost his rag and went for Hamed, later throwing his belts across the concourse and raising his hand to hit Naseem, while Hamed threw a right hook which, according to most accounts, landed flush on Eubank's lip, after which Frank Warren and others leapt in and held them apart. But even this probable version is open to dispute.

Immediately after the incident, Eubank denied Hamed's punch landed or that he had intended to hit Naseem, but insisted that his flash of bad temper had been provoked by Naseem's actions: 'He was taunting me and goading me and I'm afraid he got my goat. Unfortunately, I stooped to his level. I grabbed the belts and threw them to the floor. I realize now that I shouldn't have done it. The next thing I know he's taking a swing at me, but he missed and I didn't sustain any injury. I went as if to slap him with my open hand. I would never hit him because he's so much smaller than me. Then people dived between us. It was all very un-gentlemanly. There has been bad blood between us in the past, but professional fighters shouldn't act like that.' However, when discussing it on a television chat show five days later, he suggested his response was justified: 'When I am talking to children, I always say, "When you are faced with a bully, the thing to do is to punch him in the eye. You may pay a price, but even if he punches you back, he won't do it again." He said derogatory, terrible things to me which I don't want to repeat, and then said do I want to see his belt, and I mean, I've been there, done that, drunk that beer, so to speak, and I actually helped him and steered him in his career.' Again he claimed he didn't try to hit Hamed, implying that if had taken a serious swipe he would have broken the little man in two, but still insisted it was necessary to draw a line in the sand against a bully boy, no matter how diminutive: 'You have to stand up to them,' he said.

Hamed had a different interpretation of events, and branded Eubank a 'liar and a bully' and 'a bum, a fraud and a loser and just not on my level'. He denied he had goaded Eubank and said he had merely asked Chris whether he liked his belts, before moving on. 'Eubank moved round behind me and he obviously thought he was on my blind side, but out of the corner of my eye I saw him raise his hand and go to slap me across the face,' he said. 'The whole world knows I have the quickest reactions in boxing – I pulled back in the nick of time and the blow landed high on my chest. My natural instinct was to counter-punch. I didn't stop to think, and let go with a right hand and hit Eubank in his mouth, cutting his lip.' He said Eubank then grabbed his belts and threw them before Warren intervened. 'I was livid and in the mood to give him a real pasting,' Hamed said. 'I wanted so badly to smash his face in. He may be seven inches taller and fifty pounds heavier, but if I could have got to him I promise you I would have knocked him out.' He claimed Eubank looked shaken and wouldn't dare to try such a stunt again: 'As big as he is, I would love to fight him in the ring. Don't forget I spar regularly with heavyweights in the gym, so Eubank doesn't scare me.' He added that he felt he had responded appropriately under the circumstances: 'If I am attacked, I feel it is my right to defend myself and I don't care who it is or where.' Incidentally, Warren's version of events bore close resemblance to that of his premier boxer: 'Naz didn't throw the first punch. The first punch was thrown by Chris Eubank ... Naz showed Chris his world title belts and Eubank threw a punch and caught Naz on the shoulder. Naz retaliated and punched Eubank on the mouth.' He added that his own intervention had prevented Hamed from getting stuck in: 'I'm glad I was there. Naz had that look in his eye and I'm sure he would have laid into him if I hadn't pulled him away.'

While Hamed's guilt in this instance was in doubt, once again it led to a spate of negative publicity, with versions of the incident being repeated over the next few weeks in the national and local press and on television. The *Sun*, for example, ran two double page spreads on it, as well as an editorial comment from its boxing writer Colin Hart headed, 'Prince turning into Naz-ty bit of work', reminding him that professional boxers should not throw punches outside the ring, no matter how much they are provoked. The British Boxing Board warned both boxers that 'if there is a repetition of behaviour of this type, it would have no alternative but to take disciplinary action,' which, despite his own dislike of Eubank, Brendan Ingle said was a 'fair enough judgement'.

While this was happening, Warren was engaged in some of the most difficult, complex and challenging business and legal machinations of his thirty-year career. Shortly after the Badillo fight, the HBO contract was finalized. Lou DiBella admitted the months of talks were sometimes tough going for his company: 'We've had easier to deals to do. That's nothing to do with coming off their deal with Showtime, and Don King was irrelevant to the process, too. It was difficult because we had never done any business with Frank Warren and he had never done any business with us.' Eventually, Naseem was signed up for a six-fight, three-year deal that would see him earning a minimum of $12 million if he kept on winning. The day before the Badillo fight, Warren acknowledged the implications for his relations with King: 'Don and I have not had any arguments but Naz's career has not moved as fast as it should have done. Showtime has not been able to show his fights because of their commitment to Don's shows, so Naz has not been getting the exposure he deserves. Don King has been the greatest promoter of all time, but he is sixty-seven and I am forty-five and I refuse to be in anybody's shadow. It's very important that I move forward ... Showtime will not be very happy, but I am in the Naseem Hamed business and go where the money is. Boxing politics have prevented me making the unification matches I wanted. Now it's time to go for the big names.' He later claimed the arrangement with King regarding Showtime had been far from satisfactory: 'Naz was only shown on Showtime television once this year, when he fought Johnson. Showtime wanted to screen his fights but King was unable to provide the dates and so I have had to deal with other TV channels independently.' Showtime's Jay Larkin admitted he was 'very disappointed' about Hamed's defection.

Soon after the Badillo fight King started legal proceedings against Warren, and also launched a verbal offensive against his former partner, saying he was deeply hurt by Warren's action: 'I love Frank. I am just hurt and disappointed that he chose this road. The contract is secondary; what hurts is the disregard for a friend. Who would I have given my business to if something happened to me? Frank Warren.' For a while he continued with this tack – of the wronged lover forced to protect his rights in a messy divorce action. For example, he said he had helped Warren 'when he was on his deathbed', and that he 'brought Frank back from destitution and ill repute to high esteem and stature in the world of boxing.' But he said, with an air of great reluctance, 'Being a businessman, I must protect my interests.' What this meant was protecting his share of Hamed's largesse: 'I have 50 per cent promotional rights to Hamed all over the world. I was supposed to do all Naz's business in the United States.'

King went on to say that Naseem had actually asked him to promote his fights, a claim which prompted an angry response from the boxer who had once so admired the American promoter: 'I am very annoyed by King's claims that I approached him ... I would never agree to be promoted by King, because I don't trust him. I knew that Frank had some kind of relationship with King, but I was unconcerned, providing that King was not involved in my career in any way.' Warren, meanwhile, rejected King's backstabbing allegations. 'I have not stabbed anyone. I must be the only promoter who ever has sung Don King's praises. We had a business agreement that was good for us both, but he had ceased to deliver.' He angrily refuted the idea that King had been responsible for his rehabilitation: 'Absolute bullshit. He suggests my arse was hanging out of my trousers when we met. People forget I had fifteen years with ITV.' He said the reason for the split was King's failure to keep to his side of the deal: 'It's like a bitter divorce and it ended because of his non-action. It's a shame. I needed him for US TV but he didn't deliver.' With Warren having entered the verbal fray, King abandoned the high ground and launched a perpetual verbal tirade against his former partner, using every public forum he could find to have a go at him while employing a team of private detectives to trail his former partner and launching the ground for a concerted legal campaign to use the British courts to stop Warren. Warren soon began to reply in kind. 'My future is in the United States,' he said shortly before the Kelley fight. 'And one of the main reasons is that I am going to kick Don King's arse.' He seemed to be energized and inspired by this new battle for supremacy over a former friend. 'I'm not ruthless, I'm just determined,' he said. 'When things are easy, I don't get a buzz out of them. When things are going wrong, that's when the adrenaline goes. I thrive on what's happening with

King. It is giving me an urge to succeed, to make sure he does not knock me out of business.'

But that was precisely what his new rival had in mind. King began a series of legal sorties, the first being the much-ballyhooed threat to use an injunction to prevent the Kelley fight from taking place. He lost that one before it got to court but soon initiated another legal suit, one reaching to the heart of their partnership. He claimed that in February 1997 he had given Warren $1 million in exchanging for signing a three-year extension to their 1994 partnership contract and that he was the co-promoter of all Warren's boxers, including Hamed and others in his European stable. He also claimed that Warren's lucrative contract with Sky could not have been brokered without his ability to deliver Mike Tyson fights. These charges were rejected by Warren, who said King had benefited enormously from the Sky deal he had negotiated and that King's loss of Sky revenues would cost him $45 million over the next three years. More significantly, he claimed King had fraudulently inserted the three-year extension clause into their contract, a charge which King denied. 'I don't like what he has done and I am going to nail him down and kick him out of the business. I intend to be a big thorn in his side,' Warren snarled. 'He's finished – completely. There is no way back for Don King. How could I ever do business again with a man who forges contracts?'

While his promoter was engaged in finalizing the HBO deal and in fending off his former partner, Naseem was in the United States with his two older brothers, together with Warren, Ingle, Ryan Rhodes and Joe Calzaghe. In New York he put in several press conferences and interviews and various other media events together with Kelley to drum up interest in the fight. One of the events saw him posturing on top of a double-decker bus, which prompted sustained heckling from New Yorkers. He then flew to Los Angeles for the WBO convention and to Florida. In addition to publicizing the event and doing some impromptu house-hunting, he also spent a day with Michael Jackson at his Never Neverland ranch-cum-amusement park in Santa Barbara. This extremely odd couple seemed to hit it off surprisingly well, with Hamed impressed by Jackson's music, ostentatious wealth and celebrity status, and Jackson by the boyish boxer's moves and ebullient personality. They were first introduced after a Jackson concert in the summer of 1997 and occasionally spoke on the phone after that, leading to the day on the ranch. Shortly before the Kelley fight, when Naseem was training in New York, Jackson dropped in on one of his sessions at the Blue Bell gym, leading to a renewed bout of mutual admiration. But the US trip also prompted yet another Ingle-Hamed breakup. This time the catalyst was a quarrel in a limousine in Los Angeles, where Naseem took the opportunity to taunt his trainer in front of Calzaghe, Rhodes and Warren. He started by reminding Ingle that he had never even managed to win an area title as a professional and went on to castigate him for not standing up to bullies. Ingle was incensed and snapped back, saying that unlike the mollycoddled Naseem, he had risen the hard way. 'Eventually Frank intervened and told us to shut-up, and that we were going on like a warring married couple, and I suppose he was right,' said Ingle. But at the time Brendan felt hurt and humiliated and on the flight home he decided that this was it – his role as Naseem Hamed's trainer was over.

Hamed returned to Britain on 4 November, but the next day was off to the Netherlands to present one of the MTV music awards. The twenty-five-day British leg of his preparations for the Kelley fight began on 10 November, four weeks after the Badillo fight and five and a half weeks before his Garden date. But once his training session was over, Brendan had an un-welcome surprise for Naseem, informing him that he no longer wanted to work with. 'I said he was welcome to use the gym if he wanted, and that I would not stand in the way of him coming to an agreement to get John and Dominic to help him, but that I wanted out.' Later that day Naseem's father, Sal, came to plead with Ingle to continue as trainer, but for almost two weeks Brendan stuck to his guns, doing no more than observing while John and Dominic took Naseem through his paces, though Hamed would later admit the negative atmosphere got to him. 'It was terrible. It was like training at a funeral,' he said. Eventually, on November 23, Naseem took the initiative and asked for a meeting with Brendan at the gym, together with Riath and Sal. Brendan agreed on the condition that Riath didn't come. For over two hours Naseem, Sal and Brendan discussed their dispute. Naseem apologised for the incident in the limousine and they settled on a 10 per cent trainer's fee for the Kelley fight and agreed that Riath, who had become the bogeyman of the family in Ingle's eyes, should stay out of the gym. With this deal they were once again back in business. By then Naseem appeared to be reaching his peak, at least at the physical level. One of his main Sheffield sparring partners was Junior Witter, an unbeaten light-welterweight who, soon after, outpointed the world rated Jan Bergman. During their first two weeks together, Naseem had trouble reaching the extremely slippery Witter, but prevailed after that. 'Junior's probably the most elusive guy in the gym but still, I was surprised how well he coped,' said John Ingle. 'They sparred quite a bit but until their last few sessions together, Naz was finding difficulty catching Junior and neither of them was really dominating. But eventually Naz worked him out and then began getting stuck in and really hurting him, and then we knew he was going to be okay.'

Witter remembers these sessions with vicarious trepidation. 'I'd say I can hold my own with Naz if I'm really focused. He has a lot of unusual angles and he really does hit with a lot of power. Until I sparred with him I didn't realize just how much power he had. Even shots that don't look hard are actually very hard. The other thing is that it's psychological warfare in there with him. Usually I get on with him but he had become moody because of all the stress he was under. He's fine when there is no stress, but often when people see him in public he's stressed, and when you're working with him in the gym, you sometimes have to deal with him in this mood. As soon as he sets foot into that ring, his arrogance comes on. He's cold – no warmth, no heart; but I suppose that's how you need to be. When you're sparring with him, you can't have a split second when you are not thinking of what you are doing, and I'm just glad I've never had to do head sparring with him, because, let me tell you, you don't want to be hit in the head by Naz. Just watch him knocking Johnny Nelson about and then you'll understand why. It would be the short cut to brain damage.' When Naseem left for New York, he appeared to be in superb shape. Trim and hard, his weight within three pounds of the limit, his timing and rhythm near perfection and punching with the kind of power that astonished even seasoned Hamed-watchers. 'I have already won before I turn up,' he said on the eve of his departure. 'It may even look like a mismatch, like two guys fighting in different weight divisions, but something disastrous will happen in the third round. Kelley's world will fall apart. It could happen sooner. There is no way defeat is on my card. I am prepared; I am ready and fit and will do the business.

He has been shooting his mouth off and deserves to be taken out – and in style. I don't think about negatives.'

Naseem knew he was up against the most talented opponent of his career. The thirty-year-old New York southpaw raked up thirty-six straight wins, including victories over former world champions Harold Warren and Troy Dorsey before beating Mexico's formidable Goyo Vargas for the WBC world title in December 1993. But after a couple of defences, he lost his crown in an eleventh-round upset against Alejandro Gonzalez and went into a fourteen-month unofficial retirement. He returned to action in 1995 and had been unbeaten since, lifting the inconsequential WBU title and making four defences, including one where he came from behind with a closed eye and on the verge of defeat to knock cold the highly rated Derrick Gainer. His record stood at forty-seven wins (thirty-two stoppages), one loss and a pair of draws in fifty fights. He had extremely quick hands and feet and was one of the sharpest combination punchers in the game. He possessed the reflexes and boxing brain to use his skills effectively, and on top of that had genuine concussive power in both fists, loads of courage and vast experience at the top level. He was also a natural featherweight, having fought at the weight for his entire career, with only a handful of time-filler ventures at superfeatherweight. He was three inches taller than Naseem, as well as being broader and more muscular. All in all, he was certainly a far tougher proposition than, say, the declining, southpaw-confused Tom Johnson or the light punching Manuel Medina. And to top this, he was fighting on his home turf while Hamed was having his first fight outside of Britain and Ireland. Kelley's major fault was a tendency to go for broke and take chances – the same kind of mistake Hamed occasionally was drawn to make. As a result Kelley had been dropped five times, though never counted out, suggesting that his chin was only so-so.

For over a year Kelley had been angling for this fight, although unlike most he seemed to have a coherent strategy about how to get it. He regaled every British journalist who crossed his path about how he would approach a fight with the Englishman. I first met him in Connecticut in late 1996 and found myself doing a lot of listening and very little talking on the subject of Naseem, which was just fine because there are few more entertaining practitioners in this business than the 'Flushing Flash'. 'What am I? What is it that I do?' he asked, before providing his own answer. 'I'm an entertainer, right? That's what the public wants from a boxer – they want to be entertained. We're all like that here. It's like, I got given this video recently which showed footage of people getting killed – executed, car crashes, close-ups of ripped-up murder victims, all sorts of stuff. So, sure, I don't approve of it, but did I watch it? Of course I did, and to be honest, I was a bit disappointed because they didn't go far enough. Then I passed it on to my family and they watched it. It's a bit like that with boxing. They want to see how far you'll go. The fights of mine that people want to see are the ones that went to the edge, like when Alejandro Gonzalez beat me or my knockout over Derrick Gainer. So that's what I want to give them, entertainment.' Despite his formidable record, Kelley had no illusions about where he stood in his sport: 'I'm satisfied with what I've achieved. I'm headed for the Hall of Fame. I'm not interested in titles anymore – it's the right fights, the right opponents, the right money I want. I've done fine financially. I've got a house in Long Island, two of my four kids go to private school and HBO still love me, but when it comes down to it I'm still a blue-collar fighter. Here in America, the public, the media, whoever, pick two or three fighters who are white-collar. Today it's Holyfield, Tyson, Oscar de la Hoya, maybe Roy Jones, though he's borderline. There's no room for any more. The rest of us are blue-collar.'

And this is where his admiration for Hamed came in: 'Now it's different if you have a whole country behind you. The whole of Britain is behind him because he's the only good boxer you've got. What Hamed's done is great. Everyone involved in boxing here wants to know about him. We all want to see him beaten, you see. And his act – the way he comes into the ring – he got that from Chris Eubank and people here love it, cause they want to see how far he'll go.' At which point I interjected: 'Sure, but the difference is that Hamed can fight.' 'But can he?' Kelley asked rhetorically, before changing gear into a jingoistic stream-of-consciousness monologue. 'You see, we don't know. Because all your boxers just fight each other and then they think they're world champions. But we don't respect anyone who hasn't come and fought the best Americans in America, because this is where the real fighters are. You say he can hold his own with Johnny Nelson. Who's he? Let me tell you when I was training for Derrick Gainer I sparred with heavyweights to increase my strength – it means nothing. You want to know about *real* sparring? Speak to me.' Having laid it all on the line, Kelley went into tactical retreat: 'Don't get me wrong, Hamed's not bad. I *like* the way he throws his punches. He leaps at you, stiffens his arm and throws his whole body into it, and it's like being hit in the face by a pole. I know, because I sometimes do that. Tyson used to do it with his uppercut; Roy Jones can do it, too. It wouldn't work against me, of course, because I know how to counter it.' And finally, he reached his sales point: 'Now if Warren offered me a fight with Hamed, sure, I'd take it like a shot – if the money was right.'

The money, of course, is never right. Even though he understood the business logic behind the way things worked, Kelley resented the fact that Hamed was officially earning almost three times as much as his own $600,000 purse (and actually rather more) and also disliked how Naseem was getting all the publicity, had attracted all the lucrative endorsement deals (while he had none), had won a multi-million deal with HBO and was attracting all the headlines and the television exposure in what was after all Kelley's home town. The bill also featured Kelley's friend and fellow New Yorker Junior Jones defending his WBO super-bantamweight title against the former champion Kennedy McKinney (with Jones pencilled in as Hamed's next opponent), yet neither of these locals was getting much of a look-in either, and when Jones and Kelley compared notes their irritation was complete.

As a result of this rising resentment, Kelley put his all into his two-month training regime at a small gym in Bayside, Queens, not far from his childhood home, and restricted himself to something less than the contractual minimum when it came to the final weeks of pre-fight publicity. He gave a convincing impression of serious confidence and did not appear to have been put off his stride by Naseem's pre-fight taunts. He often watched with a kind of detached amusement as his rival prattled away, but when he wanted to, Kelley was able to give as good as he got. For instance, three days before the fight he offered a few choice remarks about his opponent's state of mind: 'I believe he's scared to death, to be honest. Why does he have to brag about everything? I don't believe he's as good as he says he is. Being a champion, he should be showing respect to other people. All he tries to do is to get under your skin, but he doesn't get under mine. I think it's nervous energy. He's human, got two legs like me, two arms. Hamed hasn't been through the things I've been through. I've been to hell and back in boxing terms, been to Vietnam, so to speak. If he's waiting for me to fall down, he's wrong. When I hit him on the chin he had better not even think about getting up, not even try it.' He went on to emphasize Hamed's obnoxious qualities: 'Fighters like Arturo Gatti, Junior Jones and James Toney have all called me up to say they hate him. They believe Hamed's constant bragging and putting me down shows no respect and they desperately want me to teach him some.' With the television executives squirming visibly, he said: 'Everytime I land their pockets are going to feel it. I'm beating their money up.' Finally, he gave his message to Hamed: 'I'm going to send you back to England all fucked up.'

By this stage, the fighters' mutual inclination to insult had descended into the realm of the distasteful. Kelley, for instance, threw in a few off-beam remarks about Naseem's Arab ancestry, while Hamed treated his rival with similar disdain: 'After this fight, I'm gonna create a nice job for you putting my posters up. Make sure there are no creases on them. Make them look fine.' Kelley's wife Val offered an even classier response: 'After the fight, you can come to my house to clean the dogshit.' But an hour later they were chatting and joking away together, suggesting that unlike at several of Hamed's previous bouts, these moments of trash-talking had more to do with one-upmanship in front of the cameras than any deeply felt animosity.

The idea of conquering New York appealed to Hamed as much as it did to Warren. For several years Naseem had spoken of his urge to overwhelm the Americans, of how they would love him, take him to heart, enjoy his ways. When he arrived, he believed this adoring relationship with America was about to be consummated. 'I know the Americans will love me – I can fight, I can talk, I can entertain and I am a 100 per cent pure British-Arab winner.' He was particularly taken by the rich symbolism of Madison Square Garden, the site of some of the sport's finest moments (though less important of late because of its lack of a nearby gambling hall). Brendan Ingle, too, had long dreamed of taking Naseem to Madison Square Garden. In his home he has a picture of his late brother, Jimmy, gazing at the New York skyline, preparing to fight at the Garden as part of an amateur team. That was in 1939, when Jimmy was 18 and Brendan was still in the womb, and fifty-eight years later he had finally arrived at what he, like everyone else, still called 'the Mecca of boxing' – this time hired for $750,000 – and the crowd would be buying the tickets to watch his little boxer perform. 'Now we are here where legends like Louis and Ali fought,' he said.

But it was becoming apparent that the locals had not taken to Naseem in quite the same way as those other 'legends'. Kelley, who still professed to be fond of his rival, stressed this point: 'I could not find anyone who liked him, and if no-one likes you there is usually a reason for it.' One reason was that even before he crossed the ocean, Naseem was busy creating controversy with his widely reported claim to be 'a young Ali coming to town'. With Ali's flaws as a boxer and a man having long been forgotten in the haze of time and retrospective glory, the impertinence behind this comparison riled New Yorkers, including Kelley, but Naseem made no gestures towards retreat on this hallowed terrain: 'I am coming back a winner. I can box five different ways, including southpaw and orthodox. Muhammad Ali could only box orthodox. After I achieve what I want, people will be saying that. I am not going to lose to Kelley. It's not bragging. It's confidence.' The Ali theme was also pressed by most of those surrounding Naseem, including HBO boss Seth Abraham who described him as a 'combination of the Beatles and Muhammad Ali', prompting the New York *Post* to respond: 'So far, Hamed fights about as well as Ringo Starr and I doubt he sings as well as Ali.' Despite such put-downs, Naseem found it difficult to restrain himself in front of his new audience. He added Michael Jordan to the list of celebrities he was 'bigger' than, and had no qualms about announcing he was a finer featherweight than Willie Pep, or anyone else for that matter. 'I'm not bragging,' he bragged the day before the fight, 'but I feel like I'm invincible – like I just can't be beaten. My feet are staying firmly on the ground. I'm going to win everything and whoever is put in front of me will get knocked out. I don't think I'm the best pound-for-pound fighter in the world today, I know it.'

By this stage his backers had poured $2 million into creating an instant celebrity. As Lou DiBella put it: 'We are in the unusual situation in having an athlete who is world renowned but not very well known in New York.' As a result, they had to swamp New York with advertising. His face was plastered all over the city (and as far afield as Sunset Boulevard) on sixty-foot bill-boards and hoardings while local television and radio stations were saturated with advertising – he appeared in six chat shows in twelve days – and on Times Square and at the entrance to Lincoln Tower huge images of Hamed gazed imperiously down on the uncomprehending natives while the real thing looked out of the twentieth-floor window of his suite at the New York Palace Hotel in Madison Avenue. Warren, in fact, booked 200 rooms in four hotels, but most of Naseem's closest chums were within reach, ready for yet another shopping expedition. There also seemed to be an endless round of media appearances, press conferences, ringside chats with Michael Jackson, Daniel Day Lewis, Quentin Tarantino, Liam Neeson and scores of other celebrities. In addition to his frequent shopping, these interruptions made it more difficult to fine-tune Naseem's final fortnight of training at the Blue Velvet gym and the plush Pier 60 gym at Chelsea Piers complex in Manhattan. Afterwards, Naseem admitted this foreign environment had put him off his stride: 'I thought it would be no different from home, that I could just get into the ring and do the business, but it wasn't really like that. There were so many distractions, and not just all the shopping.' Aside from the still-simmering conflict with his trainer, he was also brooding over the discovery that his girlfriend, Eleasha, was pregnant with his child. And then he was further shaken up six days before the fight when he listened to a telephonic transmission of the Sheffield fight between his buddy, Ryan Rhodes and Otis Grant for the WBO middleweight title. Rhodes, whom he had always seen as a larger and only marginally less skilled version of himself, was soundly outpointed after a training spell which involved its own share of distractions, including what Ingle called 'women problems'. The outcome seemed to affect Naseem by making him more power-crazy in training. Immediately afterwards, for instant, he went all-out in a sparring session with the heavyweight Clifton Mitchell and got caught in the mouth for his troubles. However, John Ingle said this should not be overstated. 'I thought he was very well prepared. Sure, there were distractions, but he liked the Blue Velvet and in some ways it was quite a lot like ours – very relaxed, with lots of fighters around.'

Most of Hamed's New York training involved winding down and staying in tune. Invariably the gym would come to a halt when he climbed into the ring, and the other fighters, like former world middleweight, super-middleweight and light-heavyweight champion Iran Barkley, and former world light-welter and welterweight champion James 'Buddy' McGirt would stop to take a look at this little boxer with his unconventional moves and astonishing speed and power. Few went away unconvinced, although former world lightweight champion Carlos Ortiz professed confusion: 'You call that sparring? It looks more like dancing. I can't make the kid out at all.' His final training session, at the cosy, closeted Blue Velvet, began on a bitterly cold evening at 5pm on the Wednesday, fifty-two hours before fight time. After warming up, he worked the pads with John Ingle, who was wearing a T-shirt saying 'Spank the Yank'. While friends like Ryan Rhodes and Johnny Nelson watched, Brendan kept time and Naseem's youngest brother, Murad, controlled the music. The lithe little boxer, looking serious but relaxed, mouthed the words as he went through his punching routine. When that was done, he stretched, loosened up, admired himself in the mirror and shadow-boxed before going into a dance routine to the sound of his chum Michael Jackson singing 'The Girl's not Good Enough' and 'Don't Stop 'Til You Get Enough'. He ended with a vigorous skipping session. It was enough to stay sharp and sweat off the last ounces, but nothing too draining. He then drove back to the hotel to 'chill out' with his mates for his final twenty-two hours of abstinence before the weigh in at 4.30pm on the Thursday – twenty-nine hours before fight-time (which was enough to take Naseem back up to 130lb and Kelley a few pounds more, without any undue strain on their bodies.)

The Madison Square Garden weigh-in itself was anti-climatic by Naseem's standards. The day before, Kelley had been fuming about the idea of waiting for Hamed during his long ring entrance. 'This time Hamed is going to be in my house,' he had said. 'If they think I am going to stand there like an idiot waiting for him to put on his show, they are sadly mistaken. I say to hell with tradition. If he's going to make his usual ring entrance, I shall be sitting in my locker room until it is all over.' But by the time he reached the Garden for his appointment with the scales, he was resigned to the inevitable. Kelley in his Y-fronts made the featherweight limit by half a pound, to the cheers of his many supporters who chanted slogans like 'Kev, King of New York, King of da world'. Naseem in his Calvin Kleins was '126, on da nose!' as the MC put it. Once that was done, they did a spot of muscle flexing and preening. 'Show me what you got,' Naseem shouted, referring to his opponent's more sculptured biceps. Kelley pretended to pinch Naseem's to indicate their lack of substance. 'Show me your legs!' Hamed suggested, as an alternative, lifting up his tracksuit trouser leg. But before Kelley could consider whether to comply, Naseem stood on the tip of his toes to get to his opponent's height, raised his arms and screamed in Kelley's face, his eyes displaying provocative aggression. Kelley refused to budge and there was a bit of light barging before Warren intervened and Kevin's wife tried hitting Naseem, without connecting. He smiled, nodded at her, grabbed the microphone and announced his 'great respect to all of you for coming here and following me' before bidding them goodbye: 'Tomorrow night I'm gonna knock Kevin Kelley spark out. When I'm doing it, I want you to be singing, "We'll be singing, when we're winning; we'll be singing when we're winning." '

The prelim to the Hamed-Kelley fight was another major league contest, between Junior Jones and former IBF world champion Kennedy McKinney, with the winner set to fight Hamed in his next bout. While HBO was banking on a Jones victory, Naseem preferred the idea of meeting McKinney. Shortly before this contest Naseem disappeared for a few minutes and Ingle said: 'Where've you been,' before seeing the look in his eye. 'You've been to see Junior, haven't you?' Naseem nodded and smiled. 'I spoke to Junior and fucked his head in. He's gonna lose.' In a wild slugfest, Jones was knocked out in the fourth round. This upset was followed by a period of confusion surrounding Naseem's ring entrance, which seemed to detract from the WBO champion's performance rather than his challenger's. When Kelley arrived, the 11,954 people in attendance (who had paid $850,000 for the privilege) were all on their feet, waving flags, clapping and stamping their feet. For Naseem, however, things failed to work according to plan. They were treated to the usual mix of ear-splitting music, strobes and fog, but also to a giant screen behind which a silhouette of a dancing Hamed could be seen. But the screen failed to open, with the result that Hamed continued grinding his hips as the crowd grew restless. Kelley worked on the pads in the ring, then climbed the ring posts and called Hamed to 'Get in here now!' Later, however, he said he was unfazed by it: 'It didn't bother me, but I don't think they liked it in New York City. It was WWF stuff. I have seen his act five times, twice live, and when you've seen it once, you don't want to see it anymore.' Hamed, meanwhile, was becoming increasingly irritated, which affected his concentration. He eventually burst through the screen on his own initiative, but his entrance took a total of almost twelve minutes, three minutes longer than HBO had planned for, at least seven minutes longer than necessary – and time enough for a brawl to start in one section of the crowd. 'There were real problems with the entrance,' said John Ingle. 'We were used to the way Sky handled it. They always had a continuity girl on hand, but with HBO it was confusing. They'd said they had the tissue-paper screen, but then no-one told Naz when to go and it didn't open like it was supposed to, so eventually Naz went through on his own initiative. And then the confetti was only supposed to drop down after he was well away from the screen but it fell too early, all over him, and we had to brush it off, and then we found the ropes were much higher than normal. So, yeah, he was a bit unsettled.' Naseem in fact, had not concentrated when the HBO officials gave him entrance instructions, and as there was no dress rehearsal, he fluffed it. He later acknowledged he allowed himself to become distracted. 'Surprisingly, I didn't feel as confident in the Garden as I thought I would have been. I had that trouble with my entrance and there were so many people in the ring and so much going on that I just wanted to get in there and get it over with. I would have been happier in Sheffield or London.'

When Naseem finally made it to the ring, the two boxers engaged in a prolonged spot of the usual eyeballing during Michael Buffer's introduction, although they both had smiles on their faces. 'We were playing,' Kelley later explained. 'There was no possibility of us throwing a punch at one another before the fight began. Naz was trying to stare me down and intimidate me, find a weak spot mentally. He wanted to show me how confident and relaxed he was, but it wasn't working. This is America, Jack. I had fifty fights against the toughest, meanest guys, so I was very relaxed; very comfortable.' With the crowd shouting 'Kelley! Kelley! Kelley!', referee Benji Estevez completed his instructions while the two little men stared again, but once more Kelley seemed more relaxed than most of Hamed's opponents while Naseem lacked his usual predator's sneer. 'I pushed him off. I was just joking with him. I was not playing his game, I was encouraging it. I was doing things to him that had never been done before. To me, this was fun. We were having a good time,' said the American. As they eyeballed each other Naseem whispered to Kelley, 'Let's see who's got the best chin ... let's have a war.' Kelley smiled and replied, 'It's a deal.'

At the bell, Kelley moved to ring centre while Hamed made his familiar, but still audacious start, a leaping right uppercut-cum-hook of the kind that ended the challenge of Said Lawal. Kelley was ready for such treatment and evaded it, replying with two right jabs which Naseem slipped, giving his statutory butt-wiggle just to show what a clever little thing he was. Before the fight, Brendan and Naseem debated tactics, with the boxer wanting to go all out and the trainer advising caution. They eventually agreed he could put everything into his opening attack, but if that failed, he would box his way to victory behind his southpaw right jab, and so what followed after that first miss was a brief right-jabbing battle, with both men doing more avoiding than landing. Two minutes and seven seconds into the round, Hamed fired with a quick three-punch combination in reply to one of Kelley's connecting punches. His left hook landed squarely but instead of covering up on the corner ropes, Kelley lashed back with his own big, fast right hook. Naseem, who had moved back with his hands at his side, sensed the arrival of this bomb a fraction of second too late and it landed squarely against the side of his chin, twisting his head around. His legs did a momentary dance and he fell, making a mockery of the 7–1 odds in his favour.

Once again, however, his powers of recovery were impressive. He leapt up with a silly smile on his face, embarrassed at being caught out in the opening round of the biggest fight of his life. Kelley had always said the moves that so confused lesser fighters were going to be a liability against him, but Hamed was determined to prove him wrong and from that moment abandoned his fight plan. 'I think it would have been different if it hadn't been for that first round knockdown, and let's face it, he was caught by a wild punch. I mean, Kelley had his eyes closed,' said John Ingle. 'He has incredible recovery powers, but when you fight with his style, it's easy to be down. He might be stunned for a second or two when his head twists and as he goes down, but as soon as he hits the canvas his head clears. But the trouble is, once Naz gets hit, he wants to fight. It was just like after the Alicea knockdown, when he went all out in the next round. This time he just stood there firing away. I asked him why he did that, why allow yourself to get into a situation which is 50–50, and he said because he was just like that, when he gets hit, he's not going to hide behind a defensive rock. If Kelley hadn't caught him with that wild punch, I think he would have boxed like he did against Badillo, taken a few more rounds and taken him out easily.' From then on Hamed abandoned his jab, forgot all Brendan had taught him about defence and began a war of position. Kelley did the same and although the round ended without any more damage, the American was clearly in command. Now both men returned to their corners with the idea they could end it quickly. Brendan looked at his charge with the idea of putting some sense into his scrambled head, but Naseem had spent too many years doing as he pleased and treating his mentor like his servant to take much notice. 'I know what I'm doing, don't worry,' he snapped. 'I'm your pal, I'm your pal,' Brendan pleaded. 'Listen to me – stop letting him hit you on the chin.'

There was little sign in the second that Hamed had taken note, as Kelley opened with a successful three-punch combination. Naseem tried moving anti-clockwise, and jabbing, but found himself being out-jabbed. Kelley was using his right as an offensive weapon and was catching Naseem frequently, sometimes snapping his head back and once driving him into the ropes. After forty-five seconds he caught an off-balance Hamed with a well-timed left lead. Naseem's gloves touched the canvas momentarily, but before referee Estevez could intervene the New Yorker struck home again as Hamed's head was coming up, this time with a right hook. Naseem was down for his second count of the fight, this time on his right knee. Again he was up immediately and nodded to his opponent, but his legs looked less than certain about what they were doing. He was now in the worst trouble of his career – his brain shaken, his defence shredded, his chin dangling invitingly, his pre-fight strategy forgotten. What he was left with was his punch and his tremendous fighting instinct, and he was assisted by Kelley's impetuous folly.

As they went for each other, Naseem connected and Kelley staggered onto the ropes. But the American was still in hot pursuit mode, convinced he could end it, and with one minute and fifteen seconds remaining in the round, he moved into Naseem's range, landed a decent right and then walked into a straight right which found the point of his chin and sent him sprawling to the canvas at ring centre. Kelley smiled in recognition of his folly and pointed with his right glove to indicate his appreciation of Hamed's success, rising at the count of four. 'I got over-excited and saw the end of the fight when I had him down,' Kelley later explained. 'I was trying to take over, but doing it carelessly. That's when he hit me with a good punch, but it was more of a case of I'm moving forward but the shot pushed me back. I wasn't discouraged by it. I was still trying to knock him out. I was thinking, "I hope you were encouraged by that knockdown." I figured if he thinks he really hurt me, he's going to open up and be knocked out. I still had the advantage because of my speed and power, but I was losing it because I was getting emotionally involved and not controlling the emotions the way I should.' They both worked feverishly for the last minute, with Hamed bundling his opponent into a corner and landing a crisp left as he regained his balance, but with one knockdown apiece it seemed that the American's earlier dominance had shaded the round. Curiously, two of the judges, Victor Salamon of Mexico and Jose Rivera of Puerto Rico, scored it 10–8 for Hamed, while the American judge, Eva Shain, made it a more credible 10–10.

In the third, which Naseem had predicted would be the last, Kelley boxed superbly, regularly beating his opponent to the punch. It was evident that Hamed was unable to slip the quick jabs and the left cross was also catching him. Hamed's own jabs seemed surprisingly tentative – he was flicking them out, looking for openings, but getting caught more than he was landing. The embarrassing truth was that Naseem was being out-boxed and out-sped by an older man and was unable to find his timing and range. At the 40-second mark, Kelley shook the champion with a solid left cross and built on this success with a heavy jab. These punches were hard and well-timed but Hamed was taking them well. 'I've never ever took a shot and thought, "That kills, that hurt," ' he later claimed. 'I wanna get on with the job and just say yeah, let's do it. He's gonna get it back.' Kelley, however, had a different explanation: 'I realized when I got back to my corner at the end of round two that the thing that was keeping Hamed up was not his ability to take a punch, but his flexibility. He reminds me of myself when I was younger. I used to have his flexibility.' In the last minute, Kelley's trainer Phil Borgia was imploring his charge to keep his head. 'Control, Kevin, just let it flow,' he shouted, but it was Naseem who suddenly seemed to find his way. He landed two hard left uppercuts and several lesser blows over the last half-minute, which was enough for Shain and Rivera to give him the round, while Salomon remembered the first two and a half minutes and justly rewarded Kelley.

Brendan seemed relieved when Naseem returned to his stool, but once again issued a warning: 'Don't get into a war. You've gotta pick him off with the jab. He's had his fun. You start giving him some.' But at the start of the fourth it was Kelley, who had been told by Borgia to 'throw, believe in it', who had the early success, catching Hamed with a pair of solid, hurtful lefts. Naseem was still looking for the pay-off, convinced he could take Kelley out, and after a minute and a half he found his mark with a right-left-left combination, with the second heavy left hook doing most of the damage. Kelley fell hard on his right side but pulled himself up and raised his arms in a desperate gesture of defiance, even if his legs looked far less sure of themselves. He held briefly and then began firing back. Naseem rushed in with a lunging punch and was clipped by a quick right hand that upset his balance, causing his glove to brush the canvas. This time, however, he was not hurt and referee Estevez's count was unnecessary. The eight-second respite was not enough for Kelley. Naseem had found his range at last and was landing heavily. Kelley fired and Naseem countered with a short left hook that landed neatly on the temple and the challenger crumpled to the canvas, his head banging the floor as he landed. He seemed to have made it to his feet fractionally before the ten-count was tolled, but referee Estevez cradled him with one arm and indicated it was over. His legs betrayed him once again and he fell into Estevez's arms, before being assisted by his seconds. Later, however, he claimed he should have been allowed to continue: 'I was okay. He should have let it go on. Benji has refereed me since the amateurs. Look at all my other fights where I was hurt and came back. This would have been no different.' However, to most ringside observers it looked like Kelley was finished and that another punch from Naseem might have caused serious damage. As John Ingle put it: 'Naz never even hit him with one of his big punches, yet afterwards Kelley's corner had to hold him up, he was so badly stunned.'

Either way, it was over and, once again Hamed had prevailed. He moved over to hug Kelley, a look of relief on his unmarked face. 'You're the best I've ever boxed and I'm the best you've ever boxed,' he said. Kelley, however, was not so sure about Naseem's claim within this equation. He was convinced he could have knocked Hamed out if he had followed his fight plan: 'He came off the floor, I take my hat off to him, but he's not the hardest puncher I ever fought. That was Goyo Vargas. I never hit him with my best shots. I didn't do a lot of stuff that I can do. There are things I can do he hasn't seen yet.' Hamed's early take on his performance was to justify his tactics: 'I wanted a war, a real fight. If I set my mind to it, I don't get hit, but I like to feel the power and see if they can take it. I proved I have the heart of a champion. You've got to nail me to beat me, to knock me clean out. I was hurt by the shots that knocked me down, but I knew I would win. It was only a matter of time. I could take his punches but he couldn't take mine.'

Brendan Ingle, however, had a very different perspective. For once he made it clear to the public what he was saying in private – that Naseem had boxed terribly and had forgotten much of what he'd been taught. 'That was the worst he's boxed,' Ingle said. 'He was tense and on edge, but he's so brave. Instead of boxing him, drawing him out and countering, he went out there throwing bombs. Sometimes he's his own worst enemy. Everything Naz could do wrong, he did wrong, and he still won. If he had done everything right, if he'd done what he should have done, it wouldn't have gone two rounds, but he cocked his chin up in the air, dropped his hands when he was in distance and didn't slip the shots. Every mistake he made, Kelley made him pay. He was on a suicide mission. He could go on to become one of the best fighters ever, but now and again he's got to listen. Naseem has got to go back to what he was doing two years ago, when nobody could hit him.'

In terms of Naseem's campaign to conquer America, he walked away with mixed results. On the one hand he had established himself as an immensely compelling force within the sport – a gutsy fighter who could hit and be hit, a showman and an entertainer, and equally important, a little foreign man worthy of serious loathing. Had he boxed cautiously, as against Badillo, he may well have had an easier ride and would have won the respect of the in-house pundits, but he would not have thrilled the punters quite so much. Instead, his tactics, or lack of them, allowed for a featherweight battle to rival the Hagler–Hearns middleweight war, which won him a measure of praise in the American print media and certainly aided HBO's campaign to make him one of the most marketable fighters on their books. An impressive 10.4 million people from 2.5 million households watched his American debut, according to Seth Abraham, setting the basis for an even larger viewership in his next bout, against a non-American in Britain. It also improved the chances of attracting 'name' opponents. He had made so many fundamental mistakes that suddenly, everyone thought they had a chance against the 'Prince' and were lining up to take it.

But on the other hand, the fight diminished his reputation as a serious rival to the likes of Roy Jones and Oscar de la Hoya as one of the best fighters in the world. As Kelley expressed it immediately after the fight: 'Hamed is a good fighter who's got a lot to learn. He could be great one day, but right now he isn't. I've got news for you, Seth (Abraham): Hamed is no Roy Jones.' Hamed's performance made a mockery of his claim to be able to move through the weight divisions with impunity, all the way through De la Hoya and beyond. If he could be dropped three times by a featherweight, how could he possibly survive against the world's best welterweight? The result was an impression that, once again, a British export had been found wanting – in this case, brave, exciting, powerful, but also defensively challenged and perhaps even a bit chinny. Michael Katz of the New York *Daily News* wrote: 'He came in like Kid Confetti and fought like Kid Counterfeit. Prince? Naseem Hamed was on his way to being as successful as George III in this country. He won but he did not conquer.' In a similar tabloid tone, Anthony Gargano of the New York *Post* sneered: 'This was not Willie Pep, this was barely Prince Charles. The wind he brought to New York proved more like a hollow breeze. He was dazzling and quick and a solid puncher, but his chin seemed more than suspect and his overall skills are rather ordinary. He is a champion, but certainly an over-rated one.' The eighty-three-year-old author Budd Schulberg offered a more balanced analysis, which reached a similar conclusion: 'He can hit hard and he got up and won, but after everything I had heard, I thought he would be more elusive and that disappointed me. Muhammad Ali at twenty-three years old would never have been hit by a jab the way Hamed caught Kelley. He looks to me as though he still has a lot to learn. Henry Armstrong and Sandy Saddler would have knocked him out. They would have just run him out of the ring. Hamed is exciting, yes, but at the moment he is simply not in the class of those guys.'

And so the biggest year of his boxing career ended on an oddly ambiguous note. No other British boxer, ever, could possibly have walked away unsatisfied after completing five fights, five wins, five knockouts within twelve months, unifying two versions of a world title, beating the two best Americans and a pair of mandatory contenders, topping a bill at Madison Square Garden and establishing himself as one of the three biggest earners in his sport and one of the ten biggest in any sport. But this was Naseem Hamed, the would-be legend. For so long he had been instructing us all to judge him by far higher fighting standards than other mortals, and by these lofty measures he had been found wanting. As soon as he'd had a few moments to think about it, he realized he had been fortunate to survive yet another bout of living dangerously. In fact, John Ingle said the minute Naseem reached the changing room he realized what he had done wrong. 'He kept on saying it, that he had been hit far too much.' So it was a more contrite Naseem who offered a balanced assessment once his adrenaline levels had subsided. 'I deserved to be criticized for fighting the way I did. You must admit it was exciting stuff and I actually enjoyed it, but I realize if I go on fighting like this I will get into trouble. I was disappointed with myself for getting hit the way I did. I must not let it happen again. I must remember to keep my head down and my hands up.' Naseem, it seemed, had learned a lesson.

9

GROWING UP?

Shortly before the Kelley fight, Naseem had broken a small piece of news to his family: he was going to be a dad. The next little earthquake was the news that the mum-to-be was none other than Eleasha Elphinstone, the woman he had supposedly separated from six months earlier. That split-up had come in the wake of pressure on both of them from some family members who couldn't abide the idea of a non-Yemeni, non-Muslim, slightly older woman, with a 'past' and a small streak of independence, entering their nest. In fact, Naseem had been seeing her on the quiet for several months and in September 1997 she had fallen pregnant with his child. When the Kelley fight was over, they both informed their families and went off together on holiday to Los Angeles and Miami. Her family seemed to have little difficulty accepting Naseem as a future son-in-law. As her stepmother Liz Creally put it during their American holiday: 'They are having a great time. Their problems are in the past now. All that matters is that they are happy. They deserve to be happy.' His family, however, had to get their heads around the idea of negotiating Eleasha's entrance to the fold, via a religious conversion on her part, followed by marriage.

Their renewed relationship delighted Brendan, who felt it would help to settle his young charge. 'I was always telling him to marry her but as you know, not everyone felt the same way and some members of his family were doing their best to get them to stop seeing each other. They really didn't like it. But after they broke up I could see he wasn't right. He was driving past her house and not focusing on his career, so when they got together again and then decided to get married I was absolutely delighted. I think she's a wonderful girl and I really hope they will be very happy together. It was the best thing that could have happened to him and things definitely improved after that.' Most of Naseem's friends seemed to like Eleasha and agreed with Brendan that she was a positive influence. As one put it: 'Naz has been under a lot of pressure to go out with a Muslim girl, but Eleasha means a great deal to him and we were pleased. She's perfect for him because she helps to keep his feet on the ground and doesn't let him get his own way all the time.'

After their return from California, the young couple moved back in together and then met with his family, when it was agreed that Eleasha would convert and they would then have an extremely low-profile wedding. On 9 February, soon after the conversion, they had their small, family wedding, conducted according to traditional Islamic Nikah rites by an imam and two male witnesses at Naseem's parents' home in Whirlow, on the outskirts of Sheffield. Brendan Ingle and close friends like Ryan Rhodes were not invited or even informed of the wedding, while even Eleasha's stepmother stayed away because the ceremony was 'strictly Muslim'.

Until he realized he was about to become a father, there was a distinctly childlike quality to Naseem's persona which survived well into adulthood and was undoubtedly part of his early appeal. As he put it in 1997: 'Actually, I do feel really young. I don't feel twenty-three inside. I feel nineteen, eighteen.' It could be detected not only in his desire to be the centre of attention but also in the tastes which expressed his desire for instant gratification and status enhancement: the car collection, his favourite music and movies (either violent or funny – *Casino, Raging Bull, Scarface* or anything with Eddie Murphy), his Disneyworld holidays, his pool hall escapades, his hero worship of other celebrities, his sense of humour, and most of all in the boyish banter of his friendships. After the Kelley fight, however, his relationship with Eleasha finally took precedence over the buddy rapport he had with his close friends and stablemates.

Perhaps a more significant strain on his relationships with his peers, however, was the way he had responded to fame and fortune over the previous two years. Some of those who knew him well detected subtle shifts within the balance of power between Naseem and his gym-mates. Whereas once they had been bantering equals, now they were more cautious with him, knowing that to a significant extent their futures rested on their proximity to him. Some of his closest friends had slipped into a praise-singing role and were reluctant to give him the kind of frank, open criticism he often needed. Having a laugh was seldom allowed to mean having a laugh at his expense, although this restriction did not work in reverse. He had not developed particularly close friendships with the more balanced and emotionally mature members of his gym, and instead relied on those who could feed his needs and desires on his terms. What emerged was a pecking order, with Naseem at the apex, and this created resentments and jealousies which had previously been more muted. At the time he won the WBO world title, Naseem's gym-mates were virtually unanimous in their praise for his personal qualities as well as his boxing abilities. By his third year as champion, however, this had changed markedly. Several of the juniors continued to hero worship him, saying he was 'brilliant' and that they trained harder than ever when he was around in a bid to catch his eye, but others had become less enamoured, and no longer felt compelled to deny it, while a few older gym members were starting to speak off the record about the changes. 'In a way it was inevitable, but still sad – he's not the same Naz anymore,' said one senior stablemate. 'Fame and fortune *have* changed him.' Or as Brendan put it to me: 'He seems to think he's chocolate and if he's not careful he will devour himself.'

One of his closest friends was Ryan Rhodes who won the British light-middleweight title at the age of twenty, in December 1996. After this, Rhodes's career took off and he began moving in his own direction rather than being seen merely as Naseem's bigger, lesser half. Some said this took the edge off their camaraderie, although they remained friends. On the one hand Naseem was always there to cheer on and back up friends and stablemates like Rhodes, Neville Brown, Tom Bradley and Johnny Nelson, often travelling across the country to give them support; but sometimes he appeared less certain about sharing the adulatory fruits of success and there was even a patronizing tone to his treatment of their efforts. As he once put it: 'Ryan and Johnny are always telling me about how they want to be rich and famous like me. I tell them it isn't easy. Never a day goes by without someone asking for something – an autograph, photo or money.' Ryan, for his part, says it is merely a question of marching to a different beat. 'I was living in his shadow but I'm on my own path now – totally different from Naz's. His is really loud. I'm not as loud as him.' However, he refuted suggestions that this created antagonism between them, and did not seem to take offence when he was not informed of his friend's wedding. 'We're still close – we're good friends and have been ever since we first met. We always wanted the best for each other. We weren't comparing or nothing. We just wanted each other to do well. We done alright to each other – and we still hang out together in Sheffield sometimes.'

While Naseem had often spoken of the gym as his second home, this was no longer the case and he often appeared far more relaxed in more neutral environments where he felt less under scrutiny. In such surroundings he was still capable of making a strong impression as a relaxed, easy-going nice guy. One of those he won over was the women's world welterweight boxing champion, Jane Couch. 'Naz has been down here in our gym and he's been really supportive of what I'm doing and women's boxing generally, she said. 'Once I was messing around with him when he was here. I was saying, 'I can knock you out, you daft cunt', and he was laughing his head off. He's brilliant, he is. He's me mate. And I've got a lot of respect for him, for what he's achieved, what he's up against. In Britain they don't like winners.'

Naseem's determination to be the nonpareil of his roost is perhaps best illustrated by his palpable dislike for Daniel Teasedale, the sixteen-year-old amateur light-heavyweight who is a national Schools and Boys Clubs champion and one of Britain's best young amateurs with Olympic ambitions. When Naseem was training for the Cabrera fight in 1997, he went as far as punching the then-14-year-old Teasedale in the stomach outside the ring after the young amateur requested Hamed to speak to him politely. Teasedale, who in recent years has regularly been described by Brendan Ingle as 'better than Naseem at the same age and stage', says he does his best to keep his distance from Hamed and suggests the senior boxer resents the praise and attention he has been getting from Ingle. 'I don't exactly get on brilliantly with him. We don't talk much at all, but sometimes he'll make negative comments to me, but I can't let it bother me because I know that one day I'll be better than him. In the past we've sparred together but Brendan always likes to keep us apart these days, because he's worried Naz will slip me one on the chin. It doesn't bother me, but he's done that before. I still rate him very, very highly as a boxer, but I wouldn't rate him as a person. I don't want to become a show-off like him.' In Ingle's view, Hamed's attitude was based on envy and resentment at being supplanted as the trainer's young protégé: 'He was jealous of Daniel. He heard me saying Daniel was better than him at 15, and he saw all the attention he was getting from me, and he didn't like it. That's why he was horrible to him. His eyes went green.'

That, certainly, is one dimension of the Naseem Hamed persona. But there is far more to him than just the egotistical swank. The boxer himself likes to stress that his private persona should not be confused with his public image. 'A lot of people think I'm cocky, but I'm not. You know, there's a certain way you come across on the television and the reason I do it that way is to make people listen up. It's purely to get their attention, so people can say, "I'm going to watch this guy, I'm going to watch his attitude," but I'm not really like that at all. When I'm outside the ring I have nothing to prove whatsoever.' Warren has endorsed this view, emphasizing qualities like Naseem's instinctive generosity. 'He can be the most charming person, very thoughtful. I've dealt with hundreds of boxers and I can think of about three who have ever picked up a restaurant bill. Naz is one of them. He's not out to prove himself to be a nice guy, but he is a nice bloke.' One example is that Naseem has been consistent in donating significant amounts of money and time to various charitable ventures. Not, perhaps, to the level of a Lennox Lewis, (who donated £3million to found a school for the under-privileged) but serious money and time nevertheless. Whatever the motivation for these ventures, some are not of the high-profile kind. Among others, he is a patron of the Teenage Cancer Trust and periodically makes appearances on its behalf, as well as assisting individual cancer victims by presenting them with boxing gloves, visiting them in hospital and driving them around in his cars, for example. He has helped to raise money for Shelter, an organisation for homeless people, and has donated large sums to the Yemeni Economic Training Centre in Sheffield and has also joined campaigns against alcohol and drug abuse and against racism.

Naseem's relations with his immediate family also suggest a less selfish side. It may be true that even the most notorious monsters look after their own, but in Naseem's case it reflects a caring dimension. For instance, he displays a genuine enthusiasm and affection when talking about his nieces and nephews, and certainly his brothers seem genuinely astonished and hurt to see him criticized for being obnoxious, while his father said of him: 'He is an incredibly generous son and we love him very much.' Much of his money has gone towards looking after his family. He bought his parents a £300,000 home in the city, along with all manner of modern conveniences, and pays the bills for their foreign travels, while lesser amounts have been spent on houses and cars for his siblings. Perhaps the most visible gesture came with his impetuous decision in May 1997 to withdraw £500,000 from his bank, place it in two black binliners and empty the contents on their sitting room floor. As he explained: 'I just wanted to give my mum and dad a surprise, so I said to them, "That's your spending money for the next six months – it's up to you what you do with it, so go and enjoy yourselves." I think they expected old beer cans or other stuff to fall out, so their eyes were popping out of their heads. They just couldn't believe what they were looking at – all that money, and all in cash. It gave me a fantastic feeling to see them so happy. I owe them such a lot, more than money can buy. You have to realize how precious our mum and dad are and how much they mean.'

Despite the tensions which his relationship with Eleasha generated, in certain respects he had grown closer to his immediate family since becoming world champion, with most of its members becoming involved in the new family business: Naseem himself. Until the Hameds' move to go it alone in late 1998, the boxing deals were all handled by Warren; the rest by Riath Hamed and his team. Naseem retained enormous pride and faith in the intellectual prowess and financial acumen of Riath, who remained one of the few people who could get away with admonishing him. As his business manager, Riath negotiated most of his brother's numerous sponsorship and advertising deals and media engagements, and played an overseer role regarding his investments, which expanded rapidly. In 1998 Riath and Nabeel, the family members most centrally involved, gave themselves new job titles. Nabeel, then 28, who had been a motor mechanic before taking over the fan club, became Promotions Director of Prince Naseem Enterprises, while former Sheffield community liaison officer Riath, then 29, became the company's managing director. In addition to purse money and advertising endorsements, Naseem Hamed Enterprises (NHE) and Naseem Hamed Promotions (NHP) are useful earners. Both took advantage of small company exemptions, which allows disclosure of abbreviated financial accounts, but it emerged that NHE made net profits of £407,000 in its first business year to April 1996 while NHP (which had £600,000 in assets) earned net profits of £158,000 in its first year to April 1997. Papers released in the course of the Warren-King legal dispute revealed that much of Hamed's earnings were channelled to an offshore tax haven-company, Striking Distance, which is registered in the British Virgin Islands and was formed in 1995 by Offshore Inc, a Hong Kong firm of company formation agents. It received $3.8 million of the $6 million paid to Hamed for his fights against Kelley and Wilfredo Vazquez (whom he fought after Kelley, in April 1998). Nabeel was responsible for the fan club and merchandising of Naseem-related products through NHE; Sal played a role in negotiating deals in the Middle East; his oldest sister Mona's film production company made documentaries about Naseem; his three other sisters assisted with the business administration; his youngest brother Murad set up a Hamed website on the internet, and his second youngest brother Ali assisted him on many of his travels and before fights. The result of this growing family business empire on the one hand, and Warren's promotional role on the other, is that Brendan had effectively been squeezed out of any managerial role. He had become no more than Naseem's trainer and at times even this was in doubt. On the eve of the Kelley fight Naseem and Riath attempted to place further restrictions on Brendan's role. He received a lengthy legal document, which set out an eight fight agreement, at £75,000 per fight, requiring him to take instructions from Hamed, to give his needs priority over those of the other boxers in his gym, only to speak to the press with written permission and not to divulge information not already in the public domain. His sons, John and Dominic were required to sign similar secrecy agreements and Brendan was required to hand over all documents relating to

Hamed, including boyhood pictures, once the contract expired. 'I simply ignored it then and refused to sign it,' Ingle told me soon afterwards (although a year later he did indeed sign a similar document, as a way of getting money owed to him for the Wayne McCullough fight). At the time he agreed to work on a fight-by-fight basis, earning what amounted to £75,000 per fight but without any formal restrictions on what he could say to the press.

The other aspect of Naseem's expanding business empire which was not neatly pigeon-holed to his best advantage was the most important of them all: who was promoting him. *De facto*, there was no confusion here: Frank Warren had been his sole promoter for over four years. *De jure*, however, this remained in dispute as a result of the intricacies of Warren's now-unravelling relationship with Don King. Shortly before his next fight, Warren experienced what he hoped was merely a temporary setback to his attempts to secure a clean break from King. In March 1998, the first round of this protracted battle went to the American promoter when a British High Court judge, Mr Justice Lightman, ruled that the three year extension of their contract had been valid. As a result, Warren 'was in breach of duties he owed to Don King Productions. Mr King is entitled to receive half the profits from all Warren promotions unless Mr Warren buys him out.' This meant King still had a claim to a piece of Naseem Hamed, although the judgement went to appeal and this had frustrating implications for Warren, whose assets were frozen, initially to the tune of £1.75 million but in July 1998 increased to £3.35 million. All his income from his boxing interests had to be paid into a City bank, effectively controlled by the court, with the result that Warren and Sports Network had to rely on a monthly allowance of £45,000.

It was becoming clear that this was going to be no quickie divorce and that the conflict could drag on for years. King used this legal victory to launch a fresh series of verbal attacks on his former partner's trustworthiness. The English promoter made it clear that a legal victory over King was his only option, and that the alternative might mark his exit from the game. 'Should the courts enforce me to remain in partnership with him, then I will quit because I do not want to be in business with Don King,' he said in an interview in *Total Sport* magazine. 'It wouldn't be the end of the world; there's other things in my life.' This, of course, would have profound long-term implications for Naseem Hamed.

Meanwhile, King himself was also facing a series of other legal actions. Most significantly, Mike Tyson left him and then sued him for lost earnings, followed by several of his other lesser stars. Despite his subsequent insurance fraud trial victory, it was hard to escape the impression that King's kingdom was in a state of decline, temporarily at least. Warren, on the other hand, gave the temporary appearance of moving to consolidate his position. In addition to the lucrative HBO deal, which opened the way for several of his other star fighters to appear on the cable network, he established a close working relationship with Spencer McPherson, a boxing manager who was an important defector from the King camp, and a promotional arrangement with the retired basketball legend Magic Johnson, while consolidating his ties with several British and European promoters and with South Africa's Rodney Berman. Warren and King's conflicting fortunes at that early stage of their power struggle were neatly illustrated by their little battle for the services of Vazquez, the World Boxing Association featherweight champion earmarked as Naseem's next opponent.

The thirty-seven-year-old Puerto Rican had lived a charmed existence by boxing standards as a result of having long been a favourite of the WBA, and more recently an acquisition of King's. Among the distinctly debatable decisions on his tally was an outrageous verdict over Nicaragua's Genaro Rios in November 1997 – his third defence of the WBA featherweight title he had lifted from Eloy Rojas in May 1996. However, when Vazquez defied and then dumped King by accepting Warren's offer to fight Hamed in a unification bout, his luck with the WBA changed instantly. They threatened to strip him of his title for delaying a defence against former super-bantamweight champion Antonio Cermeno, and when he refused to back down they carried out their threat – a decision which disgusted Naseem, who complained that the politics of boxing was the aspect of the sport he most despised: 'The WBA stripping Vazquez of his title for fighting me is rubbish. It is spoiling the sport. The public should get a chance to see one champion at each weight, but it seems the governing bodies don't want it.' What this decision revealed, once again, was that King continued to wield a dominant influence over the sport's venal control bodies. But

Vazquez's decision to defy King and the WBA and go ahead with the fight suggested that in this case at least, Warren's dollar counted for more than King's political sway. For three years, while a partner of King's, he had tried to secure Vazquez's services and had failed. Without King to impede him, he succeeded immediately with his $300,000 inducement, securing what was, in all but name, another title unification bout for Manchester on 18 April 1998.

Even allowing for the WBA's past generosity, Vazquez was a high-quality fighter, albeit one who had shown inconsistency over his seventeen-year career. The combination of the death of his father and the victory of his countryman Wilfredo Gomez over Mexico's Carlos Zarate inspired him to turn professional. He first came to prominence in February 1986 when he was outpointed by Happy Lora in a bid for the WBC bantamweight title, but twenty months later he was ready for his next try, this time for the WBA title, which he won by knocking out Korea's Chan-Yong Park in ten rounds. Six months on, however, when struggling with the weight, he lost it on points to Japan's Khaokor Galaxy. In March 1992 he won his second world title by stopping his former conqueror, the Mexican Raul Perez, in three rounds for the WBA super-bantamweight honours, and this time he put together nine defences, including one against the brilliant Texan Orlando Canizales, before dropping a close decision to Cermeno in May 1995. He then moved up in weight again, pulling off a major upset in stopping Eloy Rojas for the WBA featherweight title in May 1996 and remained champion for two years. His record stood at fifty wins (thirty-seven inside the distance), seven losses and three draws, and he had only suffered one official loss in the previous eight years. He was an excellent counter-puncher who was tricky, strong and well-conditioned, with a tight defence and an extremely reliable chin as well as world-class power and vast experience at the top level. Aside from his age, his main weakness was a lack of speed and mobility, which meant he had trouble against quick movers. This quietly spoken father of three had been in full training since January and seemed to feel he was in with a genuine chance. 'Everybody knows Hamed can go down, but now he is facing the best contender he has ever met, and the biggest puncher. I will study him for the first five rounds, then knock him out. When I nail him, I'll finish him and put him completely out. Forget my age. I am ready,' he predicted.

After four months out of the ring, Naseem needed a lot of effort to get back into shape. He worked reasonably hard by his standards, although not quite as hard as for Kelley. However, there were clear signs of a thaw with Brendan in the way he was approaching his task. Once again he was listening to his trainer, showing him courtesy in public and echoing his advice. As usual Naseem predicted a quick knockout, but also said he would avoid a Kelley-type punch-up. 'I intend to get back to my boxing skills. I made mistakes against Kelley. He wanted a war, so did I, and we decided that was the way it was going to be, but I know now that was crazy and shouldn't happen. Vazquez is experienced but I'll stop him in two rounds. I'm a lot faster than him. His time has gone, but mine is coming up.' Nevertheless, from his training sessions it still seemed that much of his emphasis was on power – trying to land single, devastating blows on the pads from different stances rather than working on the multi-punch combinations, dazzling footwork and elusive twisting of his earlier years. While many punchers become cagier and more defensively adept as they get on in the game, Naseem seemed to be moving in the opposite direction. Once more, he was loading up on everything and the speed and defensive wizardry that had been a feature of his rise seemed to have become a thing of the past, perhaps never to be reclaimed.

Partly as a result of the Kelley fight, Hamed was continuing to get his share of bad press from boxing writers who had heard it all before and were unconvinced there was a genuine change. As *Boxing Monthly* editor Glyn Leach wrote: 'I'm hearing the words "regression" and "peaked" a lot these days … Hamed is booked for defeat, say some, and he's brought it upon himself. You hear these things: Hamed doesn't train anymore; Hamed won't listen to anyone; but in case he does, he makes sure that those around him bruise his backside with their lips as much as had Kelley's fists, indirectly.' He went on to decry Hamed's love of power at the expense of defence, before asking: 'Can Hamed be put back on track? Only if he wants it himself – and the evidence suggests that he doesn't even recognize there's a problem … Hamed is all fighter and precious little boxer these days, which seems, to me at least, to be taking the lazy way out. He's in danger of selling himself short.' It was also the kind of remark many of Naseem's prospective opponents were making: recognizing his extraordinary power, but, strangely for a boxer who was once viewed as a defensive genius, seeing him as a fighter with no more than a rudimentary defence. The comments of the leading American Derrick Gainer were typical: 'He is a very, very good puncher, but as far as skills go, he doesn't have any. All he is is a puncher. If someone sticks to the game plan and boxes Hamed – Hamed's in a lot of trouble.'

There was therefore a great deal for Hamed to prove in his dealings with Vazquez, both in the way he handled himself and, more importantly for his legendary aspirations, in the way he fought. In the lead-up to the fight, Naseem seemed to be going an extra foot or two to show that he was, in fact, a decent human being, that he was training hard and in tune with his trainer. When he arrived almost an hour late at a press conference, he carefully explained his hired limousine had broken down in the snow and apologized to Vazquez, going out of his way to stress this was not a sign of disrespect. When Eubank had another verbal go at him (saying, 'I have no interest in his fight whatsoever – Naz has back-stabbed me, he has been snidey and underhand when I showed him kindness and friendship') he left it to Brendan to get stuck in with a tirade against Eubank and stayed quiet. Given their recent history, Naseem's extreme competitiveness and the fact that Eubank's fight – against WBO cruiserweight champion Carl Thompson – was once again taking precedence over Hamed's in the publicity stakes, this was quite an achievement.

The combination of Hamed and Eubank attracted a capacity crowd of 14,000 to Manchester's Nynex Arena. However, after the savage excitement of Eubank's points defeat against Thompson, they were more muted than usual when Naseem's fight arrived. Still they managed to get it up once again to boo heartily when the challenger made his entrance, dressed in a red cape and a crown, to a samba number with the refrain, 'Go Puerto Rico!' Vazquez was doing his best to make it clear he was not about to play the fall guy. His countryman Felix Trinidad, the formidable IBF world welterweight champion, joined him while a corner-man did a break-dance routine in the ring as a proxy for Wilfredo. Hamed's arrival, to a now mundane laser beam light show, was, mercifully, slightly less grandiose and time-consuming than at Madison Square Garden. When Naseem delivered his eyeballing routine, Vazquez met his stare impassively and, like Kelley, was clearly not intimidated. When Naseem raised his arms to the heavens,

Wilfredo did the same. Prior to the fight, it had seemed that for once Naseem would be fighting someone his own size in this former bantamweight, but the Puerto Rican, who scaled 1¾lb over the limit fifteen minutes before the weigh-in but returned to make the 126lb limit half an hour later, looked significantly bigger – over an inch taller, with a broader back and a more 'ripped' musculature. He said he had trained harder for Hamed than for any previous fight, and it certainly looked that way. On seeing Vazquez's forty-year-old head and twenty-year-old body, Frank Warren climbed into the ring to warn his lad to 'be smart', which is precisely what Naseem tried.

He came out as a southpaw and soon attempted a couple of the lunging knockout leads he'd been practising in training, but for the most part his opening round was marked by caution – a tickling, range-finder jab, a solitary body punch, a few solid head blows towards the end of the round and more misses than hits. He dropped his hands when he was at a safe distance, shifted stance a few times, held when Vazquez closed the gap, pushed him down in the final half minute, and took only five punches in reply – one jab, one glancing right to the head and three body blows. As the bell rang, the Puerto Rican's face had reddened from the force of a Hamed left, and the champion swaggered to his corner, content with his limited effort.

When he came out for the second, he seemed intent on fulfilling his pre-fight knockout prediction. His powerful legs were set wider apart in the position he favours for big hitting and he was fighting from closer range, using hard, accurate short lefts to counter Vazquez. A straight-left-right uppercut combination dropped the challenger momentarily but the American referee Gino Rodriguez incorrectly registered this as a slip. After Vazquez's gloves were wiped, Hamed hovered in the distance before leaping in with one of his long left leads, which missed. But he was now into his rhythm and the familiar leering smile, contemptuous hand-dropping and demeaning headshaking commenced. He was looking to fire with his big guns, but instead received a big time jolt to the chin when Vazquez unleashed a heavy, quick right cross. Hamed's head twisted round and his legs wobbled involuntarily for a second, but once again, his rapid recovery powers came to his aid and he moved out of range. It was to be his last serious mistake of the fight, as from then on the chastened champion returned to cautious mode.

Early in the third, Naseem came away from a clinch with a minor graze under his right eye – he would claim from a head butt – and as the fight progressed Vazquez homed in on it, raising an insignificant swelling. Shortly afterwards Hamed avenged this slight when he ducked a right and countered with glancing right uppercut and then a short left which landed more squarely, depositing the rock-jawed Puerto Rican on his posterior for the first official count of the fight. He was up before the referee's count reached two and looked to have recovered, indicating to his corner that he was in fine shape. Realizing this, Brendan shouted, 'Box him, box him!' from the corner, fearing that Naseem would lose his head again. This time Naseem listened and returned to his methodical boxing, trying to find openings and making his opponent miss. 'Jab, jab, jab!' Ingle screamed, and Hamed obeyed.

In the fourth, Naseem opened with a hurtful-looking left cross to the face, after which he proceeded to pick Vazquez off with ease while slipping the counters. At one point he whipped in a nicely timed leaping right uppercut, but his challenger withstood it. Towards the end of the round Vazquez finally had some success, landing a solid right cross in reply to Hamed's right hook. As the session ended, Vazquez used his head once again, rubbing it into Hamed's face, and the champion returned to his corner looking angry and eager for a punch-up. Yet, under Brendan's firm instructions, he rediscovered his composure and came out boxing from a distance, dancing and bouncing around the ring and poking out a light jab as he looked for opportunities to land more profitably. It was Vazquez's busiest spell as he went for the body with some success whenever he came close and early in the round knocked Naseem off balance, driving him towards the ropes with a long right cross. But the WBO champion was frustrating most of his opponent's major efforts, at one point making him miss by several feet, an indignity which he tried to mitigate by attempting a backhanded slap on the rebound, earning himself a caution. Still, it was Vazquez's best three minutes and the only round he had serious claim to winning.

What followed was one of the stranger moments in recent boxing history when a *deus ex machina* in the form of a snapped rope prolonged Vazquez's presence in this part of Manchester. Naseem started the sixth impressively when, after twenty-seven seconds, he dropped his opponent with a classic left cross. The punch, however, did not land squarely and Vazquez was up at two, protesting his fall was the result of a slip. This time, however, he took a count, then moved into a clinch. As the referee noticed the snapped rope and shouted break, Vazquez took advantage of the confusion by hitting Naseem, prompting an emphatic protest from the champion. The boxers were sent to neutral corners, but Naseem was incensed and walked over to rub his head into his challenger's. This, in turn, inspired Warren to climb onto the ring apron to warn Naseem to keep his cool. For over eight minutes the boxers waited and the crowd booed and hissed while the broken rope was removed and a makeshift attempt was made to close the two-strand gap. When the action resumed, Vazquez launched his final attack of the fight, landing a hard right to Hamed's body and a glancing hook to the head. At the bell, they both stood and glared at each other, sustaining the stand-off for several seconds before returning to base.

Once again Vazquez was looking competitive and there was no indication that the fight was nearing its end. It was becoming a far more trying night than most had anticipated. But Hamed is a fighter who is always full of surprises, and after twenty-five seconds he delivered one to Vazquez in the form of a heavy left hook counter which deposited him on his trunks in ring centre, prompting the usual little bum-wiggle from Naseem. Vazquez was up quickly and walked around the ring to get some life back into his legs. 'Break him up!' shouted Brendan, and Naseem moved in for the kill. His first effort failed when a leaping right missed and the momentum carried him into the ropes, but from then on he was rampant, wounding his prey with his next punch, a left hook, and then battering him with huge hooks and uppercuts with both hands. Vazquez's legs were starting to give and a cracking left hook drove him to the canvas for the fourth knockdown. Once again Vazquez hauled himself up for the count, but it needed only two more huge hooks for referee Rodriguez to decide he'd seen enough. At two minutes and twenty-nine seconds of the seventh round, Naseem scored his thirtieth win and his twenty-eighth stoppage.

As he was hoisted aloft, he held one glove with the other and it was later confirmed that he had suffered another hand injury late in the fight. Immediately afterwards he went through his usual 'I was wicked, I'm too strong for these featherweights, when I start punching them they're going out' routine, but once he was showered and changed, he was ready for a more mature self-assessment. 'I didn't box my best, but I boxed alright. I had to take my time to take him out because he was cleverer than I thought. I took some good shots – he caught me with one very good right – but I wouldn't say he rocked me to my boots. He was very, very strong inside, he used his head and he tried to manhandle me, and he seemed to have a good chin on him. He came to win – you could see it in his eyes.' Ingle, who looked far happier than he had done for some time after a Hamed bout, described the bout as 'a game of chess', full of subtle moves and counters. 'You can't afford to make a mistake against Vazquez. In the far corner Naseem did make a mistake and bang, he got caught, but he took it.'

The official Sky punch count showed that Naseem had attempted 261 punches during the seven rounds, landing 92 – a success rate of 35 per cent. Of those, 88 were headshots (including 32 jabs) and only four were body blows. Vazquez threw 243 punches, landing 53 (22 per cent), of which 27 were head shots (6 jabs) and 26 body blows. By the end of the sixth, Naseem was ahead by margins of 59-53, 58-54 and 58-55. There were two ways of looking at the performance behind these statistics. One could make a sound case that this was yet another indicator of Naseem's slippage. Once again he was hit more often than in his youth, suggesting his defensive decline had not been reversed. He veered from his strategy and paid for it. He was still neglecting body punching and the scintillating speed and reflexes of old were not in evidence. How would the Hamed of, say, three or four years earlier have coped with Vazquez? The form line suggested a lot more easily than in 1998. Juan Polo-Perez, who beat Vazquez without getting the decision in 1994 and was still good enough to hold Wayne McCullough to a split decision four years later, was despatched by Hamed in two rounds without landing a punch. Freddy Cruz, who held Vazquez to a disputed majority decision, also failed to land a telling blow on Hamed in six rounds. Steve Robinson, who had defended his WBO title eight times, beating a trio of former world champions, was knocked out in eight after landing barely a handful of punches. Yet in 1998, the slow, thirty-seven-year-old Vazquez landed fifty-three times, rocked Hamed, bruised his eye and survived several rounds longer than anyone, including Naseem, had predicted.

On the other hand, there was a legitimate case for saying the bout indicated a reversal of his decline. He took fewer clean, hard head shots than against Kelley, Medina and Alicea, and with only one, brief, lapse, stuck to his pre-fight strategy. It could also be borne in mind that the Vazquez who struggled against Polo-Perez and Cruz was weight-weakened whereas against Hamed he was in excellent shape, completely focused and in perfect tune. Yet Naseem not only stopped him for the first time in his career, he also had him on the canvas five times. This was certainly the approach taken by Vazquez himself. Asked whether there were any featherweights around who could beat Hamed, he replied: 'No. He's an excellent fighter, a very uncomfortable fighter to box – so unorthodox and very hard to deal with. He's the hardest-hitting fighter I have fought, which is why he was able to knock me down three times (sic). Now he's beaten me, I like him. He's a funny guy – not a bad boy – and I'm his fan now.'

George Foreman, who was doing HBO's inter-round commentary, relied on flattering hyperbole to announce his verdict. 'Naz has the ability to be the best in the world, not just for now but for the next ten years. His personality is attracting so many new fans, his fame could transcend the sport. He can do for boxing what Muhammad Ali did.' Naseem responded with equanimity, rather than the sneering pomposity he usually displayed after a fight. 'I hope George is right, and it is kind of him but my feet are on the ground and nothing will go to my head,' he said, before adding, 'I'm not sure I would want to box for another ten years.' This impression of maturity – or at least a serious attempt in that direction – was enhanced by his response to the announcement of an 18 July date in the United States for his next fight. Naseem firmly made it clear that whatever HBO or Warren wanted, where and when he fought would be for himself to decide. 'I don't want to make any decisions yet. I will make it when I feel right and ready,' he said, stressing he would be at his wife's side when his baby was born. After that he apologized for his early departure, saying he wanted to go home to be with the woman he loved. As he left, Brendan Ingle beamed, raised his arms and said, 'We're back in business' – a signal of relief that a measure of normality had returned to the life of his top boxer. For the moment at least.

The surprise viewing figures for the Vazquez fight – attracting higher ratings in America than fights featuring Oscar de la Hoya, Lennox Lewis and Evander Holyfield, and also pipping the

estimated 10.4 million who had watched the Kelley fight –
convinced HBO to launch an advertising campaign focusing on
Hamed's boxing skills rather than his flamboyance in preparation
for his next bout. 'The fact that so many Americans took time out
to watch a fight going ahead 3,000 miles away is incredible,' said
Seth Abraham. 'The only person who would have attracted a
greater audience is Mike Tyson. It shows Naz is catching on
quickly in America.'

But Naseem was more concerned about matters closer to home.
'I want to be there at the birth. I want to deliver it,' he explained.
On June 8, Naseem shadowboxed with delight outside the
delivery room at King's Mill Hospital in Nottinghamshire, after
witnessing the birth of his first child, a 6 lb 10 oz boy, born
naturally and without complications. Eleashas sister Maria, who
is a midwife, returned to the hospital from her own maternity
leave to help with the delivery, and it was Naseem who cut the
umbilical cord. After a week of deliberation about names, they
decided to give the boy a non-Muslim first name, followed by
family middle names: Sami Naseem Salem Hamed. Watching
Naseem gently cradling his boy it was clear he loved his son and
was delighted with fatherhood, and that it offered him a new
perspective on life. As he put it: 'This was the best thing ever to
happen to me – far, far better than winning the world title.' Some
of Naseem's associates said at the time that they detected a new
maturity about the boxer – a sense that while his egotism was not
necessarily diminished by creating someone in his own image, at
least he had a sense that there was more to the world than his self-
gratification. By then he had long given up his night clubbing
ways, but with the birth of Sami came a greater sense of
responsibility about his career, and he frequently spoke about the
necessity of not slipping up, so that Sami could always look on his
father's career with pride. This Naseem, the responsible, loving,
caring father seemed so far from the crass, aggressive narcissist of
old, that, for a few months, it was tempting to believe that a
genuine and fundamental change had come over him.

There were few more delighted well-wishers than his old
mentor, Brendan: 'Unlike some of his siblings his wasn't an
approved or arranged marriage, so it showed a sign of independence. The next best thing to happen to Naz was becoming a
father. I think it has matured him and it should help his career
because it will give his life stability, and another dimension, if he

does it right." By that stage Naseem had been absent from the gym for most of the intervening six weeks and there were concerns he would not be in peak shape by 18 July. Soon after, to the intense irritation of the HBO executives, his date with McKinney was scuppered – officially because of his hand injury involving a small bone at the back of his hand which was making it painful for him to hit with full power, although his desire to stay at home with Eleasha and his new baby was certainly a contributing factor. It was apparent that his duty to his wife and child were more important than his obligations to his paymasters, who reluctantly set a new date of 31 October 1998 for Naseem's next performance.

After negotiations with Kennedy McKinney's management broke down, they settled on his old rival Wayne McCullough, whose bargaining power had been significantly diminished over the previous two years (meaning he could be paid $500,000 – half what Warren promised him two years earlier, and a quarter of Naseem's purse). The Las Vegas-based Ulsterman relinquished his WBC bantamweight title as a result of weight problems and in January 1997 moved up in weight to challenge Daniel Zaragoza for the WBC super bantamweight title, but lost on a close points decision. A severe shoulder injury followed by a break-up and eventual make-up with his promoter Matt Tinley put him out of action for 15 months. He returned as a featherweight in 1998, but did not look impressive in his two points wins, the last being a split decision victory over former Hamed victim, Juan Polo Perez.

McCullough was a remarkable character, in terms of what he represented. He was raised as an Ulster Protestant, just off the fiercely loyalist Shankill Road, but from early in his amateur career took a strong stand against sectarian loyalties. In 1988 Olympics he carried the Tri-Colour for Ireland at the Olympic opening ceremony, and four years later won Olympic silver in the Irish singlet. By then Irish nationalists had adopted him as a hero, but right up to the Hamed fight he continued to resist pressure to become a political symbol, preferring to fight in neutral black rather than green, for instance. 'The Pocket Rocket' was also an exceptional boxer – an all-action buzzsaw, always extremely well conditioned and able to throw over 100 punches per round. But he had several weaknesses, which seemed made to order for Hamed. In particular, he was relatively easy to hit and lacked the power to place Naseem in serious danger. Also, despite being over four inches taller than Naseem, he was a natural super bantamweight. His high profile, his support among the Irish-American community, his Olympic pedigree and his record of 22 wins in 23 fights made him credible and highly marketable, but his lack of power and form, and his break-ups with two highly respected trainers, suggested he posed no threat to Naseem, despite the six month layoff.

Two weeks after Sami's birth, Naseem decided that his right hand was in reasonable working order and that it was time to get back to the gym. The fused metacarpal bones, which left a large residue of grizzle, meant that it would probably never again be perfect and would always be painful to use at full force. It therefore required ongoing physiotherapy and ultrasound treatment, but unless he was to agree to surgery that carried a significant risk, it was as good as it would get. His return to action was more gradual than this early enthusiasm suggested but by early September he seemed to have worked his way back into reasonable condition, although having arrived at the gym weighing over 140 lbs his weight was a worry for his training team. 'He's really back into it,' Brendan enthused two weeks after training started. 'I'd say he's training *nearly* right, not perfect by any means because of his weight and his timing is not quite right, but he's better than I expected and he is hitting so hard it's unbelievable.'

From the way they worked in training, it seemed that the relationship between the two men appeared to have settled down again to something approaching a workable understanding. But it was not to last. At the heart of their next dispute was the personal and financial power struggle which had festered over the previous three years, but its form was influenced by their diametrically-opposed methods of dealing with the press. Naseem seemed unable to get away from his preconception that the media, and particularly the British media, should play the role of loyal subjects to their prince. When they showed their reluctance to fulfil this destiny, he seemed to regard them as inherently antagonistic, unworthy of his attentions – the enemy, even. Questions at press conferences were treated with naked contempt and aggression and individual journalists who had dared to second guess his behaviour were publicly or privately castigated in a way some regarded as intimidatory. The result was that with a few exceptions, his idea of the press as an enemy became a self-fulfilling prophecy. He had developed the knack of transforming supporters into opponents.

Brendan, on the other hand, cultivated the press assiduously – providing open access to his gym, charming journalists with his homespun wisdom, making them feel special and speaking with apparent frankness about the problems he faced. Until the Kelley fight, he had tended to be circumspect about openly discussing his troubles with Naseem, restricting his criticisms only to well-trusted journalists on an off-the-record basis. However, after that fight he spoke more freely, as did several of his boxers. The result was that his opinions about his fraught history with his most successful boxer came into the public domain, prompting a new crisis between the two men. After a series of newspaper articles alluding to these tensions, Nick Pitt's book *The Paddy and the Prince* provided Ingle's take on their conflicts. It quoted Brendan on the history of their financial and personal disputes prior to the Kelley fight, and was followed by a spate of press and television reports discussing their break-ups and make-ups.

This 'betrayal' by Brendan incensed Naseem, his brothers and his father and the family pulled even closer together in a concerted fight-back campaign. Initially Naseem chose to play the wronged son and benefactor role for all it was worth. 'I am absolutely devastated by what Brendan said,' he said soon after the news of the dispute broke. 'For a man who I thought was a father to me, to do this is unbelievable. This is a man who I have made the richest boxing trainer in the world. He has been able to earn more money than he would ever have expected to do otherwise; then he does this. It hurts to think someone as close as Brendan would say things like this.'

Riath also broke his silence on the dispute by castigating Ingle. 'Naz is hurt that someone who has known him for most of his life, who has been through thick and thin with him, would come out and say the things that he has said. Brendan is financially secure because of Naz but he wanted everything and that was not acceptable. He seems to be fixated on money. The thing that is so devastating is that most families have squabbles and arguments and they get over them. My dad and Frank Warren got involved to try and make sure he was happy with the money he was getting. Naz is big enough to take this kind of thing from Brendan and the thing about all this is that he still wants the relationship to continue. It is something Brendan and Naz have to work out between them now. Things are not looking good between them but we want to work it out. I really hope there can be a solution to this and that the relationship will continue.'

Soon after, when Ingle was about to leave for Telford to assist Junior Witter in beating Mark Winters, Naseem arrived at the gym. For the next four hours they thrashed out their differences, forcing Brendan to miss Witter's victory. Naseem was still irate, calling his trainer a 'Judas' and a 'traitor' in earshot of other boxers and castigating him for revealing secrets which he had no right to expose. As Ingle recalls: 'I said to him, "You can call me a traitor if you like. In fact why don't you call me a Judas Paddy traitor. I don't mind. I am not a Judas, but I may have saved your career." I told him he'd been a horrible person for the past four years, and my job had been to save him from himself. I reminded him I'd said he could be as good, better even, than Ali or Sugar Ray Robinson – the perfect fighter, and that I'd kept him winning despite all his problems, and then I asked him what he would have achieved if he trained right. He then said he was going to rise above this because he was married and had a son, and I said, "marvellous, because if you don't get bigger than Ali and Robinson, he'll say to you, 'dad, what went wrong?' and I'll say to your son, 'he wouldn't listen'." He then reminded me he didn't smoke or drink and was happily married, and even claimed that he didn't want yes-men around him, and when we finished talking he said would forgive but not forget. He might still regard me as a Judas and a traitor – which I'm certainly not and never have been – but end of the day, I'm relieved it all came out in the open because it was the worst-kept secret in the game. We decided to do it fight by fight and see how it went from here. I didn't have to talk to Riath. I was dealing with Naseem, and as far as I was concerned at that point, that was just great.'

Hamed's initial response revealed a maturity not previously evident. Under Riath's guidance, he continued positioning himself on the moral high ground, stressing that while Brendan should not have 'betrayed' him by revealing details of their conflict, he had no plans to sack him. He implied he was a bigger, more loyal person than his one-time mentor – that he had grown up and become more sensible, and that fatherhood had given him a new direction life – and was therefore after reconciliation.

Brendan too was happy to stress the positive, emphasising that the Pitt book went no further Kelley fight in 1997, and that since then their relationship had improved. But he was not prepared to withdraw his criticisms. As he put it a few days after their four-hour gym meeting: 'I have to say to Naz, that was my opinion. I'm entitled to it and he's entitled to his. I haven't got a problem with all this. It may even make him a better fighter and a better person. My job is not to be nice. You can't have yes-men around you. But as far as I am concerned it is all water under the bridge now. We had our differences at the time of the Kelley fight but those are in the past now, and I've been working with Naz since. This is something we have to work out between us.'

But despite these words of reconciliation, it was clear that the remaining trust in their relationship had evaporated, and that Naseem was no more prepared or able to forgive than he was to forget. In an interview with Sky a month later, he returned to his more familiar vitriolic tone, speaking with a bitterness that had evidently not subsided: 'I have realised after 17 years, Brendan is totally and utterly money oriented, money motivated. I am not an angry. I am a mature man who is more mature and wiser at 24 than Brendan and he is 58. Any other person would have sacked him. I made him a millionaire. It was like a marriage, like a bond. I feel betrayed. He is a Judas.' He went on to ridicule Ingle's training methods, saying that up until then he had been prepared for fights like an amateur, without any specialist tuition – using this claim as evidence that his achievements were purely the result of his innate, God-given talent. 'In 30 fights I have never had one-on-on tuition as a world champion. I've gone into the gym and done a set routine like any other kid. The truth is that I've never had a proper trainer.' And despite the fact that Ingle had produced a 20-year stream of champions, he reiterated his view that he reached the top despite Ingle, not because of him. He also made it clear that he had discovered in times of trouble only his 'blood' family could be relied on.

Subsequently, however, Naseem seemed to regret the way he had come across, and was furious with the interviewer, Adam Smith for using it in unedited form. This brought a strong riposte from Sky's boxing commentator, Ian Darke, who wrote in *Boxing News*: 'He had the choice to say what he wanted with the camera rolling and chose to get stuck into Brendan. But now he wanted to shoot the messenger, refusing to give Smith another interview. He launched a vicious verbal attack on a reporter who had been one of his closest allies, claiming a breach of trust, when in fact all Sky had done was broadcast the words the fighter himself had spoken.'

Back at the gym, it was soon clear that the relationship had changed, even though the day to day exchanges between Naseem and Brendan seemed amicable enough. For his promised £75,000 Ingle was playing what he called a 'supervisory background role' and what Naseem called 'basically not much'. The bulk of the condition work was done by Dominic Ingle, who also put Hamed on a diet with protein powders, amino acids, fat burning ingredients, vitamin supplements and a carbohydrate drink. While the main emphasis was on weight reduction, Dominic also increased his strength work and built on his aerobic fitness, while John Ingle continued to do the padwork. Every morning Naseem would arrive at the gym at 7 a.m. for a two-hour session, with a second session at 3 p.m. Naseem was clearly delighted with the benefits of the change, showing off his more defined musculature and claiming he had never been fitter and better prepared. 'My recovery rate was remarkable,' he said after a month of this routine. He also made a regular point of heaping praise on the Ingle brothers at the expense of their father.

The tensions with Ingle were not the only new distraction for Naseem. It was also becoming clear that Frank Warren's battle with Don King was doing nothing to enhance his relationship with his top fighter. For five years Warren and Hamed had developed an affectionate relationship which had gone well beyond their business dealings. Naseem recognised something of himself in Warren's risk-taking, big-thinking aggression while admiring the older man's business acumen and worldly wisdom. Warren enjoyed Naseem's boundless self-confidence, his cockiness and the respect he was willing to show. Now and then they exchanged expensive gifts (the jeep, the Aston Martin and a few top of the range watches from Warren; a statue of Naseem from Naseem, with the inscription: 'To the best promoter in the world from the best boxer in the world'), but they also exchanged jokes and personal confidences. Throughout 1998, however, there were signs that the relationship was cooling. Warren was no longer being asked to play a mentor's role, and no longer praising and defending his young charge with quite the same conviction as before, and it was apparent that Naseem had withdrawn much of his admiration for his 'main man'. He therefore became even more reliant on his immediate family for advice.

In the background was the sense that despite his early victories, Warren had been premature in launching his war with King. With his greater financial muscle, the American was winning the major battles and the Englishman was clearly in retreat on this front, while at the same time he acknowledged he was preparing himself for charges of VAT evasion from the IRS, of which he said he was innocent. His most pressing problem, however, was that as a result of his dispute with King, his assets had been frozen by the High Court, which meant his business interests had to run on a shoestring retainer. One of these was his rugby club, Bedford, which was in a state of revolt because of late payment of wages. But far more serious was the Hamed fallout.

The court order effectively restricted Warren's ability to promote Naseem, with the result that Warren initially chose to use an American company, Sports International, to do the honours, while acting as a 'consultant' himself. King returned to the High Court to object to this arrangement and HBO became concerned that the fight would not materialise. As a result, Cedric Kushner, the New York-based promoter who had close relations with HBO as well as with Warren's South African partner, Rodney Berman, was brought in at the last moment as the official promoter.

It was hardly surprising therefore that Hamed became concerned he would not be paid in full, and on the Friday before the fight refused to depart for the United States until receiving confirmation that his $2 million was deposited in his bank account. Soon after it emerged that Naseem's work permit in the United States had not been secured with the result that he missed several crucial pre-fight engagements, which angered HBO, Kushner and Bally's Casino Organisation, which underwrote the event. Both Warren and Riath Hamed denied blame for this oversight but what may have exacerbated the problem was Naseem's own tardiness on the bureaucratic front.

A week after being asked by the Sports Network office to provide the required documentation, this little task had still not been completed. He also failed to turn up to two appointments at the American embassy, eventually making it – a couple of hours late – on the third try. He finally arrived on Concorde four days after the rest of his entourage and four days before the fight, and

immediately demanded that everyone be removed from the
Atlantic City gym so that he could train. But despite his
impressive workout, it quickly became clear that the un-
certainties of the previous month had upset him far more than he
was prepared to acknowledge. The effect was to undo the carefully massaged image repairing work that Riath had been
masterminding.

For a start, he returned to his old mode of using unsavoury
insults against opponents. Still smarting from the time
McCullough upstaged his weigh-in for the Manuel Medina
fight in Dublin two years earlier, he went way beyond his
prediction of 'three rounds or earlier, depending on how I feel'
(and later 2 min 28 of the third, to be precise) to talk with relish
about the kind of physical damage he would dish out. He spoke
of his desire to 'seriously hurt' McCullough, adding, 'I'm going to
beat him like his daddy.' Later, at the final head-to-head press
conference, he told his understated opponent: 'I stretched Kelley
and I'll stretch you. Then you'll be just a couple of old bums. This
could be your last fight.'

The lack of dignity in these insults was exacerbated by
McCullough's good-natured and thoroughly professional
response. Despite the distracting presence of his manager-wife,
Cheryl, and baby Winona in his hotel bedroom in the lead-up to
the fight, and his own history of trainer troubles, the adopted
Irishman appeared calm and focused about the job at hand. He
insisted he had 'nothing personal against Naseem' and refused to
rise to Naseem's bait. Instead he focused on the champion's
technical shortcomings and on his own strengths. 'Sure he'll hit
me. But what if he can't move me? What if I don't go down where
the others do? Then we'll see how good he is.'

But if Hamed's verbal treatment of McCullough was crass, his
handling of the press was astonishing, even by his own
standards. On at least two occasions Sal advised his son to ease off
on the vitriol. 'I told him he's got to calm down. I told him to be
nice to people,' Sal said.

But instead of listening to the man he claimed to respect more
than any other, Naseem let loose a stream of abuse, aimed at
specific journalists. At the final head-to-head press conference
there were insulting or belittling titbits for the likes of Barry
McGuigan (whom he wished was still boxing so that he could
'batter him'), former IBF cruiserweight champion Glenn McCrory

and several British and American journalists before he turned his chair to face the *Sun*'s highly respected boxing writer Colin Hart and vomited out a sustained torrent of abuse, beginning with: 'I don't like you Colin. You are a fool. You are an idiot.' This seemed to be drawn from the fact that 'Colin Fart', as he charmingly proceeded to call him, had the temerity to criticise him.

For the rest of the week Naseem continued in this vein, picking on Sky television commentators, British journalists and everybody else who crossed his path. When it was over, he had lost the ground he had regained with the British press over the previous nine months while securing his reputation for nastiness with the Americans. Despite the efforts of his family, he was viewed as out-of-control and dangerously self-obsessed and several journalists were itching to get their own back.

Meanwhile, behind the scenes Riath, with his lawyer in tow, was renegotiating Naseem's contract with HBO, pointing out that Warren's contract with his brother had expired in August and that HBO's existing six-fight deal was with Warren, rather than Naseem, and therefore demanding rights to television sales outside of America. In the course of these spats, both Warren and Ingle had become exasperated with the situation. Warren described it as his worst experience in his 20-year association with the sport and considered returning to Britain and taking his staff with him. In public he continued to mouth the Hamed cause, but it was clear he was merely going through the motions by this stage. In private it was a different story. As Brendan Ingle recalls: 'The day before the fight Frank told me he was seriously considering pulling out. You can't believe the pressure he was under. Of course, he stuck it out but he said to me: "Brendan, I don't need this", and I replied, "Neither do I, neither do I". I made my decision then that I would never work with him again, even though I'd choose my own time to announce it – only after I was paid what was owed to me. What happened then – the way they treated people – was as bad as I've seen in half a century in this game. All of the worst elements of human nature came out and I just couldn't put up with it any more.'

But it was Naseem's performance in the ring that set the seal on his rapidly declining reputation. Following two impressive wins by potential rivals – South Africa's Vuyani Bungu outscoring America's Danny Romero to retain his IBF super bantamweight title for the 12th time and Mexico's Marco Antonio Barrera regaining the WBO version by stopping Britain's Richie Wenton in three rounds – Hamed was expected to close the show in spectacular fashion. And that was the way it appeared until the fight passed the opening rounds. To the sound of Michael Jackson's 'Thriller' Naseem confidently danced his way past HBO's grotesque mock Halloween night graveyard (originally set to include the names of his past victims on the gravestones, until, in a moment of good taste, Naseem refused). To a mixture of Irish boos and Arab cheers from the 8,138 crowd (well short of the 15,000 capacity), he whacked a gravestone before proceeding with his usual entrance. Weighing in at 125 lbs – his lightest in over three years – he looked svelte, taught and, as usual, supremely confident. In contrast, McCullough, who weighed in at 124 lbs (the midpoint between the super bantam and feather-weight limits), looked frail, nervous and drawn while his pale wife Cheryl appeared terrified about what would happen to her man.

This impression of a gulf in confidence was reinforced when McCullough emerged jabbing tentatively from behind his peak-a-boo guard, only to be whacked by a hard three punch combination, ending with a hurtful left. Another flurry raised expectations of an early night. Within a minute the right side of the challenger's face was already an angry red, but instead of pressing his advantage, Naseem chose to dance and play with his hands dangling, saying, 'Come and fight' before looking casually backwards, smiling at the press rows before leaping in with a left hook to the body. All Wayne could manage in reply was a light-fisted body flurry on the ropes and a solitary right to the head. At the bell the laughing champion was convinced it was as good as over.

Early in the second he connected with a hefty left hook, fired from chest level but McCullough revealed he possessed one of the soundest chins in the business by absorbing it and replying with a left-right combination, followed by a left hook that surprised Naseem. Soon after, he evaded a left, before following Hamed's momentum and patting the champion twice on his bottom. Naseem response was to push Wayne down and hit him while his gloves were still on the canvass. Midway through the round the challenger landed several light body blows and exchanged a pair of rights for Hamed's two left hooks. The round ended with Wayne digging in a decent right cross and then matching Hamed punch for punch at the bell.

In the third, Naseem came out with the intention of fulfilling his prediction, but it was Wayne who landed first, with left hook. This success encouraged a determined effort to get inside and he eventually landed a hard right cross. This prompted another moment of clowning, followed by a heavy uppercut and a solid straight left, none of which moved the Irishman. When the champion touched down from a slip, the tricolour contingent at the back of the hall roared. The last seconds of the round were marked by desperation from Naseem who, after exchanging some elbow blows on the inside, landed a heavy right. However, he had failed to make good on his prediction, and returned to his corner with a depressing announcement. 'I've knocked up my left hand. I'll have to box from here.'

After the fight, when Brendan removed the bandages, it was clear that three of the knuckles were severely swollen while his right hand was also in some pain. From then on, Hamed's sense of purpose evaporated. He refused to listen to his corner, contemptuously looking into the middle distance when Brendan tried to address him and specifically ignoring advice to move in and 'break him up with the jab'.

In the fourth he indulged in prolonged mockery, looking out of the ring, grinning away while throwing little of consequence. His reluctance to put weight behind his jab allowed Wayne to get closer, and, eventually, to land a right cross which rocked Naseem's head back. The champion came back by landing an uppercut with his bruised left, but once again Wayne was unmoved. He was finding his range, while at the same time making Hamed miss with effective head movement. He started the fifth by snapping Naseem's head back with a jab, and then made him swipe air with several punches, although he had to absorb a double right for his troubles. Later, McCullough landed a right cross and a left, to win the round.

The sixth and seventh followed a similar pattern. Between rounds Hamed made a point of standing when he was asked to sit, all the while smirking to make a showy point of his attitude to his trainer. By then he was pawing with his jab and measuring for the big shots, confusing McCullough without doing much damage. He managed to land flush with a right cross in the sixth and despite all his movement he looked the fresher of the two. But in the seventh he went back to demeaning the occasion and himself by looking away from him and into the booing crowd while laughing at the frustrated Wayne and he kept it up in the eighth – dancing, pawing, clinching, taunting and missing far more than he was accustomed to. At the end of the round Naseem sat again, with his familiar, smug smile on his face. Despite the fact that he was showing no signs of wear and tear, or even breathing heavily, this seemed to encourage McCullough's corner towards the view that Hamed was fading, and they implored their man to greater efforts. Responding to this advice, Wayne upped his workrate. After a frustrating minute, a sharp McCullough right got Naseem's attention, and the challenger followed this by working his way inside and then landing an even bigger right cross which sent the sweat flying and forced Hamed to keep his guard up. He responded with several hard punches of his own which landed on McCullough's sturdy chin, but the Irishman was into his stride and kept marching forward. Shortly before the bell Wayne connected with a decent left hook that raised a small red blotch on the side of the champion's cheek.

Naseem was purposeful at the start of the 10th, bettering Wayne in a mid-rung exchange. He followed that with a hurtful right but McCullough responded with a left-right combination drawing a sustained cheer from the mainly anti-Hamed crowd. But it was a brief moment of glory. The champion came back with a stiff right to the nose which forced his opponent to take a half step backwards to retain his balance and later a left hook which wobbled McCullough. Towards the end of the round Wayne landed his left hook but it was becoming clear that the effects of this kind of punishment, the frustration of missing so often and his own high WordArt, were taking the snap out of his blows. Hamed on the other hand, still looked fresh and tried to reinforce this impression by standing in the middle of the ring when the bell sounded, taunting the Irishman.

Realising he was ahead and that the prospect of a knockout was fading, Naseem eased off again in the penultimate round. This allowed McCullough to land a stiff right cross which shook him momentarily. Spurred into belated action, Naseem landed three heavier blows, drawing blood from Wayne's nose. When the round ended McCullough's left eye was swelling, and his face was covered with welts and blotches, while Hamed had a cut inside his mouth and a few blotches and bruises on his face.

Once again Naseem elected to remain standing between rounds, and pushed Brendan away when he implored him to sit and listen. He made no attempt in the final round to change the pattern of the fight – merely dancing evasively, prodding out his right to measure his man, and pulling away at the first sign of trouble.

Eventually McCullough raised a roar when he connected with a right cross, which Hamed paid back via a heavy left but after that, Naseem refused to fight, holding or backing off and drawing a warning from the referee to do more. McCullough, on the other hand, did all he could to make an impression and managed to connect with a right cross and left hook. In the last seconds the frustrated Irishman performed a mock Riverdance shuffle that seemed to amuse Michael Flatley at ringside, and then threw his arms up at the bell before lifting Hamed into the air.

Hamed's heavier artillery and superior evasive powers had won the fight with plenty to spare. The CompuBox punch statistics showed he landed 46 percent of his 742 punches (a figure inflated by his many prodding little jabs) while McCullough landed 23 percent of his 740 punches. Judge John Steward's score of 118 – 110 (10 rounds to two) was too wide and a more accurate interpretation probably fell between the scores of Nelson Vazquez (117 – 111 or nine rounds to three) and Clark Sammartino (116 – 112 or eight rounds to four). Still the crowd booed the result heartily and at least one newspaper, the *Atlantic City Press*, gave it to the Irishman.

In all this there were a few positives worth mentioning. By going 12 rounds without any sign of exhaustion Naseem had revealed that concerns about his stamina after six months of inactivity were misplaced. Dominic Ingle's fitness programme and dietary supplements had evidently played their role in his victory. Naseem demonstrated that his ability to dance had not been lost, and dispelled some of the doubts about his ability to take a punch. Despite his record of 14 stoppages in 22 victories, the 'Pocket Rocket' was not a particularly heavy hitter, but he did connect with several full-blooded right crosses and handful of left hooks without seriously inconveniencing Hamed. As with previous below par showings, there may have been plausible reasons for suggesting this was a temporary aberration. With Alicea it was his failure to take his training seriously. With Medina it was his lung infection. With Kelley it was the novelty of New York, the problems with his ring entrance and the upset of his break-up and make-up with Brendan. There were similar excuses in Atlantic City – his late arrival that, he claimed, upset his body clock, the troubles in his camp, the confusion and aggravation around the promotion and his hand troubles.

Overall, however, it was hard to escape the impression that it was his most dismal showing to date. He was clearly in peak fitness yet his timing was off, both defensively and in attack, and he seemed to have little stomach for a close range shootout with his lighter adversary. It is true that he hurt his left in the third round, but until then he had failed to dent his hard-headed opponent, and after that his right made little serious impression either. More surprising was that an uncomplicated boxer like McCullough was making Hamed miss spectacularly. With his early tactics having failed, Naseem seemed to have no other answer but to dance on retreat, and once again he virtually ignored his opponent's body.

McCullough's own verdict was that while Naseem was strong and hit hard, he had taken bigger punches from the bantam-weight Victor Rabanales and the super bantamweight Daniel Zaragoza. 'Naseem ran away. He ran like an amateur. He was stealing the fight. There was nothing I could do but run after him. He never hurt me once, and I'm a bantamweight,' he said. Later he added: 'If I'd stood off Naseem there wouldn't have been a fight. I could have sat in my corner and had a cup of tea.' As a result, many drew the conclusion that either Hamed's decline was more rapid and absolute than previously assumed or he was incapable of boxing at his best without a harmonious relationship with his trainer. Unlike his focused performances against Badillo and Vazquez, when, by fight time, he was willing to listen to Ingle, his bleak showing against McCullough had more in common with the Kelley fight in this respect. On both occasions his trainer had played a backseat role for much of the build-up and both times he was determined to ignore his advice. The result was that he was distracted and was unable to adjust tactics when his initial plan failed.

'There is no question that a major reason for his poor per-formance was that he was ignoring all my advice and trying to make a point about doing it his way,' said Ingle, 'but I think all the distractions – from Riath in particular – had their effect and also you have to bear in mind that while he was obviously fit, most of the training he did was aimed at getting the weight off to make the featherweight limit again, rather than getting him in tune for a boxing match. His weight had risen to over 145 lbs and it was a real job knocking off 20 lbs.'

Naseem, however, was having none of this. Until six weeks after the fight he did not accept there was reason for criticism either of his showing in the ring, or his performance outside the ring over the previous week. When Sky's Ian Darke asked him if he had any regrets about the way he'd treated the press he replied: 'Not at all. I'm so happy. I said what I said. I got it off my chest.' He was prepared to give no more than a backhanded compliment to McCullough: 'He was quite strong. I tried to knock him out in the third round. What can I say? He's got a hard head. He's Irish, you know.' And he would not countenance any criticism of his own display. 'I thought I did very, very well. I boxed to the best of my ability. I boxed his head off. I haven't really got a problem. I'm still undefeated. I had a ball in there. It was willed by God to go 12 rounds and it went 12 rounds. I'm still the best in the world. He took a beating. Look at his face and look at mine. I won easy.'

Soon after, he walked out on the Darke interview, saying it went on too long. Darke subsequently complained in person to Naseem, but as he put it, 'my comments were not well received.' This incident and the events of the previous week, prompted Darke to make an unprecedented attack on Hamed in print. Using *Boxing News* as his vehicle he wrote: 'His American dream is just not happening. His relations with the British media are at an all-time low ... There have been murmurings from the Hamed camp of an orchestrated campaign by the British media to attack him. That is palpable nonsense. The reportage from Atlantic City was purely a reaction to the way Naz behaved and fought there. What is more, his general complaint that he gets unfair coverage takes no account of the fact that publicity has helped make him a star. Perhaps he would like to join the 90 per cent of British boxers who never get a mention in the papers ... Ignoring the heaps of praise he gets for his talent, he chooses only to hear the odd word of valid criticism that comes his way. Part of being a high-profile personality involves taking the rough with the smooth ... ' He went on to acknowledge Naseem's finer qualities before concluding with the question: 'So why does he keep showing the world his ugly profile? Someone call a spin doctor because the self-styled Prince appears to be under the misapprehension that he is really royalty.'

Meanwhile his beleaguered backers were still going through the motions of putting brave faces on it all. HBO boss Seth Abraham, who was no doubt soothed by the news that pay-per-view takings were far better than expected (beating Oscar de la Hoya's much vaunted defence against Patrick Charpentier earlier that year), said: 'He looked rusty. I still think the US fight fan does not know what to make of him.'

Adidas acknowledged being disappointed by his behaviour but insisted they had no plans to drop him. As Robin Money, their head of corporate relations put it six weeks later: 'Unfortunately, sometimes he doesn't come across well, like in Atlantic City. He didn't behave well there and he knows it, but we will continue using him in the long term, whatever that means in boxing, because he's a very special sportsman, who boxes in a unique, exciting way, and also because he appeals to the 80 per cent of non-sports people who use our products, particularly the youth market. In fact, that's the real reason why we chose him.'

He went on to stress Naseem's positive side. 'I've got to know him very well and he's a lovely character, a real, genuine guy and he's a good father and son. His own son is the greatest thing that has ever happened to him, including his fights, and that speaks volumes for him as a person.'

Warren also refrained from public criticism after the fight. 'He won comfortably enough. It's hard for him. He's 24 and you're asking him to be perfect.' In the changing room however he implored Naseem to be more contrite, and to admit he had a bad night, with better things to come. But it took over a month before the boxer was prepared to admit his performance was well below par (citing his hand injury, his late arrival and the tensions around the fight as reasons). He also acknowledged he had been 'out of order' in his behaviour, but by then the damage was done.

Meanwhile, with Naseem, Eleasha and Sami on holiday in Palm Springs, Riath was making his move. Having previously applied for a British promoter's license, and having already assumed a managerial agent's role with other boxers, including the WBC super middleweight champion Richie Woodhall, it was clear Riath wanted a larger slice of the boxing action. Ten days after the McCullough fight he announced he was ready to start making his own deals. 'As from today Naz is a free agent in the boxing world. Naz is exercising his right to retain his worldwide rights and control his own destiny. We have four years' experience in boxing management now and Naz has 17 years' experience of promoters and managers. Whatever decisions we make will not be done on a whim. We will be taking advice from lawyers and commercial experts. This is not about great. It is about Naz being paid what he is worth in the world market. Naz is hot property – 13 million people watched the Wayne McCullough fight live – and we are being besieged by offers.' He went on to claim his brother would earn '£50 million plus' through relying on his family and doing away with the middlemen and explained that his own role would involve hiring other promoters to deliver opponents, venues and ticket sales.

This announcement seemed to have seriously jeopardised the relationship with Warren, who by then was already promoting his WBO super middleweight champion Joe Calzaghe as his next big thing. Ingle meanwhile pre-empted any moves to oust him, by stating that whatever happened he would stick with Warren. 'Wherever Frank goes, we go,' he announced. Privately, he said at the time that he was incensed about the Hameds 'disloyalty' to Warren. 'For the last two years Frank was the peacemaker between me and Naz, but he's turned on the peacemaker. But far more than that, the promotional job Frank done for him, no-one else could have done. Naz is one of the best-paid boxers ever but they just have no loyalty, so I'm absolutely disgusted. They say it has nothing to do with greed, but it's clear it has everything to do with greed. Money has become their god. I said that before and I've been proved right. Now they want to cut out the so-called middle men and do everything from being the boxer to the manager to the promoter.'

At the end of the year Warren's bargaining power was further eroded when he lost an appeal against the High Court judgement freezing his assets. Lord Justice Morritt's judgement also confirmed King's view that he had a half share of the European boxers in Warren's stable prior to the break-up of the partnership. A month later the British promoter decided to throw in the towel rather than continue with a series of legal appeals he was not expected to win, and which had already cost him over £500,000. As a result, on January 12 1999 the former partners met again at the High Court where it was announced that Warren had agreed to pay King £7.2 million for his share of the partnership, and to withdraw all the allegations he had made against King including his claim that the American promoter had fraudulantly inserted a clause into their contract). Warren put a brave face on his predicament, claiming the settlement was 'cheap at the price' before announcing: 'I am free. I am glad this is all behind us but it looks as if I shall be eating soup in a basket tonight.' King's lawyers said Warren had agreed to sell his 16th century Hertfordshire mansion if necessary to make the first of a series of payments.

Yet throughout this period of successive legal defeats, Warren still managed to retain a tenuous connection with Naseem. When the Hameds returned from their post-McCullough holiday, Naseem spoke with Warren for an hour on the telephone after which he emerged with the surprise announcement. 'I want to be with Frank Warren and he wants to be with me. I believe he is a great promoter and there is no split and there is no split with Brendan Ingle.' Riath, however, quickly made it clear that retaining links with Warren was merely one option they were considering, and reasserted that whoever they worked with, it would be Naseem and his family who would be taking the risks, calling the shots and reaping the rewards. A month later, at the end of January 1999, his view of the future was confirmed when the relationship with Warren was formally severed and it was announced that Naseem's next fight, in London, would be promoted by none other than Barry Hearn, the Essex man who had started him out on his professional career seven years earlier.

Despite Naseem's assertion that there was no split with Ingle, his trainer decided he was not prepared to continue working with Hamed. 'During the McCullough fight I said to my wife that after this is finished I don't want anything more to do with him, and I would not change my mind. It might have meant a loss of money but I just couldn't handle the aggravation and as soon as that decision was made I felt much happier about my life.'

But he held back from making any announcement until he was paid the £75,000 plus VAT owed to him for the McCullough fight. As he later explained: 'I waited six weeks for my money, so eventually, after he returned, I went up to Naz's house with my son, John, and we had a bit of a ding-dong. Sal, Nabeel and Naz were there and they wanted to pay me only £30,000 and said I hadn't done the training, that I was away some of the time and that Dominic had done most of the work. I said I had worked it all out beforehand with Dominic and pointed out that they had already agreed to pay me the £75,000. Then they said they would only pay it if I signed that same gagging document I'd ignored before the Kelley fight a year earlier. I could see they wanted to finish with me without paying the full amount, and that I would then have to go through a lengthy court case, so in the end I signed their piece of paper and they gave me my cheque – if I wanted my money I had no option.'

Finally, on December 8 1998 the relationship formally came to an end, seventeen and a half years after it started. In public Ingle wished Hamed the best of luck but could not resist mentioning that their parting was a relief, observing that Naseem would have to learn to behave himself with whoever took over his training and noting in passing that his own role in revealing all about Hamed's past, as well as Naseem's marriage had 'saved his career'. 'There will be life after Naz and, for him life after Ingle,' he said, before bestowing a final double-edged blessing. 'If any trainer can take him to a higher plane then I'll take my hat off to him.'

Beyond the microphones, he was rather more frank in his opinions. 'I don't think they know what they're doing in the promotional and managerial sense, and I think whoever trains him may have trouble. Naz has matured physically so he's stronger than ever, but he doesn't put in the consistent, day-to-day hard work anymore, and that gave him his speed and timing. He may still be the best featherweight in the world, but he has developed an attitude of superiority and I think it will end in tears. But for myself, I'm happy. I've got five wonderful kids and two grandchildren to focus on, and I've still got a marvellous stable of boxers including top fellas who have learnt from Naseem's mistakes, and I feel like a weight has been lifted from my shoulders.' Immediately after this announcement Brendan took a delighted Alma out for a celebratory dinner. A couple of weeks later it was announced in the New Year's Honours List that he would receive an MBE for services to disadvantaged young people and boxing.

Naseem, who also received an MBE, did his best to hold back on the vitriol. 'I met with Brendan in my office and we agreed to go our separate ways,' he began. 'I want to make it absolutely clear there is no animosity. We have had what could be called a civilised divorce. It was like father and son in the beginning. It lasted for 17 years and I can't forget that.' However, when asked who had been at fault he could not quite let it pass. 'I'd say the blame lies mainly with Brendan,' he insisted, adding that Brendan's decision to spill the beans publicly on their relation-ship was 'the last straw'. After that, however, he withdrew from the fray, noting that they had both found it difficult to work with each other at times. 'I think it's for the best. We parted on good terms and good luck for him.' He added that while he would miss the camaraderie of the gym, 'it will all happen for me in the best way.' He went on to reiterate his belief that a new trainer could offer him the intense, one-on-one focus he needed to progress, and to confirm that he would continue to train in Sheffield. Soon after he moved his training base to a gym run by former Ingle protégé and subsequent enemy Glyn Rhodes (assisted by Herol Graham) and retained the services of an obscure Puerto Rican trainer, Oscar Suarez.

And so, as 1998 ended, Naseem's future had once again been thrown open. It had been a momentous year in every respect. He had ended an intense and formative relationship with a man who was far, far more than merely a trainer. He had come close to ending a five-year relationship with the promoter and friend who had transformed him from a rising star to one of the richest sportsmen in Britain. He had parted ways with a gymnasium that had been his second home since the age of seven, and a stable of boxers who had formed his prime friendship group. He had placed increasingly large slices of his boxing career in the hands of a brother who had never managed or promoted a fighter before, and had drawn far closer to a family whose advice he still occasionally ignored. He had abandoned his tomcat days to become a husband and father. He had been exposed by Ingle's revelations about their conflicts, then had won ground with the media by displaying his nicer side, only to lose it all again in a week of madness. And in all this time he had boxed only twice – first a sound but unspectacular stoppage over an ageing champion; then a disappointing points win over a smaller former champion, and in between he suffered further damage to his precious hands. One sensed that the grand plans for eternal wealth were resting on an edifice no longer as secure as we were once led to assume. To most analysts it seemed that, at the age of 25, Naseem Hamed MBE had passed his prime. But then again, in boxing, as in life, all is not as it seems.

10

MYTHS AND LEGENDS

We should not be surprised that most of the sport's elite do not match up to Ali's genuine warmth, generosity of spirit and love of people, nor that the line demarcating their place of work from the rest of their lives is not as defined as is often assumed. Many boxers are no more able to switch off from their fury in the ring than the rest of us can switch off when leaving our offices. Most boxers enter their sport by chance rather than inclination – because there's a gym in their neighbourhood, or because their father did it – but once there, they have to enter into its amoral logic. They are trained to score points off other people's heads and bodies, or better still, to hit them hard or often enough to make a points tally unnecessary. This means hurting people, finishing them *off*, knocking them *out*, being ruthless. Some boxers acquire this 'instinct', but the best usually arrive with it in uncut form, after which their trainers 'channel' it. However we choose to frame it, cruelty, or at least the temporary absence of mercy, is an essential of boxing greatness. We may like to believe that bullies are really closet cowards, but some of the most courageous boxers have been men with an inclination for bullying inside and outside their line of work. Certainly there are many examples of boxers whose extra-mural lives are the epitome of gentility, but this hardly comes with the territory. The best boxers are seldom the best people and one only has to search beneath the hyperbole in the lives of past 'legends' to realize that the violence of the ring is not easily switched off once the bell rings.

It should not astonish us when a brilliant young fighter like Naseem Hamed does not quite measure up to his word about being 'a completely different person' outside the ring. You look in his eyes when he's cutting down an impudent press conference questioner and it's the same look he has when he's dropping Steve Robinson or Billy Hardy. And when there are reports of the odd 'altercation', of an 'incident' at an airport, or when journalists complain he's behaving like a bit of a 'prat', or write about the contradictions between his religious faith and his day-to-night behaviour, or complain that his demeanour here, there and the next place is not what we'd expect from a world champion, we should not assume he's become some kind of fallen angel, or that fame and fortune have soiled him beyond recognition. They may well have done their share of soiling, but the capacity for cruelty has always been there, sitting alongside his capacity for self-love and some rather more endearing qualities. And besides, the contemporary standard set by the 'greats' is not exactly lofty: drug addiction, alcoholism, wife-beating, assault, kidnapping, to take a few examples from the recent heavyweight top drawer. Against these, Hamed's sins of dangerous driving, Eubank-bashing, press-berating and naked narcissm seem pathetically trifling. With Naseem we can take additional solace in the knowledge that his 'Mr Hyde' side has always been balanced if not by a Dr Jekyll, then certainly by other, admirable dimensions: love of family, hatred of racism, ability to show kindness, sense of community, spurts of generosity, bursts of altruism. One has to concede there may be 'nicer' human beings in his business, but more significant is that there are very few better boxers, and it is primarily in these terms that he should, and will, be judged.

From the start of his career, Naseem has been in a position that for most sportsmen would be extremely invidious. He has been so showered with superlatives by his own people, by the press, and most notably by himself, that it would seem almost impossible for him to meet expectations. Which other boxer – after only fifteen fights – has been compared favourably with the likes of Sugar Ray Robinson and Muhammad Ali at their peaks? Which other bantamweight has had his trainer say he's capable of winning world titles all the way up to middleweight? Which other British fighter has said of himself that he would be the only pugilistic legend his country had ever produced? It was quite a tall order really.

All we can go on is what we've seen so far, which is not enough to be able to judge him as a certainty for 'greatness', whatever that overused word means. Certainly from what I have seen of him so far – through watching him in most of his professional fights and in the gym – I would still say that in nearly thirty years of following this sport I have never seen a boxer, anywhere in the world, who has arrived with his level of *potential*. But – descending for the moment into the silly game of rating fighters of different weights and eras against each other – that doesn't mean we can be sure Hamed is destined to join the company of the Robinsons, the Alis, the Harry Grebs, Henry Armstrongs and Roberto Durans. Not by a long way.

Donald 'The Cobra' Curry was almost universally rated as the best boxer, pound for pound, in the mid eighties, until Lloyd Honeyghan and then Mike McCallum exposed a certain physical frailty that had previously been concealed; Mike Tyson seemed unstoppable in the late eighties until Buster Douglas and then Evander Holyfield exposed his vulnerability when faced with exceptional boxers who were stronger than himself; George Foreman seemed like an unstoppable wrecking bull in the early seventies until Muhammad Ali and then Jimmy Young out-thought him and exposed his lack of stamina; Julio Cesar Chavez seemed like an invincibly complete boxer-puncher until Pernell Whitaker exposed a lack of pace in his fighting rhythm. And there are plenty of warning signs that it could happen to Naseem Hamed too.

Until recently he has been such an original, so gifted with natural ability, power, co-ordination, timing, physical strength, stamina, resilience and determination that he may still remain the best fighter of his weight in the world, although his claim to this title has become increasingly precarious. But it is also true that since he won his world title in 1995, we have seen more of the worst than his early rise had led us to anticipate. He hits harder than ever, but he is also slower of foot and reflex and no longer displays the same flexibility, timing and speed as before. He may, indeed, have peaked. The weakness comes through his declining inclination to work as hard now as he did a few years ago. With each near disaster this is temporarily reversed, only for the habit to re-emerge. He no longer lives for the gym. He no longer enjoys training as he used to. And if he continues along that trajectory, it could prove dangerous. Then there is the matter of his hands, injured as an amateur and then broken and re-injured as a professional, which, if they continue to show frailty, could upset the rhythm and momentum of his career and one wonders how he will cope if the decline in his relationship with Brendan Ingle leads to a complete severing of his ties. It also has to be conceded that he has yet to face, in competition at least, a fighter who is favoured to beat him, and there are several styles he has not been confronted with. From the way he has handled extremely capable big men in the gym, one can tentatively assume he would have little problem moving up a couple more weight divisions. But that's as far as we can take it. So far, betting on Naseem to become, as he likes to put it, a 'legend', is more like trading against your broker's advice in a futures market than investing in blue chip stock.

Until now, he has preferred to leave his future in the hands of destiny, and to test the patience of the Almighty in the ring and behind the wheel. For too long he has carried an aura of a disaster waiting to happen – and there is still ample capacity for catastrophe. If the petulant narcissist prevails, there is a real danger of him ending his reign, or his days, through a 'lucky' punch, or an 'unlucky' turn in the road. The picture of Naseem spread across the canvass, or across the tarmac as part of a smoky mass of molten metal, has become harder to dispel.

But there is also a different Naseem who has started to emerge – a husband, a father, one who takes his responsibilities seriously and has given up childish indulgences, and he is firm in his insistence that this is the 'real' man. Then again, that thrusting, thirsting ego is also far more than just an act. The praise-sucking habits of a lifetime require its constant feeding, while the slightest hint of disapproval raises an aggressively defensive shield. Despite the aura of absolute self-assuredness, the thin-skinned version of Naseem does not always give the appearance of being a person entirely at ease with who he is. In a streetwise way he's an intelligent young man, but still, his self-identity wrests too heavily on a single faculty: his ability to fight. Aside from the signs that this extraordinary faculty may one-day desert him, it is not exactly a sound basis to build a happy life. One suspects that these two Naseem Hameds will be competing for some time to come – in the ring, as in life. No doubt, the boy racer's sneering, slashing, burning, bullying alter ego will have his moments, but there are also occasional indications that the other fellow – the brain-cell-protecting family man – might tentatively prevail. If it is legends, rather than myths, which he is after, then there really is no other way.